xxxHOLiC Rei

4

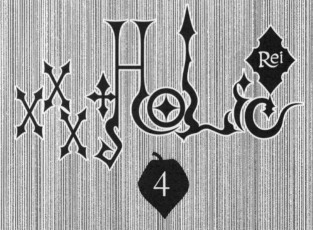

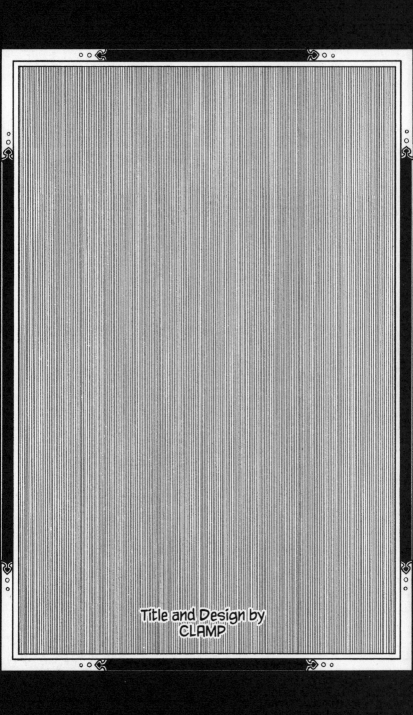

Title and Design by
CLAMP

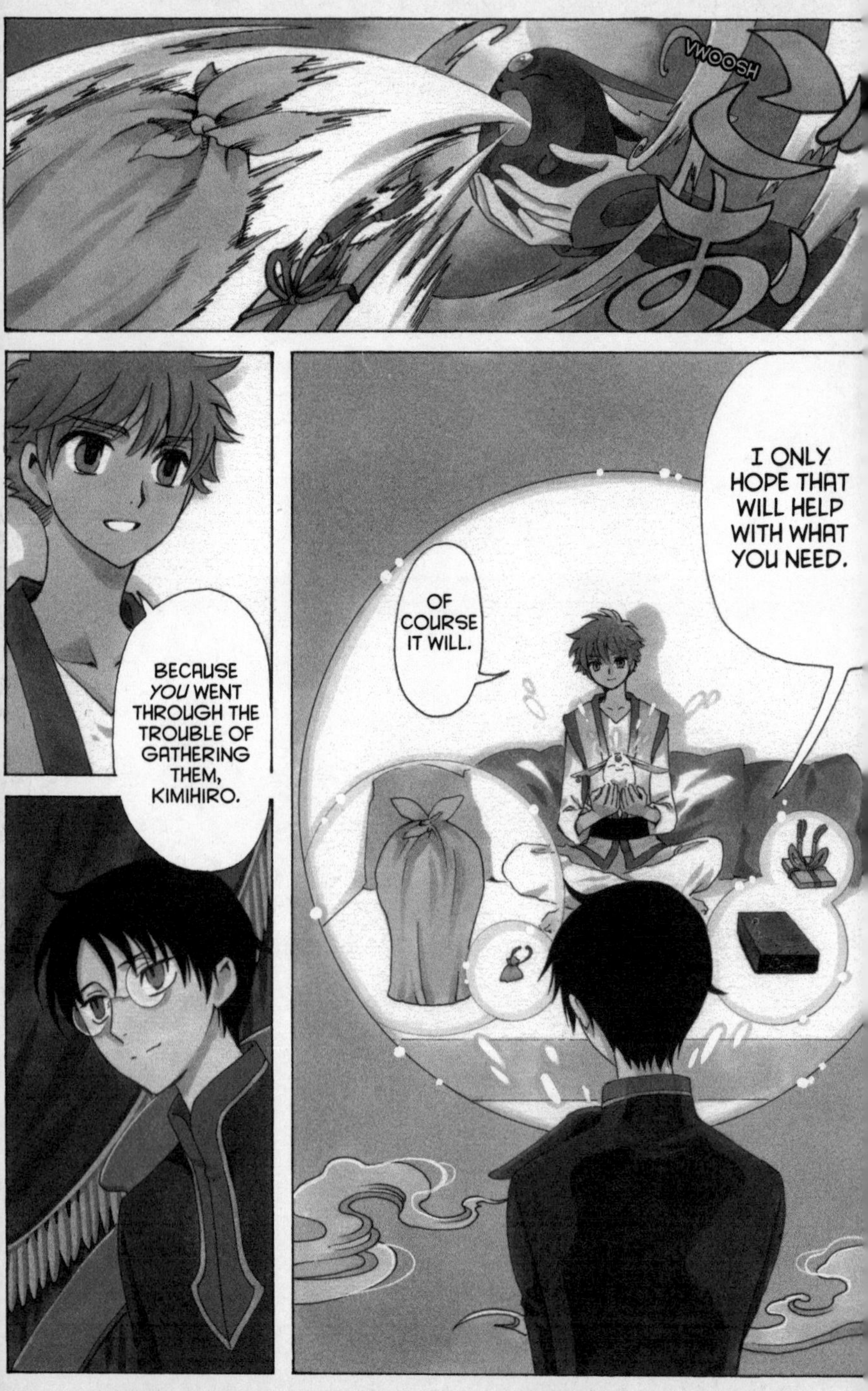
VWOOSH
I ONLY HOPE THAT WILL HELP WITH WHAT YOU NEED.
OF COURSE IT WILL.
BECAUSE *YOU* WENT THROUGH THE TROUBLE OF GATHERING THEM, KIMIHIRO.

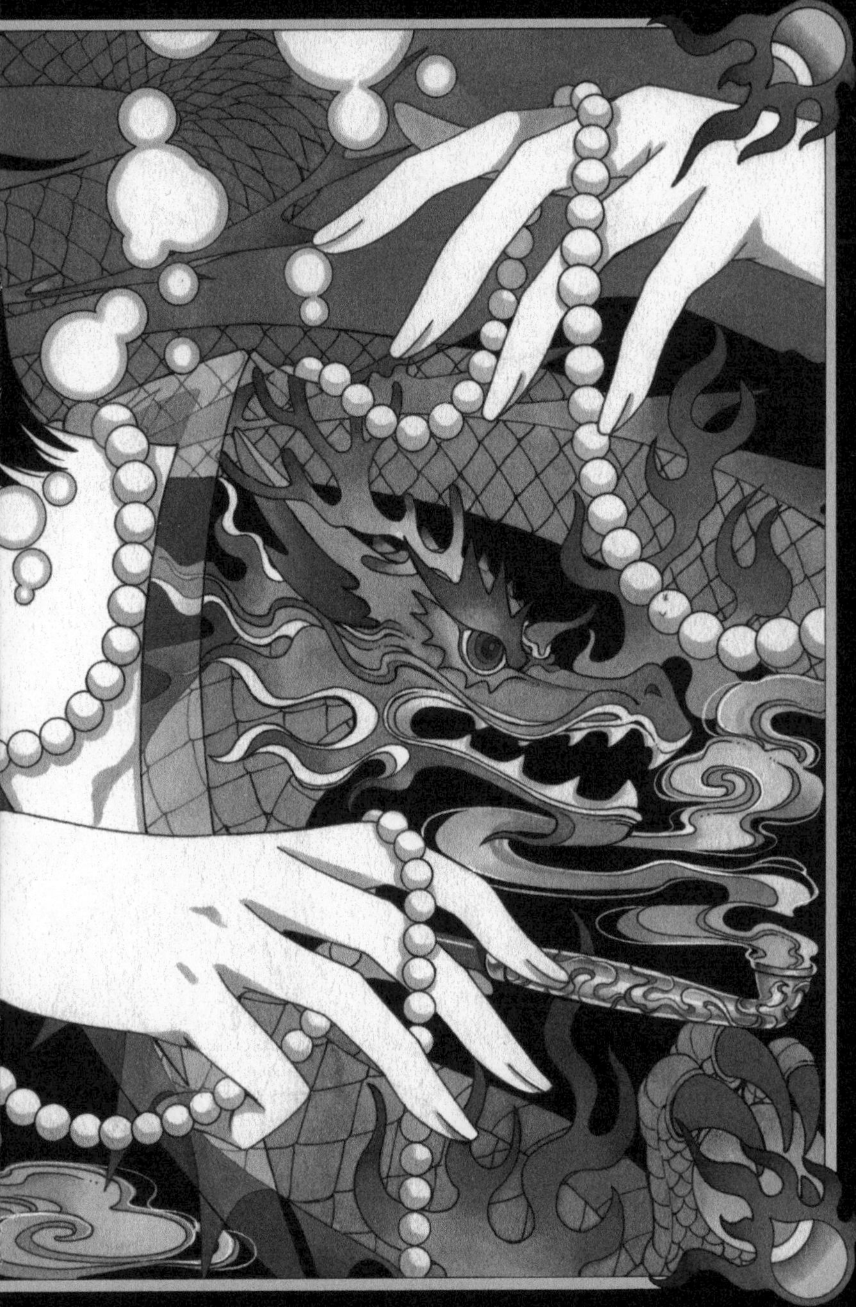

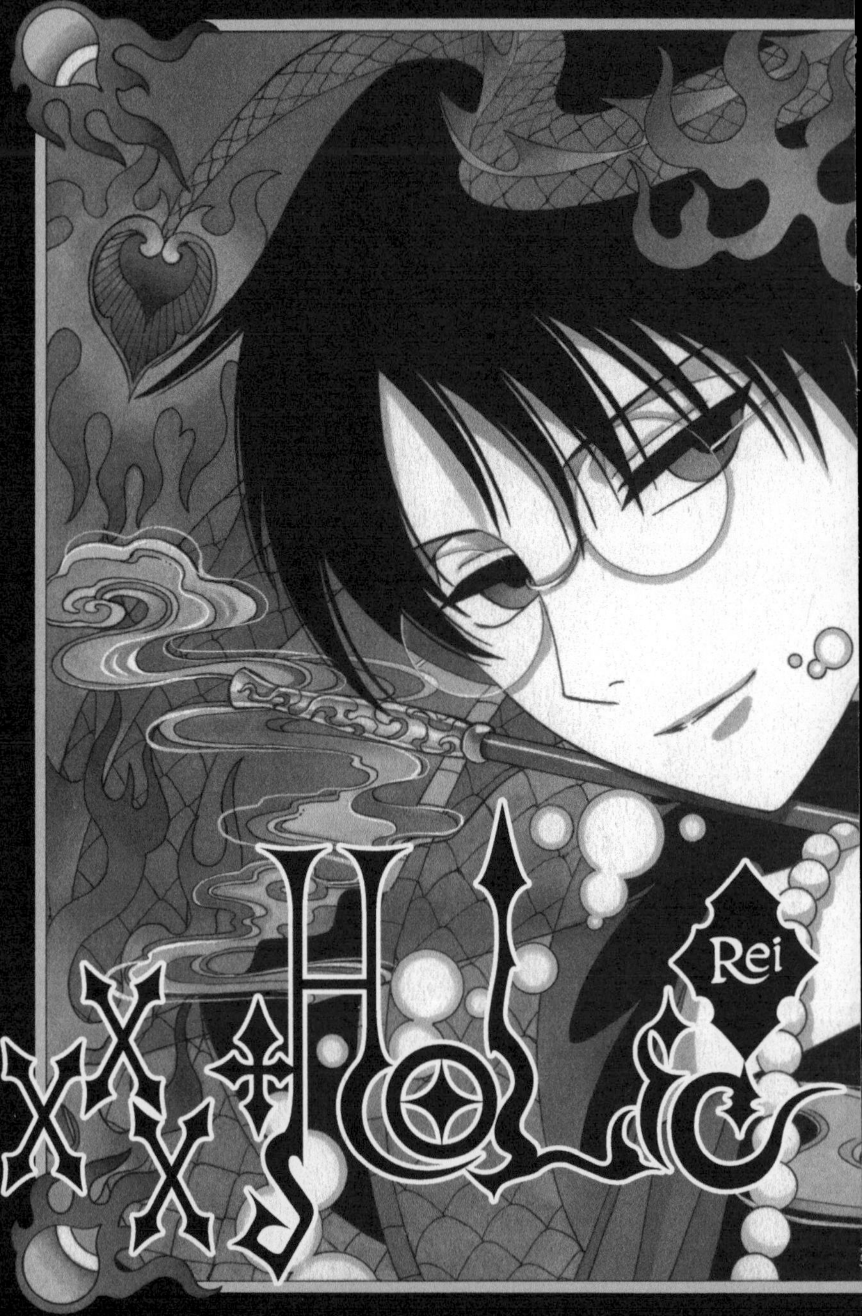
xxxHOLiC
Rei

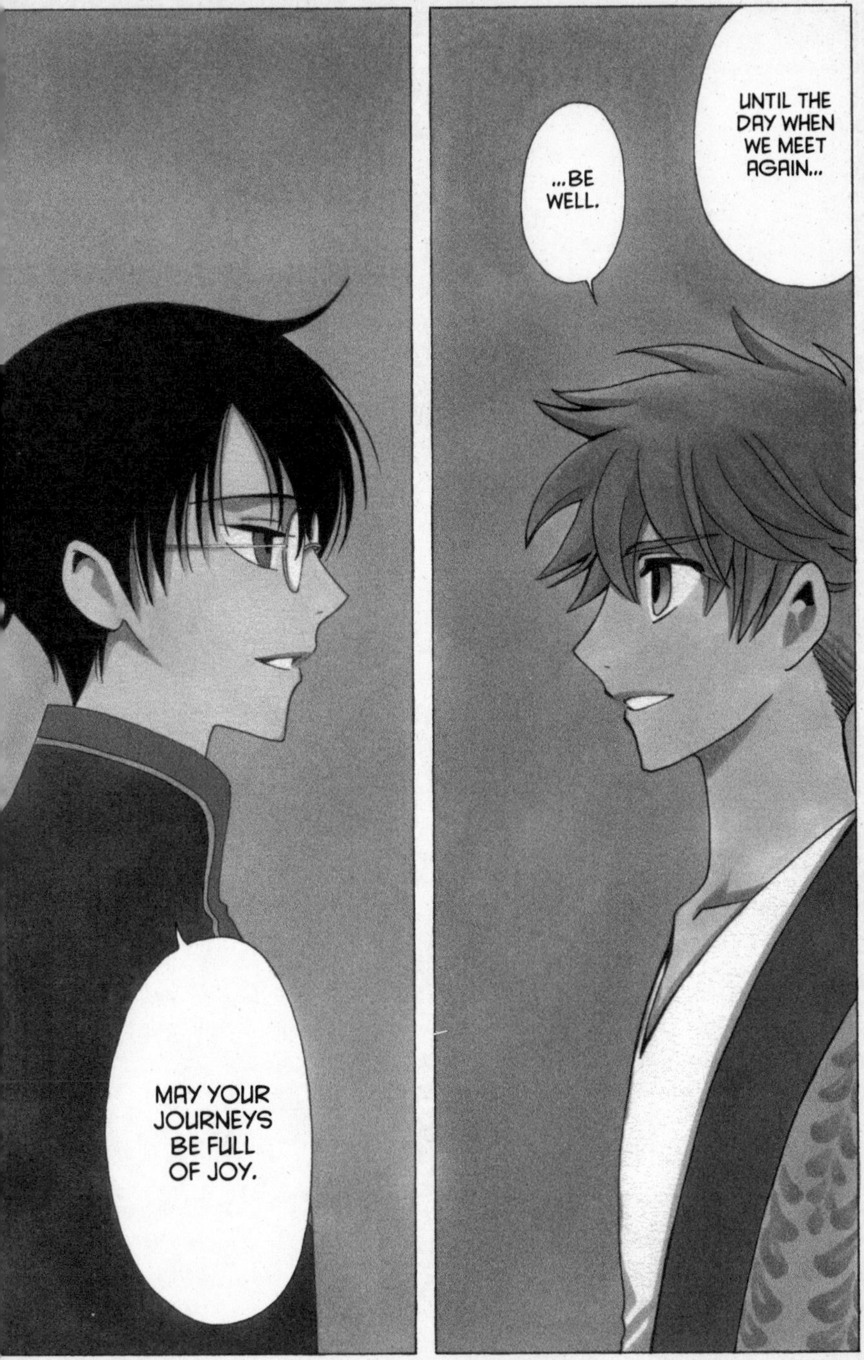
UNTIL THE DAY WHEN WE MEET AGAIN...
...BE WELL.
MAY YOUR JOURNEYS BE FULL OF JOY.

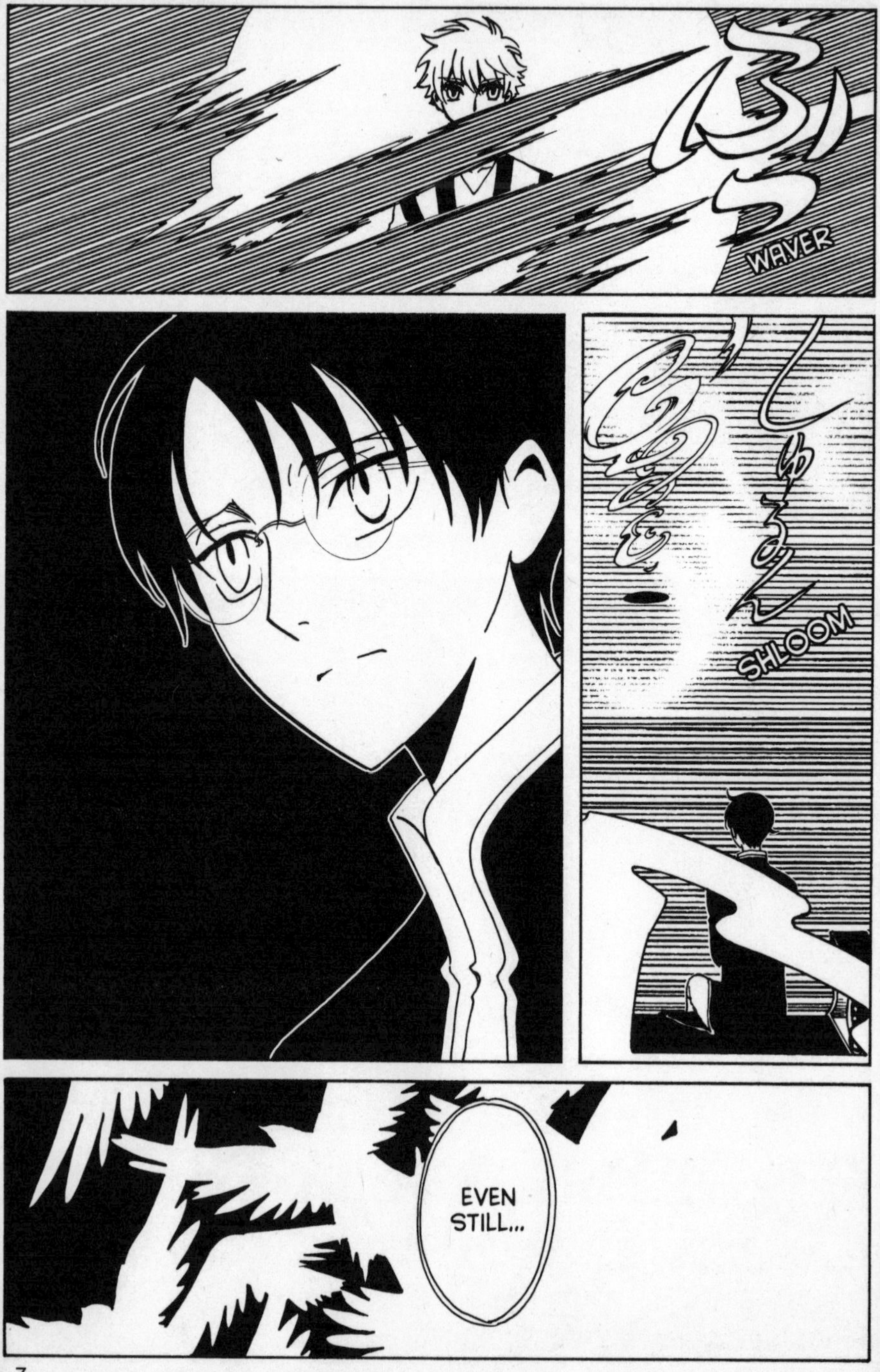
WAVER
SHLOOM
EVEN STILL...

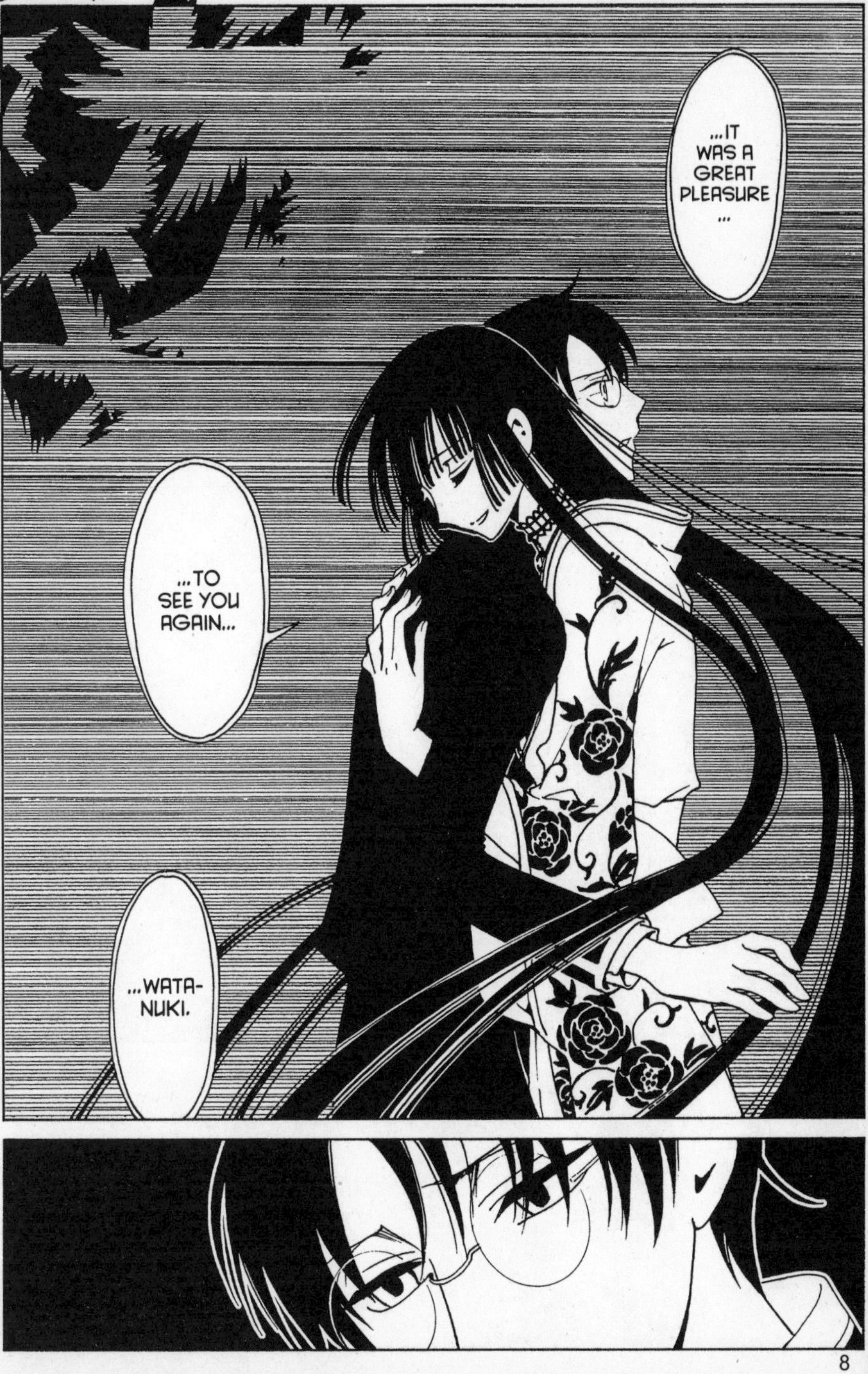
...IT WAS A GREAT PLEASURE ...
...TO SEE YOU AGAIN...
...WATA-NUKI.

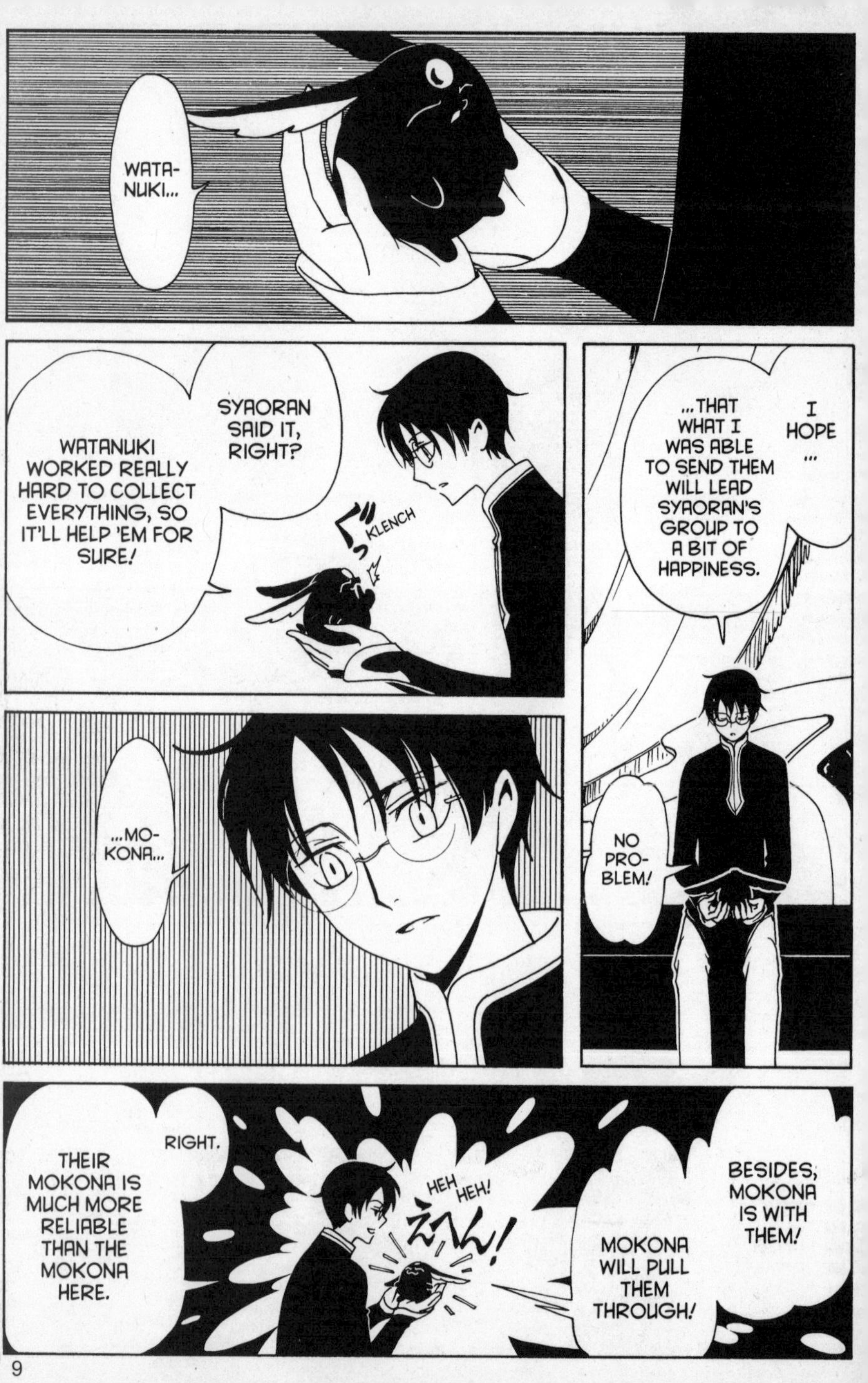
WATA-NUKI...
I HOPE...
...THAT WHAT I WAS ABLE TO SEND THEM WILL LEAD SYAORAN'S GROUP TO A BIT OF HAPPINESS.
NO PROBLEM!
SYAORAN SAID IT, RIGHT?
WATANUKI WORKED REALLY HARD TO COLLECT EVERYTHING, SO IT'LL HELP 'EM FOR SURE!
KLENCH
...MO-KONA...
BESIDES, MOKONA IS WITH THEM!
MOKONA WILL PULL THEM THROUGH!
HEH HEH!
えへん!
RIGHT.
THEIR MOKONA IS MUCH MORE RELIABLE THAN THE MOKONA HERE.

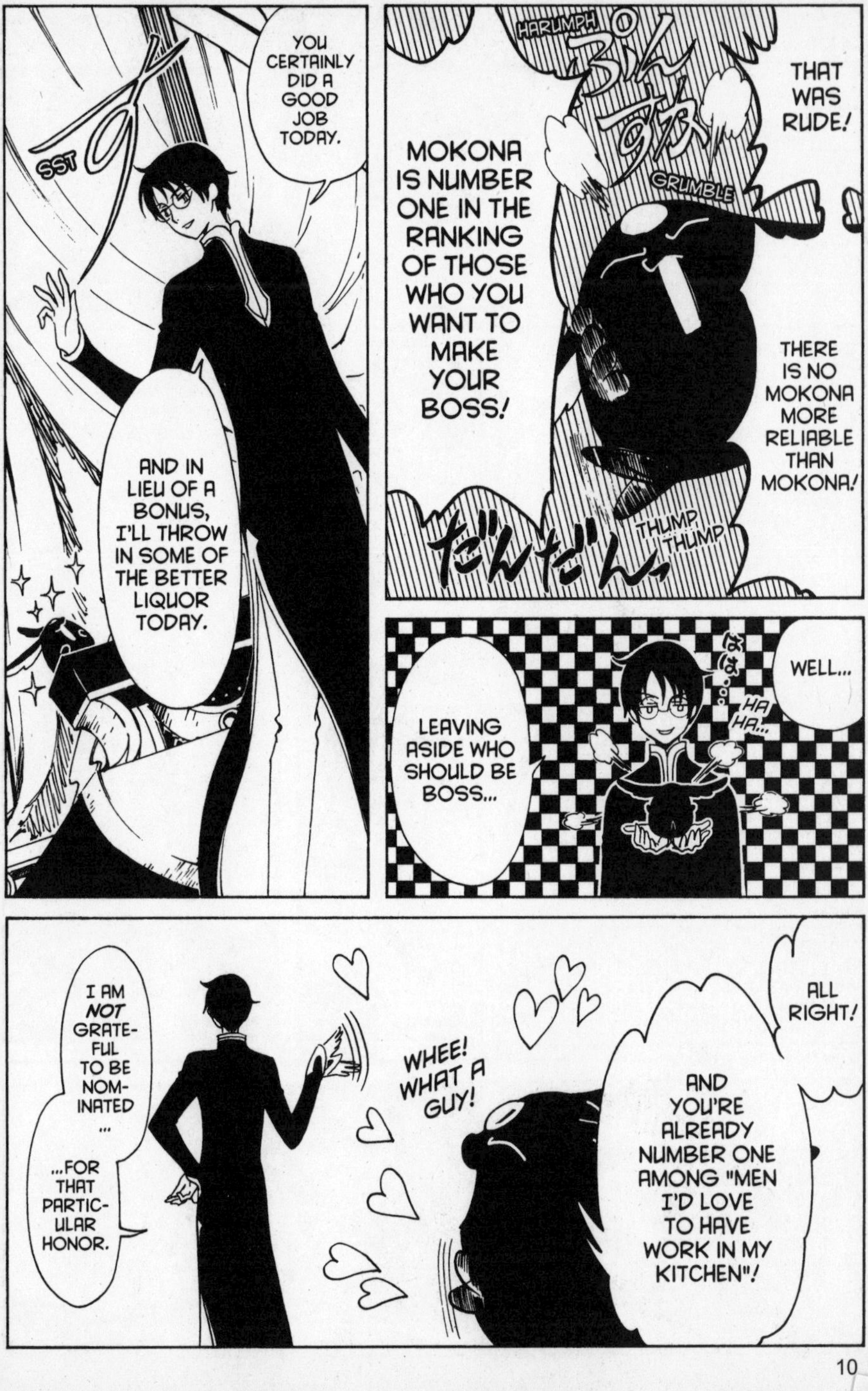
THAT WAS RUDE!
HARUMPH
ぷんすか
GRUMBLE
MOKONA IS NUMBER ONE IN THE RANKING OF THOSE WHO YOU WANT TO MAKE YOUR BOSS!
THERE IS NO MOKONA MORE RELIABLE THAN MOKONA!
THUMP THUMP
だんだん
WELL...
はは
HA HA...
LEAVING ASIDE WHO SHOULD BE BOSS...
YOU CERTAINLY DID A GOOD JOB TODAY.
SST
AND IN LIEU OF A BONUS, I'LL THROW IN SOME OF THE BETTER LIQUOR TODAY.
ALL RIGHT!
AND YOU'RE ALREADY NUMBER ONE AMONG "MEN I'D LOVE TO HAVE WORK IN MY KITCHEN"!
WHEE! WHAT A GUY!
I AM NOT GRATEFUL TO BE NOMINATED...
...FOR THAT PARTICULAR HONOR.

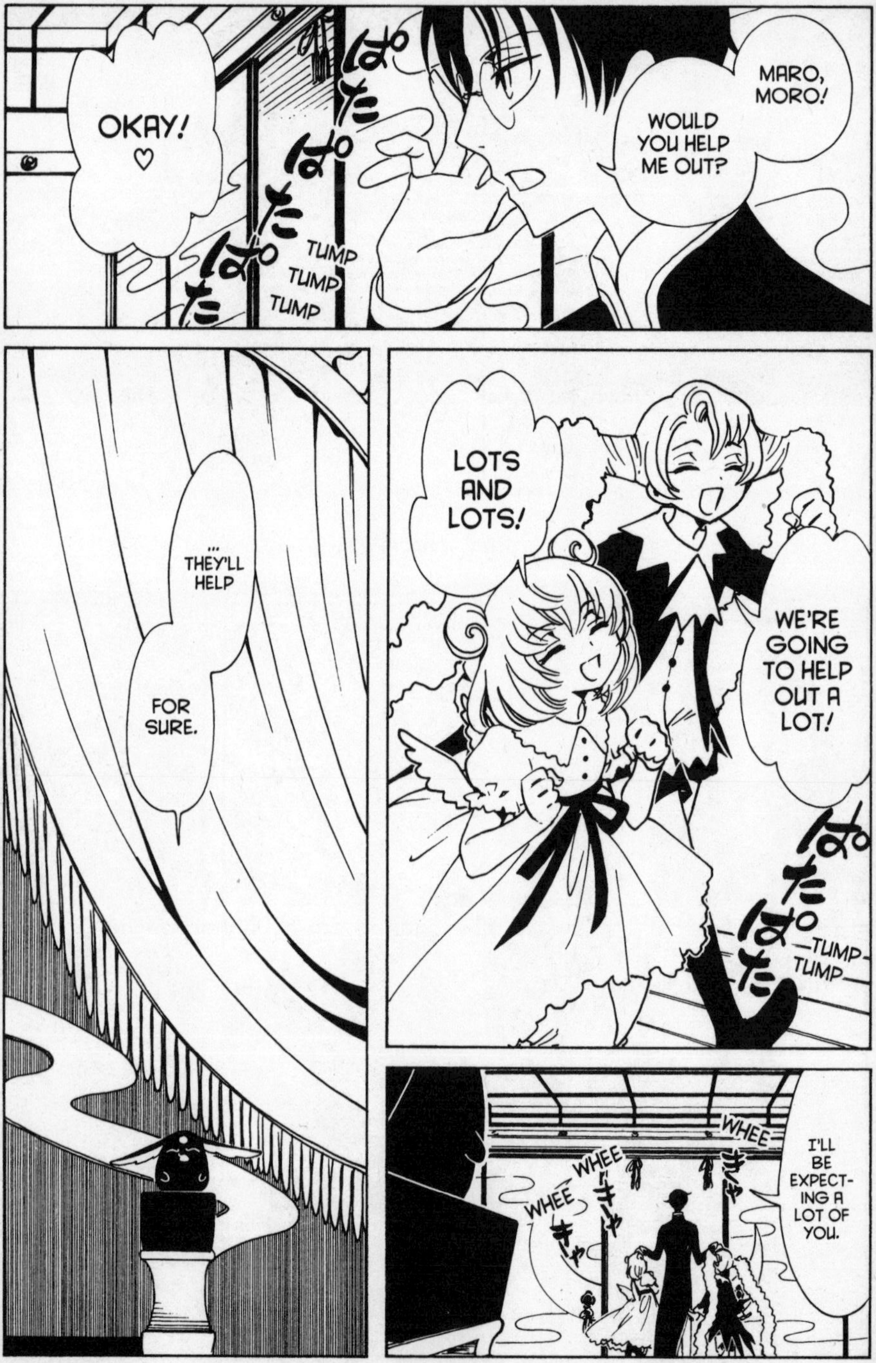
MARO, MORO!
WOULD YOU HELP ME OUT?
ぱたぱたぱたぱた
TUMP TUMP TUMP
OKAY! ♡
WE'RE GOING TO HELP OUT A LOT!
LOTS AND LOTS!
ぱたぱた
TUMP TUMP
I'LL BE EXPECT-ING A LOT OF YOU.
WHEE きゃ
WHEE きゃ
WHEE きゃ
... THEY'LL HELP
FOR SURE.

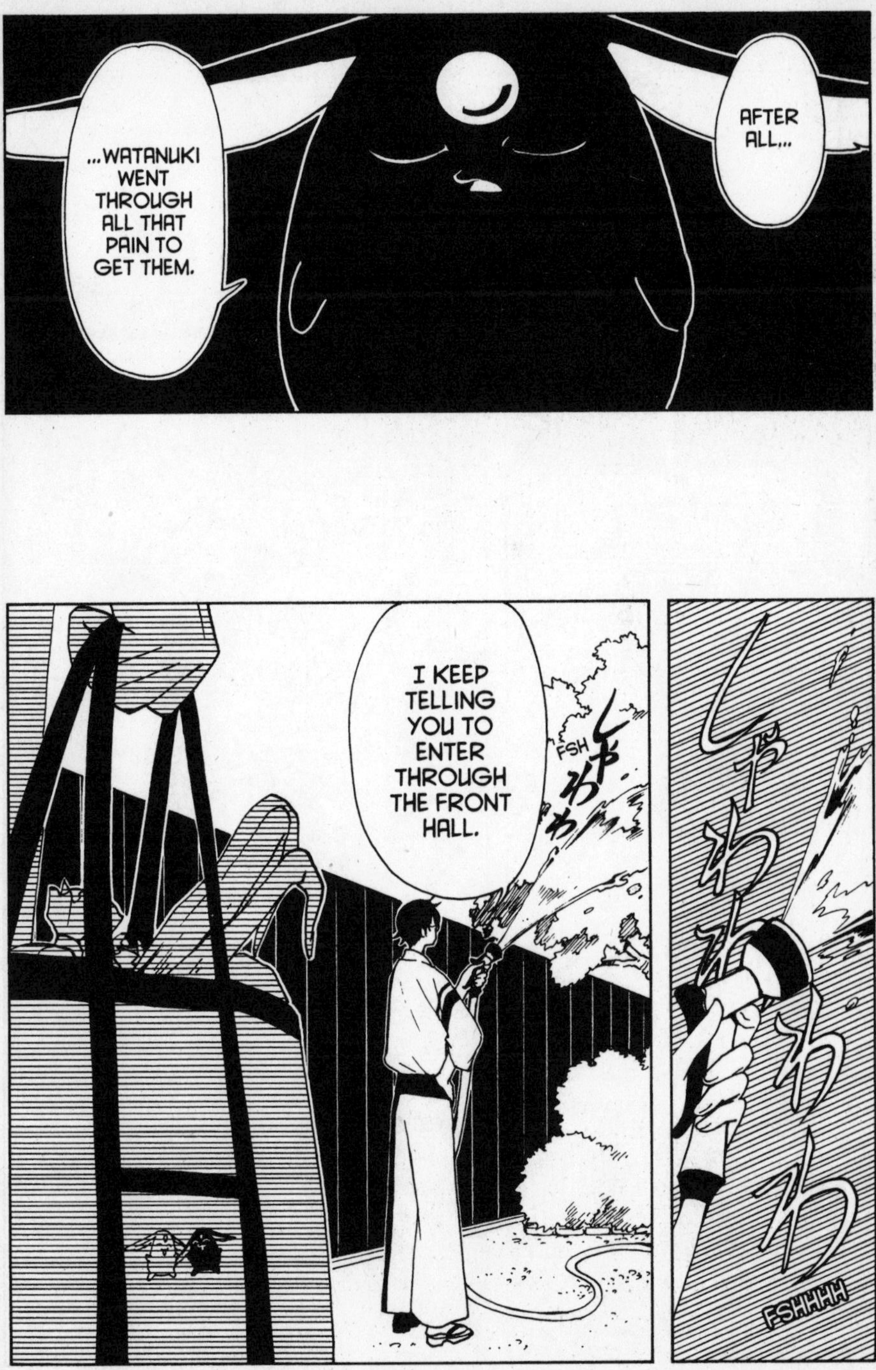
AFTER ALL...
...WATANUKI WENT THROUGH ALL THAT PAIN TO GET THEM.
FSHHHH
FSH
I KEEP TELLING YOU TO ENTER THROUGH THE FRONT HALL.

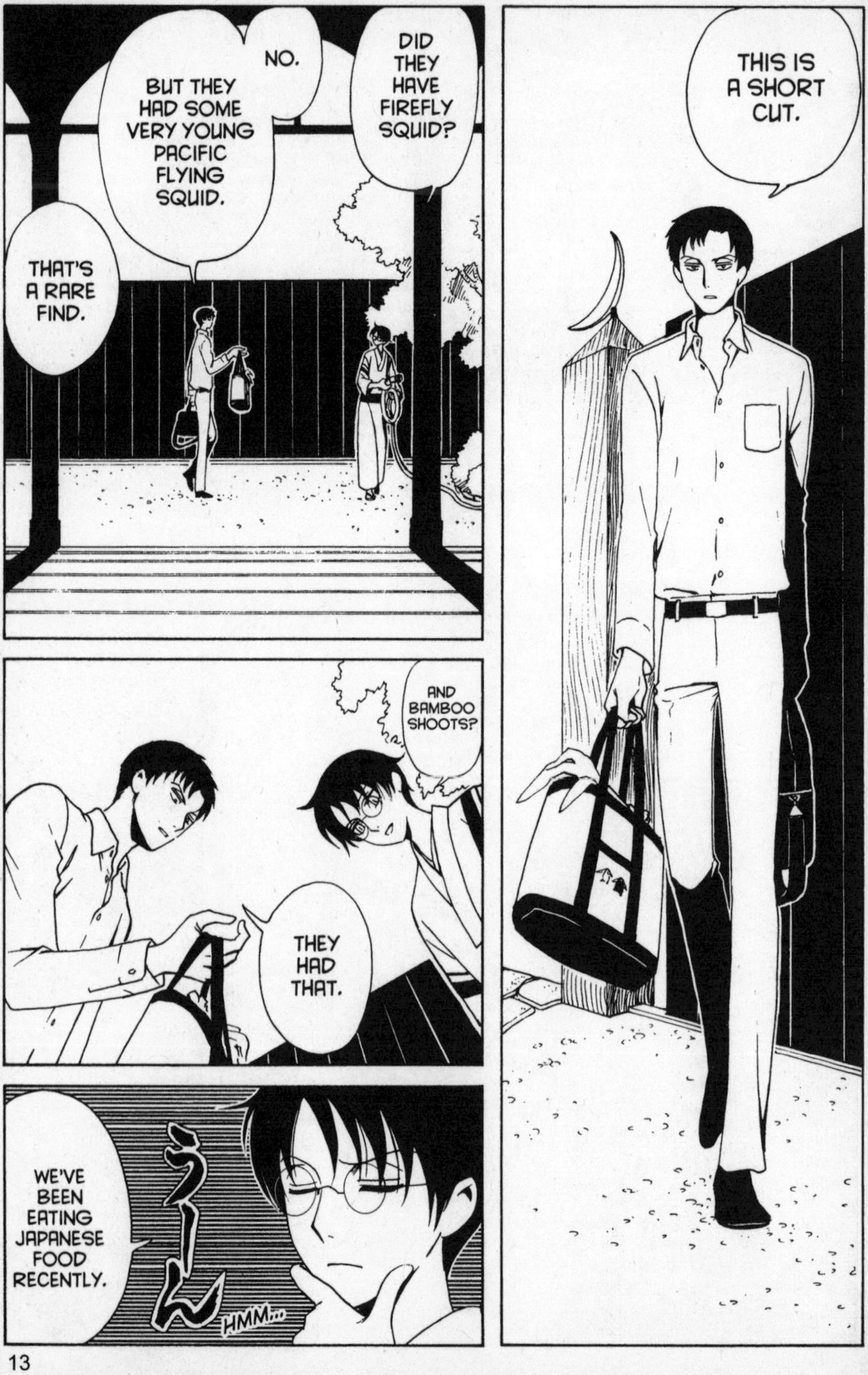
THIS IS A SHORT CUT.
DID THEY HAVE FIREFLY SQUID?
NO.
BUT THEY HAD SOME VERY YOUNG PACIFIC FLYING SQUID.
THAT'S A RARE FIND.
AND BAMBOO SHOOTS?
THEY HAD THAT.
うーん
HMM...
WE'VE BEEN EATING JAPANESE FOOD RECENTLY.

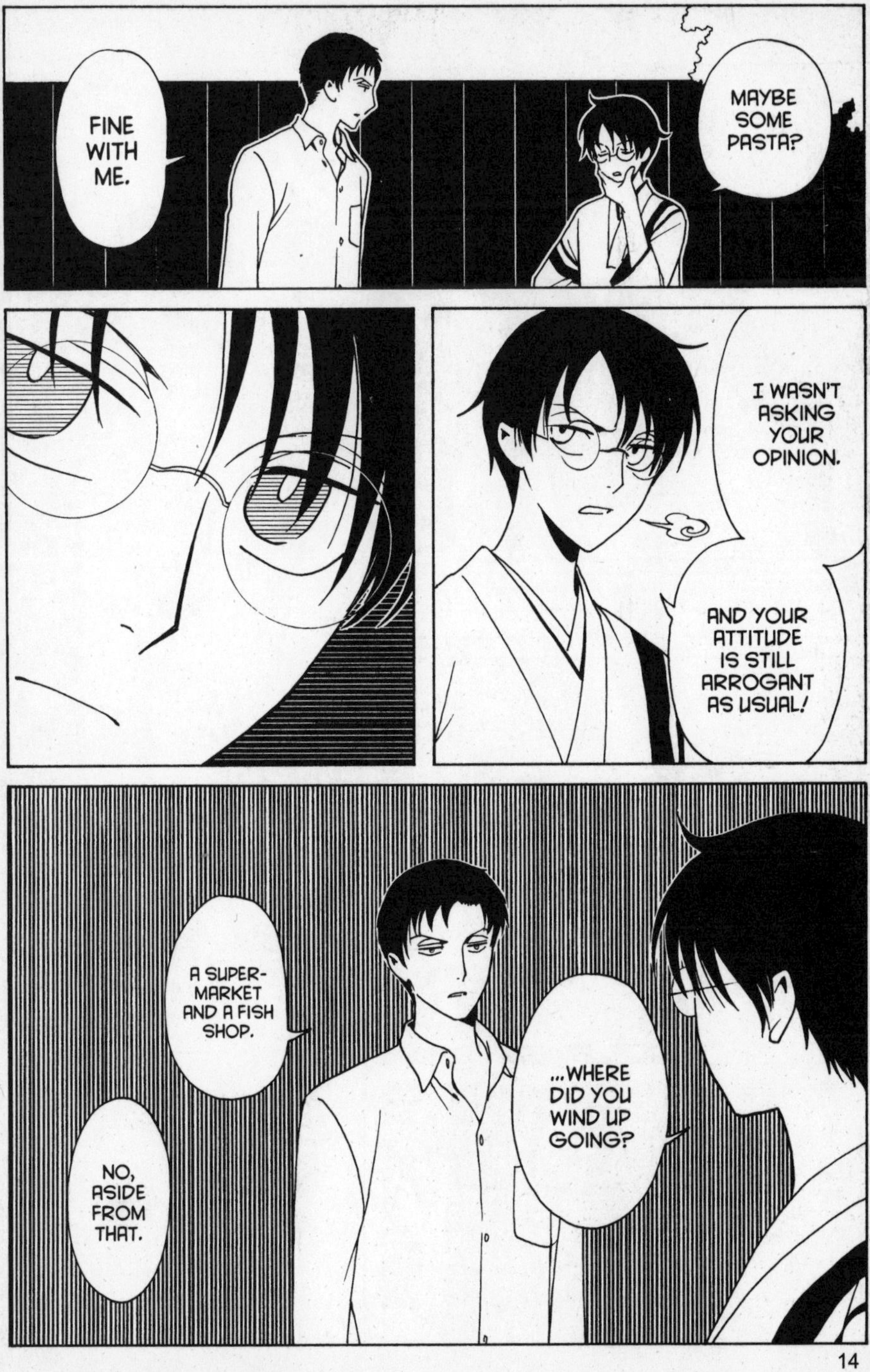
MAYBE SOME PASTA?
FINE WITH ME.
I WASN'T ASKING YOUR OPINION.
AND YOUR ATTITUDE IS STILL ARROGANT AS USUAL!
...WHERE DID YOU WIND UP GOING?
A SUPER-MARKET AND A FISH SHOP.
NO, ASIDE FROM THAT.

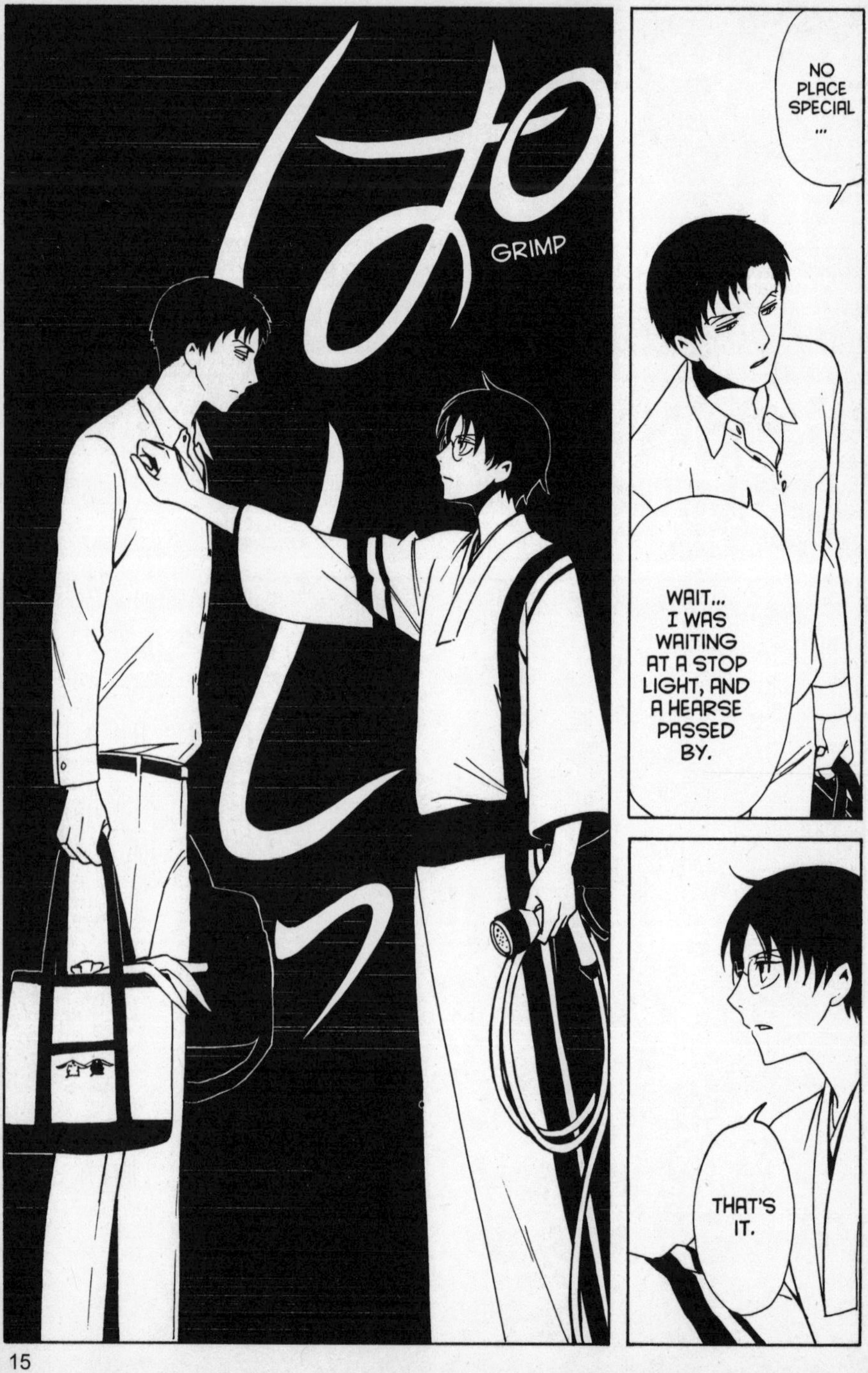
NO PLACE SPECIAL ...
WAIT... I WAS WAITING AT A STOP LIGHT, AND A HEARSE PASSED BY.
THAT'S IT.
GRIMP

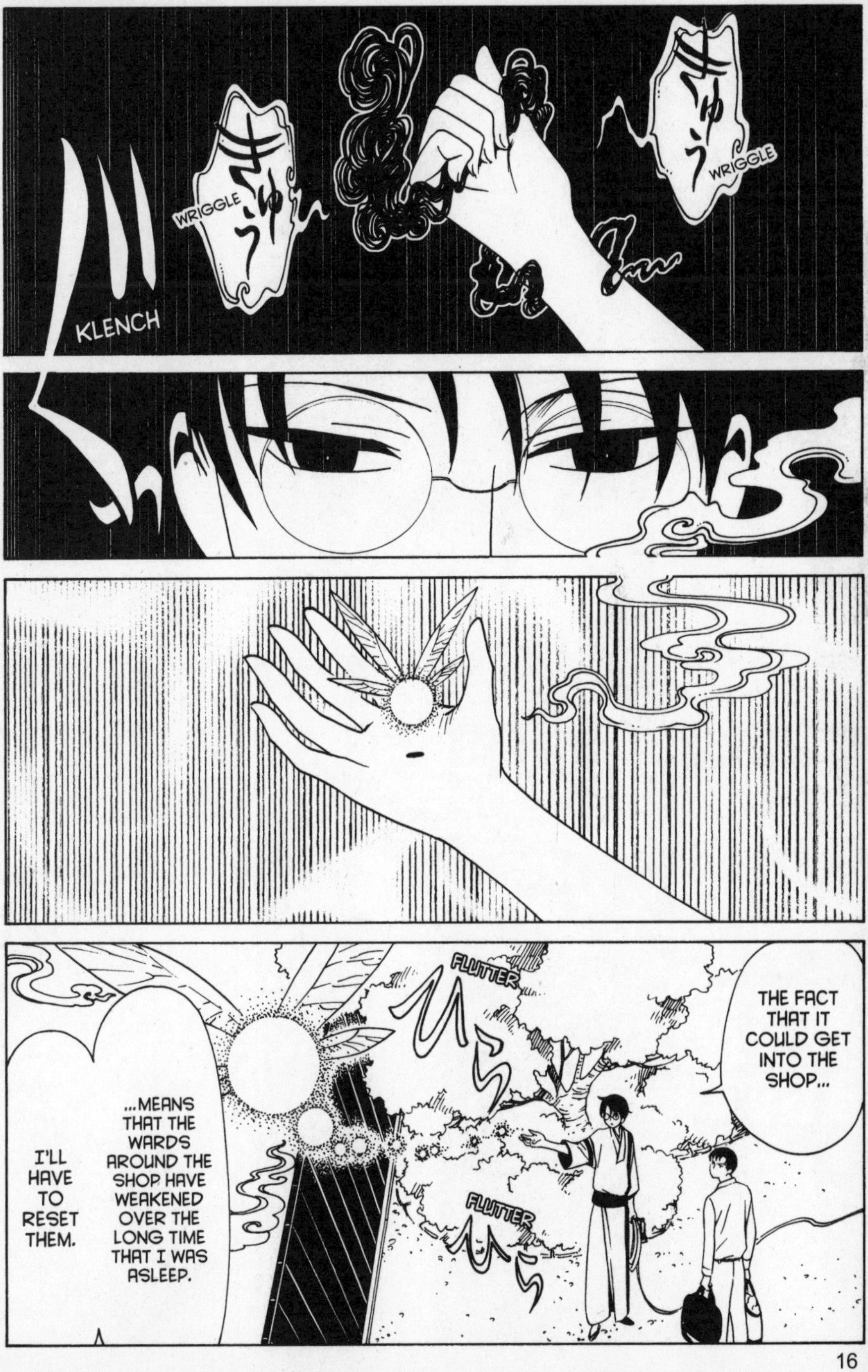

きゅう
WRIGGLE
きゅう
WRIGGLE
KLENCH
THE FACT THAT IT COULD GET INTO THE SHOP...
FLUTTER
ひら
...MEANS THAT THE WARDS AROUND THE SHOP HAVE WEAKENED OVER THE LONG TIME THAT I WAS ASLEEP.
FLUTTER
ひら
I'LL HAVE TO RESET THEM.

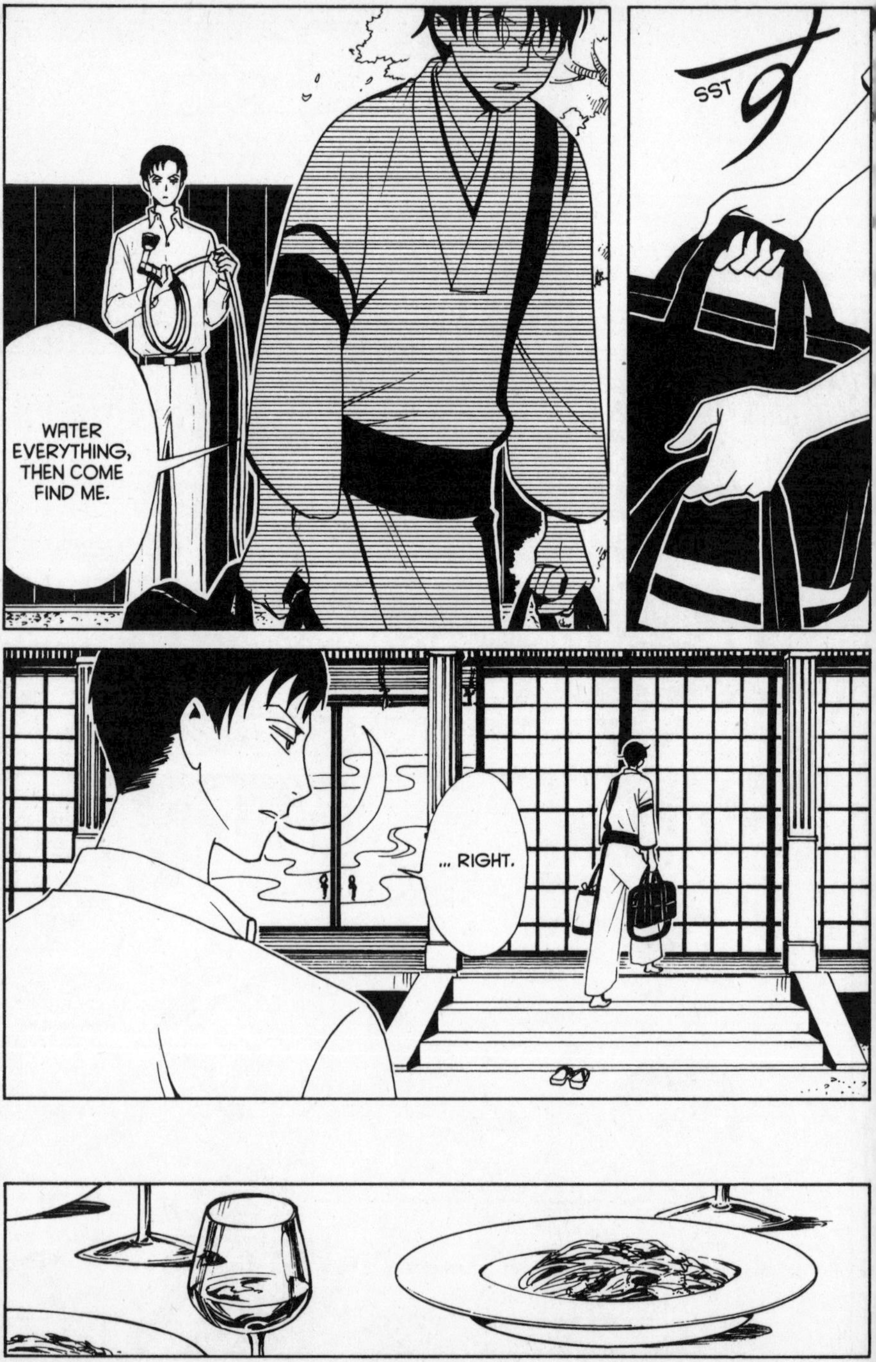
す
SST
WATER EVERYTHING, THEN COME FIND ME.
... RIGHT.

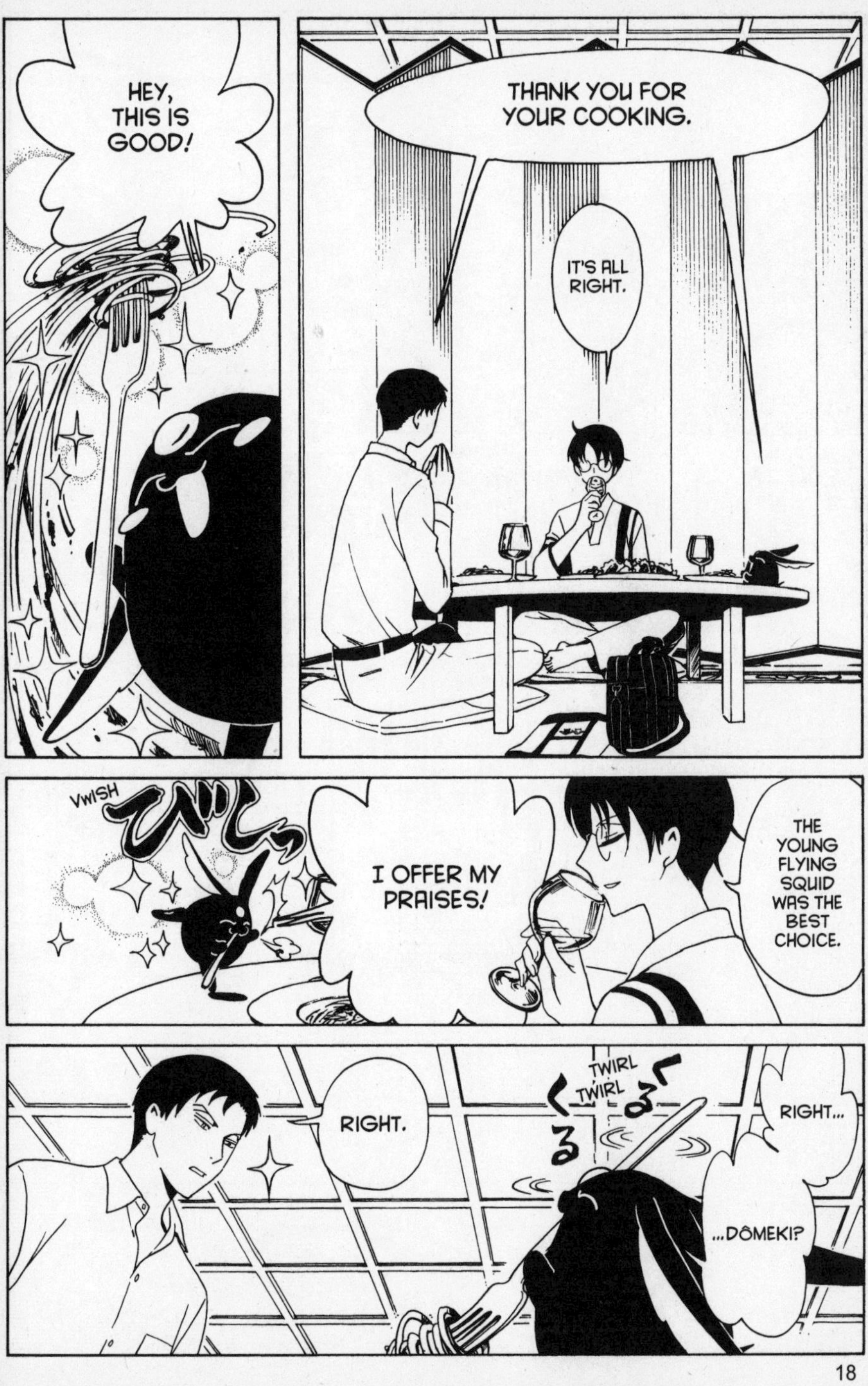
THANK YOU FOR YOUR COOKING.
IT'S ALL RIGHT.
HEY, THIS IS GOOD!
THE YOUNG FLYING SQUID WAS THE BEST CHOICE.
I OFFER MY PRAISES!
VWISH
RIGHT...
...DÔMEKI?
TWIRL TWIRL
RIGHT.

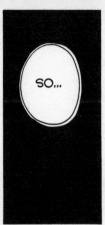

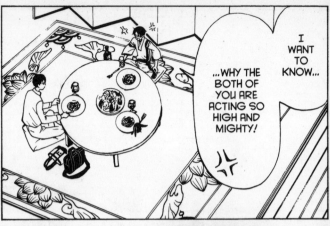

I WANT TO KNOW...
...WHY THE BOTH OF YOU ARE ACTING SO HIGH AND MIGHTY!
SO...
...YOU SAID THERE WAS SOMETHING YOU WANTED TO SHOW ME?
YES.
RUSTLE
WAIT! YOU PUT IT IN THAT?
THESE REUSABLE BAGS ARE WONDERFUL FOR THE ENVIRONMENT!

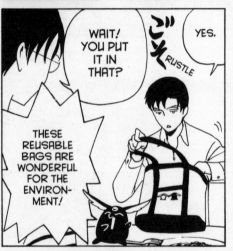

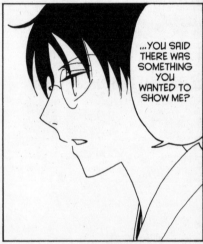

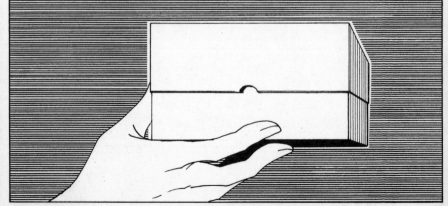

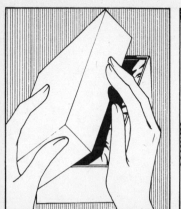

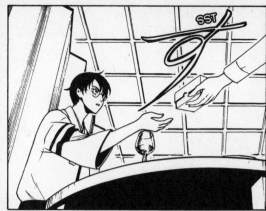

SST

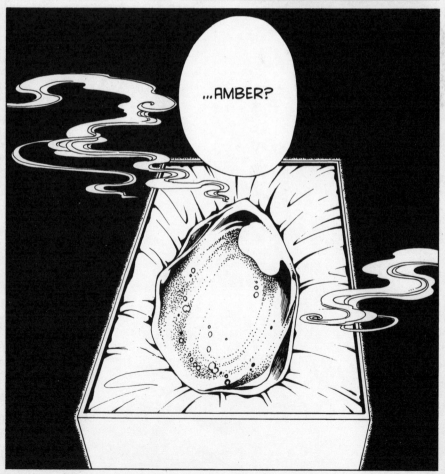

...AMBER?

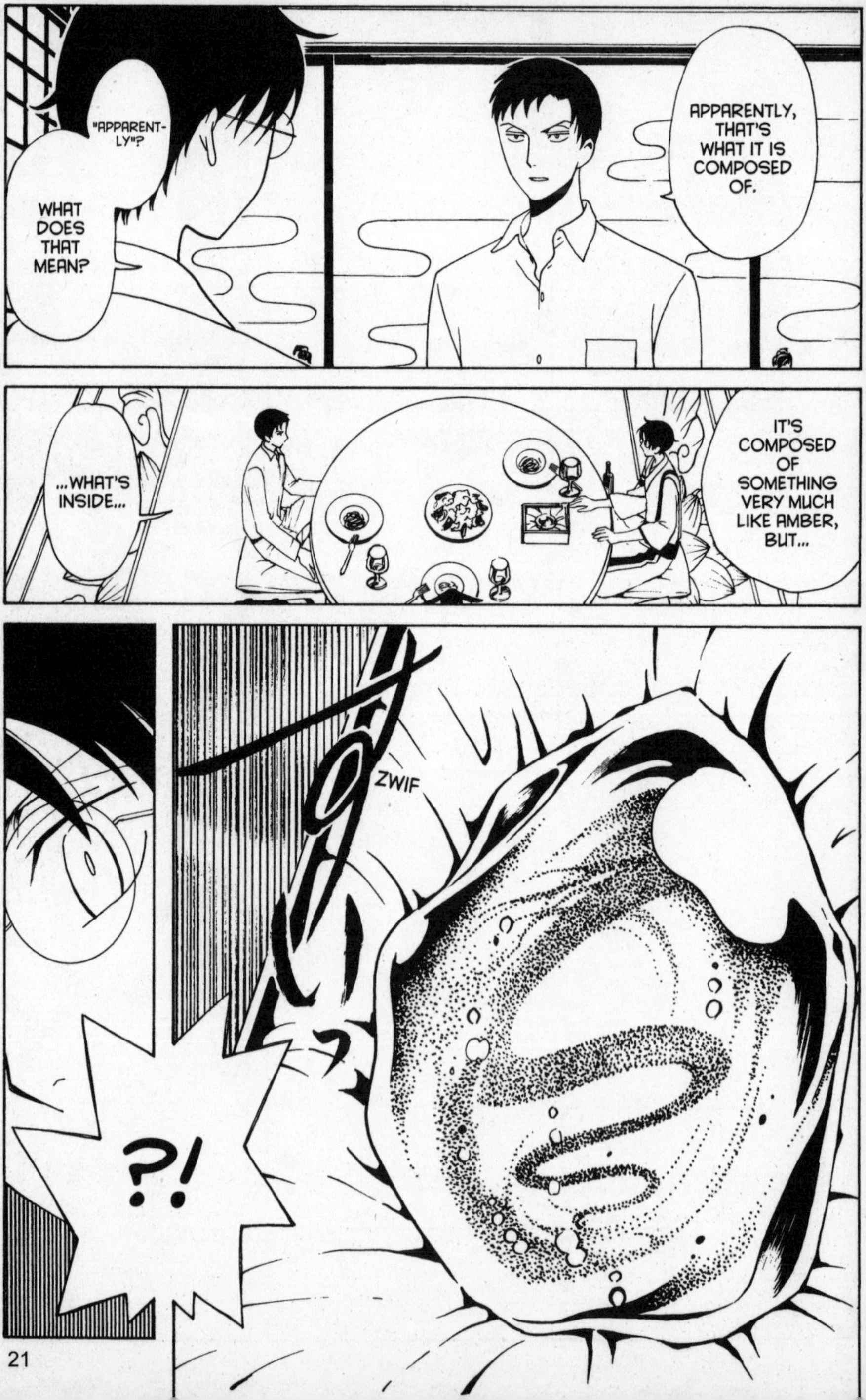
APPARENTLY, THAT'S WHAT IT IS COMPOSED OF.
"APPARENT-LY"?
WHAT DOES THAT MEAN?
IT'S COMPOSED OF SOMETHING VERY MUCH LIKE AMBER, BUT...
...WHAT'S INSIDE...
ZWIF
?!

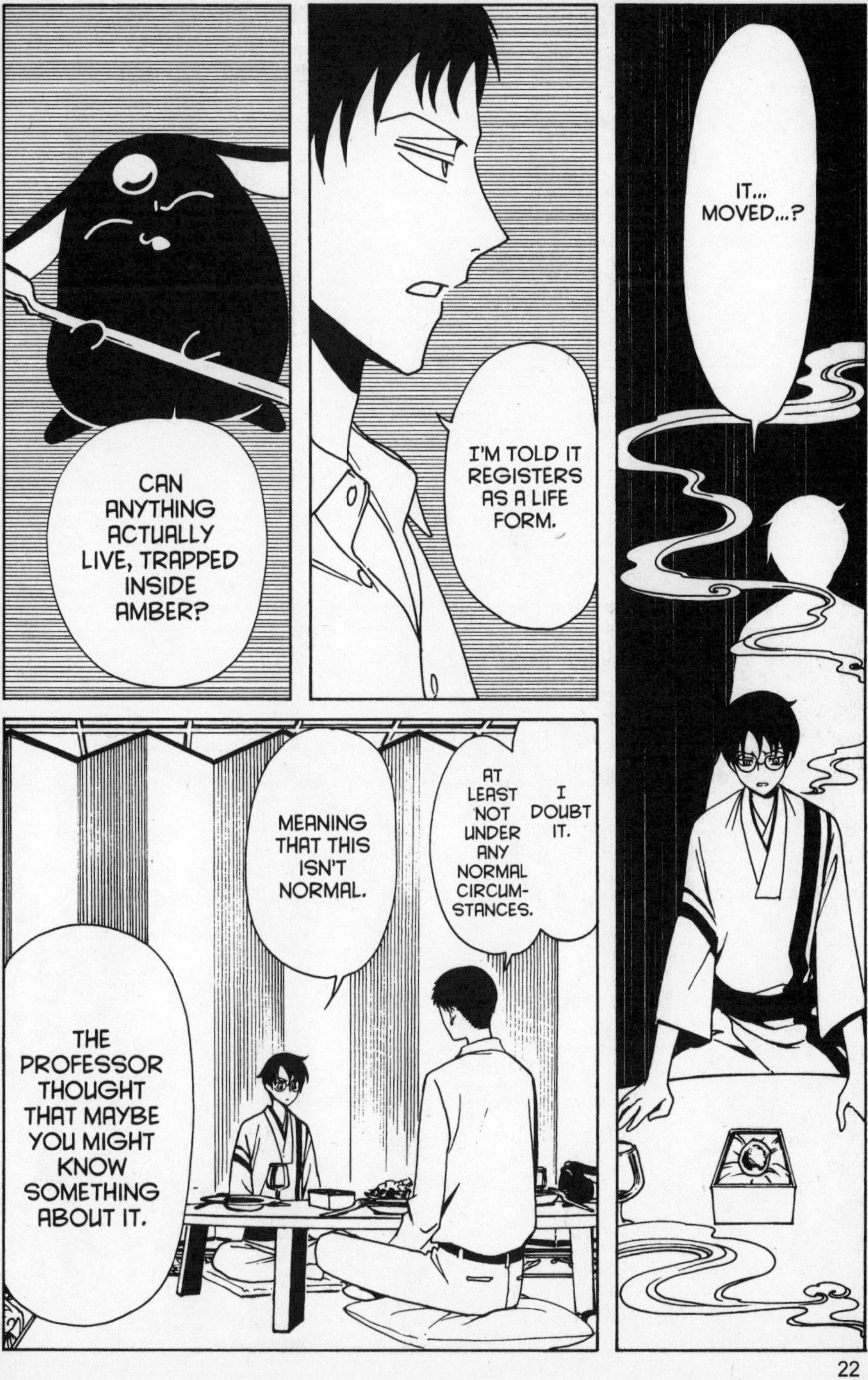
IT... MOVED...?
I'M TOLD IT REGISTERS AS A LIFE FORM.
CAN ANYTHING ACTUALLY LIVE, TRAPPED INSIDE AMBER?
I DOUBT IT.
AT LEAST NOT UNDER ANY NORMAL CIRCUM-STANCES.
MEANING THAT THIS ISN'T NORMAL.
THE PROFESSOR THOUGHT THAT MAYBE YOU MIGHT KNOW SOMETHING ABOUT IT.

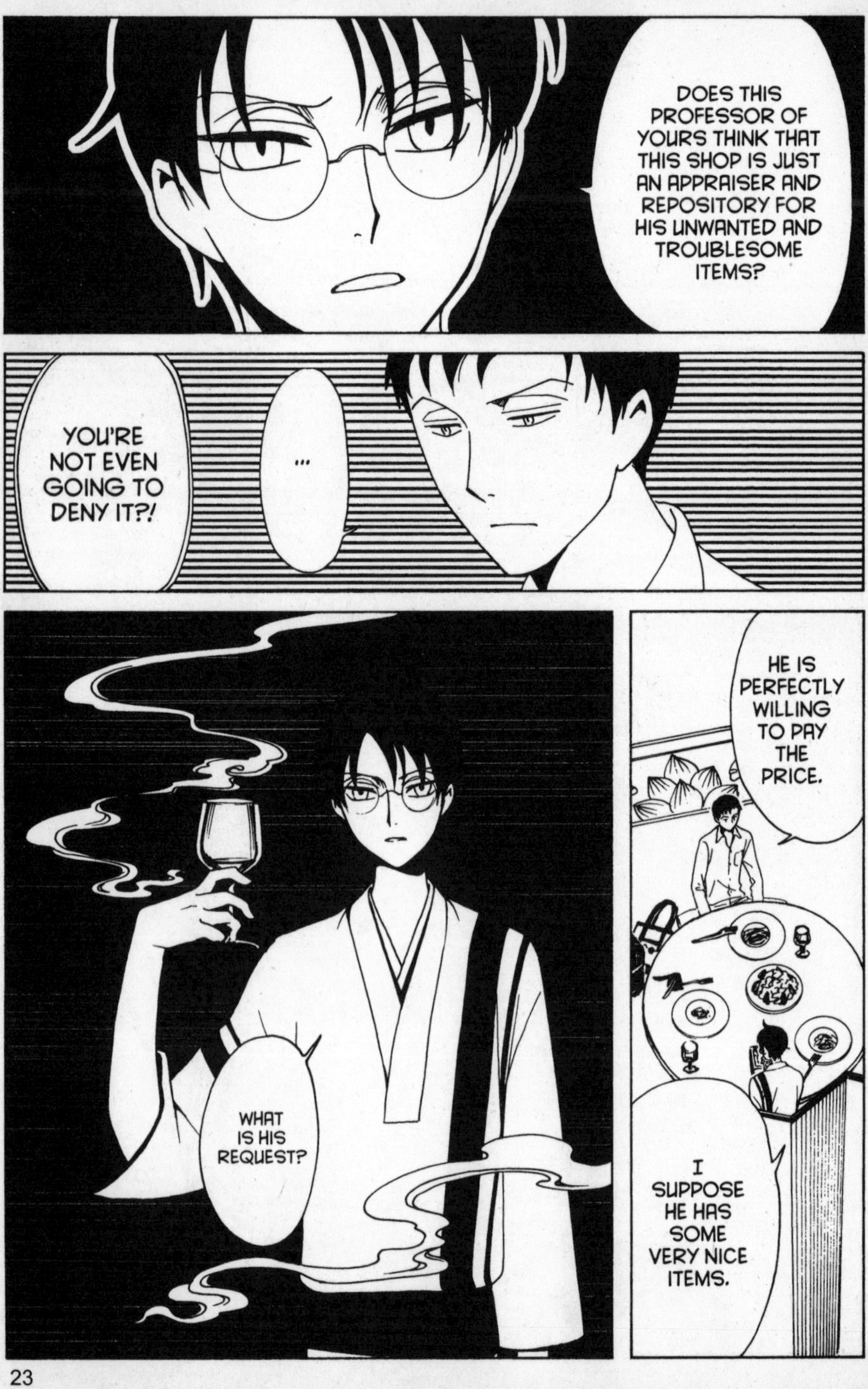
DOES THIS PROFESSOR OF YOURS THINK THAT THIS SHOP IS JUST AN APPRAISER AND REPOSITORY FOR HIS UNWANTED AND TROUBLESOME ITEMS?
...
YOU'RE NOT EVEN GOING TO DENY IT?!
HE IS PERFECTLY WILLING TO PAY THE PRICE.
I SUPPOSE HE HAS SOME VERY NICE ITEMS.
WHAT IS HIS REQUEST?

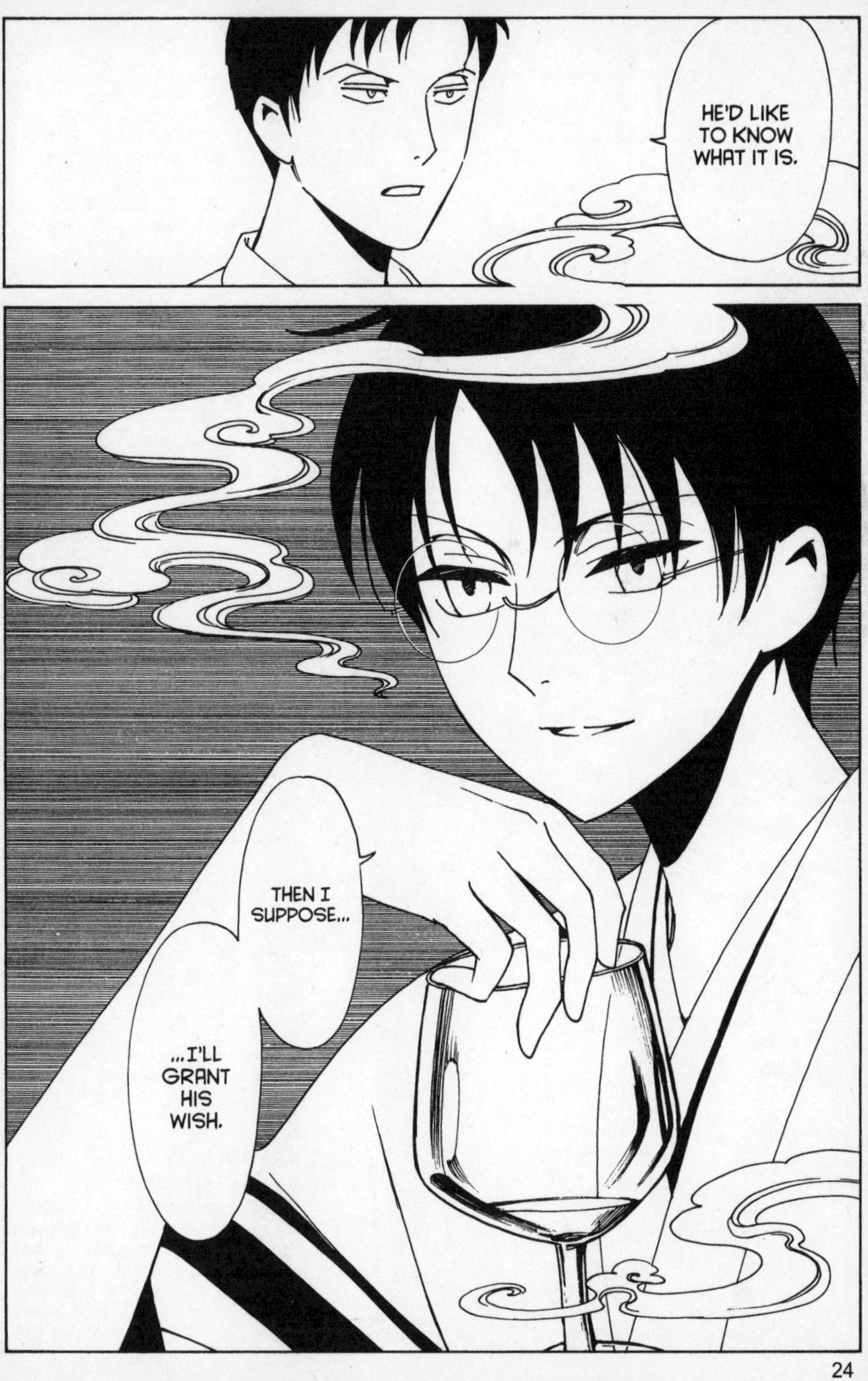
HE'D LIKE TO KNOW WHAT IT IS.
THEN I SUPPOSE...
...I'LL GRANT HIS WISH.

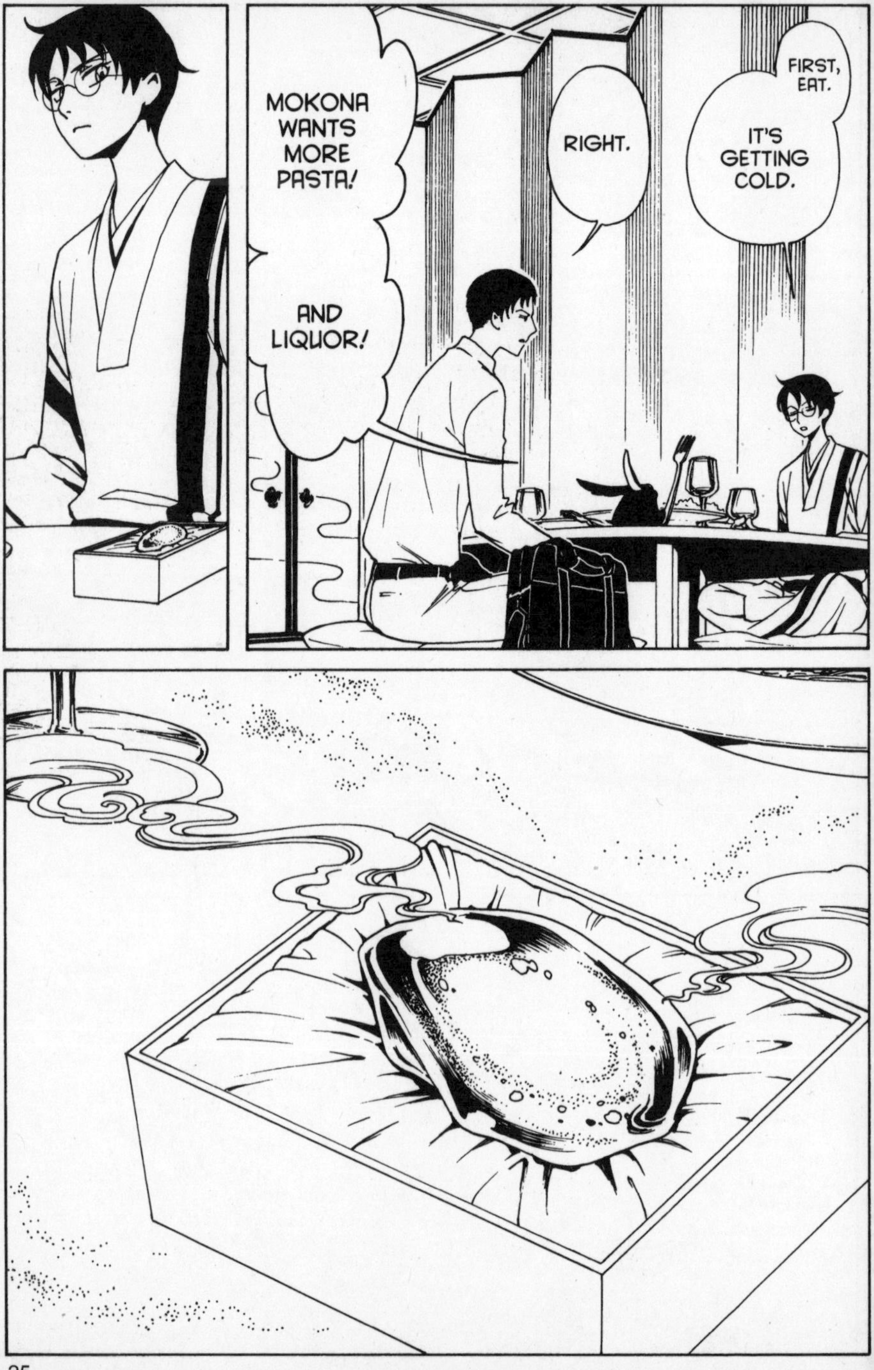
FIRST, EAT.
IT'S GETTING COLD.
RIGHT.
MOKONA WANTS MORE PASTA!
AND LIQUOR!

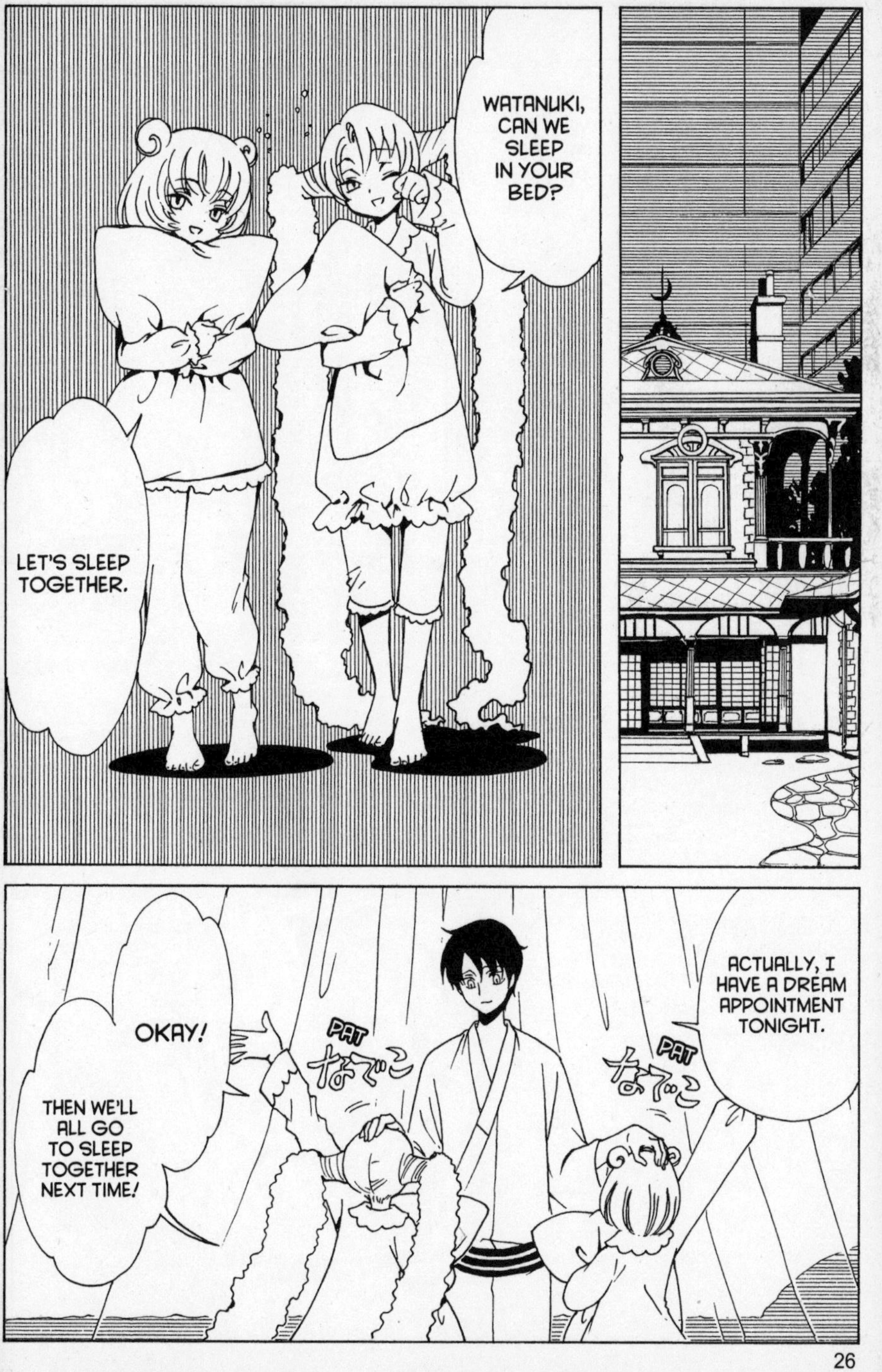
WATANUKI, CAN WE SLEEP IN YOUR BED?
LET'S SLEEP TOGETHER.
ACTUALLY, I HAVE A DREAM APPOINTMENT TONIGHT.
PAT
なでこ
PAT
なでこ
OKAY!
THEN WE'LL ALL GO TO SLEEP TOGETHER NEXT TIME!

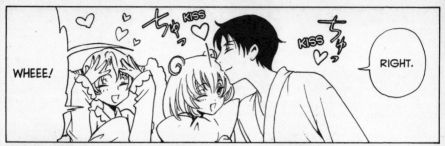

WHEEE!

ちゅっ KISS

KISS ちゅっ

RIGHT.

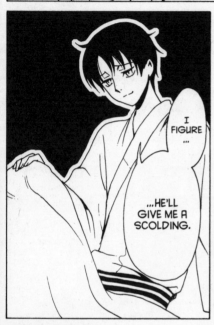

I FIGURE...

...HE'LL GIVE ME A SCOLDING.

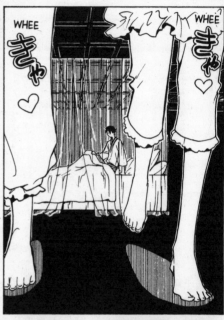

WHEE

きゃ

WHEE

きゃ

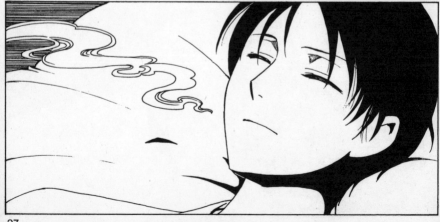

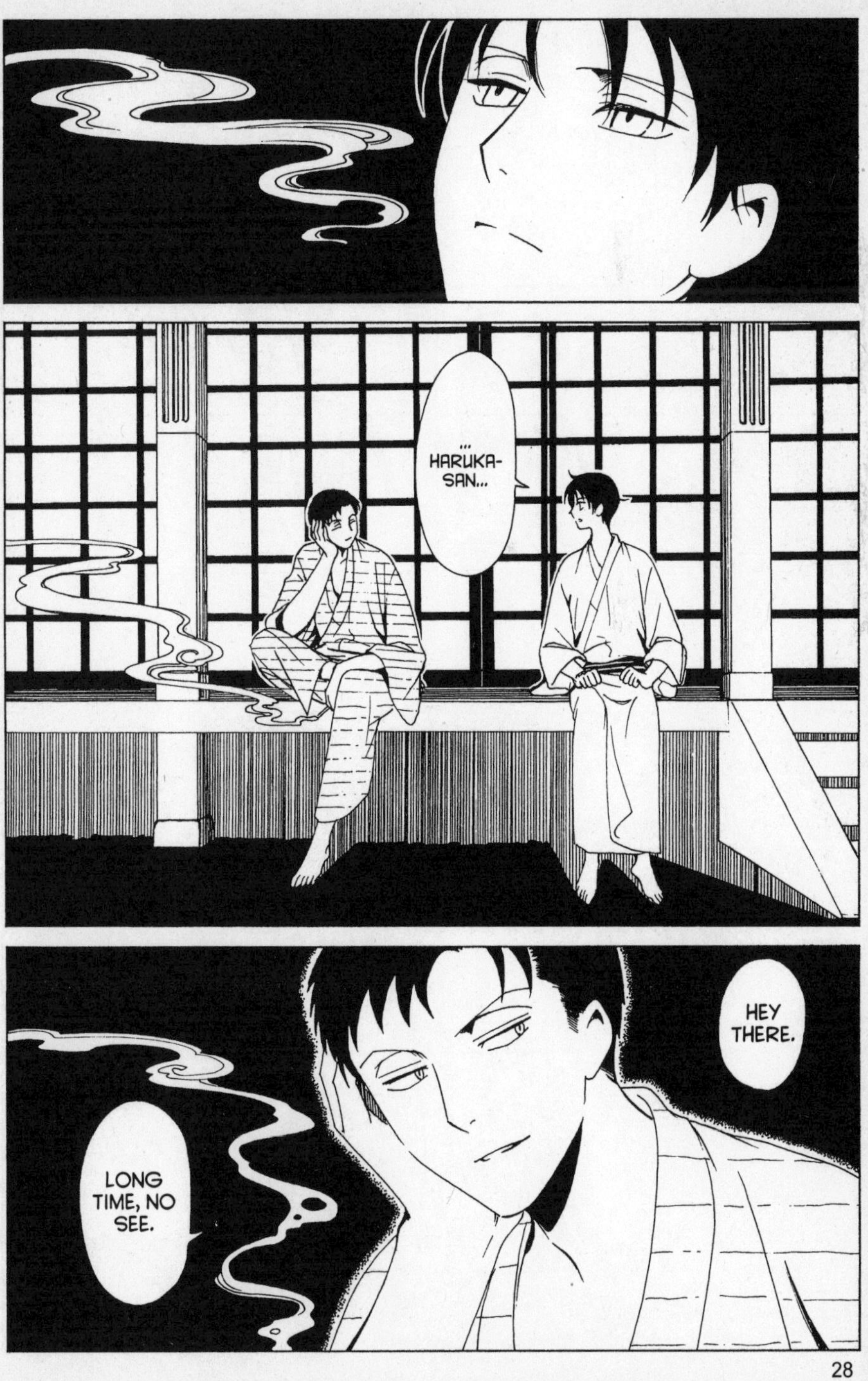

... HARUKA-SAN...
HEY THERE.
LONG TIME, NO SEE.

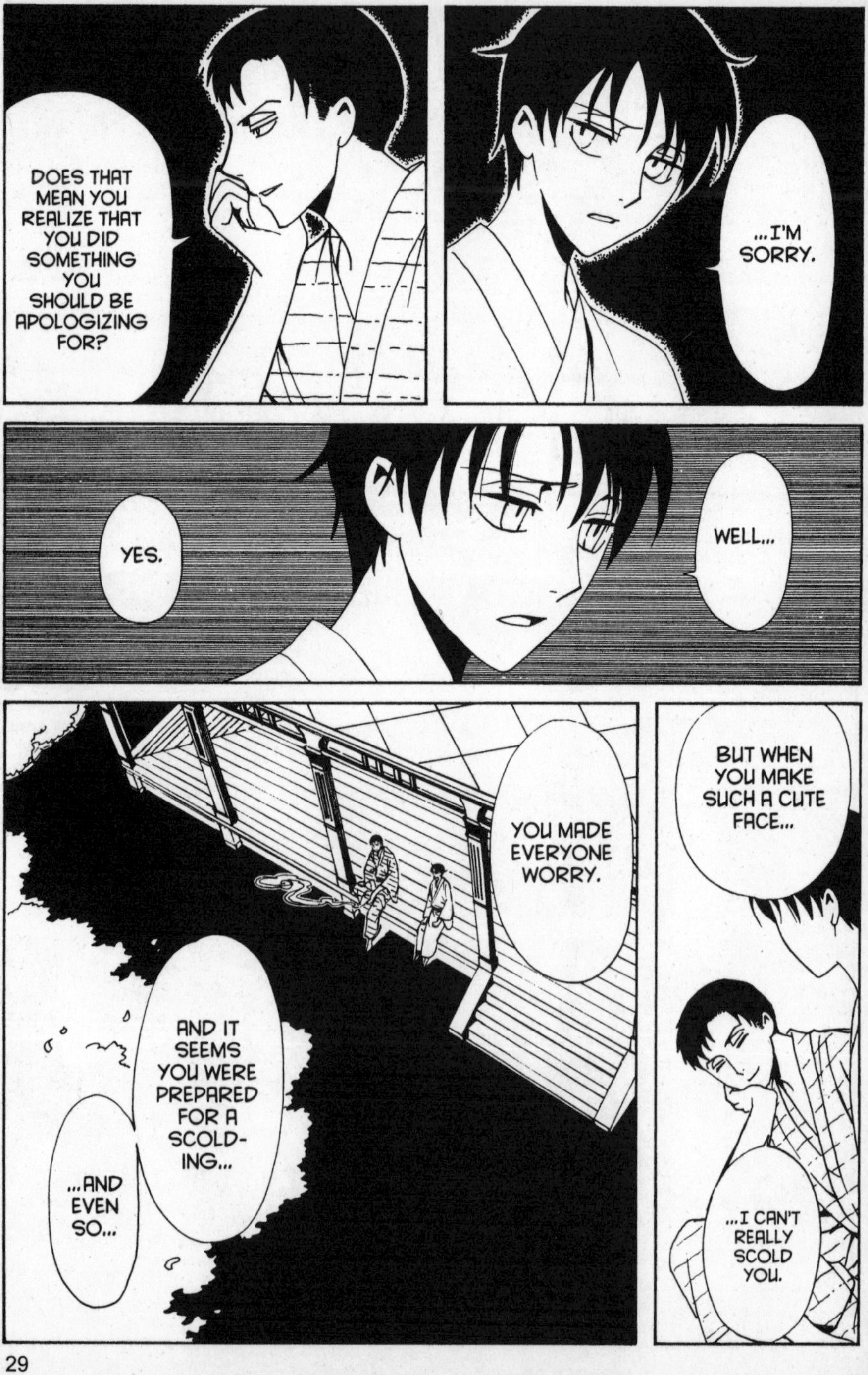
DOES THAT MEAN YOU REALIZE THAT YOU DID SOMETHING YOU SHOULD BE APOLOGIZING FOR?
...I'M SORRY.
YES.
WELL...
YOU MADE EVERYONE WORRY.
AND IT SEEMS YOU WERE PREPARED FOR A SCOLD-ING...
...AND EVEN SO...
BUT WHEN YOU MAKE SUCH A CUTE FACE...
...I CAN'T REALLY SCOLD YOU.

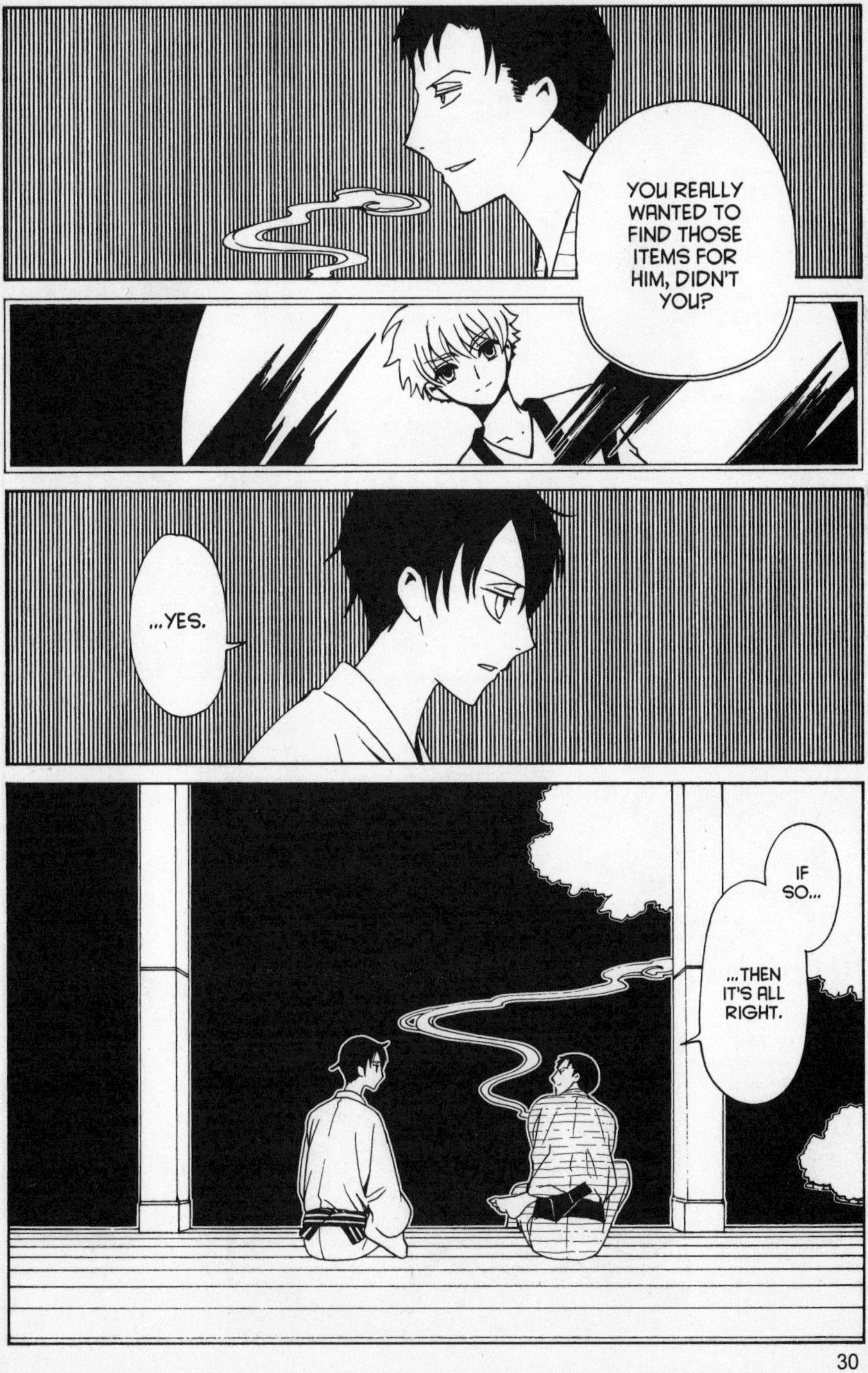
YOU REALLY WANTED TO FIND THOSE ITEMS FOR HIM, DIDN'T YOU?
...YES.
IF SO...
...THEN IT'S ALL RIGHT.

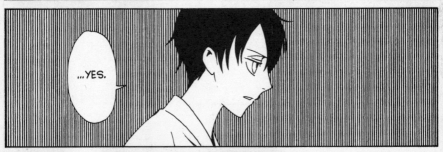

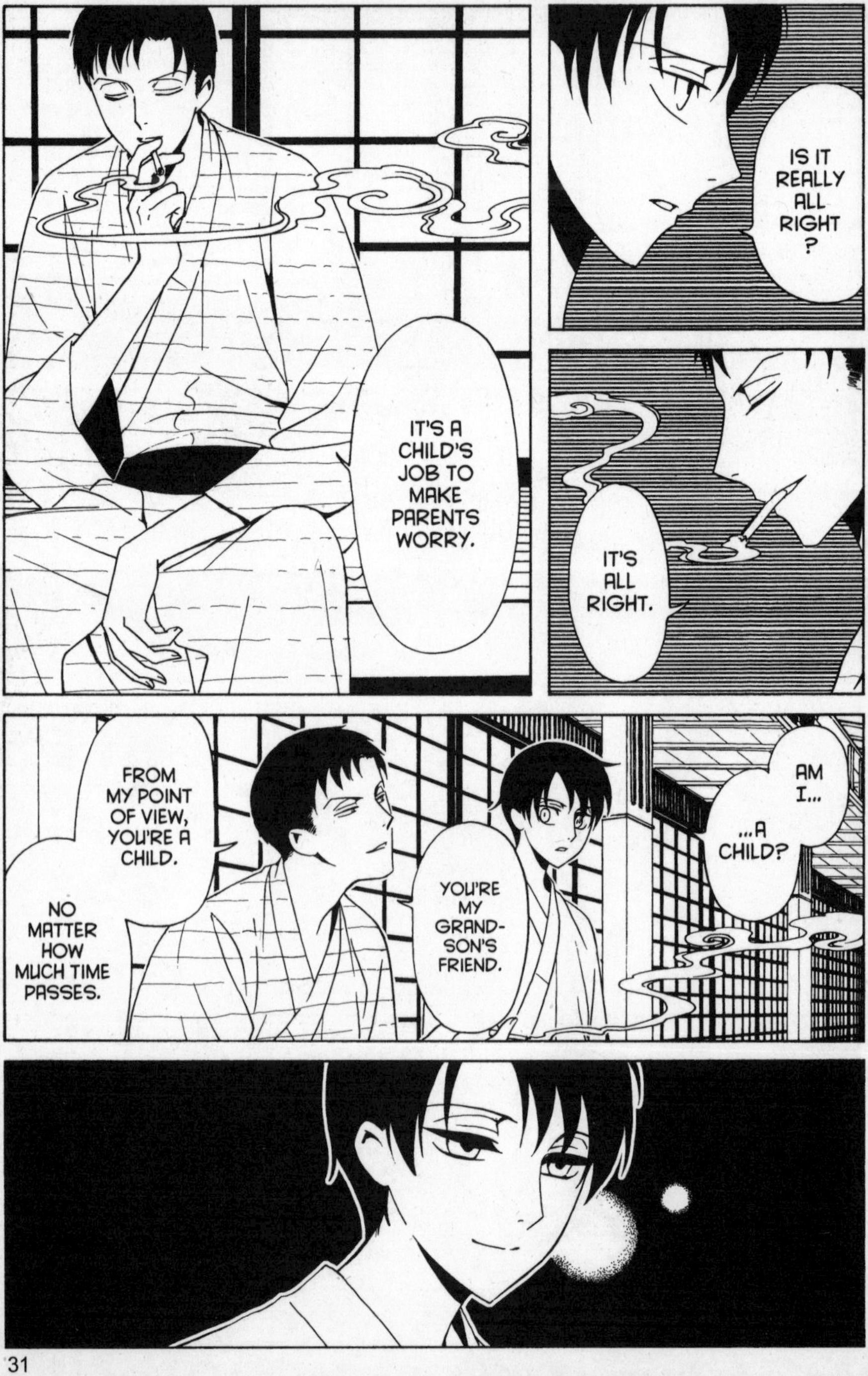
IS IT REALLY ALL RIGHT?
IT'S ALL RIGHT.
IT'S A CHILD'S JOB TO MAKE PARENTS WORRY.
AM I...
...A CHILD?
YOU'RE MY GRAND-SON'S FRIEND.
FROM MY POINT OF VIEW, YOU'RE A CHILD.
NO MATTER HOW MUCH TIME PASSES.

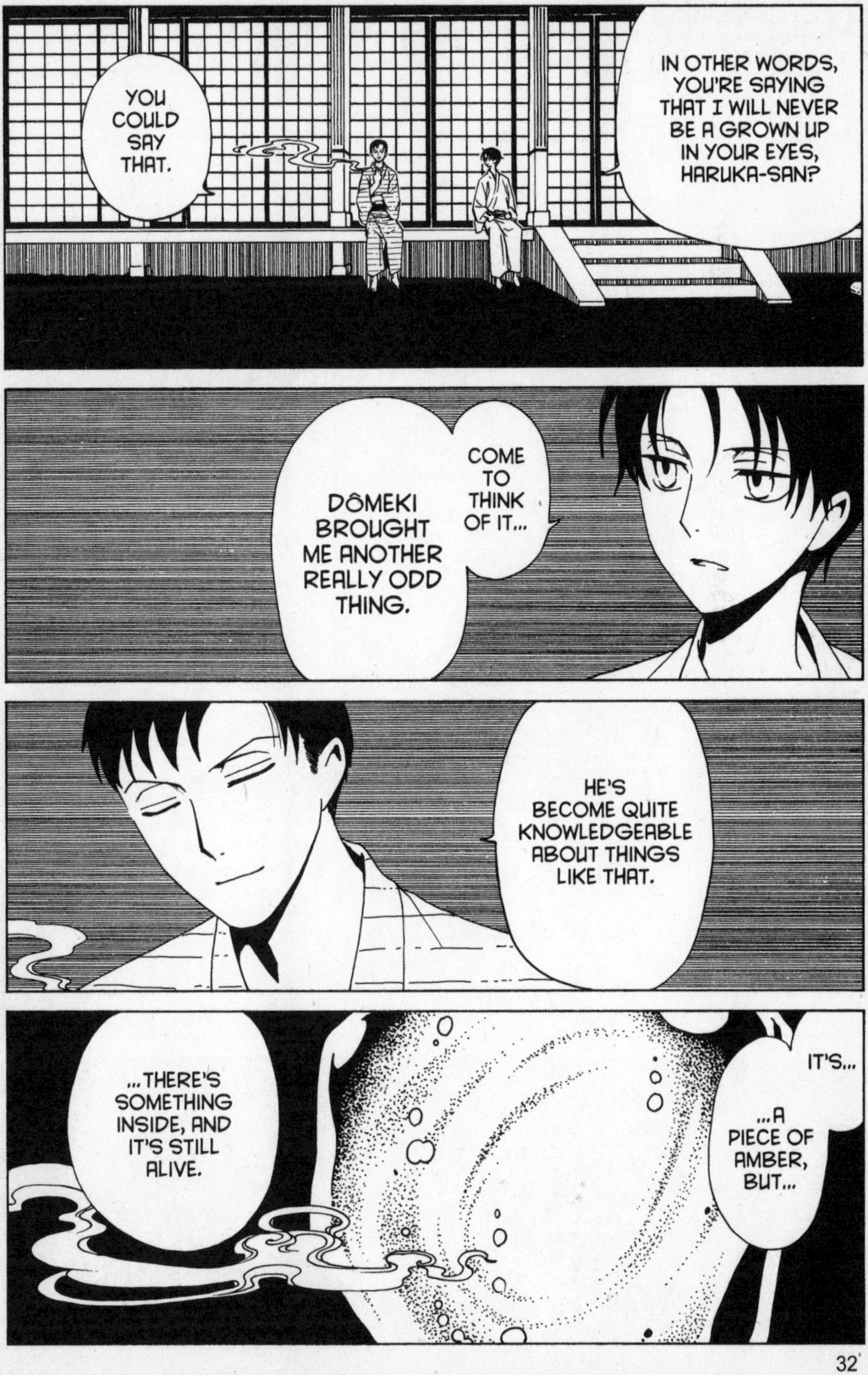
IN OTHER WORDS, YOU'RE SAYING THAT I WILL NEVER BE A GROWN UP IN YOUR EYES, HARUKA-SAN?
YOU COULD SAY THAT.
COME TO THINK OF IT...
DÔMEKI BROUGHT ME ANOTHER REALLY ODD THING.
HE'S BECOME QUITE KNOWLEDGEABLE ABOUT THINGS LIKE THAT.
IT'S...
...A PIECE OF AMBER, BUT...
...THERE'S SOMETHING INSIDE, AND IT'S STILL ALIVE.

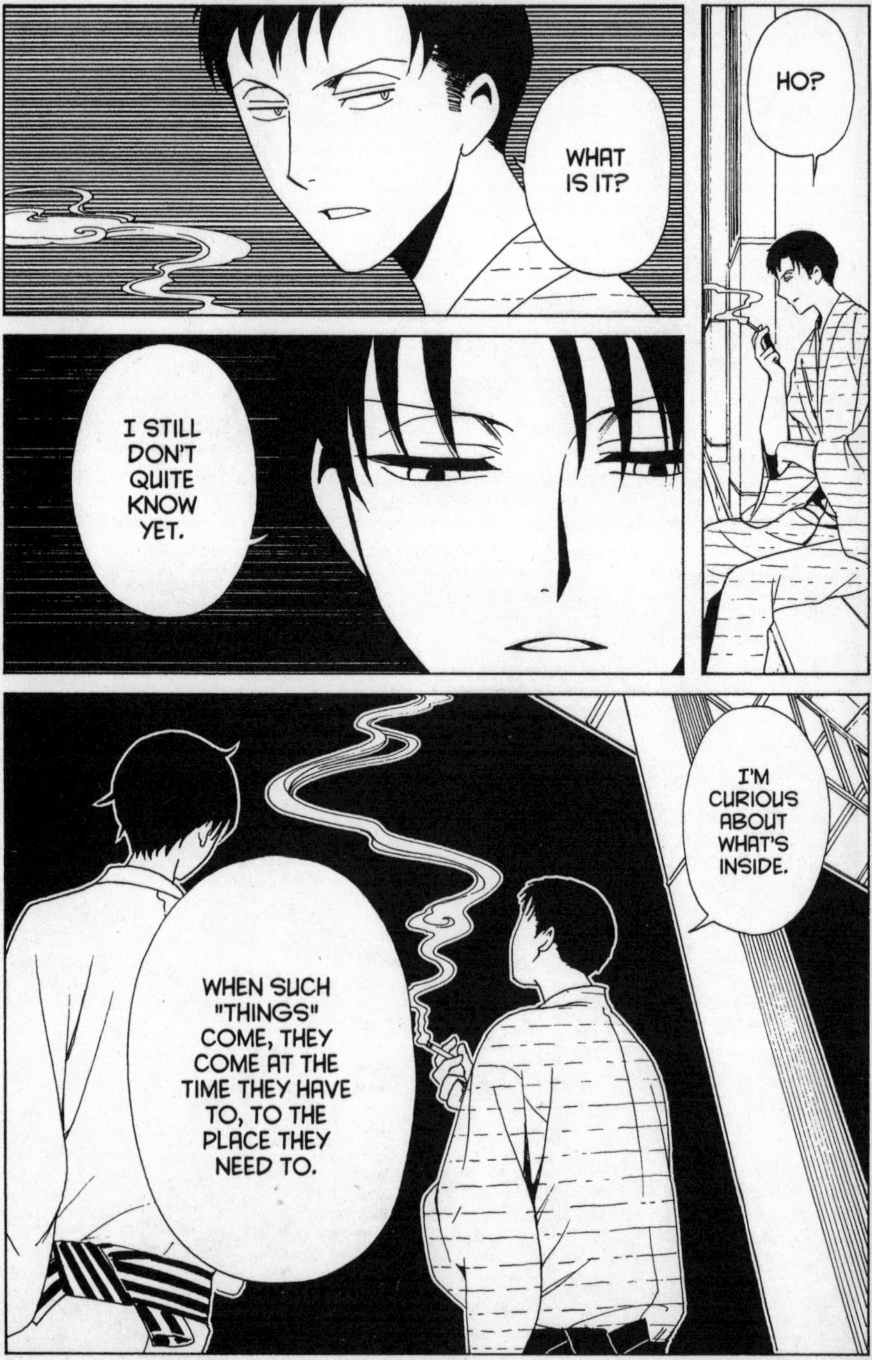
HO?
WHAT IS IT?
I STILL DON'T QUITE KNOW YET.
I'M CURIOUS ABOUT WHAT'S INSIDE.
WHEN SUCH "THINGS" COME, THEY COME AT THE TIME THEY HAVE TO, TO THE PLACE THEY NEED TO.

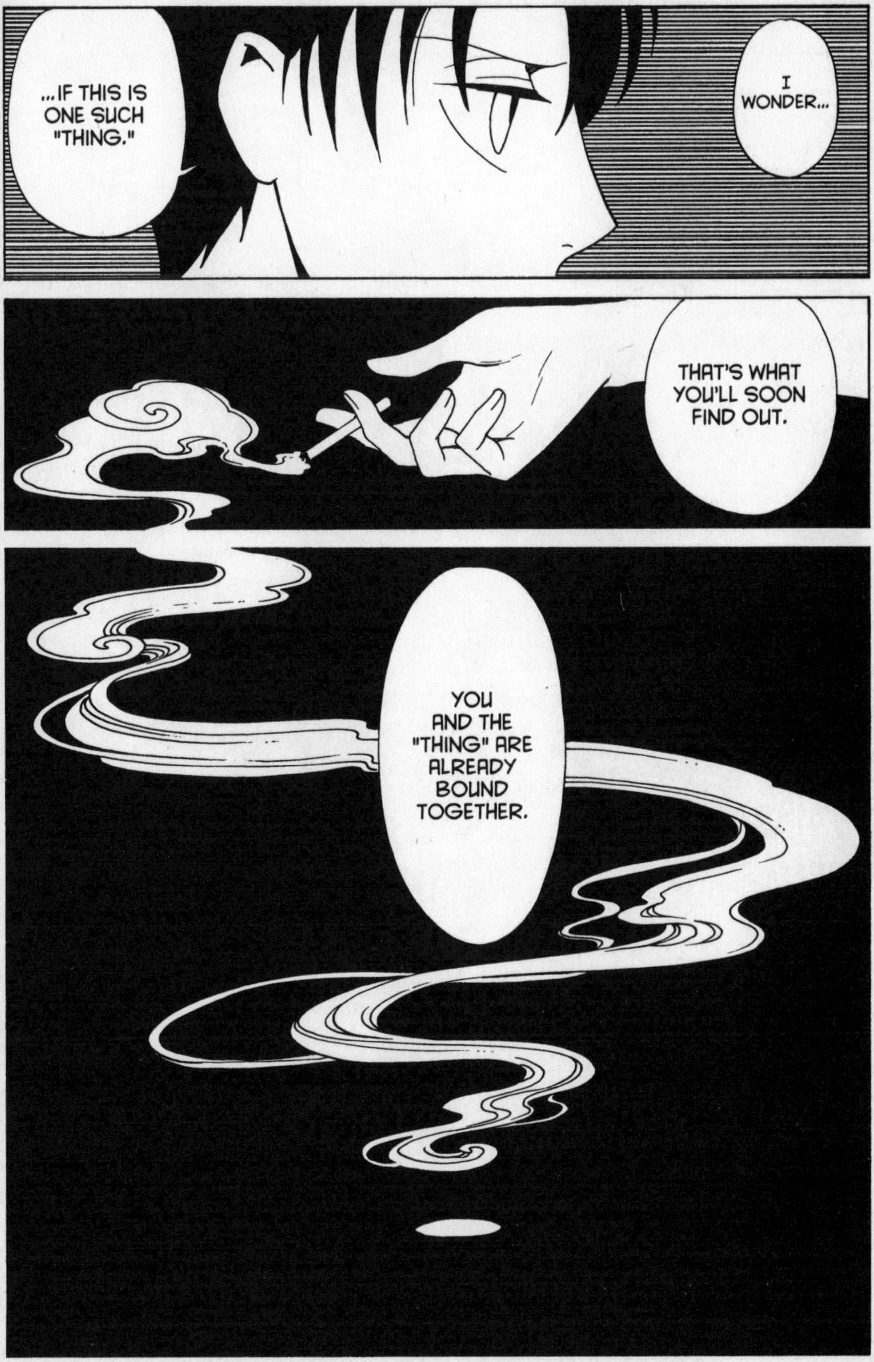
I WONDER...
...IF THIS IS ONE SUCH "THING."
THAT'S WHAT YOU'LL SOON FIND OUT.
YOU AND THE "THING" ARE ALREADY BOUND TOGETHER.

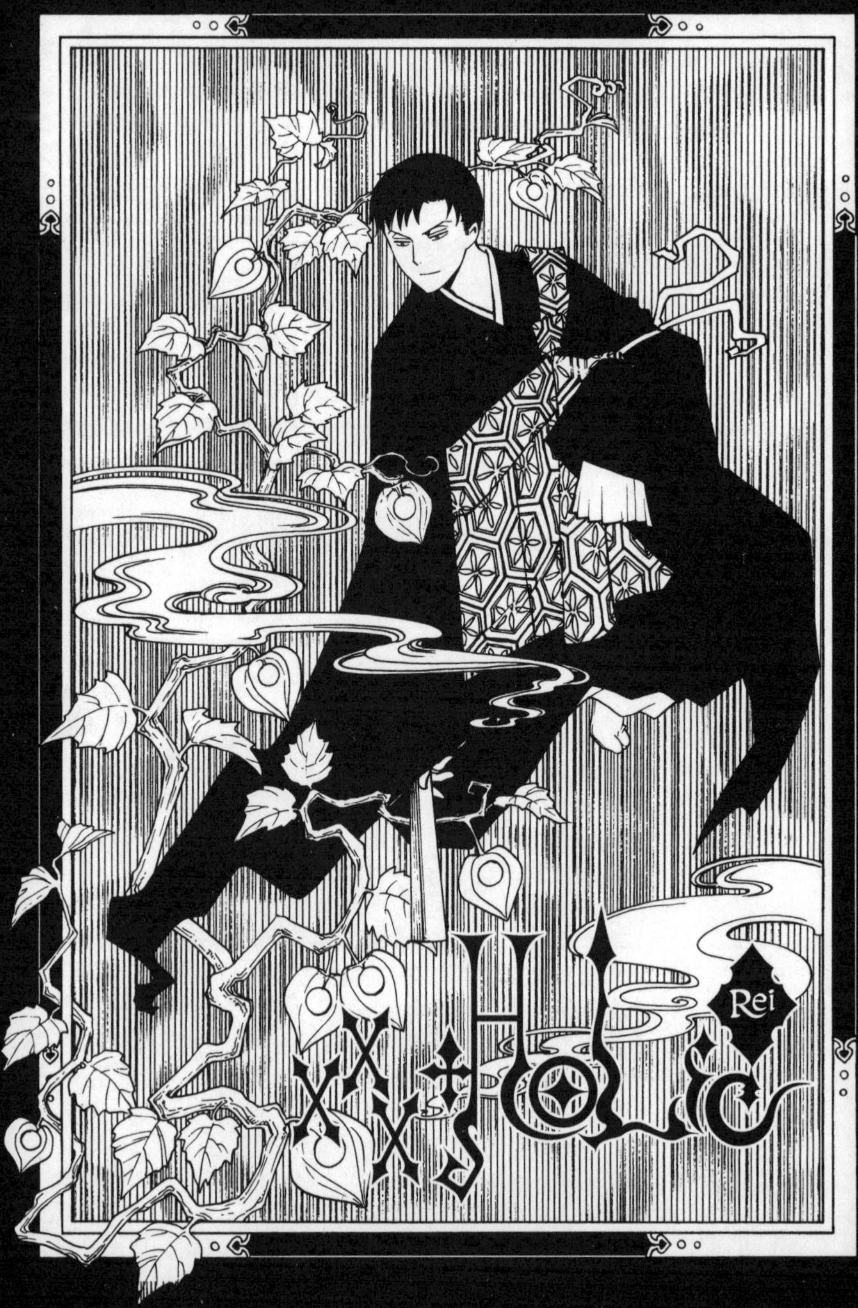
xxxHolic
Rei

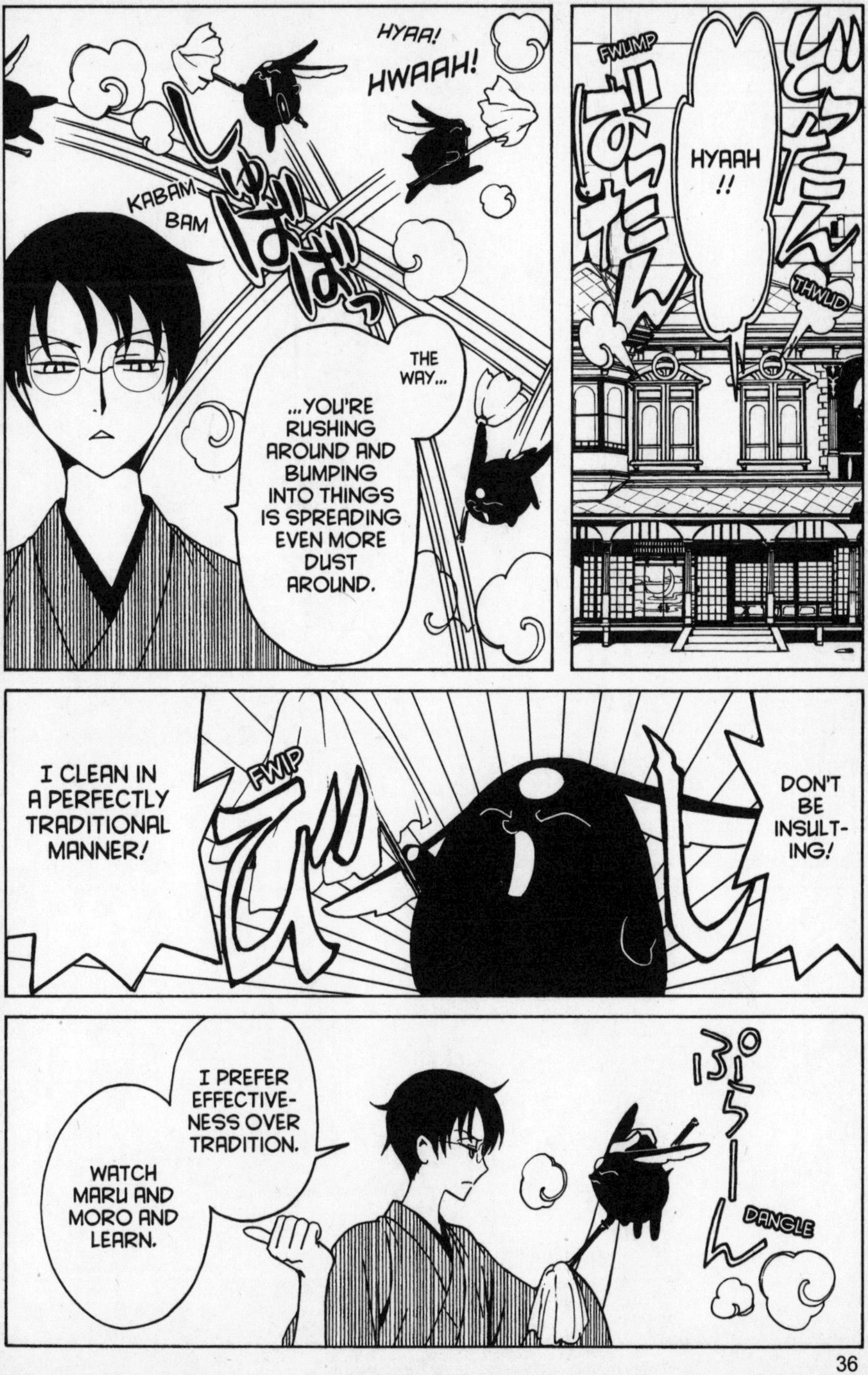
FWUMP
HYAAH !!
THWUD
HYAA!
HWAAH!
KABAM
BAM
THE WAY...
...YOU'RE RUSHING AROUND AND BUMPING INTO THINGS IS SPREADING EVEN MORE DUST AROUND.
DON'T BE INSULT-ING!
FWIP
I CLEAN IN A PERFECTLY TRADITIONAL MANNER!
DANGLE
I PREFER EFFECTIVE-NESS OVER TRADITION.
WATCH MARU AND MORO AND LEARN.

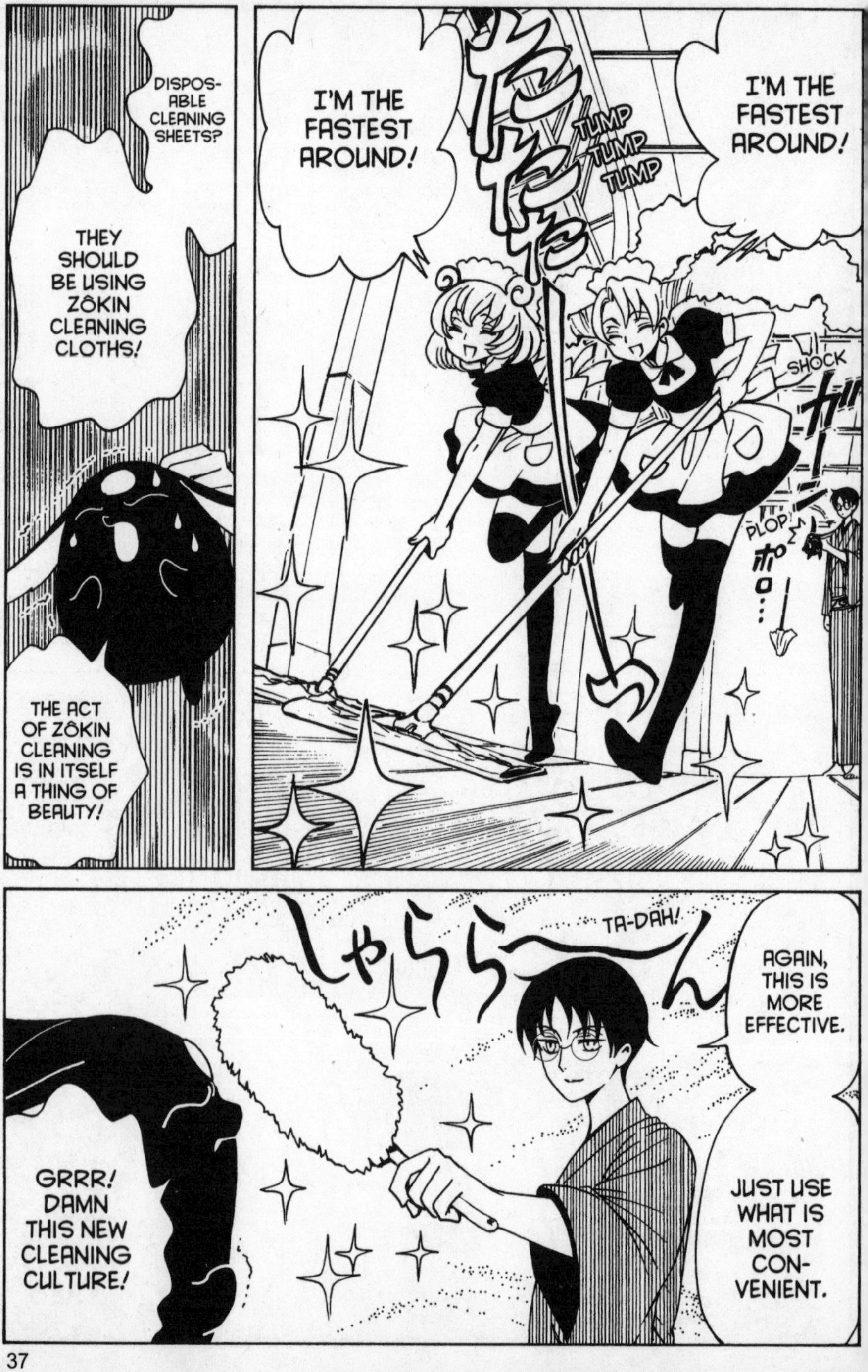
I'M THE FASTEST AROUND!
TUMP TUMP TUMP
I'M THE FASTEST AROUND!
SHOCK
PLOP
DISPOS-ABLE CLEANING SHEETS?
THEY SHOULD BE USING ZÔKIN CLEANING CLOTHS!
THE ACT OF ZÔKIN CLEANING IS IN ITSELF A THING OF BEAUTY!
TA-DAH!
AGAIN, THIS IS MORE EFFECTIVE.
JUST USE WHAT IS MOST CON-VENIENT.
GRRR! DAMN THIS NEW CLEANING CULTURE!

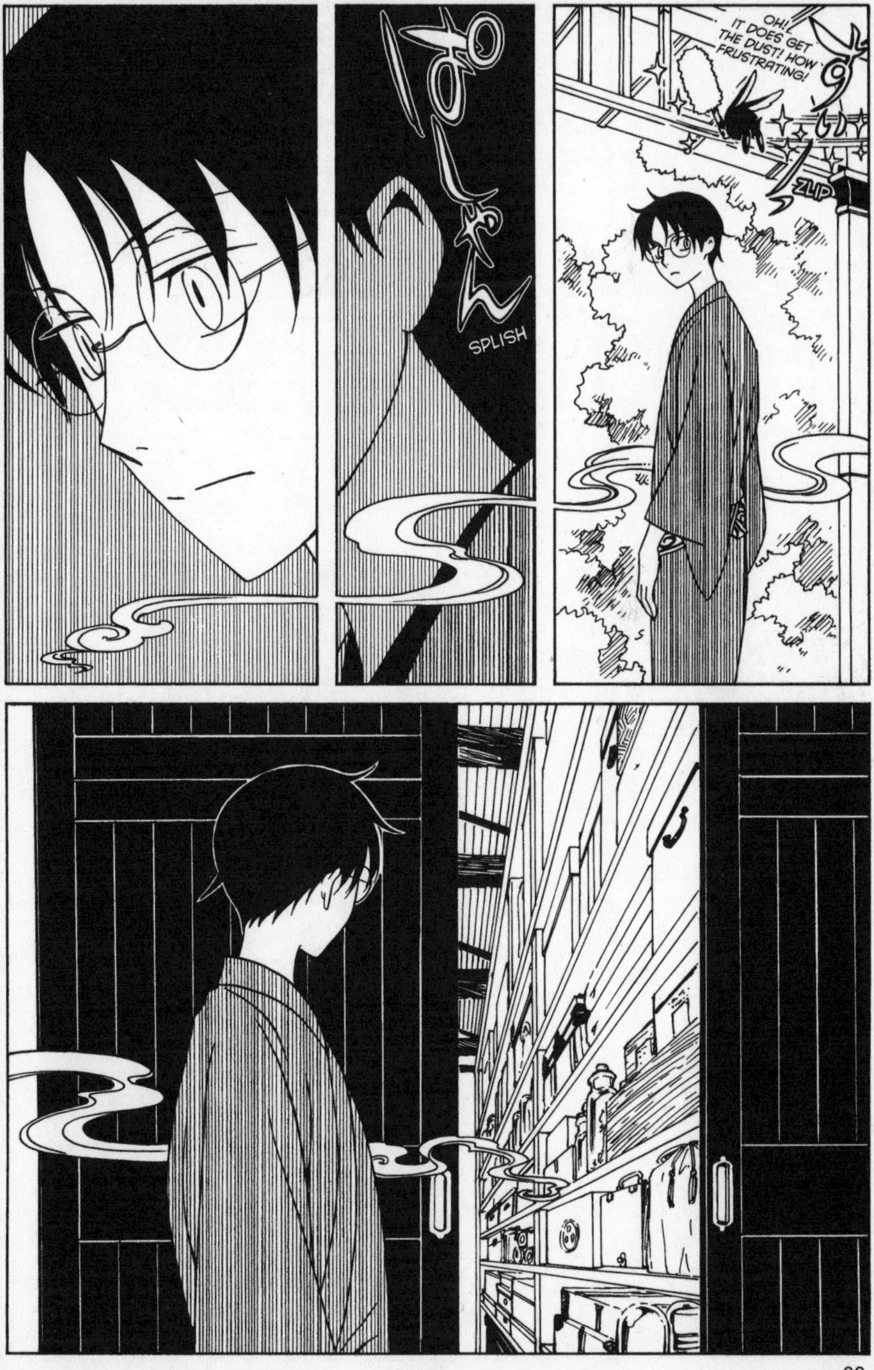
OH! IT DOES GET THE DUST! HOW FRUSTRATING!
ZLIP
SPLISH

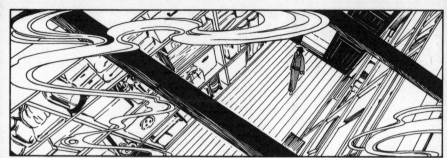

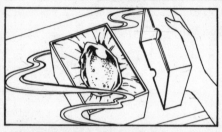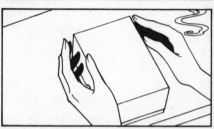

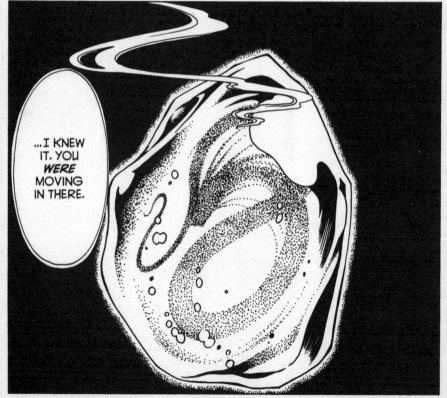

...I KNEW IT. YOU *WERE* MOVING IN THERE.

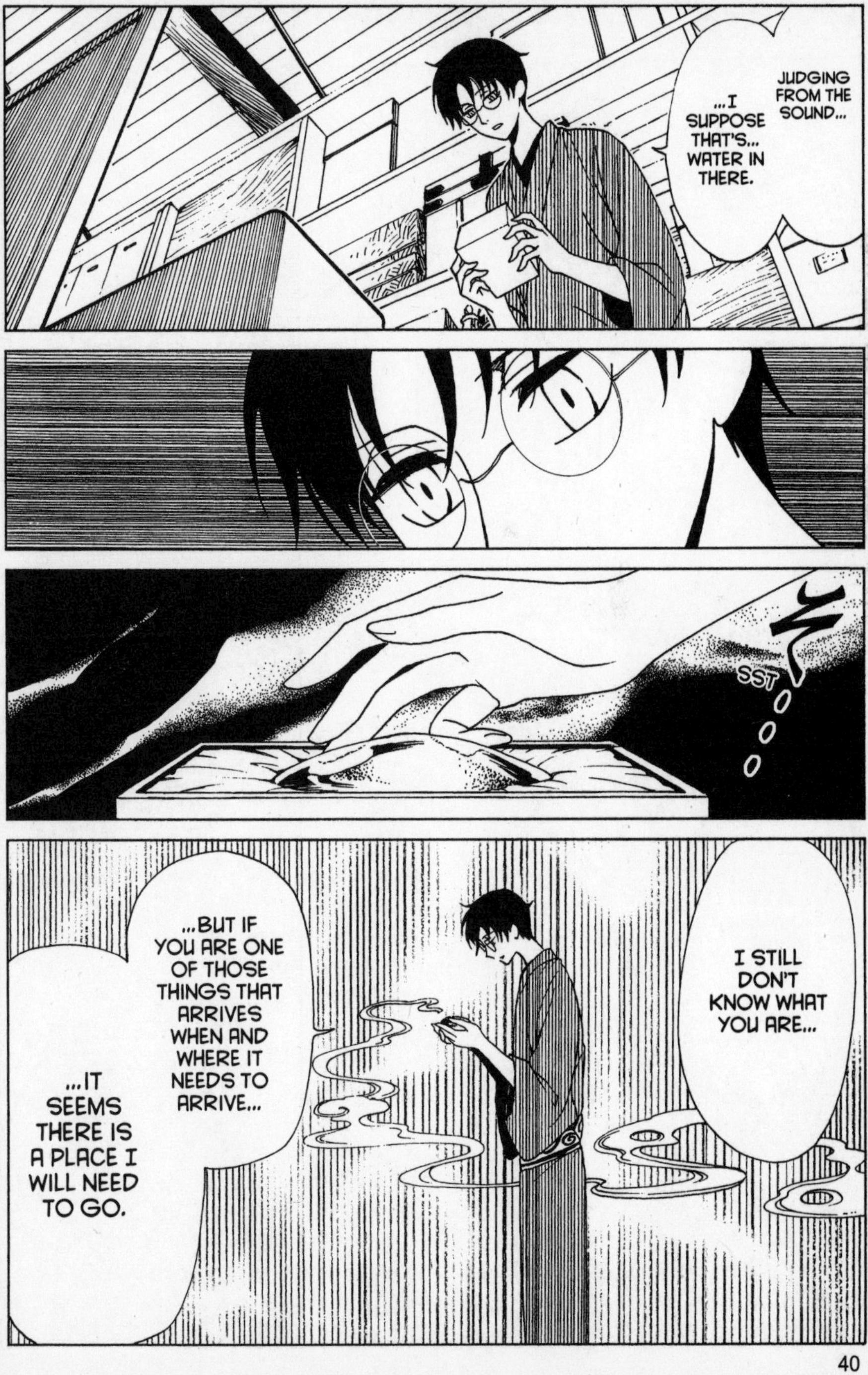
JUDGING FROM THE SOUND...
...I SUPPOSE THAT'S... WATER IN THERE.
SST
I STILL DON'T KNOW WHAT YOU ARE...
...BUT IF YOU ARE ONE OF THOSE THINGS THAT ARRIVES WHEN AND WHERE IT NEEDS TO ARRIVE...
...IT SEEMS THERE IS A PLACE I WILL NEED TO GO.

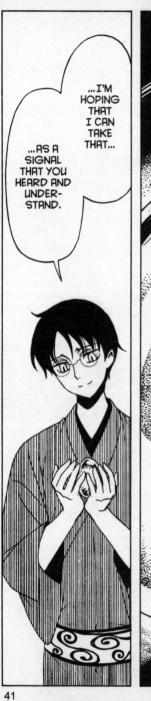

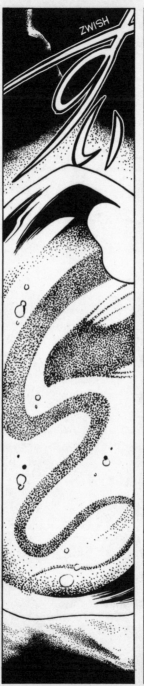

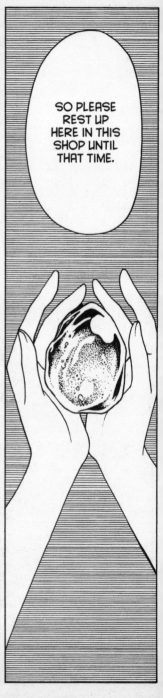

SO PLEASE REST UP HERE IN THIS SHOP UNTIL THAT TIME.
ZWISH
...I'M HOPING THAT I CAN TAKE THAT...
...AS A SIGNAL THAT YOU HEARD AND UNDER-STAND.

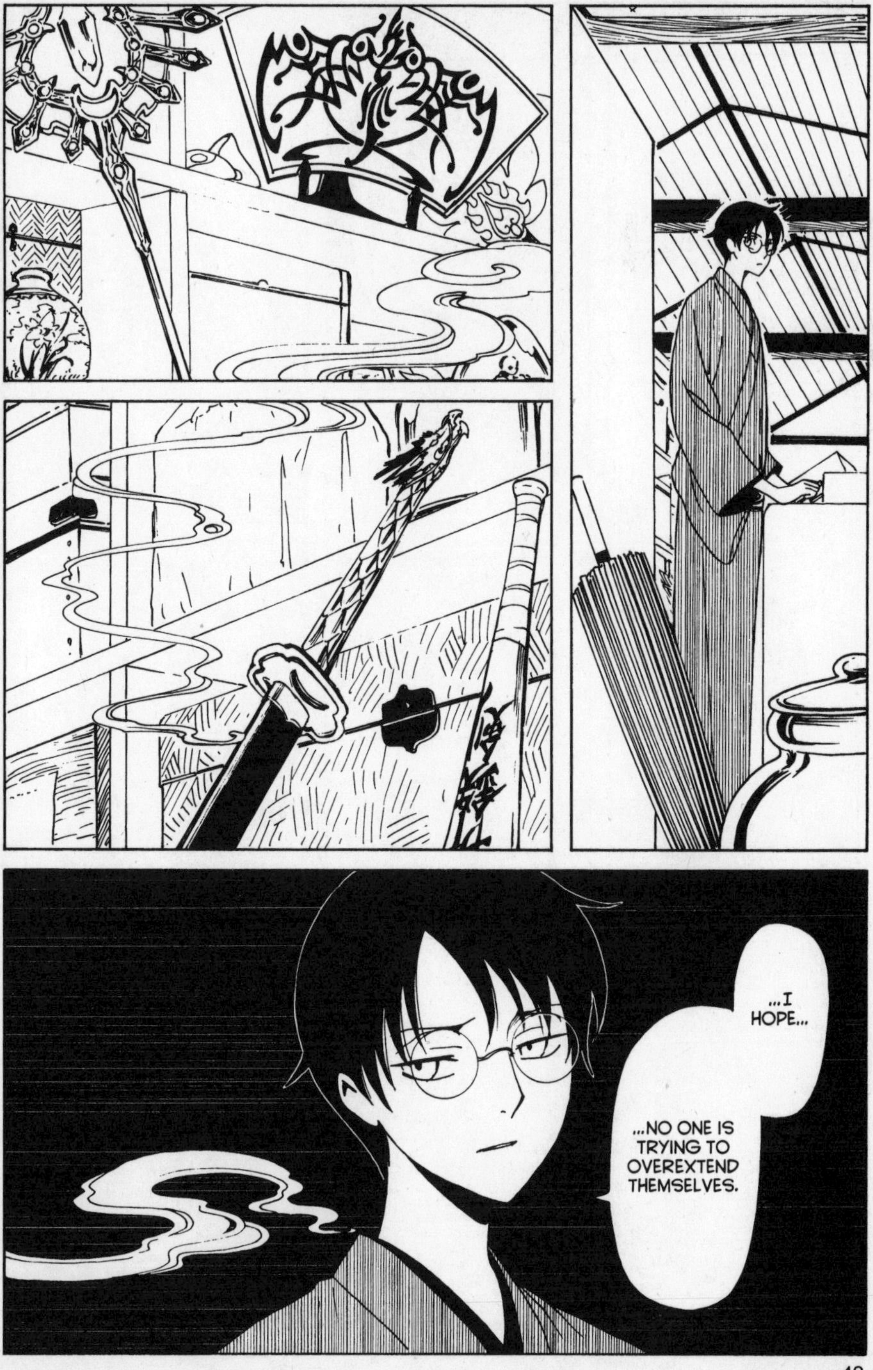
...I HOPE...
...NO ONE IS TRYING TO OVEREXTEND THEMSELVES.

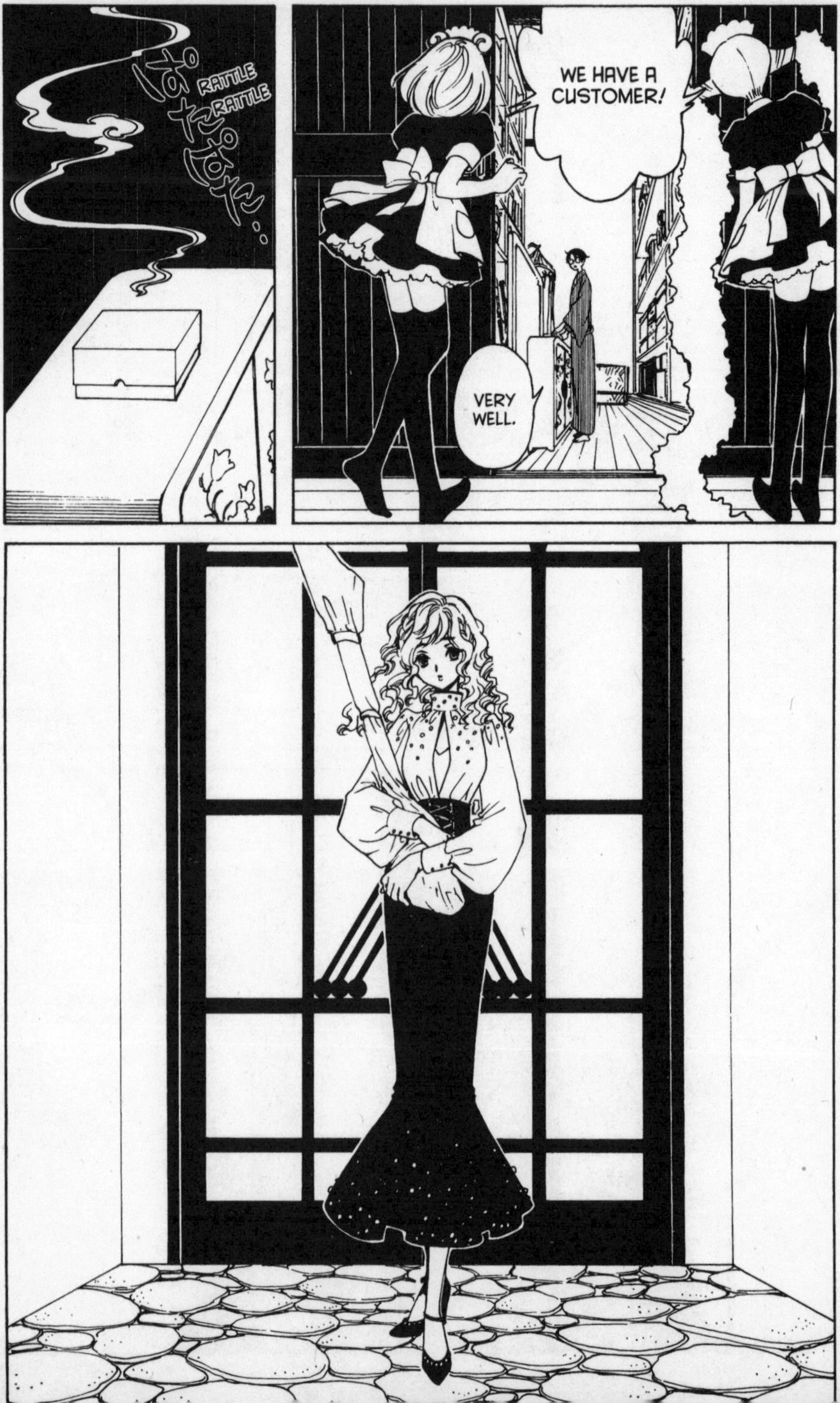
WE HAVE A CUSTOMER!
VERY WELL.
ぱたぱた..
RATTLE RATTLE

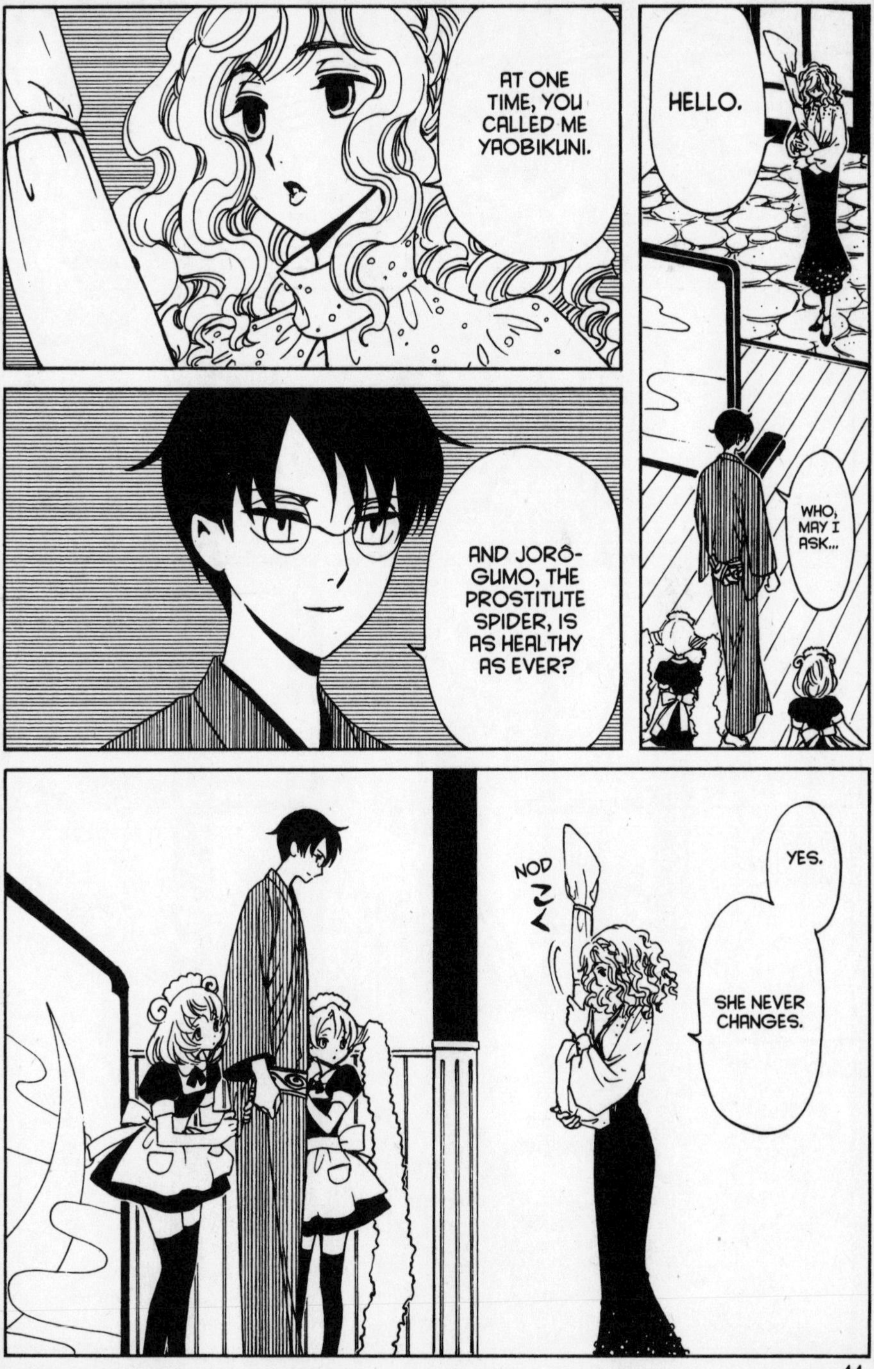
HELLO.
WHO, MAY I ASK...
AT ONE TIME, YOU CALLED ME YAOBIKUNI.
AND JORÔ-GUMO, THE PROSTITUTE SPIDER, IS AS HEALTHY AS EVER?
YES.
SHE NEVER CHANGES.
NOD

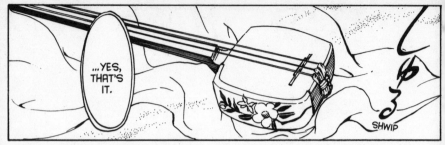

...YES, THAT'S IT.
しゅる
SHWIP
THAT IS THE SHAMISEN I LOANED HER.
AND IT'S NOW BEEN RETURNED.
BUT, MAY I ASK WHY JORÔ-GUMO FELT THE DESIRE...
...TO PLAY THE SHAMISEN?
SHE DOES EVERYTHING ON A WHIM.
DID SHE GET IT TO PLAY? IT IS A FINICKY INSTRUMENT.
NOT AT FIRST...
BUT JORÔ-GUMO SAID SOMETHING ABOUT TALKING TO IT FOR A WHILE...
...AND SHE TOOK IT OFF SOMEPLACE. THEN, WHEN SHE RETURNED, SHE HAD MANAGED TO GET SOUNDS OUT OF IT.

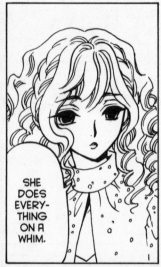

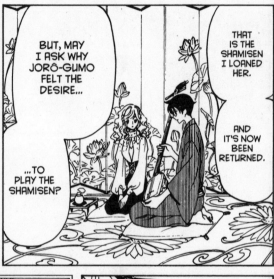

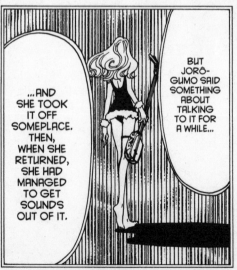

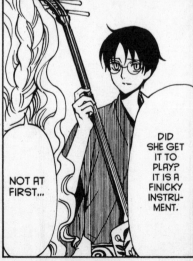

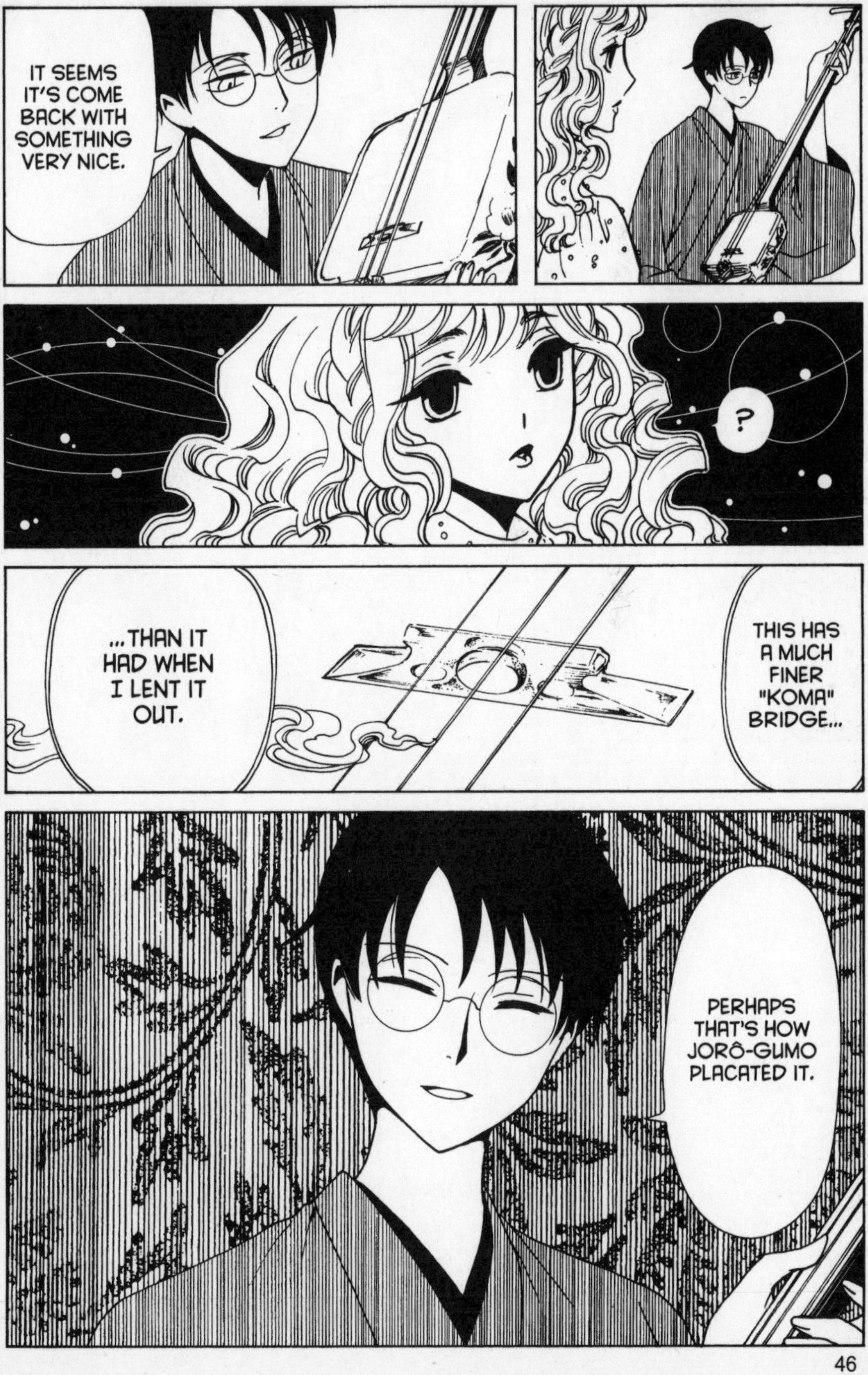
IT SEEMS IT'S COME BACK WITH SOMETHING VERY NICE.
?
THIS HAS A MUCH FINER "KOMA" BRIDGE...
...THAN IT HAD WHEN I LENT IT OUT.
PERHAPS THAT'S HOW JORÔ-GUMO PLACATED IT.

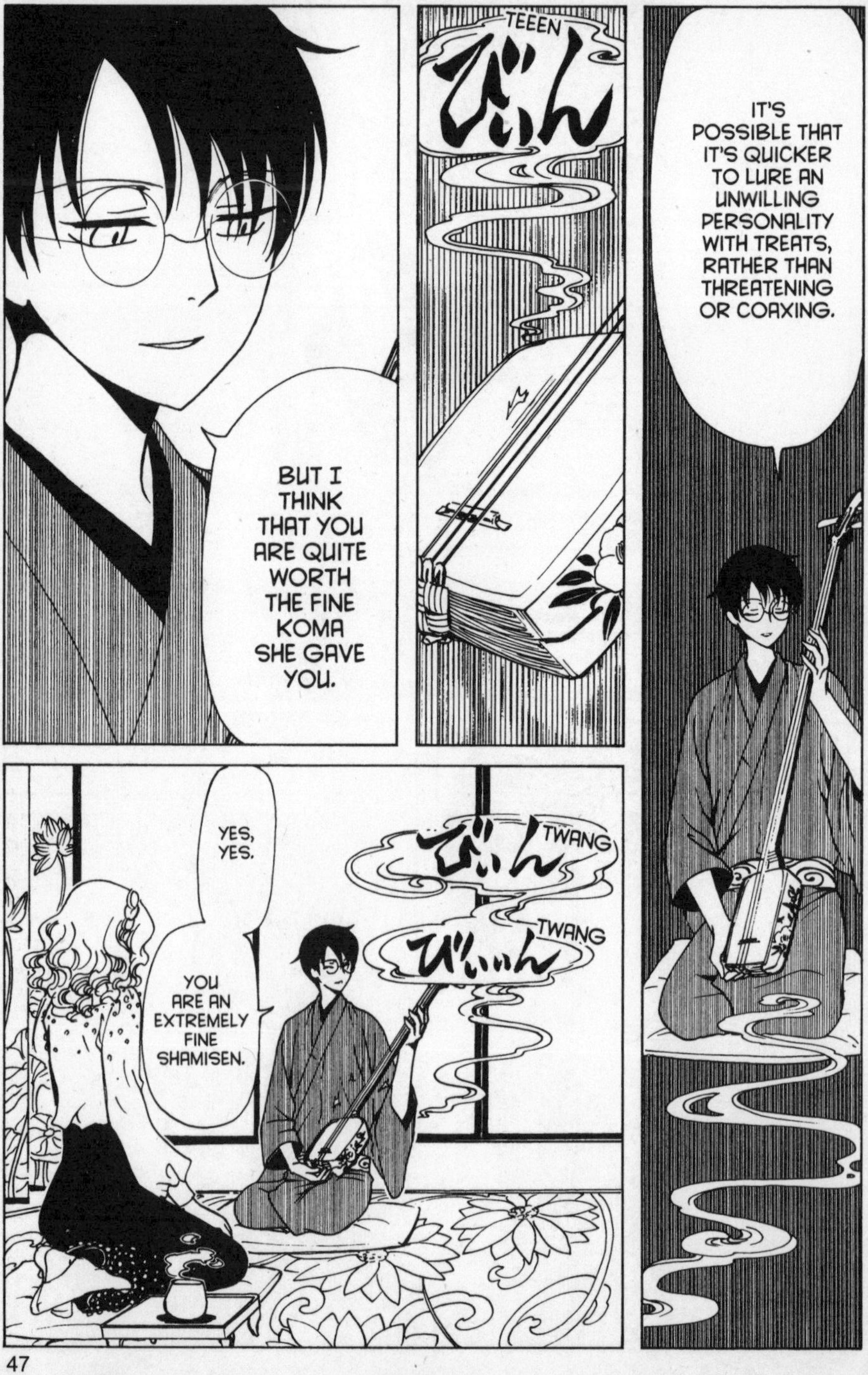
IT'S POSSIBLE THAT IT'S QUICKER TO LURE AN UNWILLING PERSONALITY WITH TREATS, RATHER THAN THREATENING OR COAXING.
TEEEN
びいん
BUT I THINK THAT YOU ARE QUITE WORTH THE FINE KOMA SHE GAVE YOU.
びぃん
TWANG
びぃぃん
TWANG
YES, YES.
YOU ARE AN EXTREMELY FINE SHAMISEN.

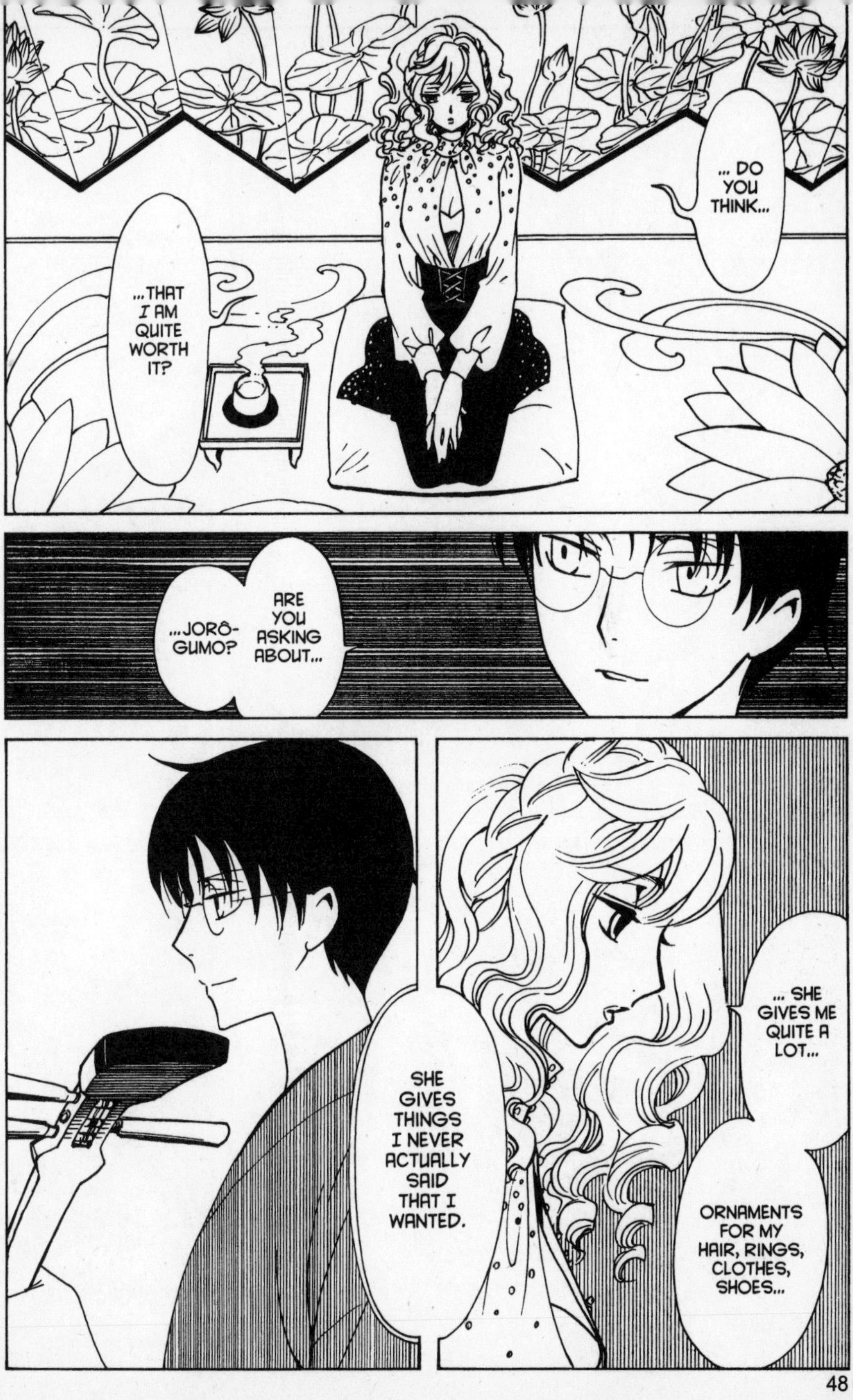
... DO YOU THINK...
...THAT I AM QUITE WORTH IT?
ARE YOU ASKING ABOUT...
...JORÔ-GUMO?
... SHE GIVES ME QUITE A LOT...
ORNAMENTS FOR MY HAIR, RINGS, CLOTHES, SHOES...
SHE GIVES THINGS I NEVER ACTUALLY SAID THAT I WANTED.

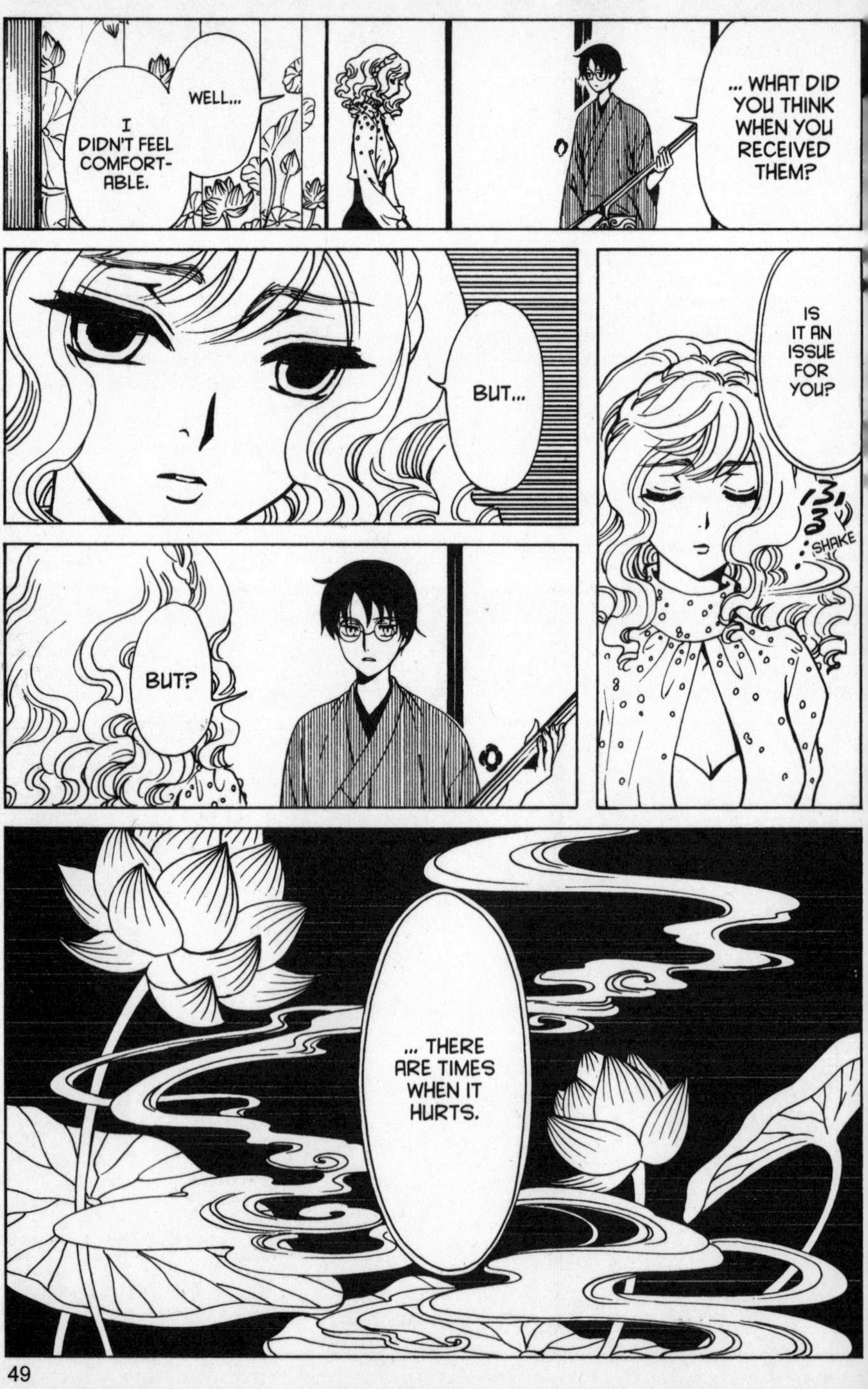
... WHAT DID YOU THINK WHEN YOU RECEIVED THEM?
WELL...
I DIDN'T FEEL COMFORT-ABLE.
IS IT AN ISSUE FOR YOU?
SHAKE
BUT...
BUT?
... THERE ARE TIMES WHEN IT HURTS.

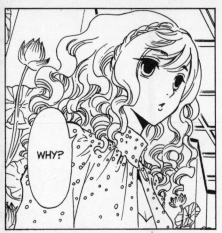

WHY?

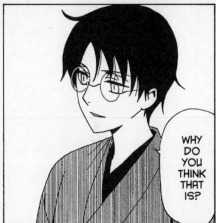

WHY DO YOU THINK THAT IS?

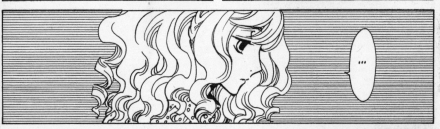

...

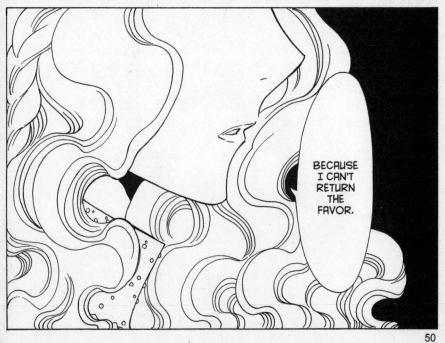

BECAUSE I CAN'T RETURN THE FAVOR.

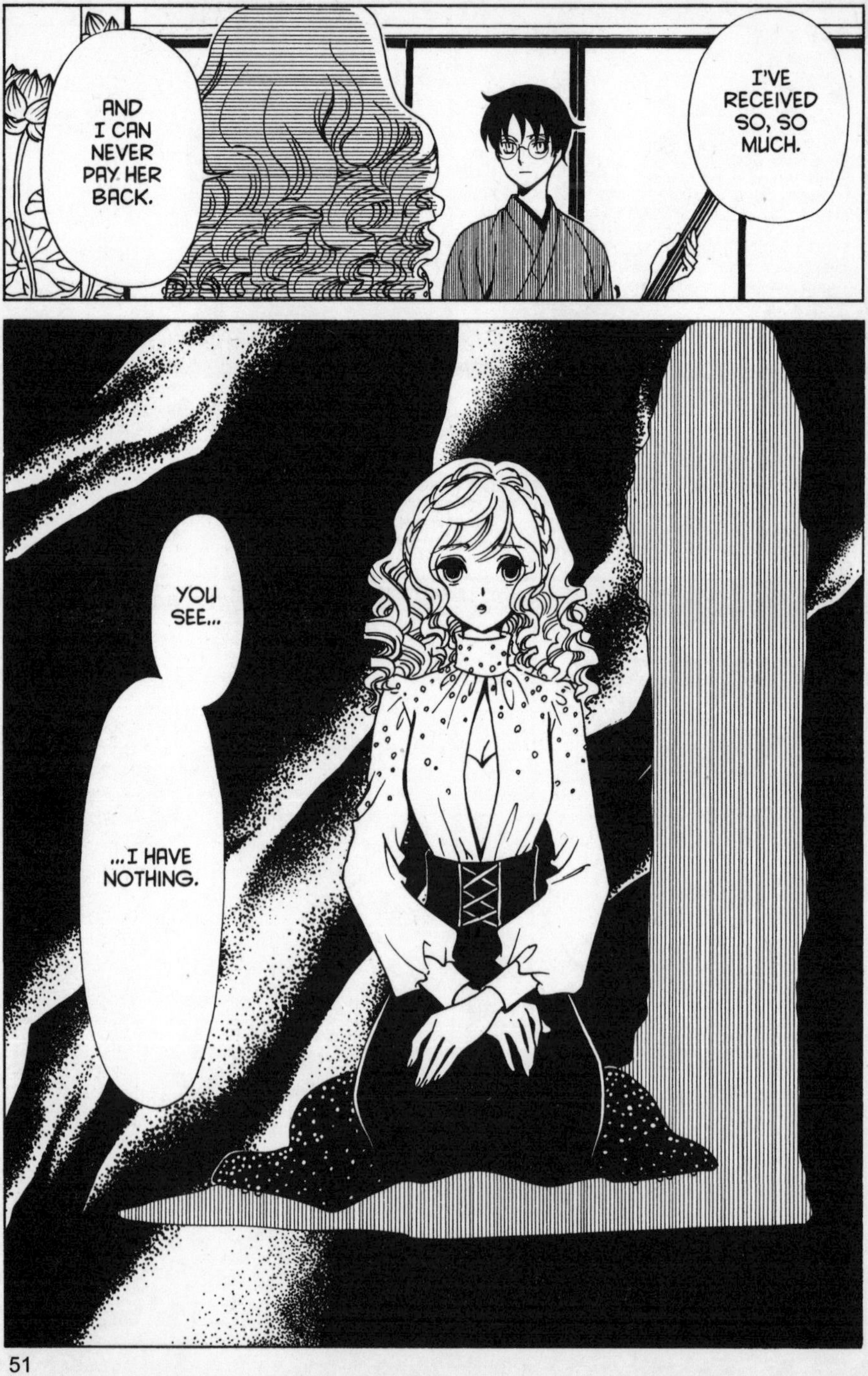
I'VE RECEIVED SO, SO MUCH.
AND I CAN NEVER PAY HER BACK.
YOU SEE...
...I HAVE NOTHING.

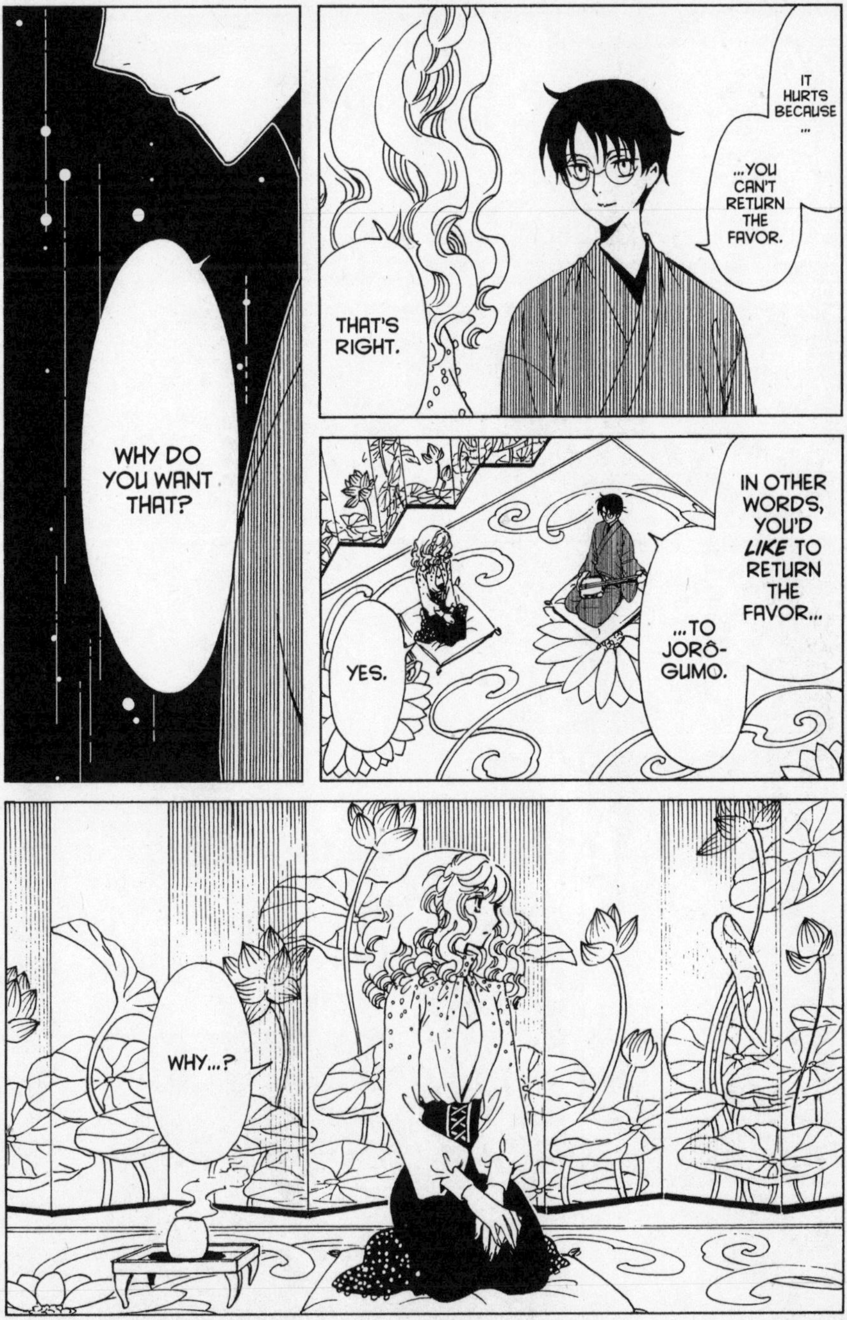
IT HURTS BECAUSE ...
...YOU CAN'T RETURN THE FAVOR.
THAT'S RIGHT.
IN OTHER WORDS, YOU'D *LIKE* TO RETURN THE FAVOR...
...TO JORÔ-GUMO.
YES.
WHY DO YOU WANT THAT?
WHY...?

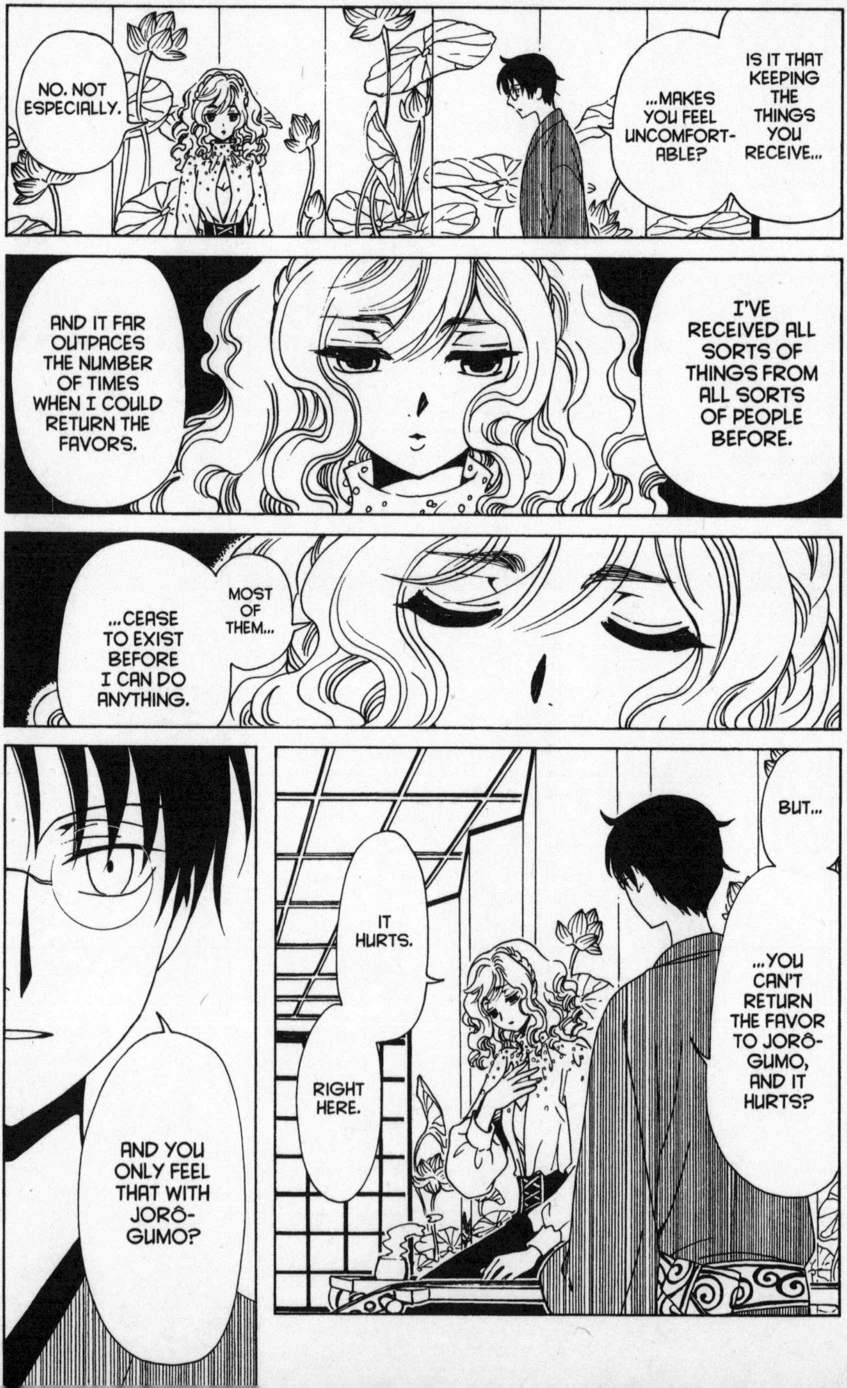
IS IT THAT KEEPING THE THINGS YOU RECEIVE...
...MAKES YOU FEEL UNCOMFORTABLE?
NO. NOT ESPECIALLY.
I'VE RECEIVED ALL SORTS OF THINGS FROM ALL SORTS OF PEOPLE BEFORE.
AND IT FAR OUTPACES THE NUMBER OF TIMES WHEN I COULD RETURN THE FAVORS.
MOST OF THEM...
...CEASE TO EXIST BEFORE I CAN DO ANYTHING.
BUT...
...YOU CAN'T RETURN THE FAVOR TO JORÔ-GUMO, AND IT HURTS?
IT HURTS.
RIGHT HERE.
AND YOU ONLY FEEL THAT WITH JORÔ-GUMO?

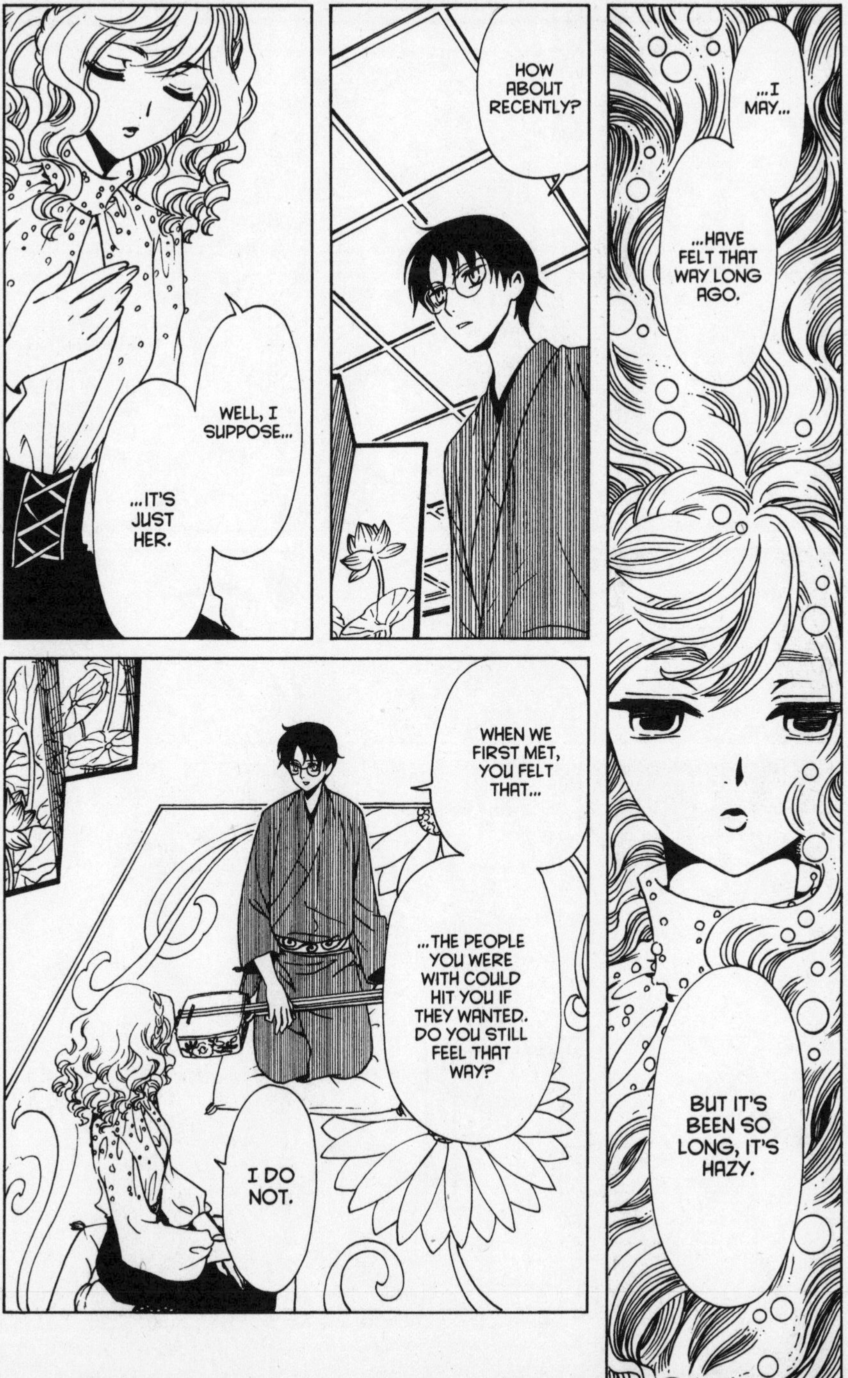
...I MAY...
...HAVE FELT THAT WAY LONG AGO.
BUT IT'S BEEN SO LONG, IT'S HAZY.
HOW ABOUT RECENTLY?
WELL, I SUPPOSE...
...IT'S JUST HER.
WHEN WE FIRST MET, YOU FELT THAT...
...THE PEOPLE YOU WERE WITH COULD HIT YOU IF THEY WANTED. DO YOU STILL FEEL THAT WAY?
I DO NOT.

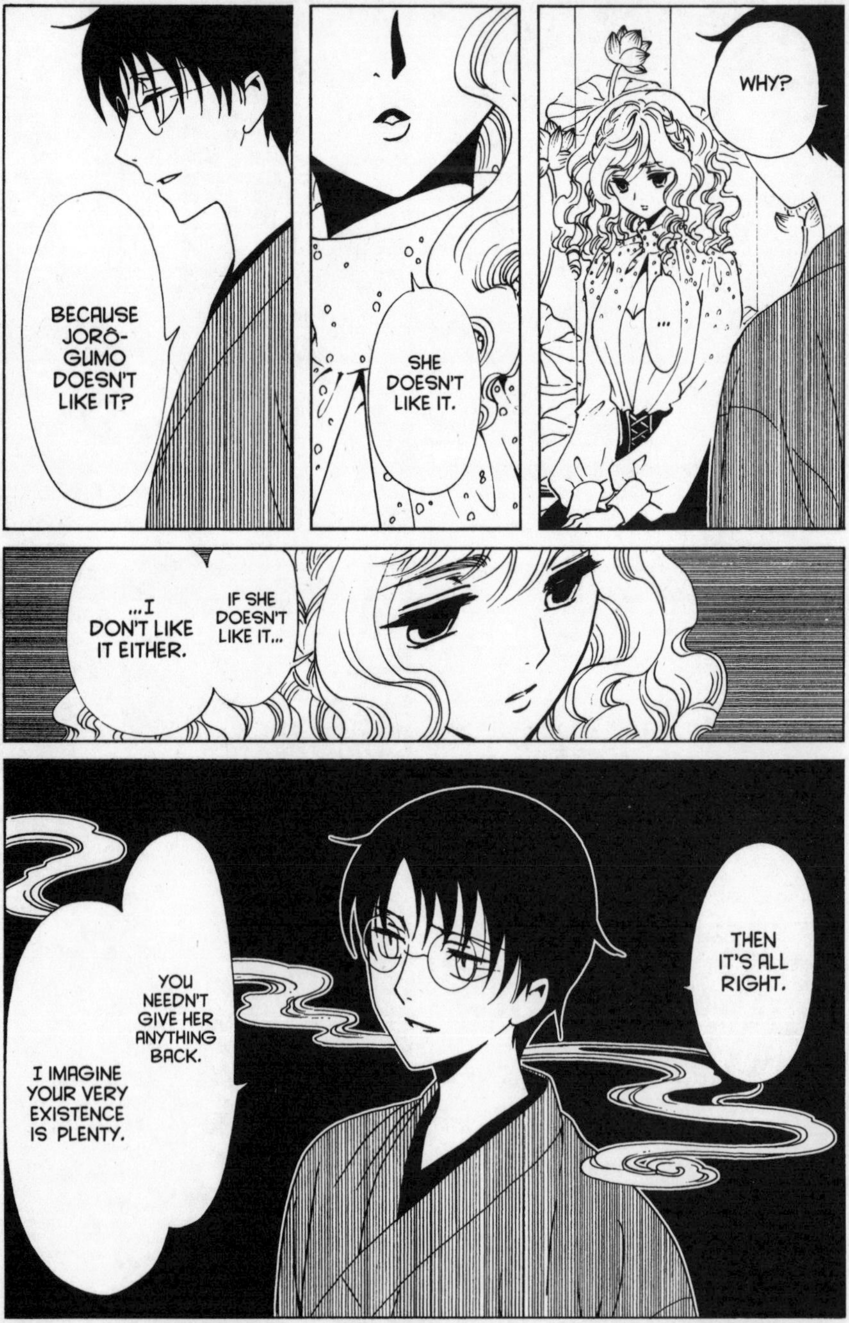
WHY?
...
SHE DOESN'T LIKE IT.
BECAUSE JORÔ-GUMO DOESN'T LIKE IT?
IF SHE DOESN'T LIKE IT...
...I DON'T LIKE IT EITHER.
THEN IT'S ALL RIGHT.
YOU NEEDN'T GIVE HER ANYTHING BACK.
I IMAGINE YOUR VERY EXISTENCE IS PLENTY.

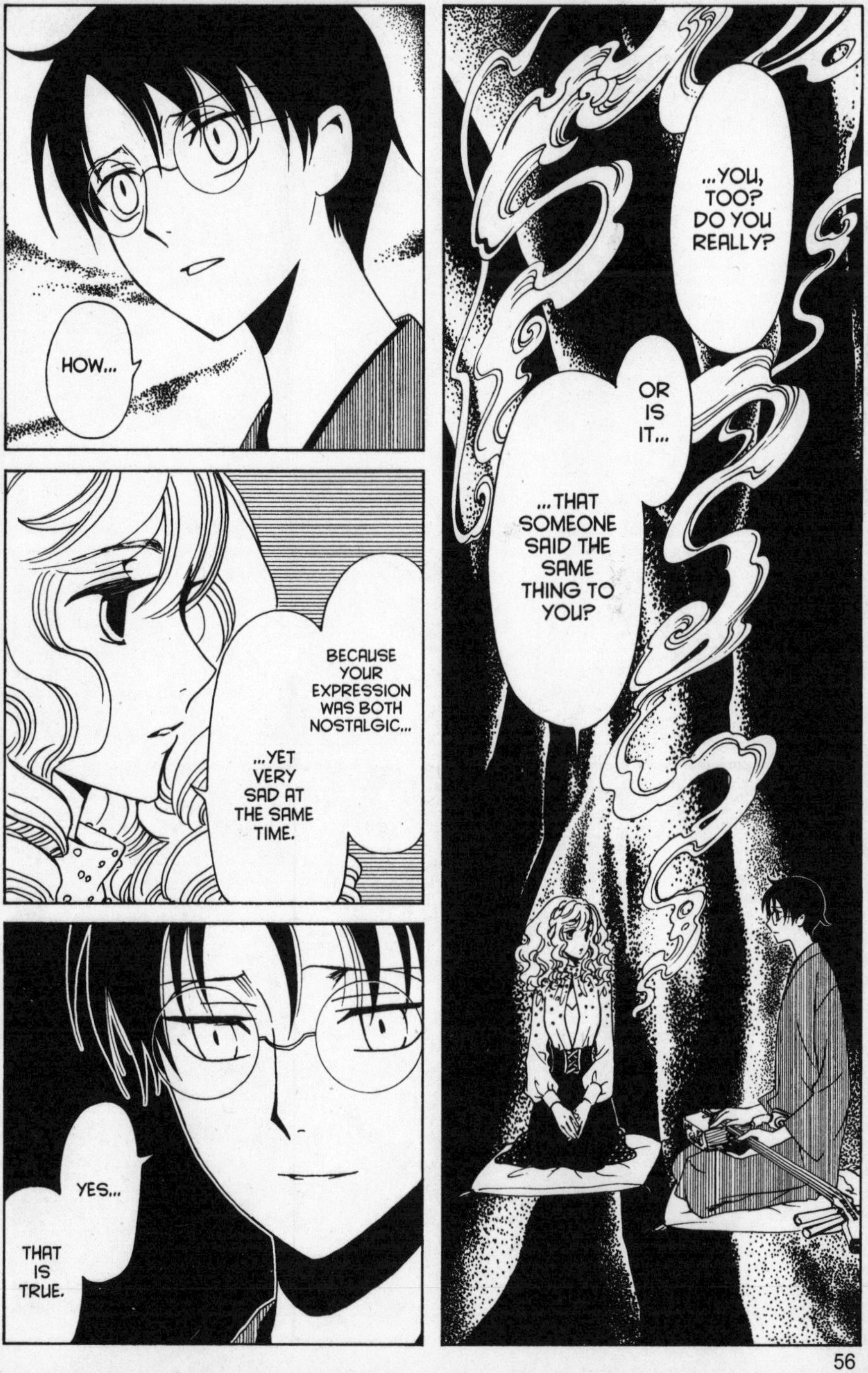
...YOU, TOO? DO YOU REALLY?
OR IS IT...
...THAT SOMEONE SAID THE SAME THING TO YOU?
HOW...
BECAUSE YOUR EXPRESSION WAS BOTH NOSTALGIC...
...YET VERY SAD AT THE SAME TIME.
YES...
THAT IS TRUE.

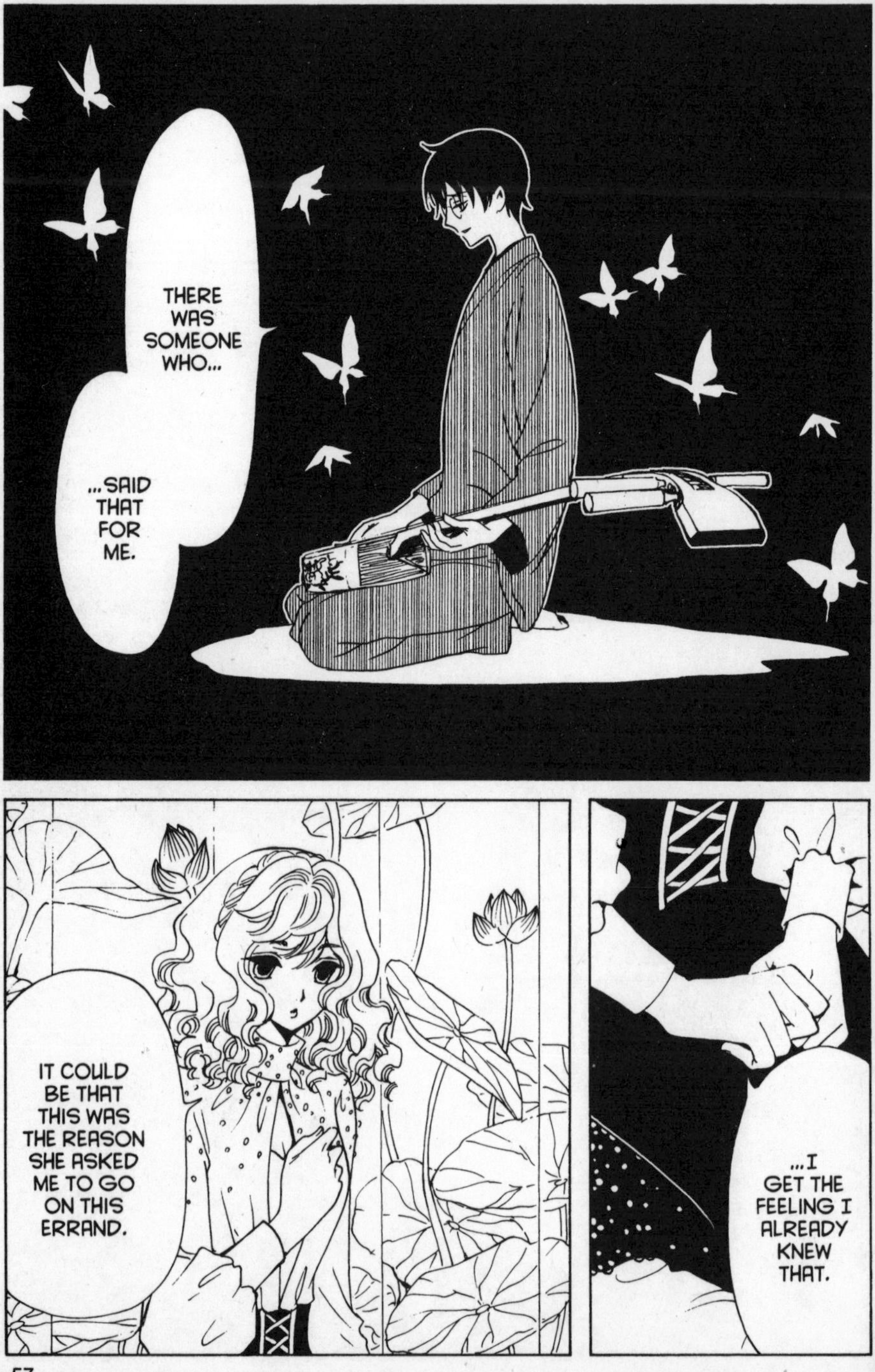
THERE WAS SOMEONE WHO...
...SAID THAT FOR ME.
...I GET THE FEELING I ALREADY KNEW THAT.
IT COULD BE THAT THIS WAS THE REASON SHE ASKED ME TO GO ON THIS ERRAND.

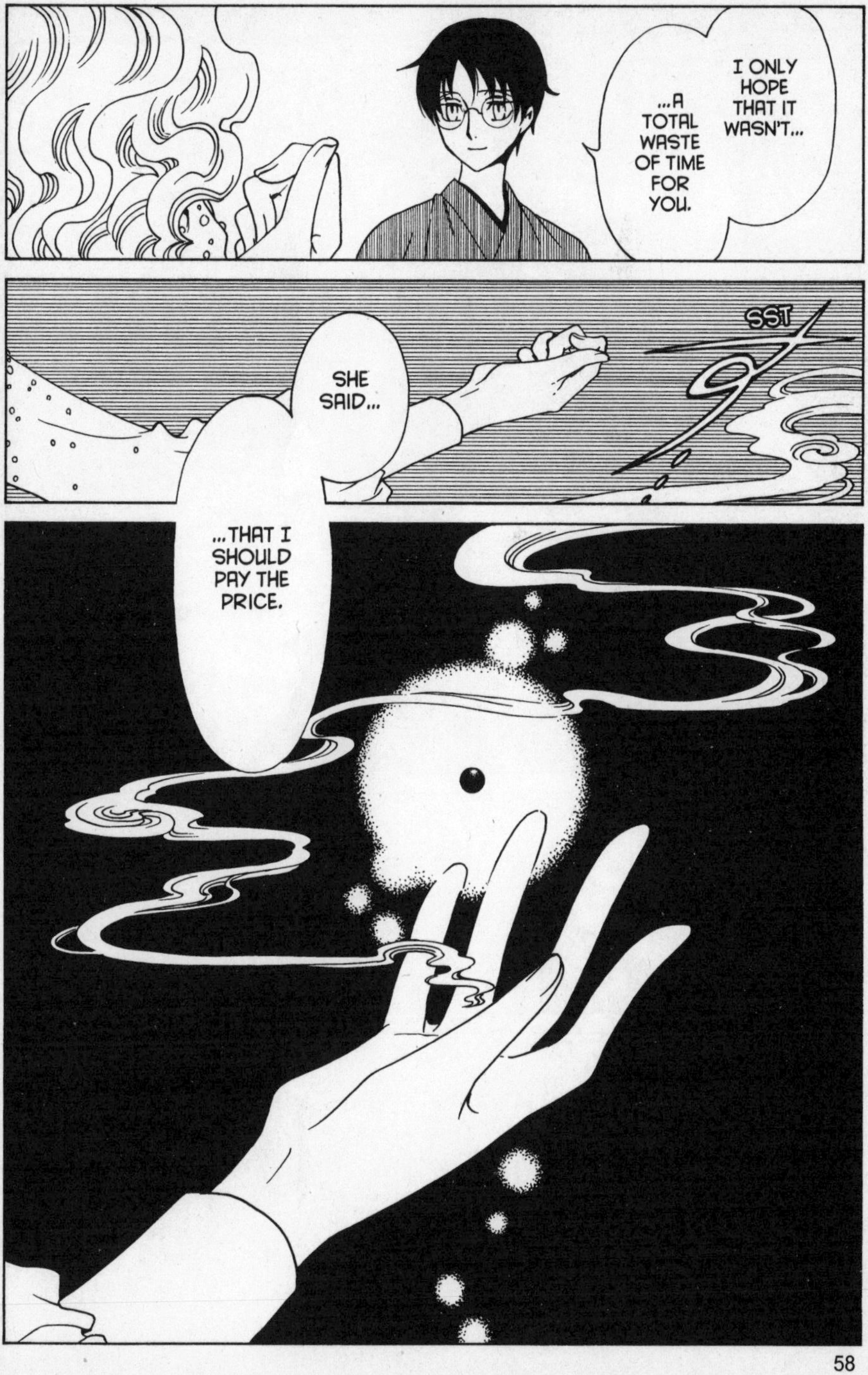
I ONLY HOPE THAT IT WASN'T...
...A TOTAL WASTE OF TIME FOR YOU.
SST
SHE SAID...
...THAT I SHOULD PAY THE PRICE.

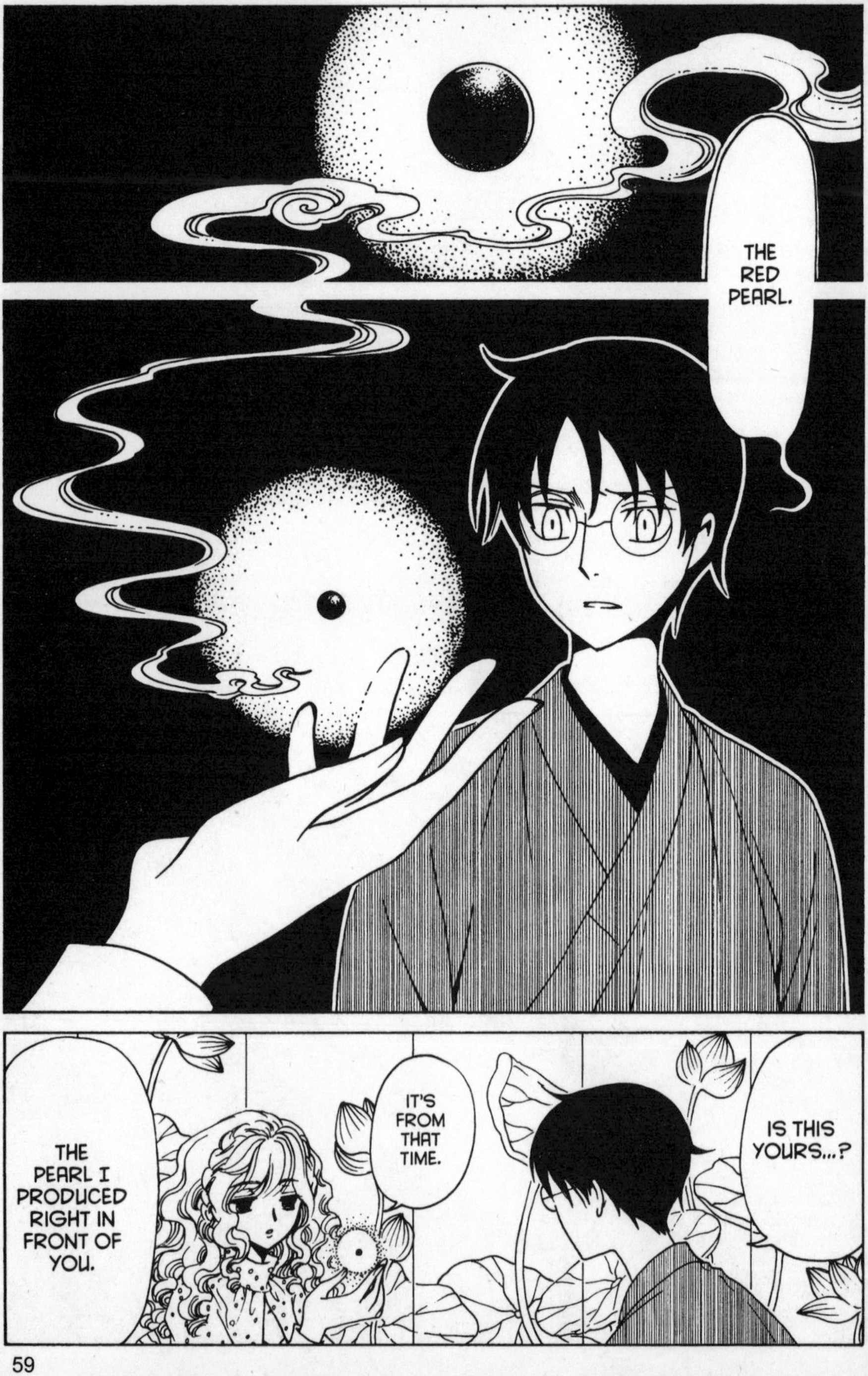
THE RED PEARL.
IS THIS YOURS...?
IT'S FROM THAT TIME.
THE PEARL I PRODUCED RIGHT IN FRONT OF YOU.

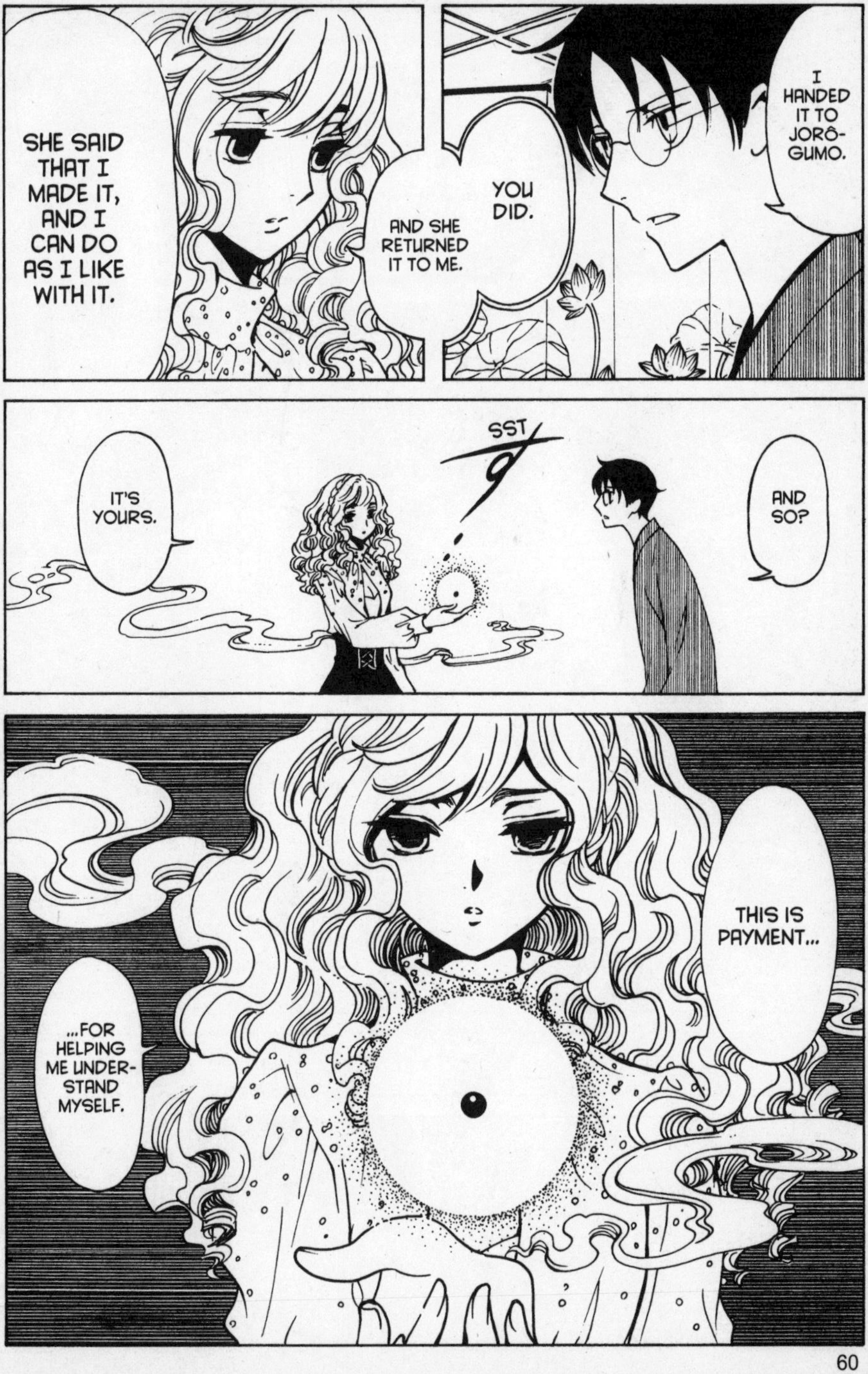
I HANDED IT TO JORÔ-GUMO.
YOU DID.
AND SHE RETURNED IT TO ME.
SHE SAID THAT I MADE IT, AND I CAN DO AS I LIKE WITH IT.
AND SO?
SST
IT'S YOURS.
THIS IS PAYMENT...
...FOR HELPING ME UNDER-STAND MYSELF.

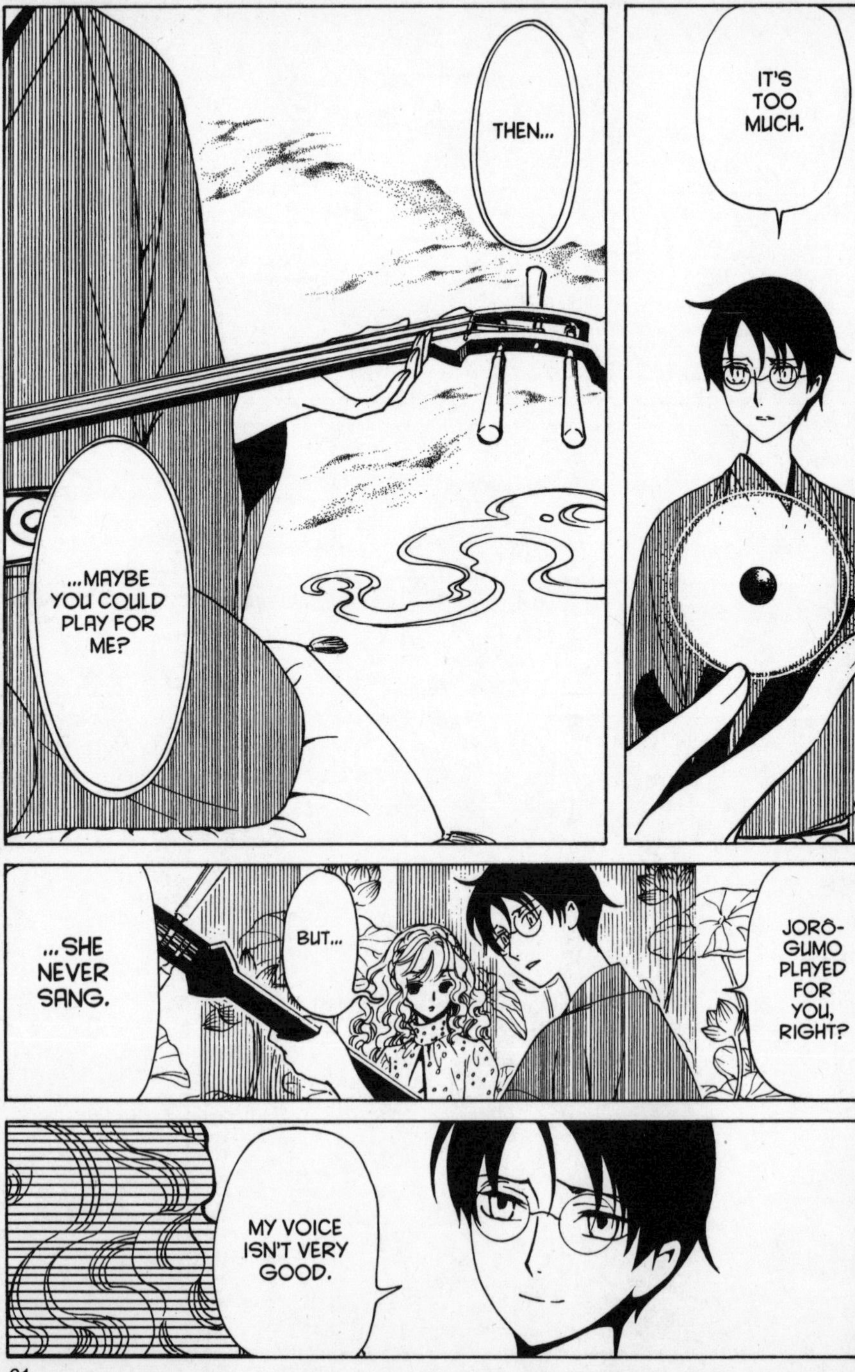
IT'S TOO MUCH.
THEN...
...MAYBE YOU COULD PLAY FOR ME?
JORÔ-GUMO PLAYED FOR YOU, RIGHT?
BUT...
...SHE NEVER SANG.
MY VOICE ISN'T VERY GOOD.

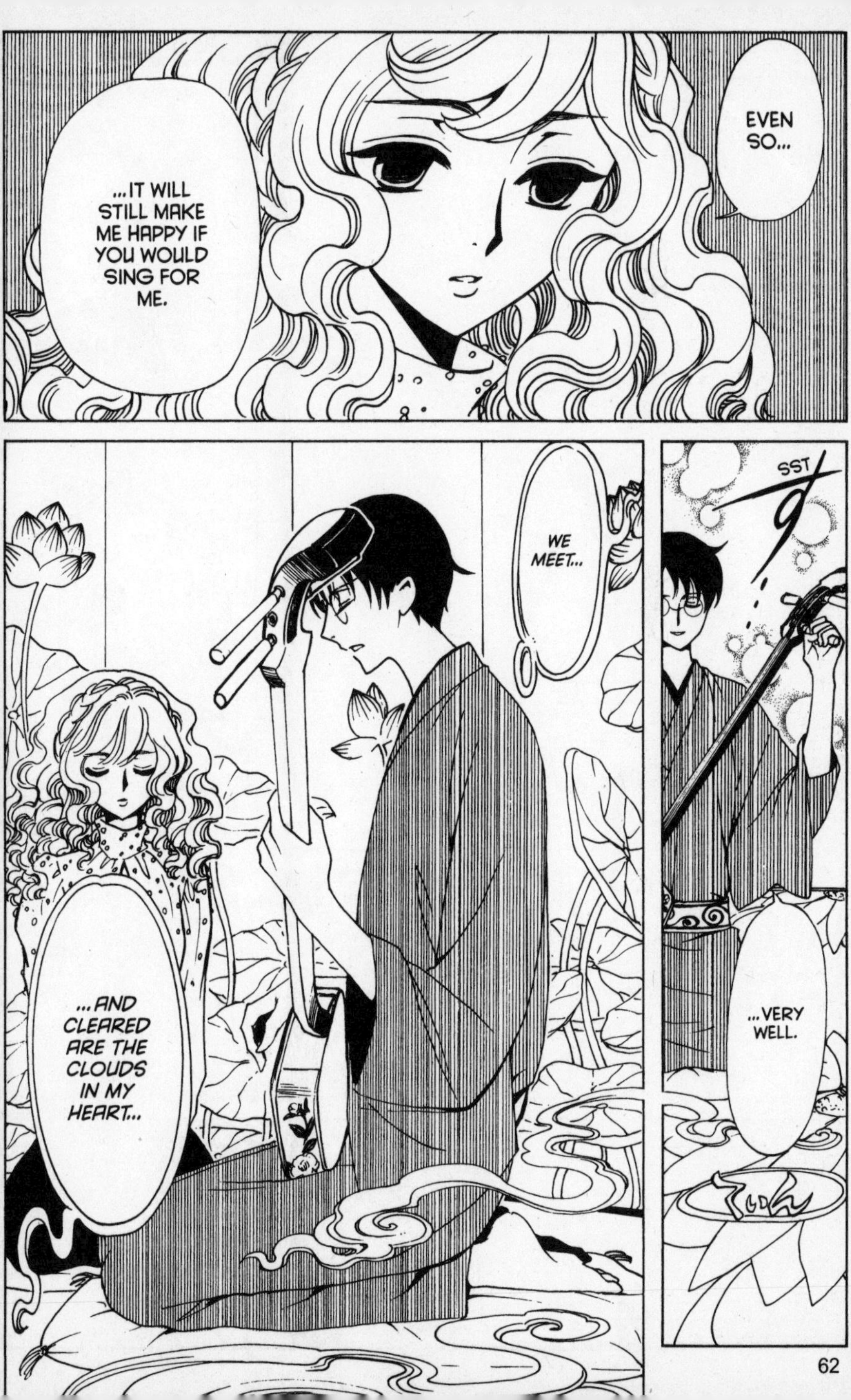
EVEN SO...
...IT WILL STILL MAKE ME HAPPY IF YOU WOULD SING FOR ME.
SST
...VERY WELL.
WE MEET...
...AND CLEARED ARE THE CLOUDS IN MY HEART...

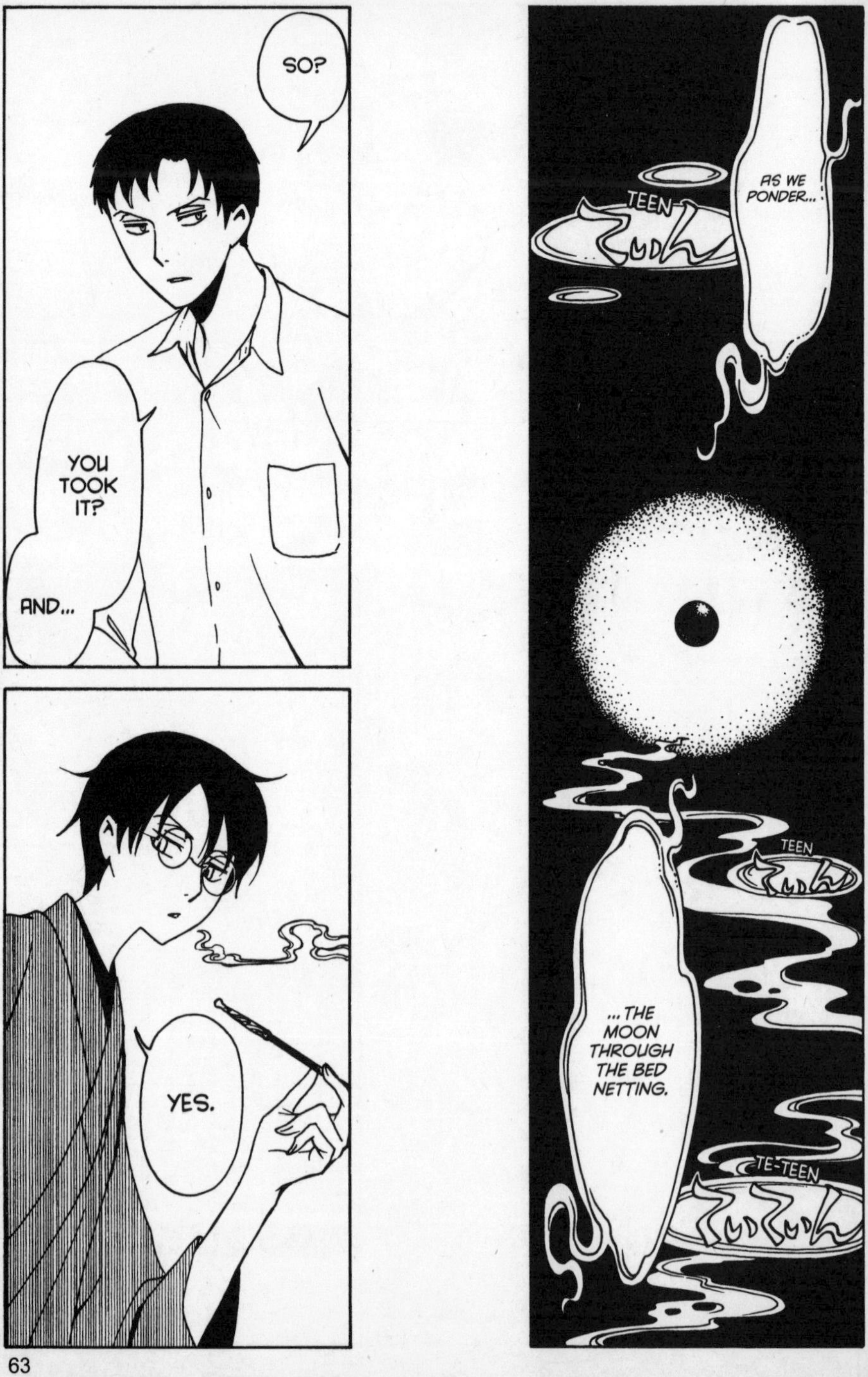
AS WE PONDER...
TEEN
TEEN
...THE MOON THROUGH THE BED NETTING.
TE-TEEN
SO?
YOU TOOK IT?
AND...
YES.

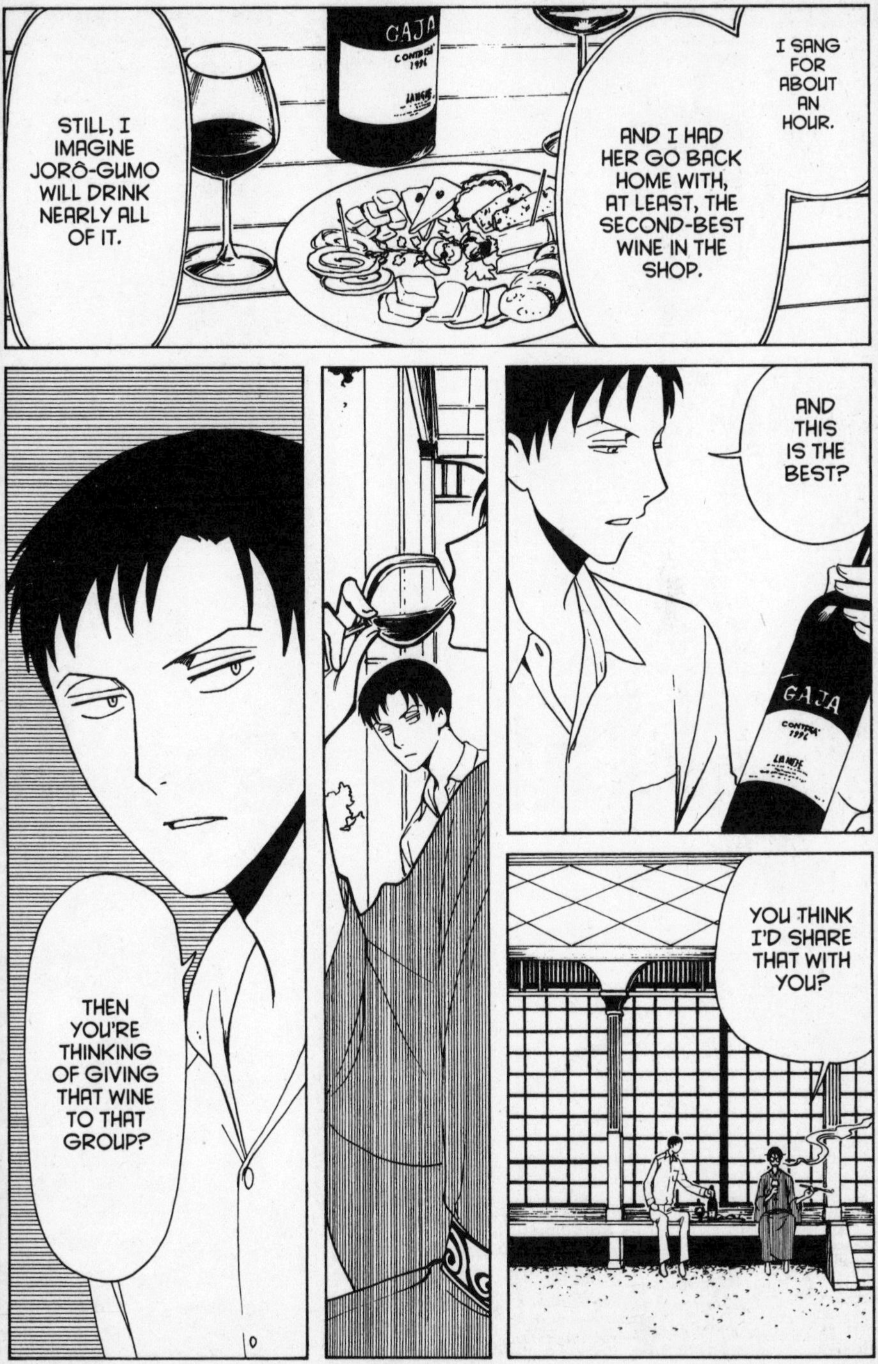
GAJA
I SANG FOR ABOUT AN HOUR.
AND I HAD HER GO BACK HOME WITH, AT LEAST, THE SECOND-BEST WINE IN THE SHOP.
STILL, I IMAGINE JORÔ-GUMO WILL DRINK NEARLY ALL OF IT.
AND THIS IS THE BEST?
GAJA
YOU THINK I'D SHARE THAT WITH YOU?
THEN YOU'RE THINKING OF GIVING THAT WINE TO THAT GROUP?

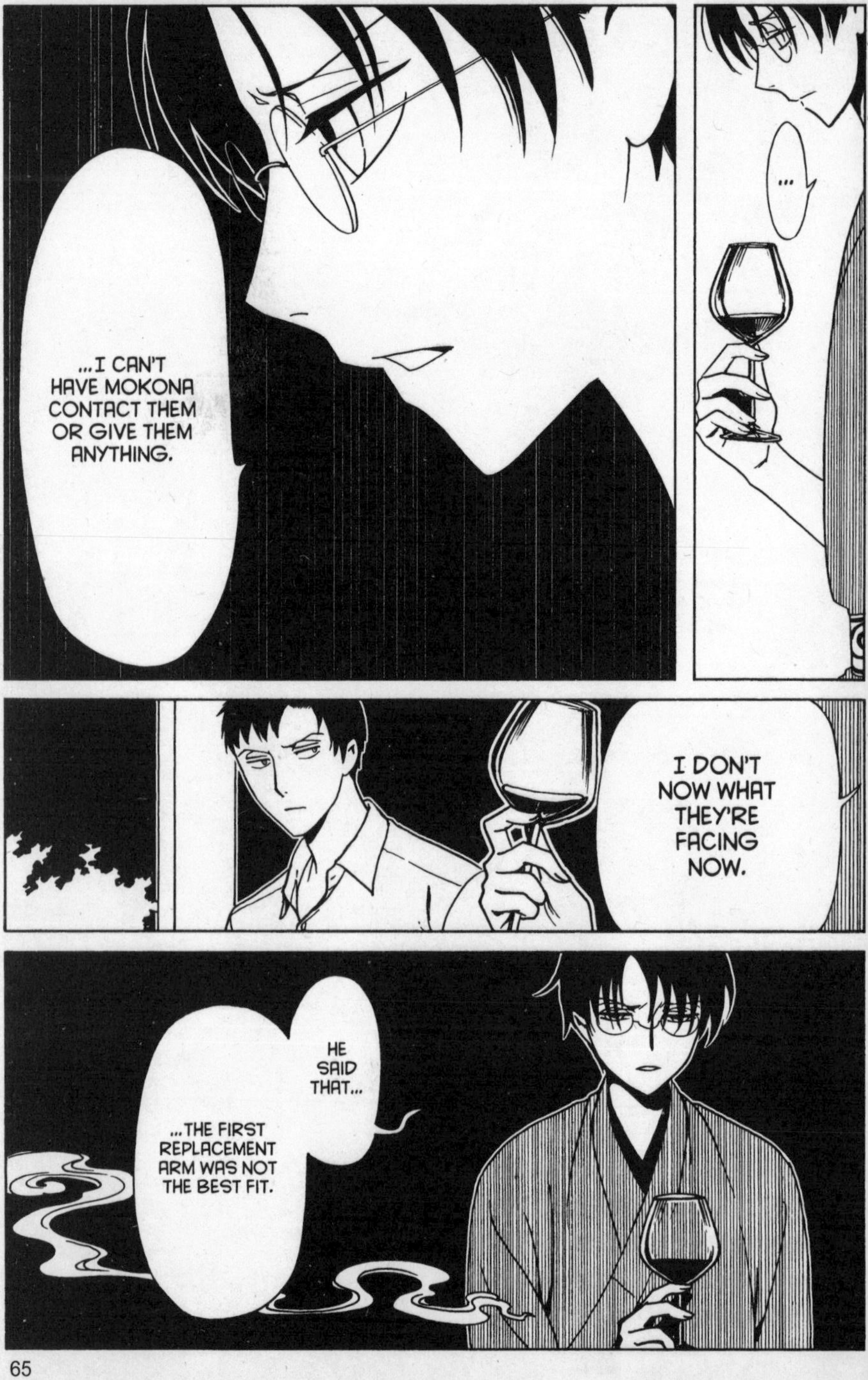
...
...I CAN'T HAVE MOKONA CONTACT THEM OR GIVE THEM ANYTHING.
I DON'T NOW WHAT THEY'RE FACING NOW.
HE SAID THAT...
...THE FIRST REPLACEMENT ARM WAS NOT THE BEST FIT.

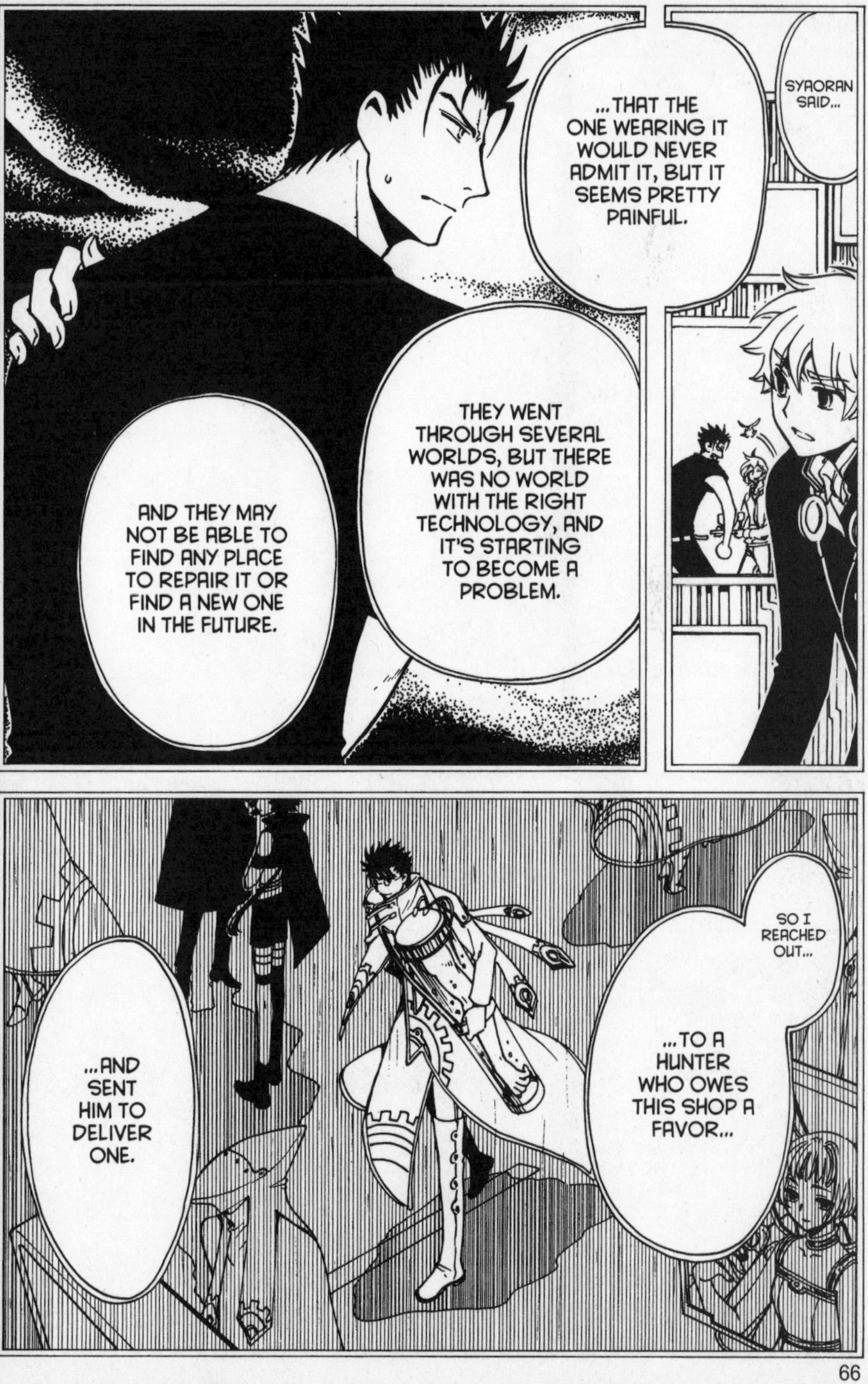
SYAORAN SAID...
...THAT THE ONE WEARING IT WOULD NEVER ADMIT IT, BUT IT SEEMS PRETTY PAINFUL.
THEY WENT THROUGH SEVERAL WORLDS, BUT THERE WAS NO WORLD WITH THE RIGHT TECHNOLOGY, AND IT'S STARTING TO BECOME A PROBLEM.
AND THEY MAY NOT BE ABLE TO FIND ANY PLACE TO REPAIR IT OR FIND A NEW ONE IN THE FUTURE.
SO I REACHED OUT...
...TO A HUNTER WHO OWES THIS SHOP A FAVOR...
...AND SENT HIM TO DELIVER ONE.

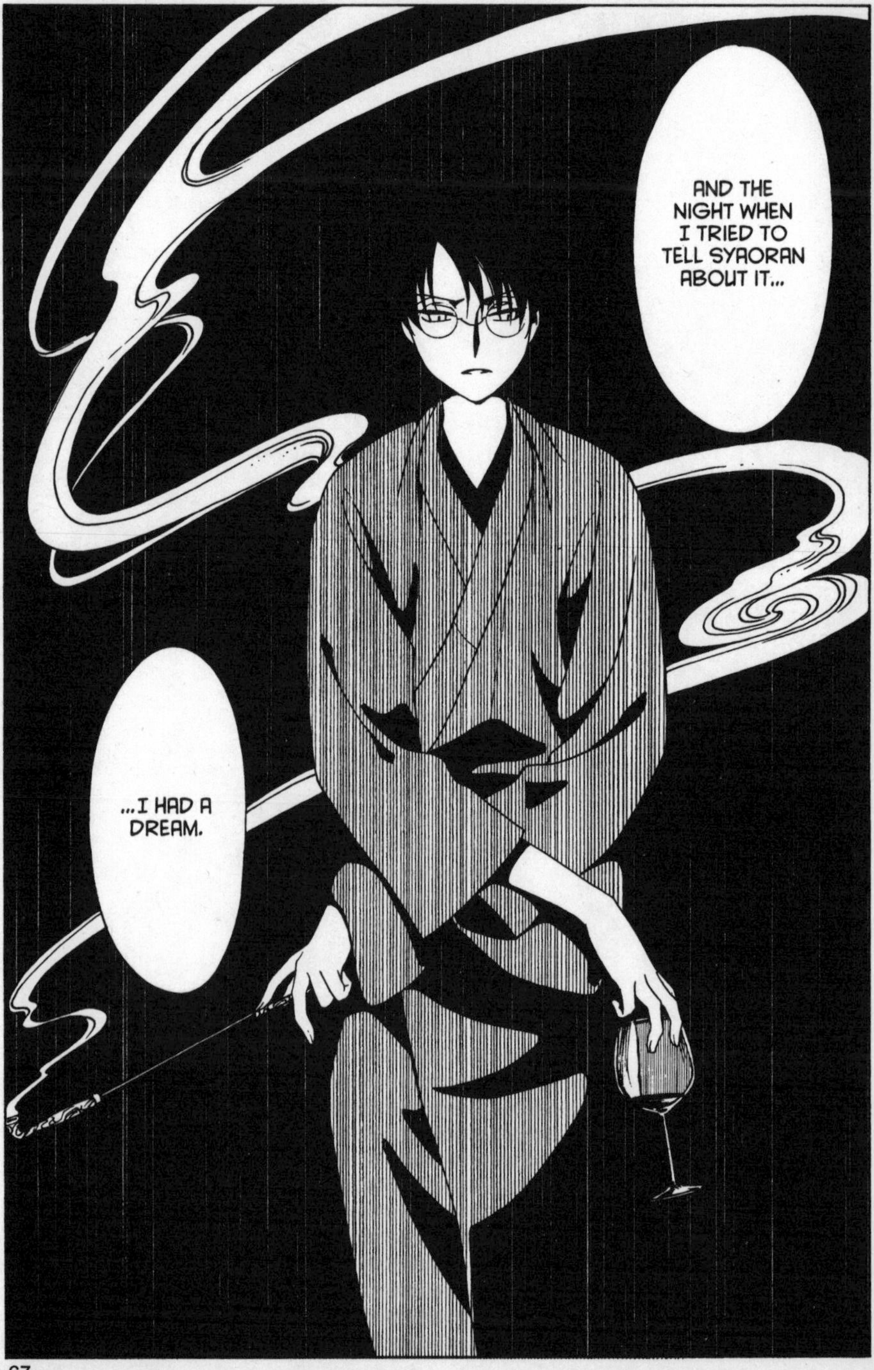
AND THE NIGHT WHEN I TRIED TO TELL SYAORAN ABOUT IT...
...I HAD A DREAM.

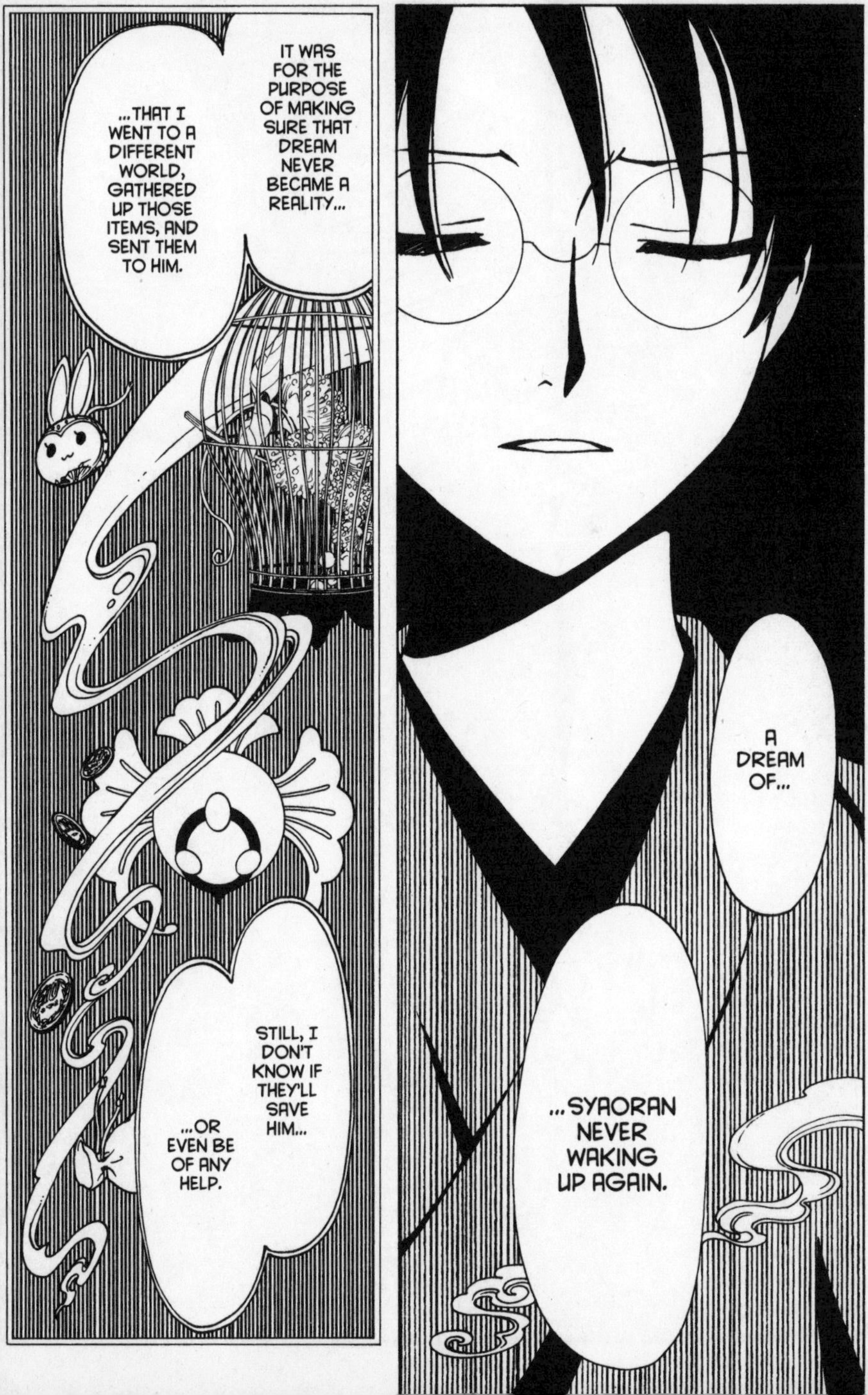
A DREAM OF...
...SYAORAN NEVER WAKING UP AGAIN.
IT WAS FOR THE PURPOSE OF MAKING SURE THAT DREAM NEVER BECAME A REALITY...
...THAT I WENT TO A DIFFERENT WORLD, GATHERED UP THOSE ITEMS, AND SENT THEM TO HIM.
STILL, I DON'T KNOW IF THEY'LL SAVE HIM...
...OR EVEN BE OF ANY HELP.

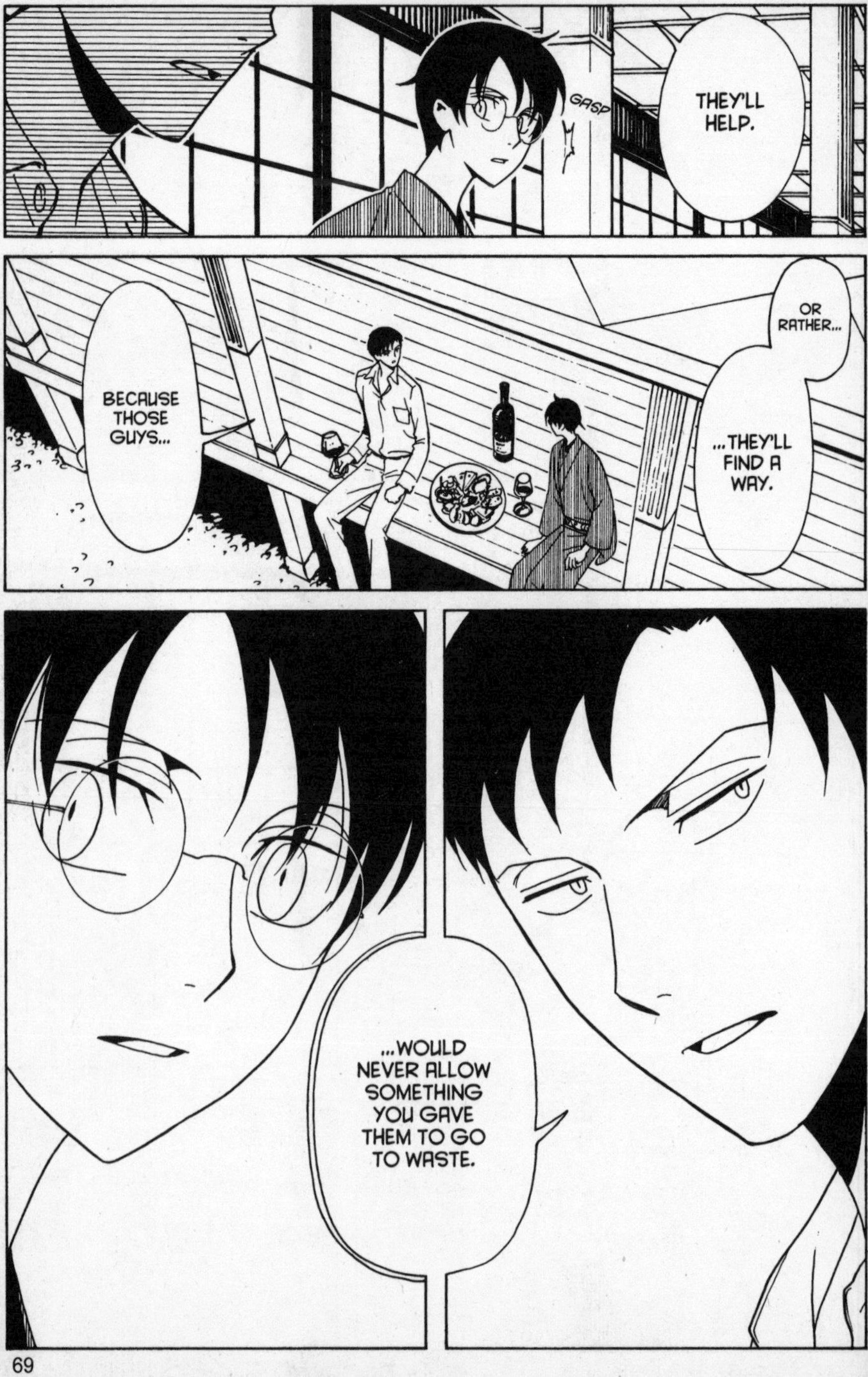
THEY'LL HELP.
GASP
OR RATHER...
...THEY'LL FIND A WAY.
BECAUSE THOSE GUYS...
...WOULD NEVER ALLOW SOMETHING YOU GAVE THEM TO GO TO WASTE.

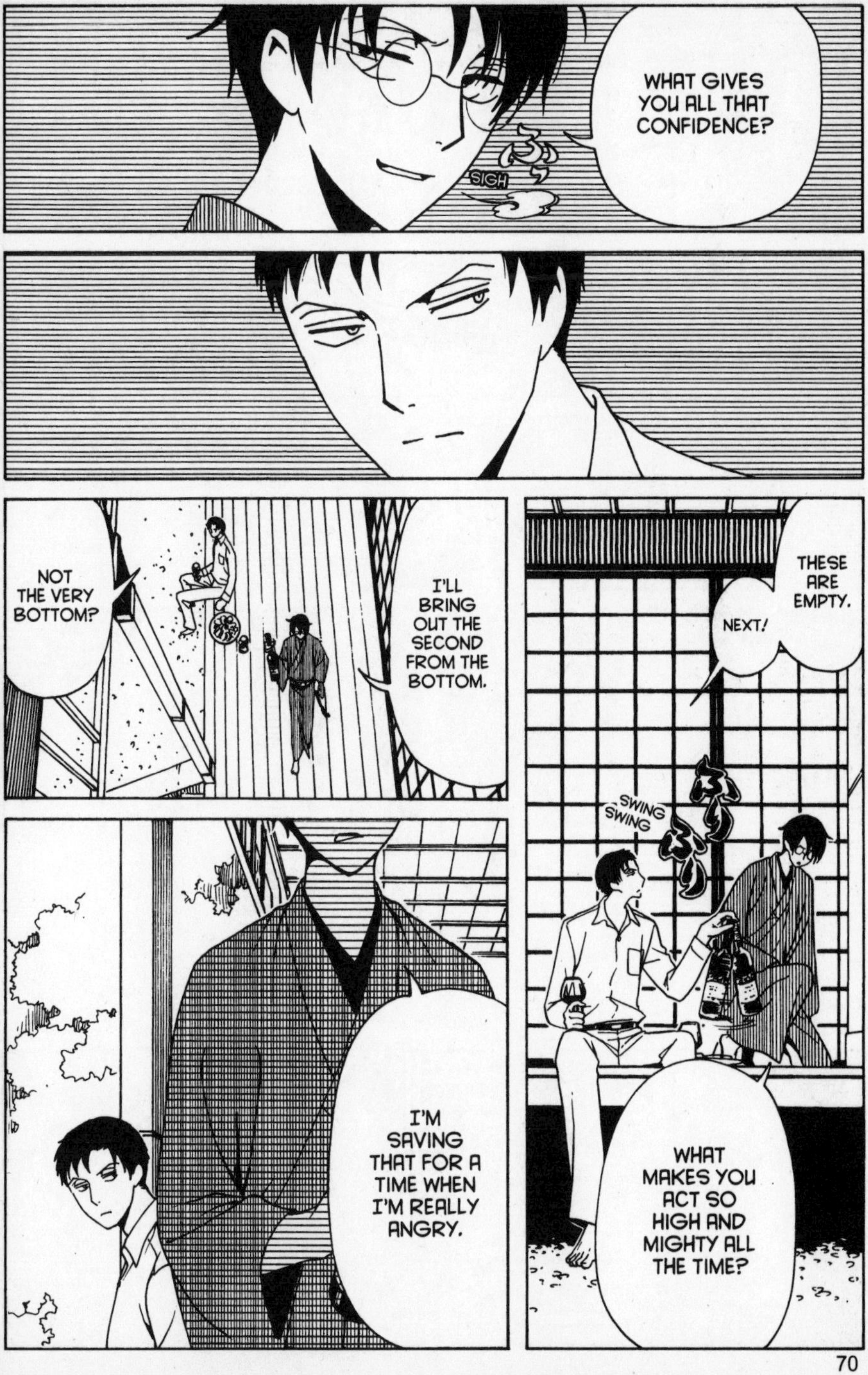
WHAT GIVES YOU ALL THAT CONFIDENCE?
SIGH
THESE ARE EMPTY.
NEXT!
SWING SWING
WHAT MAKES YOU ACT SO HIGH AND MIGHTY ALL THE TIME?
I'LL BRING OUT THE SECOND FROM THE BOTTOM.
NOT THE VERY BOTTOM?
I'M SAVING THAT FOR A TIME WHEN I'M REALLY ANGRY.

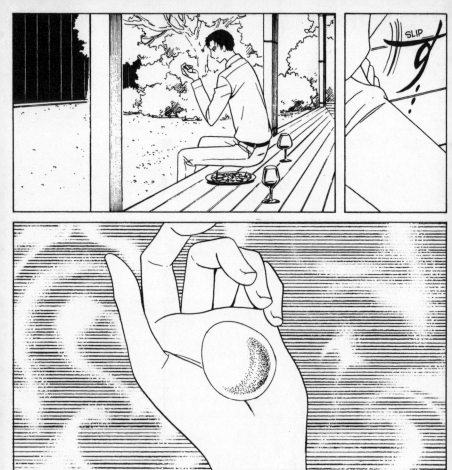

SLIP

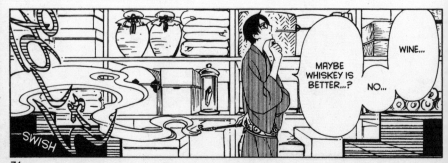

WINE...

MAYBE WHISKEY IS BETTER...?

NO...

SWISH

71

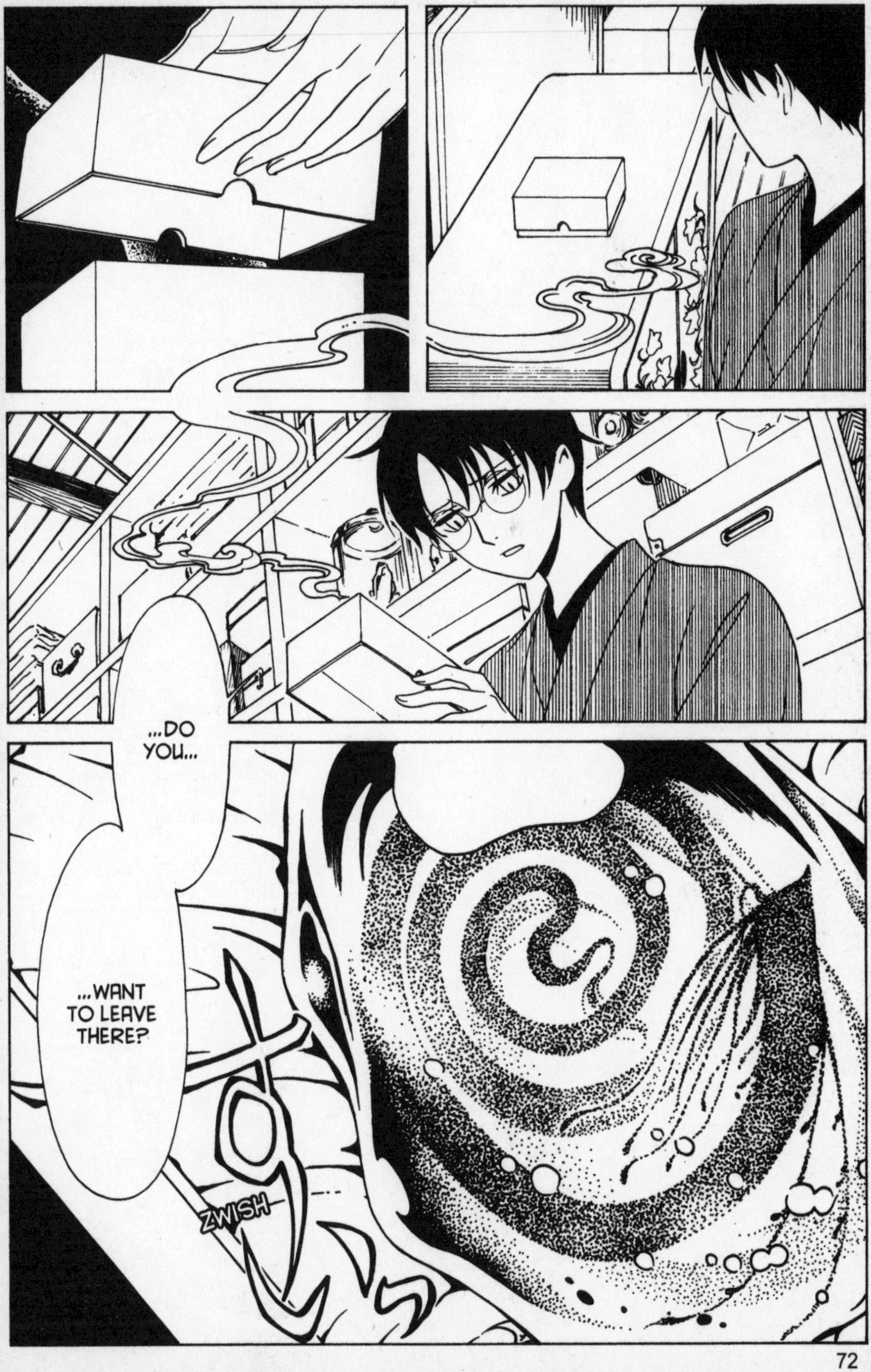
...DO YOU...
...WANT TO LEAVE THERE?
ZWISH

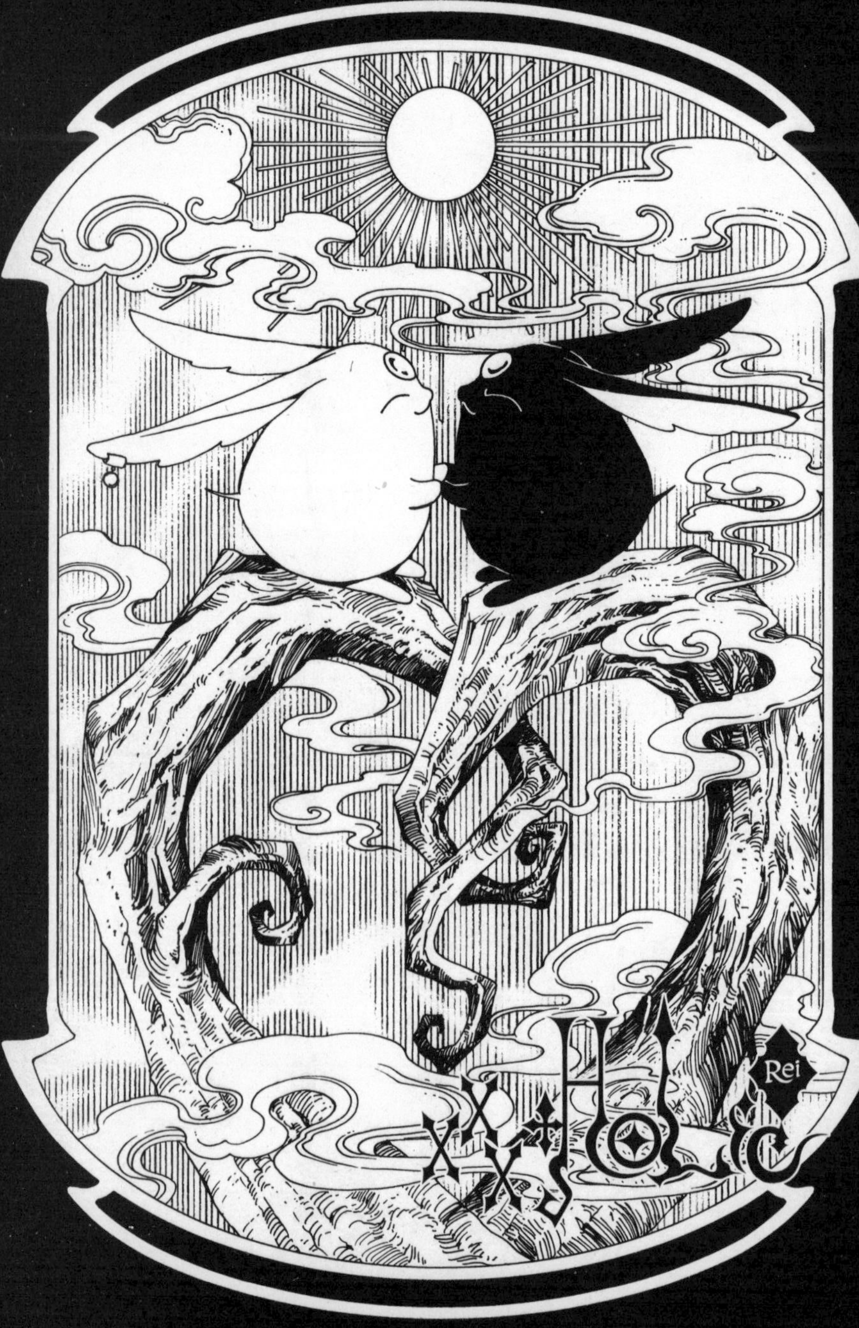
xxxHOLiC
Rei

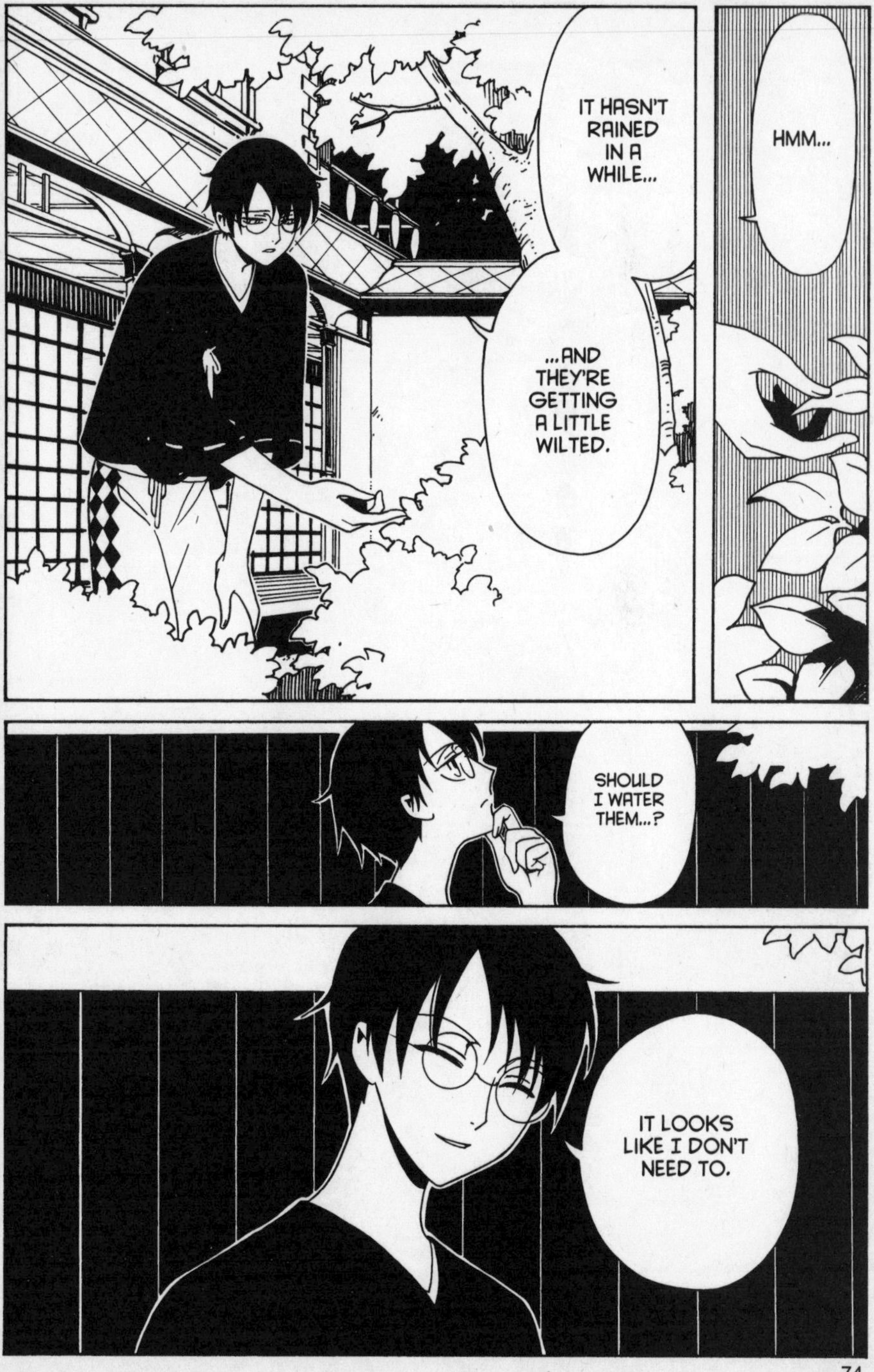
HMM...
IT HASN'T RAINED IN A WHILE...
...AND THEY'RE GETTING A LITTLE WILTED.
SHOULD I WATER THEM...?
IT LOOKS LIKE I DON'T NEED TO.

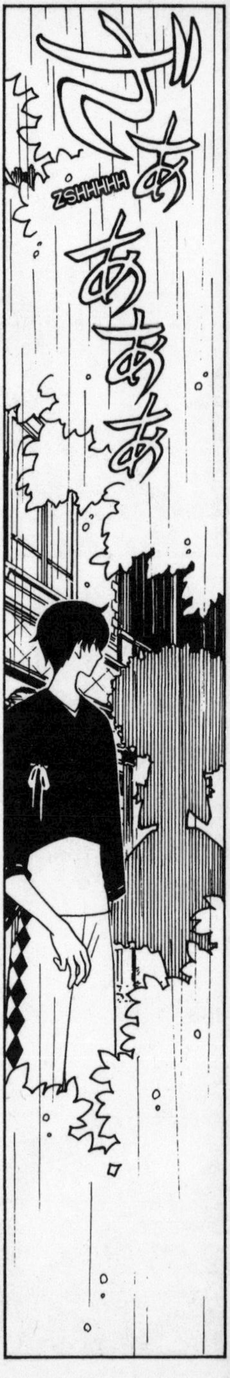
ざあああ
ZSHHHH

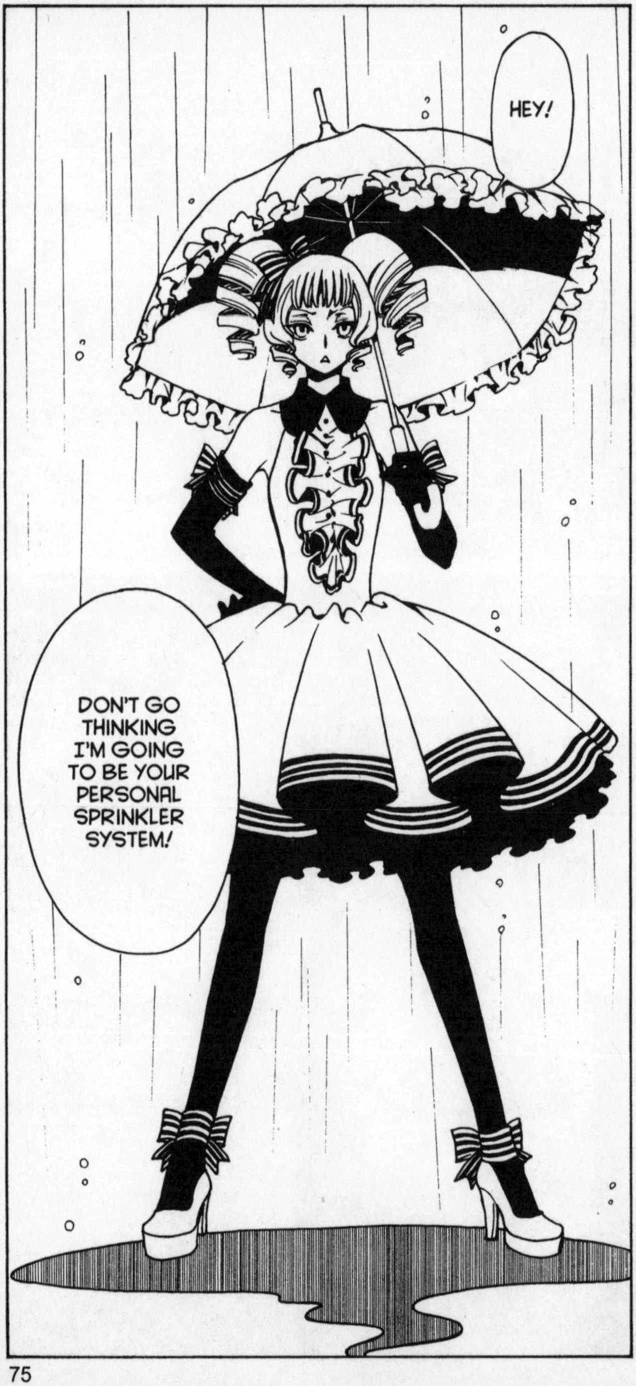
HEY!
DON'T GO THINKING I'M GOING TO BE YOUR PERSONAL SPRINKLER SYSTEM!

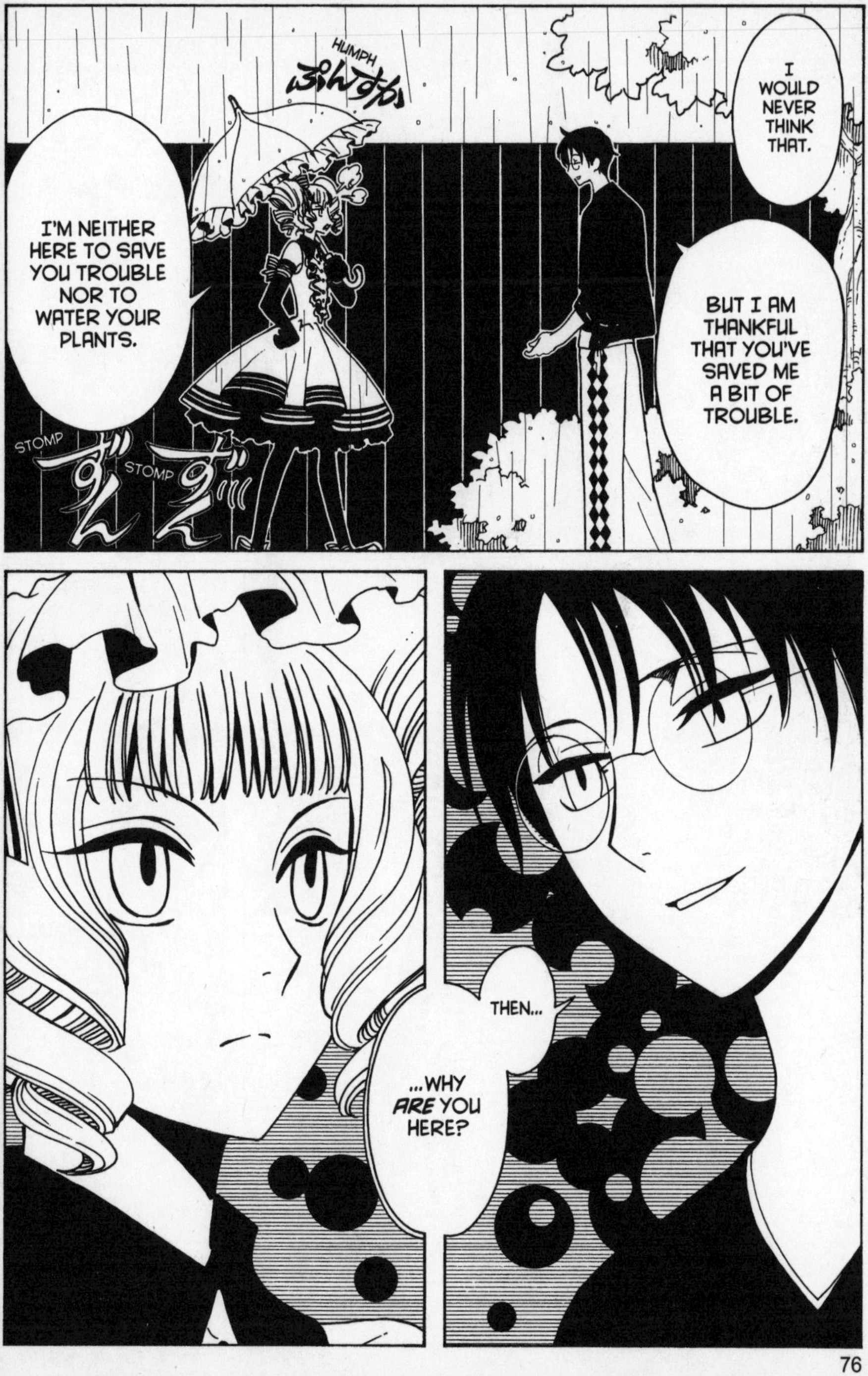
I WOULD NEVER THINK THAT.
BUT I AM THANKFUL THAT YOU'VE SAVED ME A BIT OF TROUBLE.
HUMPH
ぷんすか
I'M NEITHER HERE TO SAVE YOU TROUBLE NOR TO WATER YOUR PLANTS.
STOMP
STOMP
ずん ずん
THEN...
...WHY *ARE* YOU HERE?

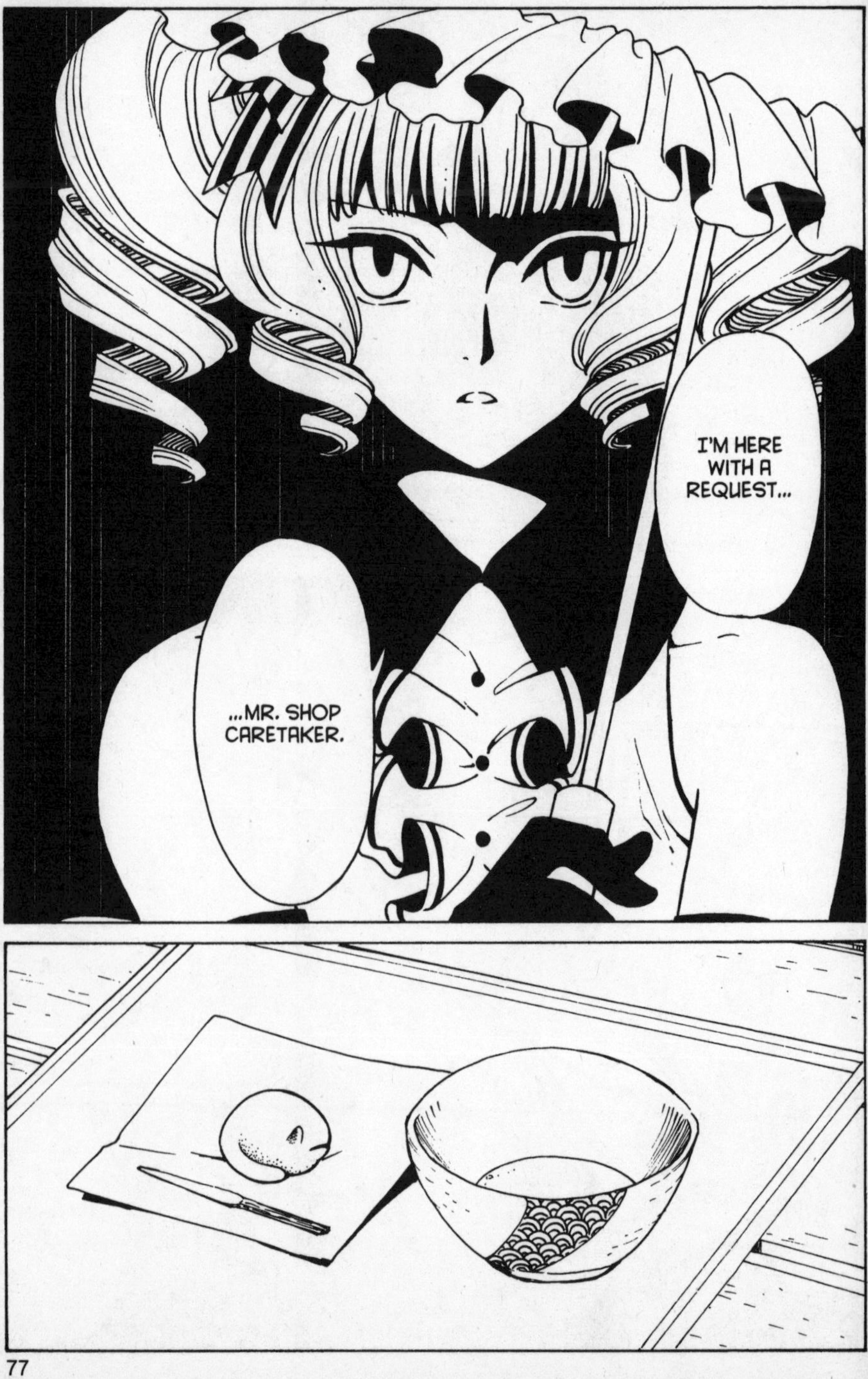
I'M HERE WITH A REQUEST...
...MR. SHOP CARETAKER.

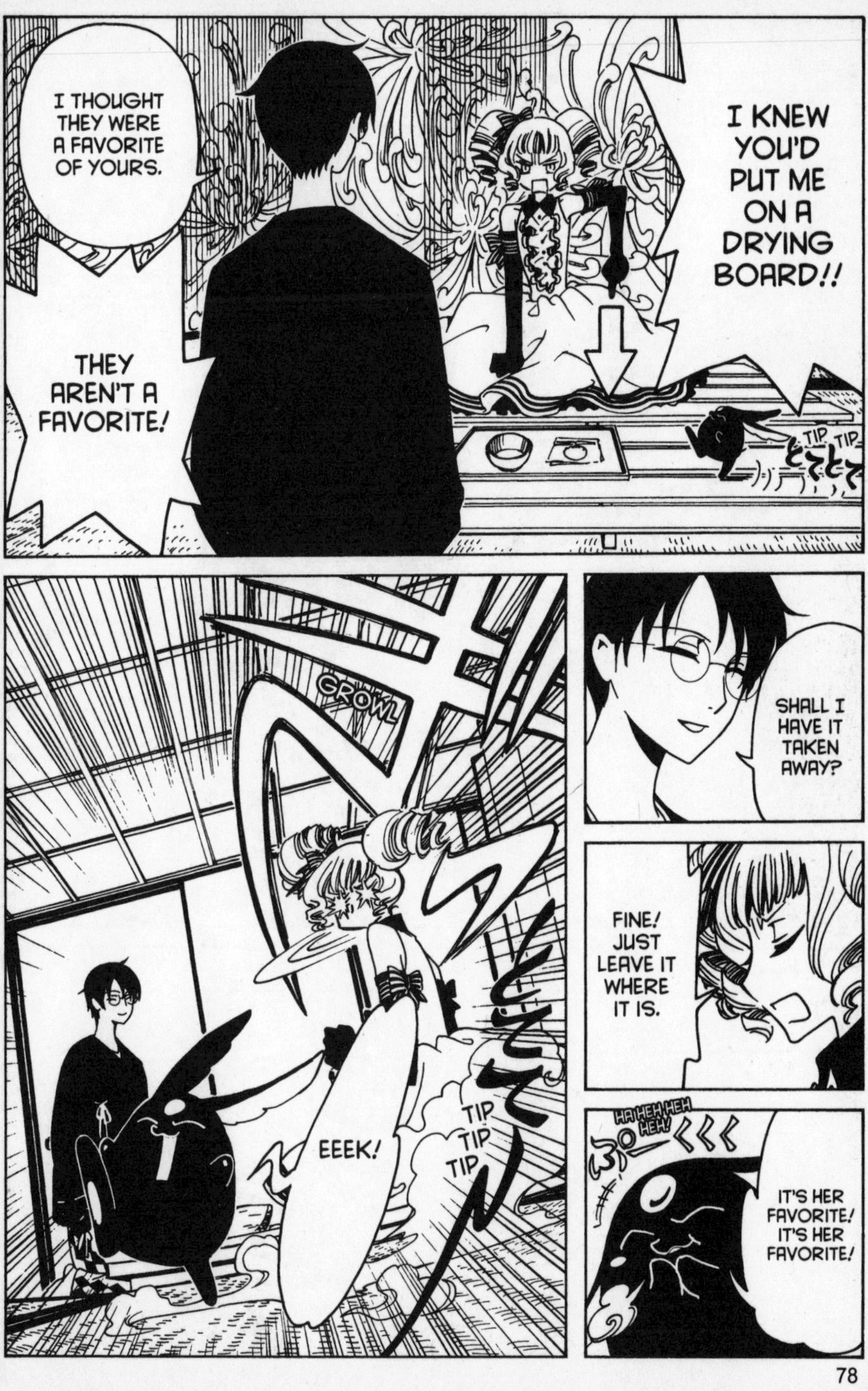

I KNEW YOU'D PUT ME ON A DRYING BOARD!!
I THOUGHT THEY WERE A FAVORITE OF YOURS.
TIP TIP
THEY AREN'T A FAVORITE!
SHALL I HAVE IT TAKEN AWAY?
FINE! JUST LEAVE IT WHERE IT IS.
HA HEH HEH HEH!
IT'S HER FAVORITE! IT'S HER FAVORITE!
GROWL
EEEK!
TIP TIP TIP

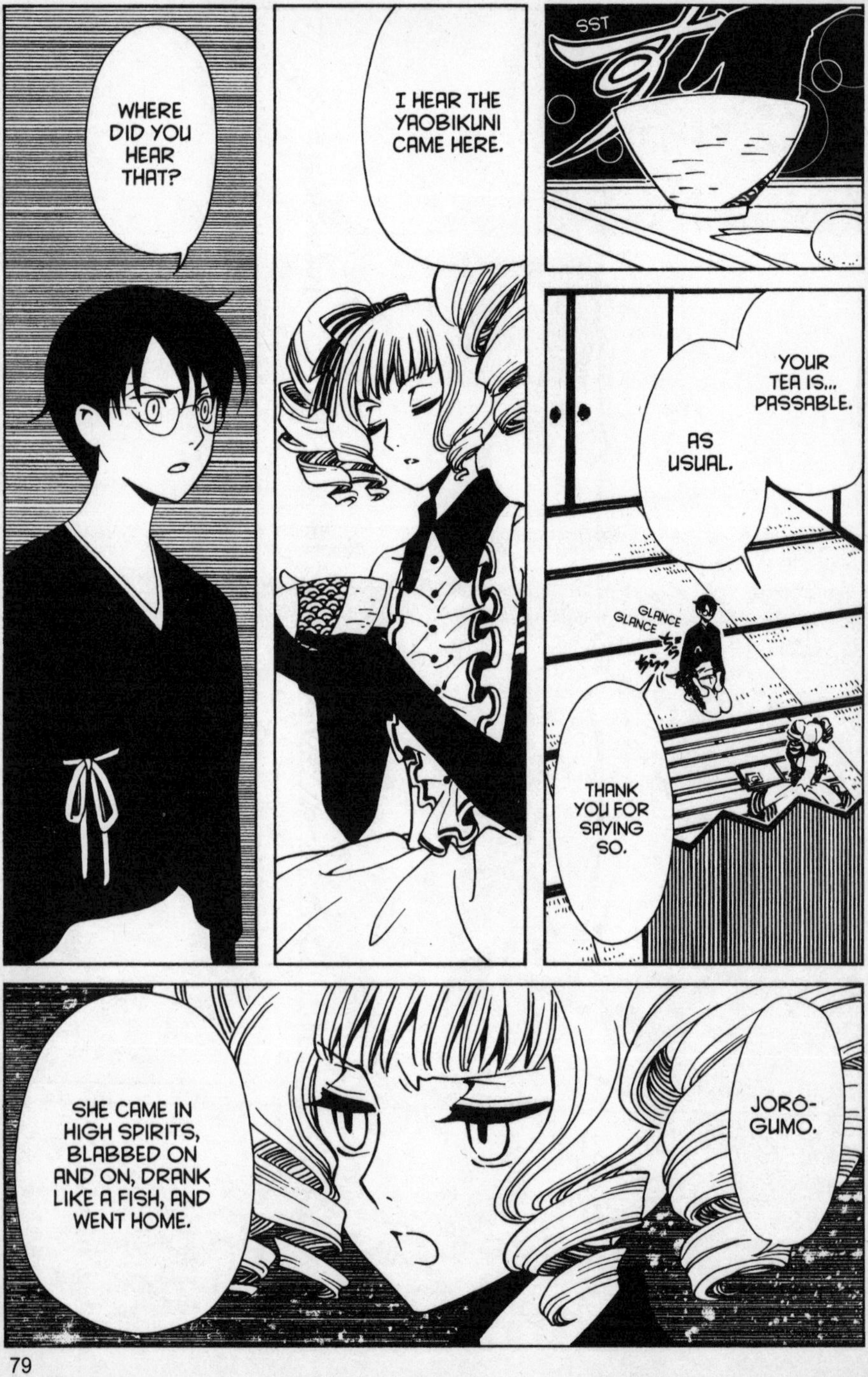
SST
YOUR TEA IS... PASSABLE.
AS USUAL.
GLANCE GLANCE
THANK YOU FOR SAYING SO.
I HEAR THE YAOBIKUNI CAME HERE.
WHERE DID YOU HEAR THAT?
JORÔ-GUMO.
SHE CAME IN HIGH SPIRITS, BLABBED ON AND ON, DRANK LIKE A FISH, AND WENT HOME.

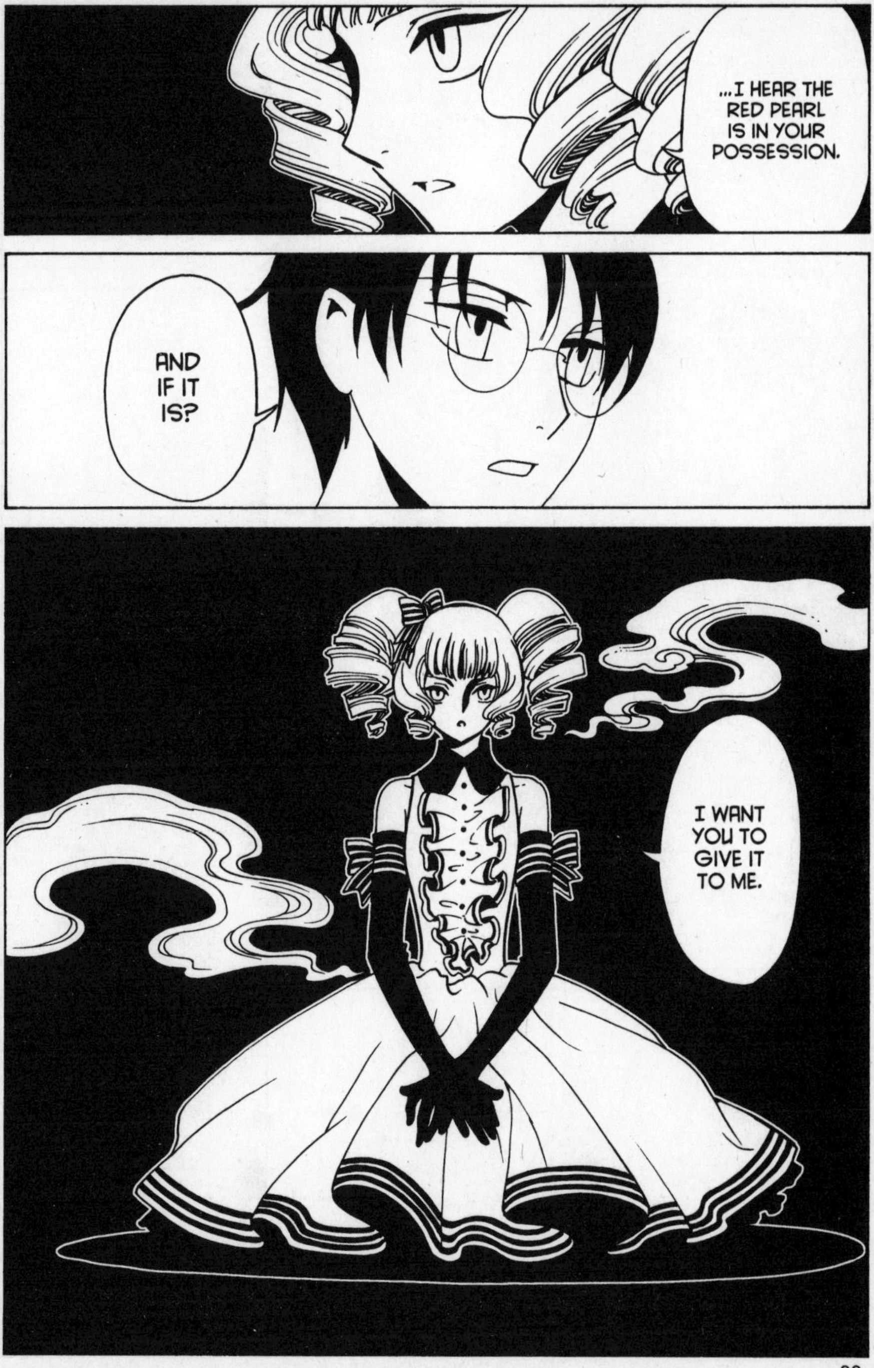
...I HEAR THE RED PEARL IS IN YOUR POSSESSION.
AND IF IT IS?
I WANT YOU TO GIVE IT TO ME.

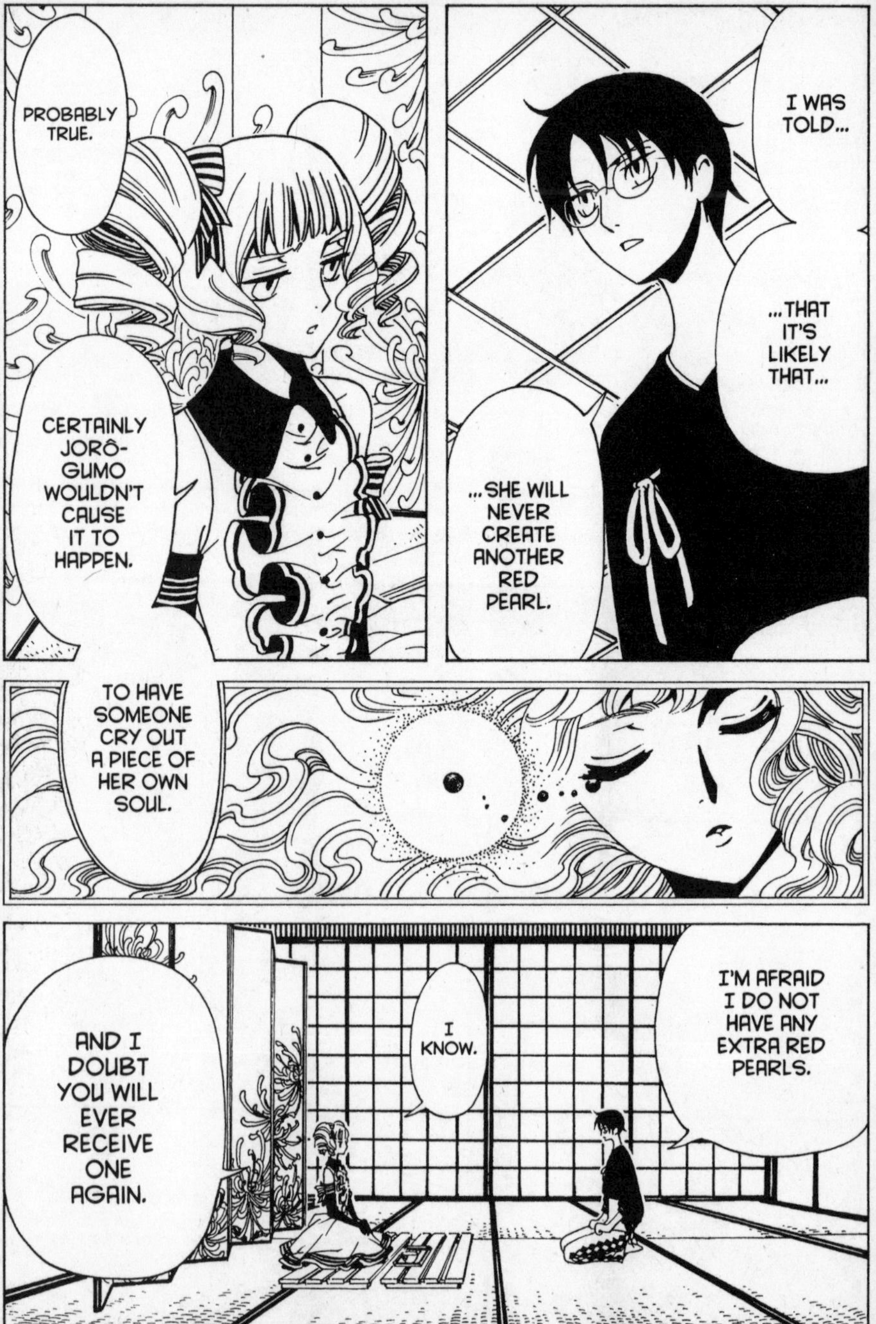
I WAS TOLD...
...THAT IT'S LIKELY THAT...
...SHE WILL NEVER CREATE ANOTHER RED PEARL.
PROBABLY TRUE.
CERTAINLY JORÔ-GUMO WOULDN'T CAUSE IT TO HAPPEN.
TO HAVE SOMEONE CRY OUT A PIECE OF HER OWN SOUL.
I'M AFRAID I DO NOT HAVE ANY EXTRA RED PEARLS.
I KNOW.
AND I DOUBT YOU WILL EVER RECEIVE ONE AGAIN.

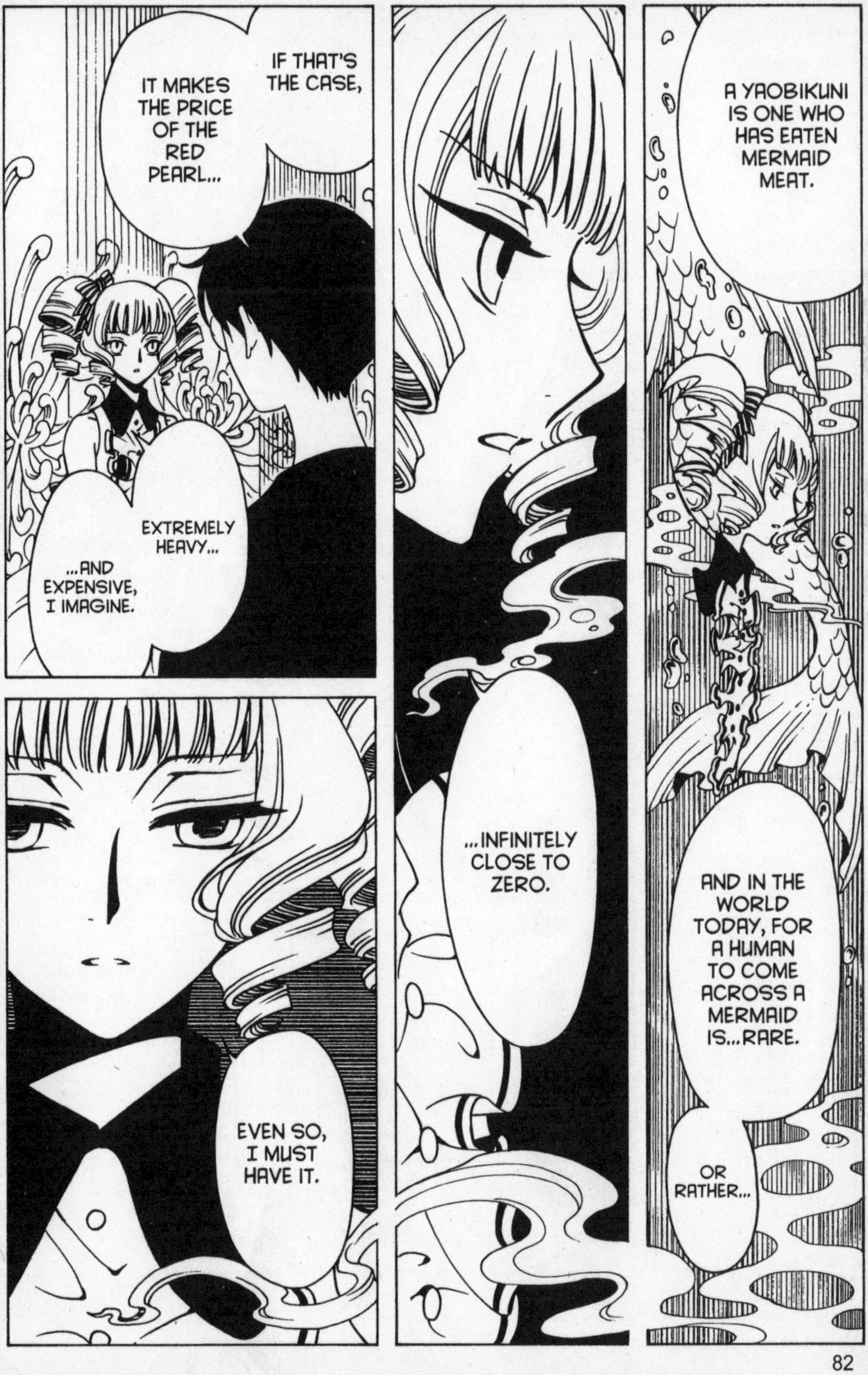
A YAOBIKUNI IS ONE WHO HAS EATEN MERMAID MEAT.
AND IN THE WORLD TODAY, FOR A HUMAN TO COME ACROSS A MERMAID IS...RARE.
OR RATHER...
...INFINITELY CLOSE TO ZERO.
IF THAT'S THE CASE,
IT MAKES THE PRICE OF THE RED PEARL...
EXTREMELY HEAVY...
...AND EXPENSIVE, I IMAGINE.
EVEN SO, I MUST HAVE IT.

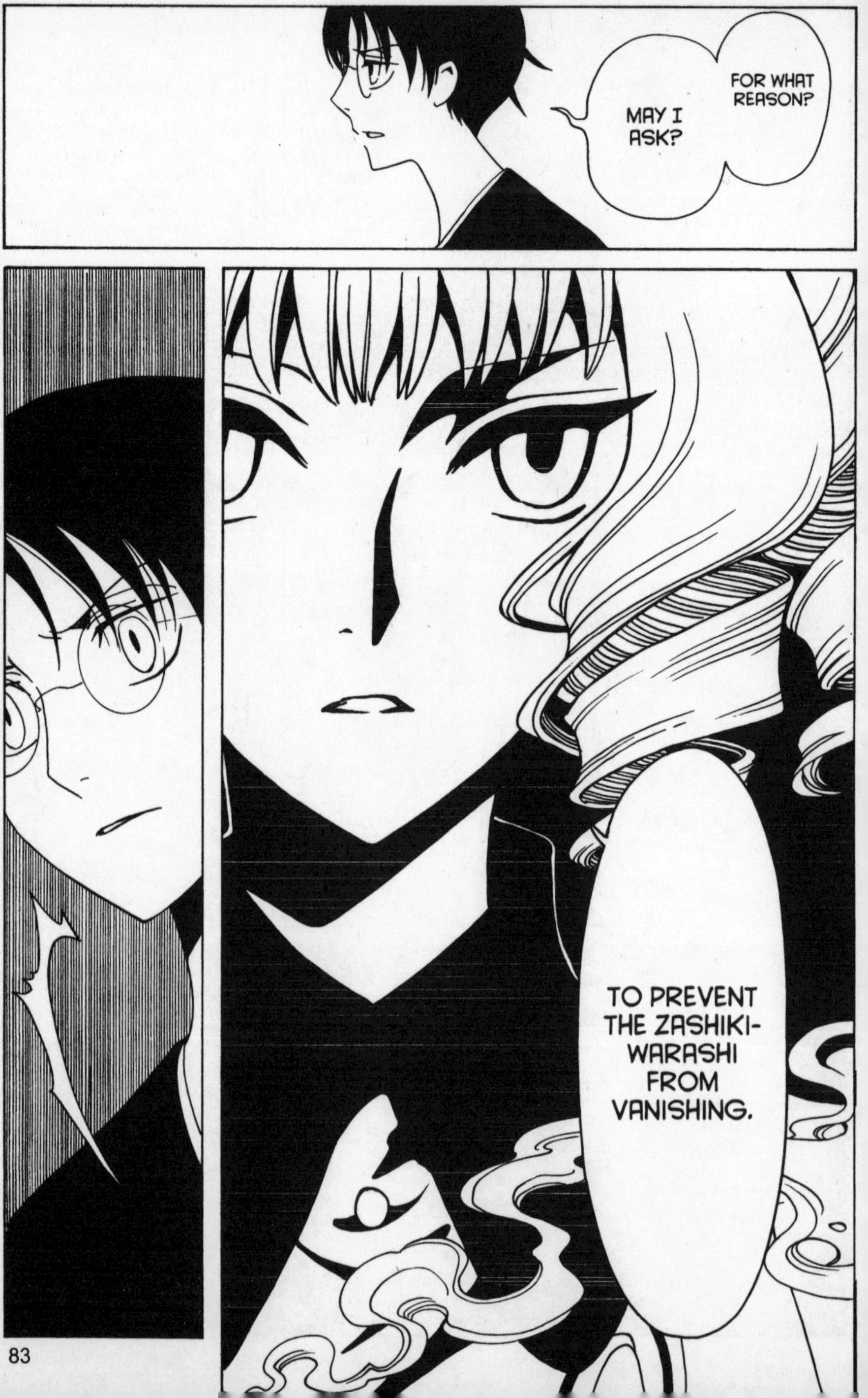
FOR WHAT REASON?
MAY I ASK?
TO PREVENT THE ZASHIKI-WARASHI FROM VANISHING.

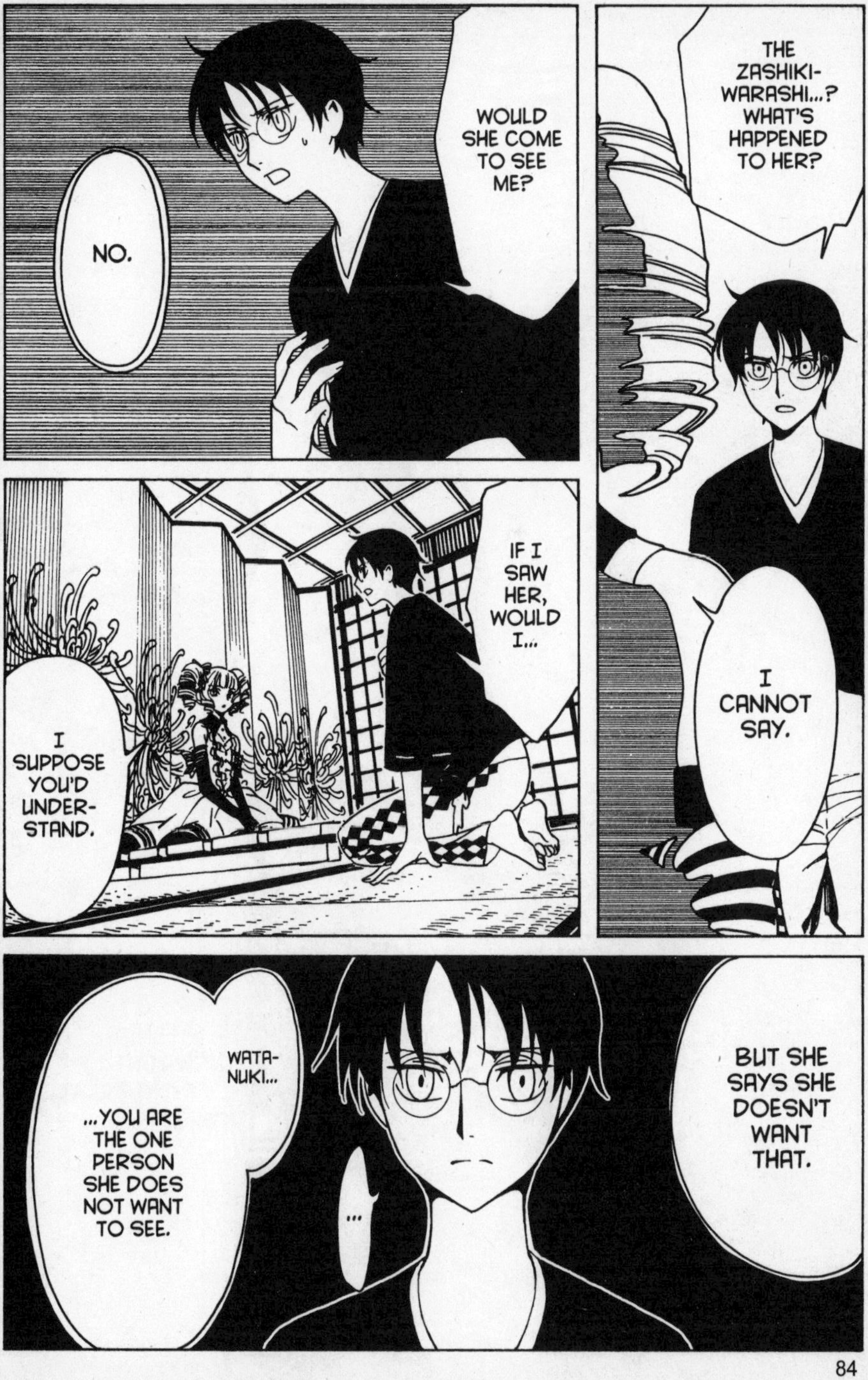
THE ZASHIKI-WARASHI...? WHAT'S HAPPENED TO HER?
I CANNOT SAY.
WOULD SHE COME TO SEE ME?
NO.
IF I SAW HER, WOULD I...
I SUPPOSE YOU'D UNDER-STAND.
BUT SHE SAYS SHE DOESN'T WANT THAT.
WATA-NUKI...
...YOU ARE THE ONE PERSON SHE DOES NOT WANT TO SEE.
...

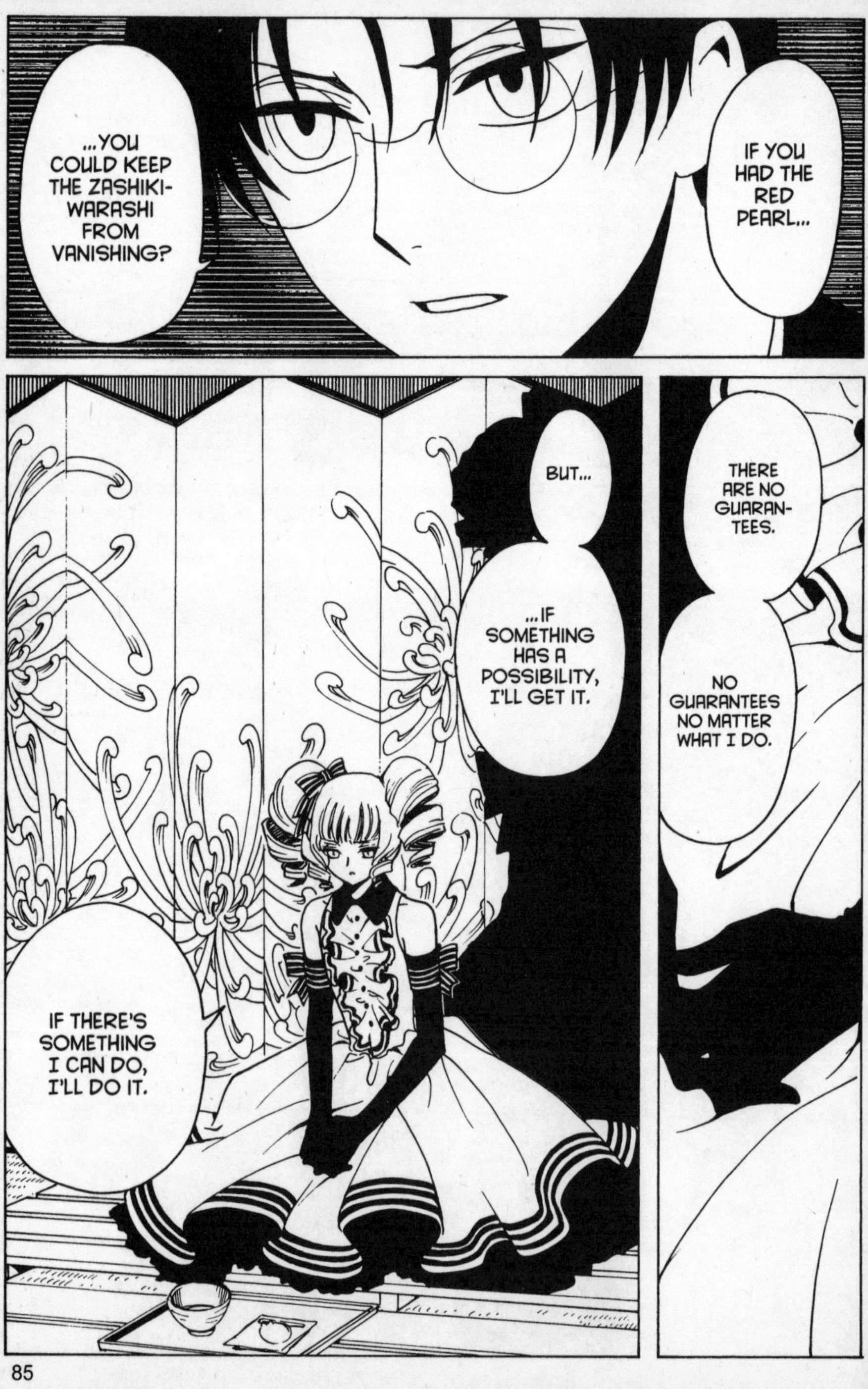
IF YOU HAD THE RED PEARL...
...YOU COULD KEEP THE ZASHIKI-WARASHI FROM VANISHING?
THERE ARE NO GUARANTEES.
NO GUARANTEES NO MATTER WHAT I DO.
BUT...
...IF SOMETHING HAS A POSSIBILITY, I'LL GET IT.
IF THERE'S SOMETHING I CAN DO, I'LL DO IT.

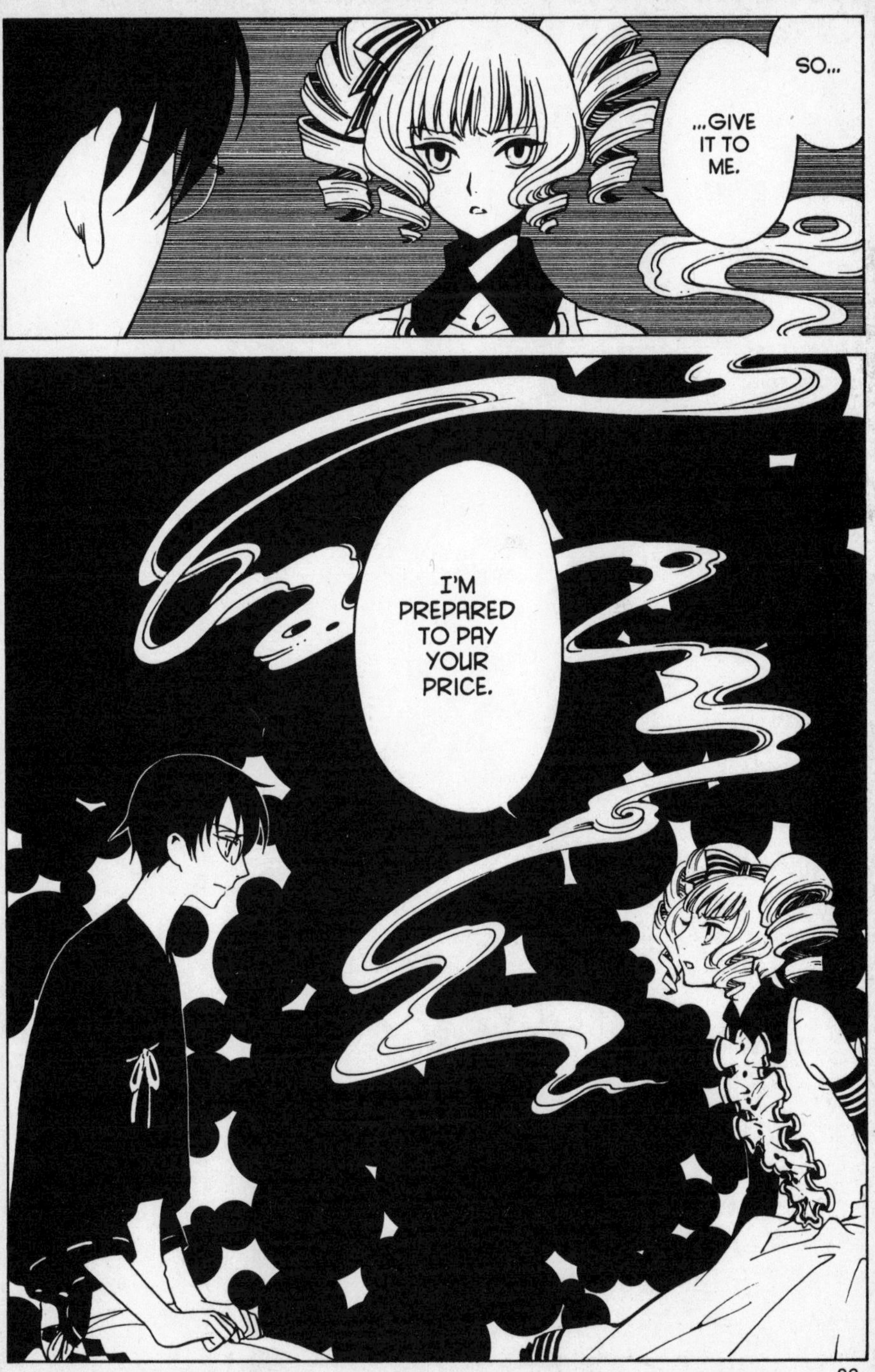
SO...
...GIVE IT TO ME.
I'M PREPARED TO PAY YOUR PRICE.

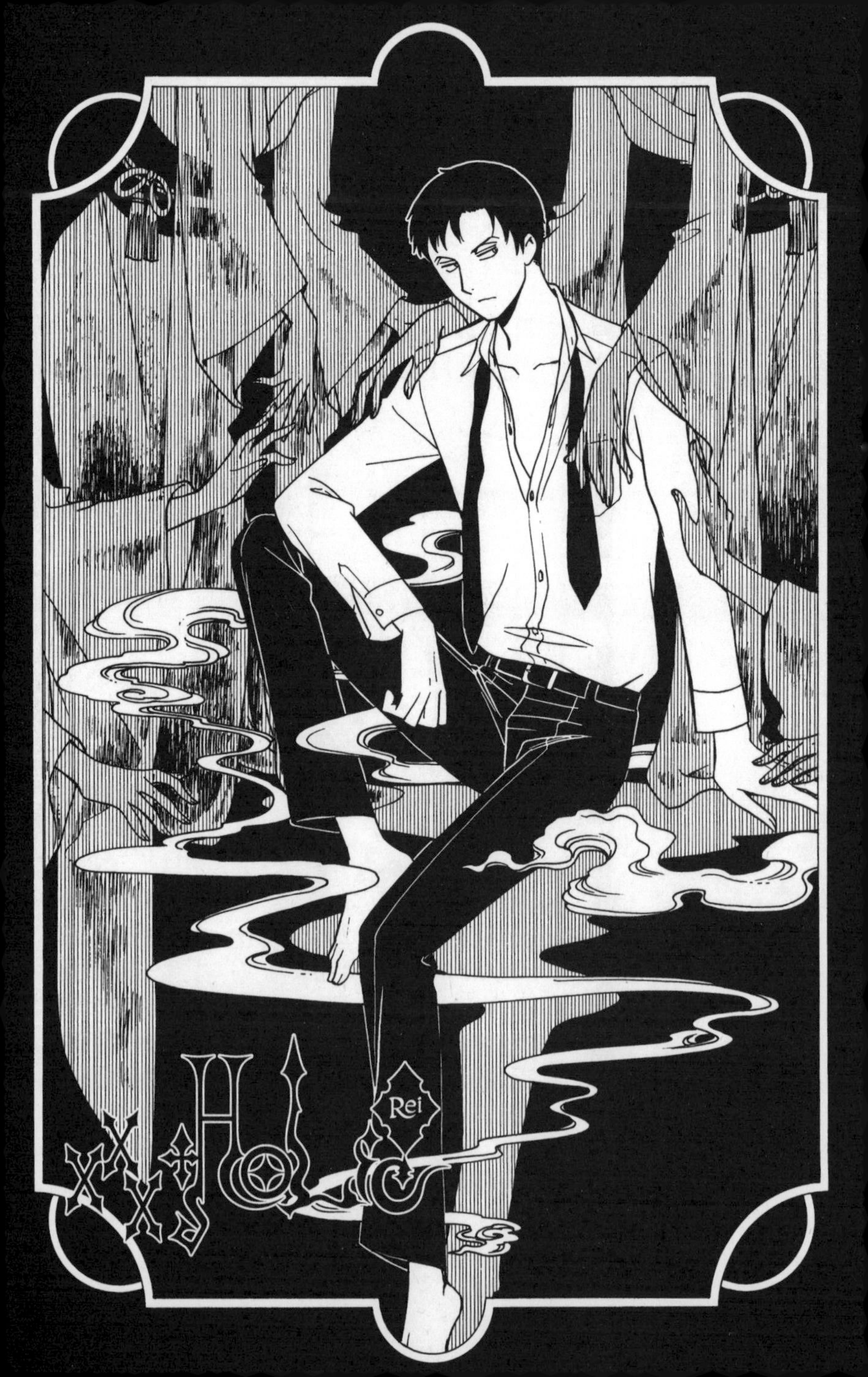
xxxHOLiC
Rei

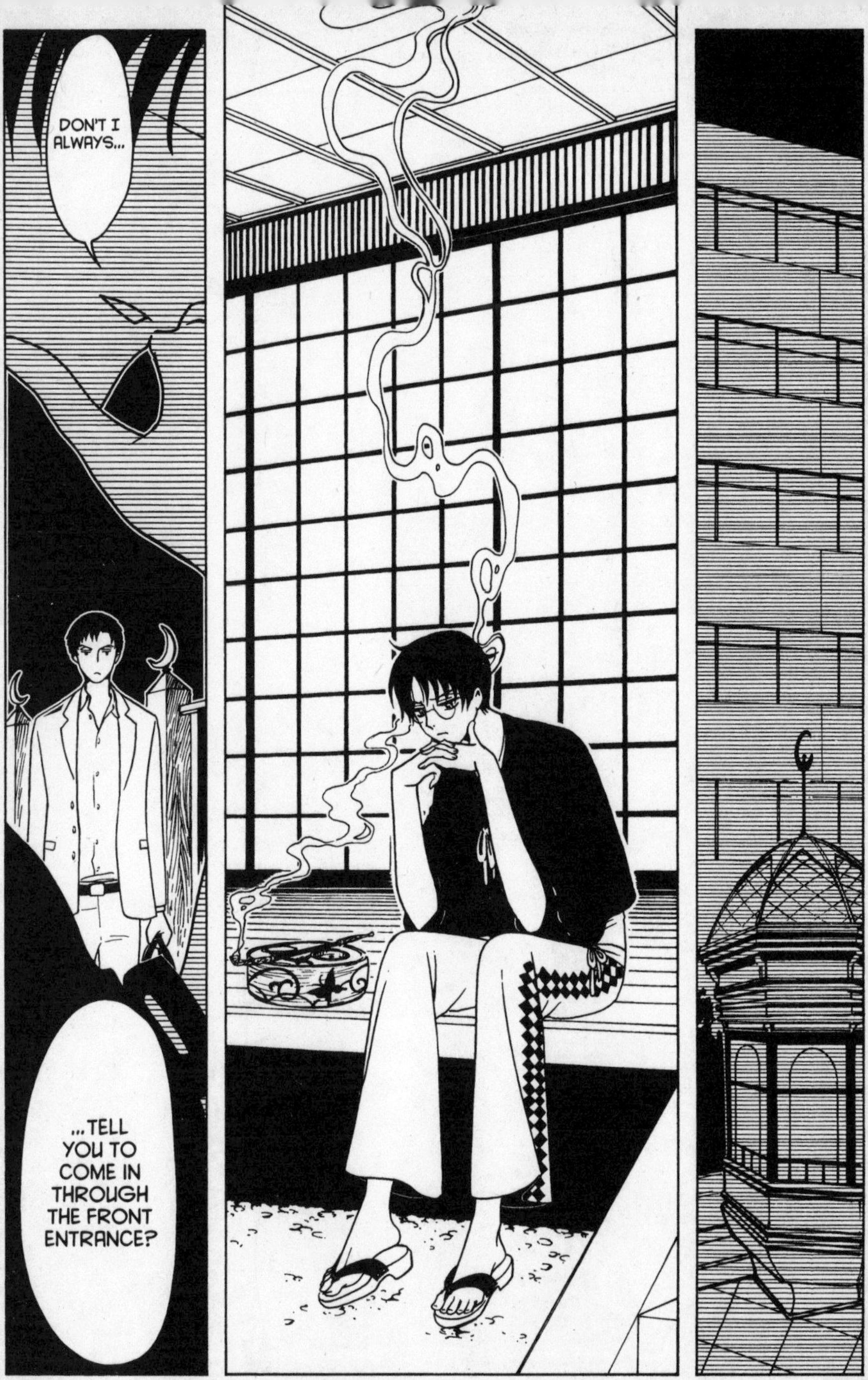
DON'T I ALWAYS...
...TELL YOU TO COME IN THROUGH THE FRONT ENTRANCE?

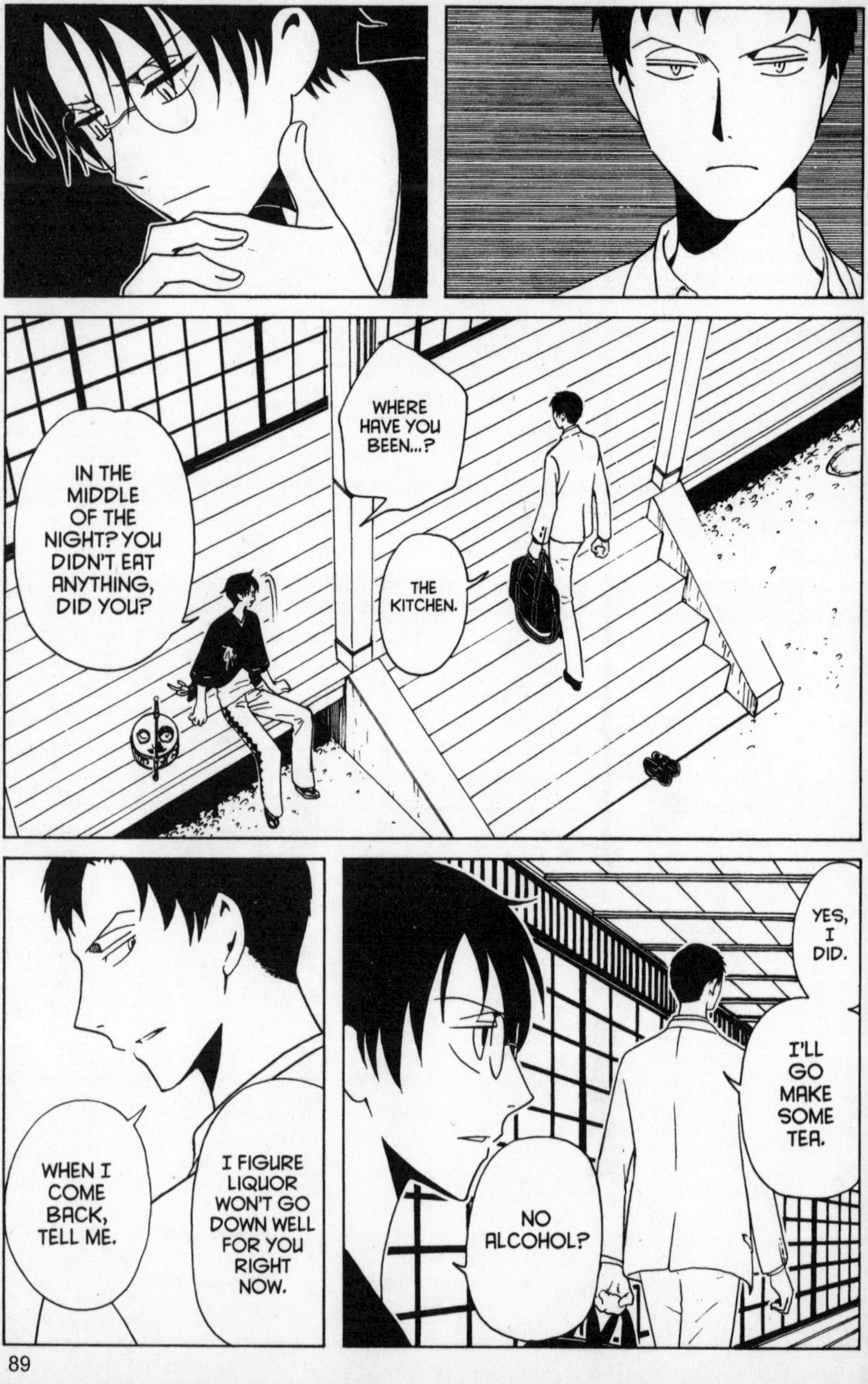
WHERE HAVE YOU BEEN...?
THE KITCHEN.
IN THE MIDDLE OF THE NIGHT? YOU DIDN'T EAT ANYTHING, DID YOU?
YES, I DID.
I'LL GO MAKE SOME TEA.
NO ALCOHOL?
I FIGURE LIQUOR WON'T GO DOWN WELL FOR YOU RIGHT NOW.
WHEN I COME BACK, TELL ME.

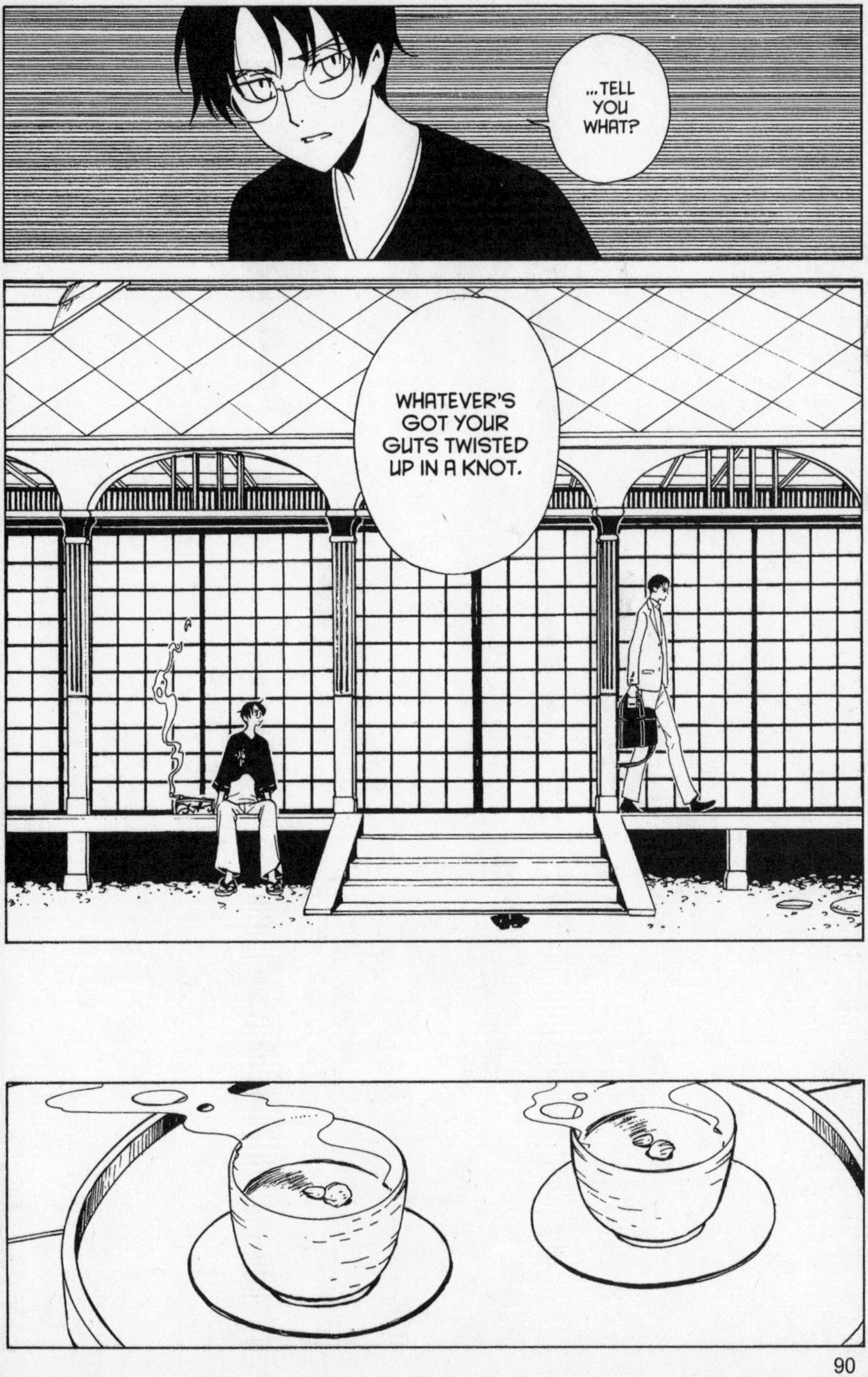
...TELL YOU WHAT?
WHATEVER'S GOT YOUR GUTS TWISTED UP IN A KNOT.

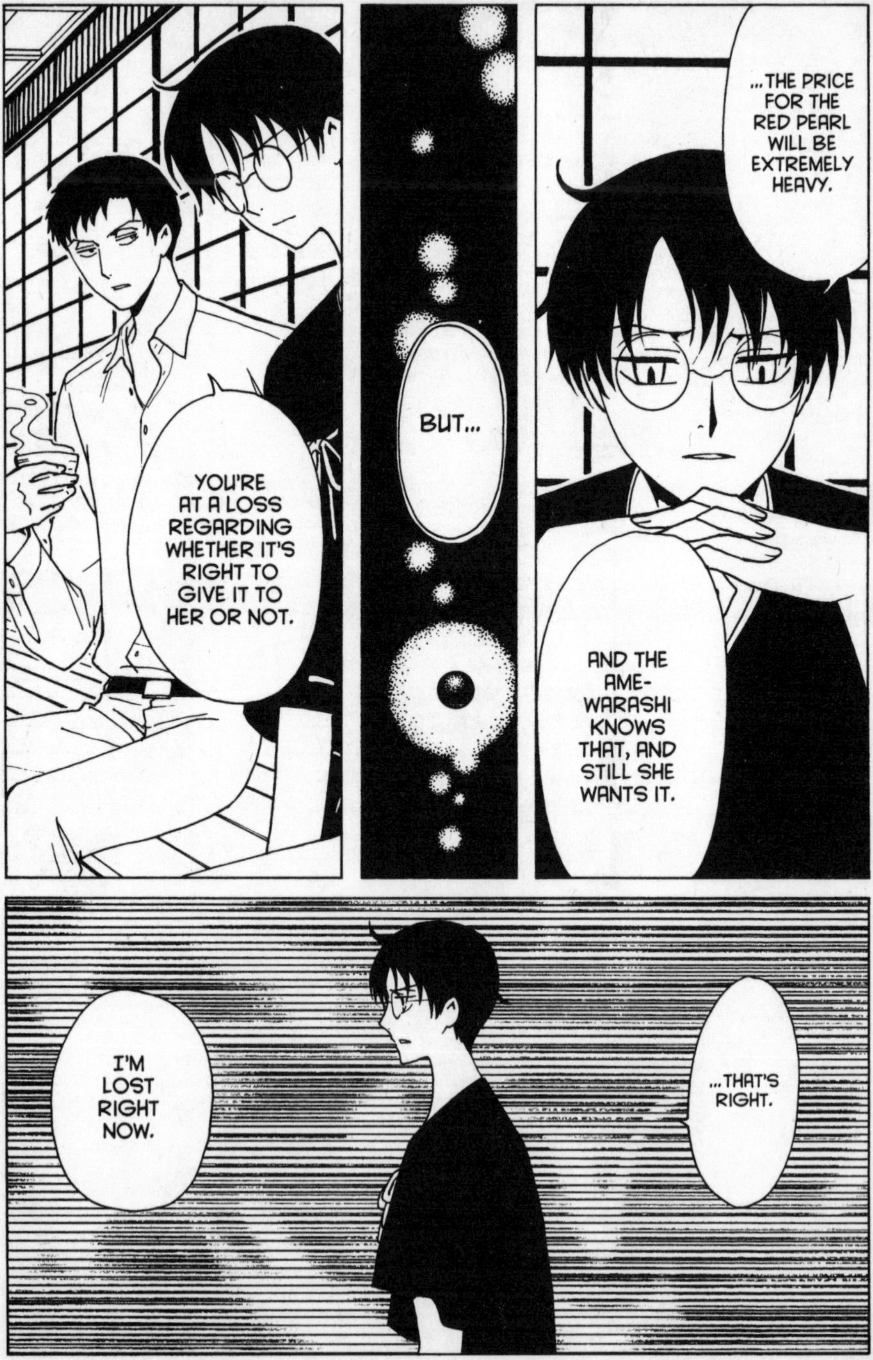
...THE PRICE FOR THE RED PEARL WILL BE EXTREMELY HEAVY.
AND THE AME-WARASHI KNOWS THAT, AND STILL SHE WANTS IT.
BUT...
YOU'RE AT A LOSS REGARDING WHETHER IT'S RIGHT TO GIVE IT TO HER OR NOT.
...THAT'S RIGHT.
I'M LOST RIGHT NOW.

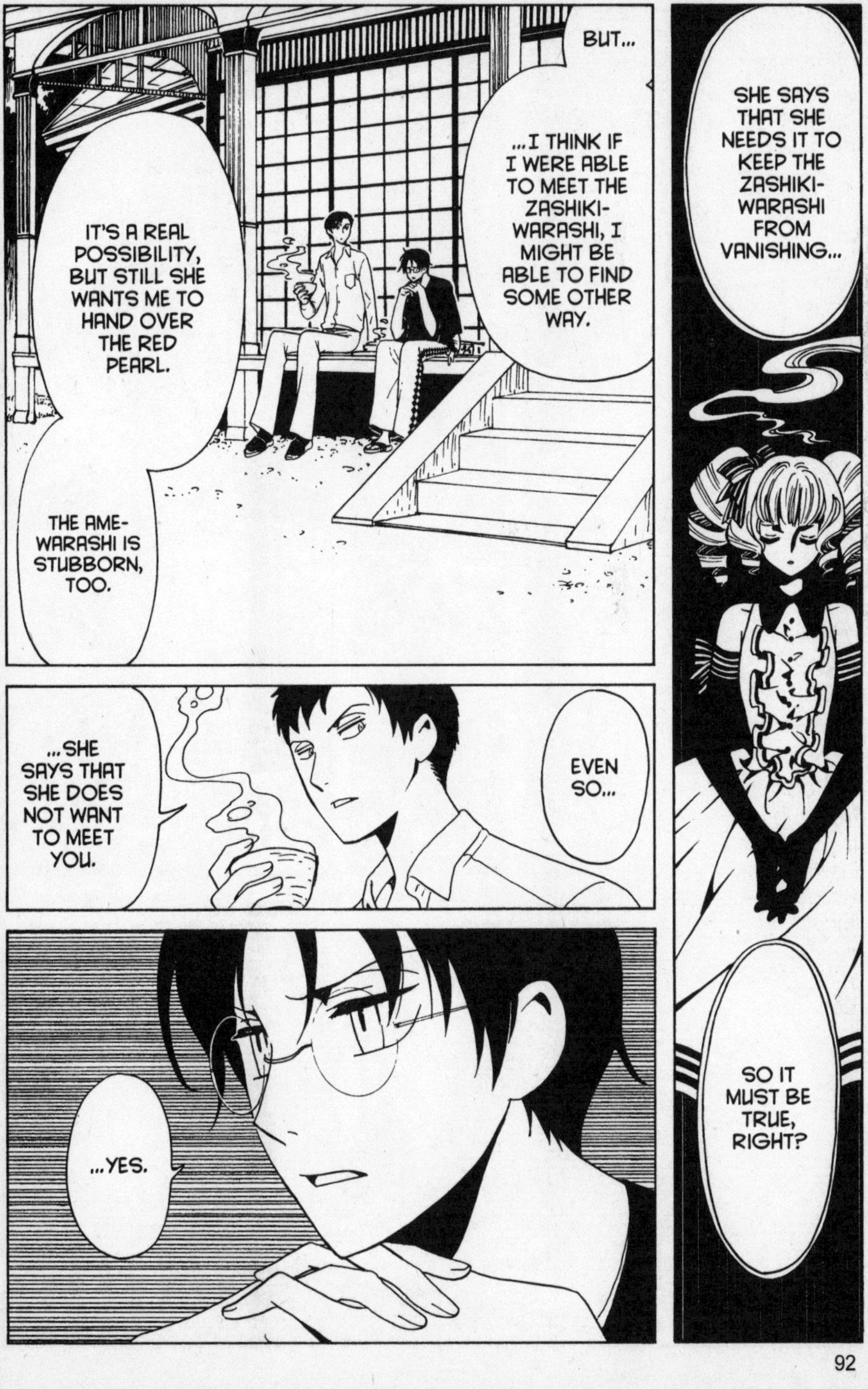
SHE SAYS THAT SHE NEEDS IT TO KEEP THE ZASHIKI-WARASHI FROM VANISHING...
SO IT MUST BE TRUE, RIGHT?
BUT...
...I THINK IF I WERE ABLE TO MEET THE ZASHIKI-WARASHI, I MIGHT BE ABLE TO FIND SOME OTHER WAY.
IT'S A REAL POSSIBILITY, BUT STILL SHE WANTS ME TO HAND OVER THE RED PEARL.
THE AME-WARASHI IS STUBBORN, TOO.
EVEN SO...
...SHE SAYS THAT SHE DOES NOT WANT TO MEET YOU.
...YES.

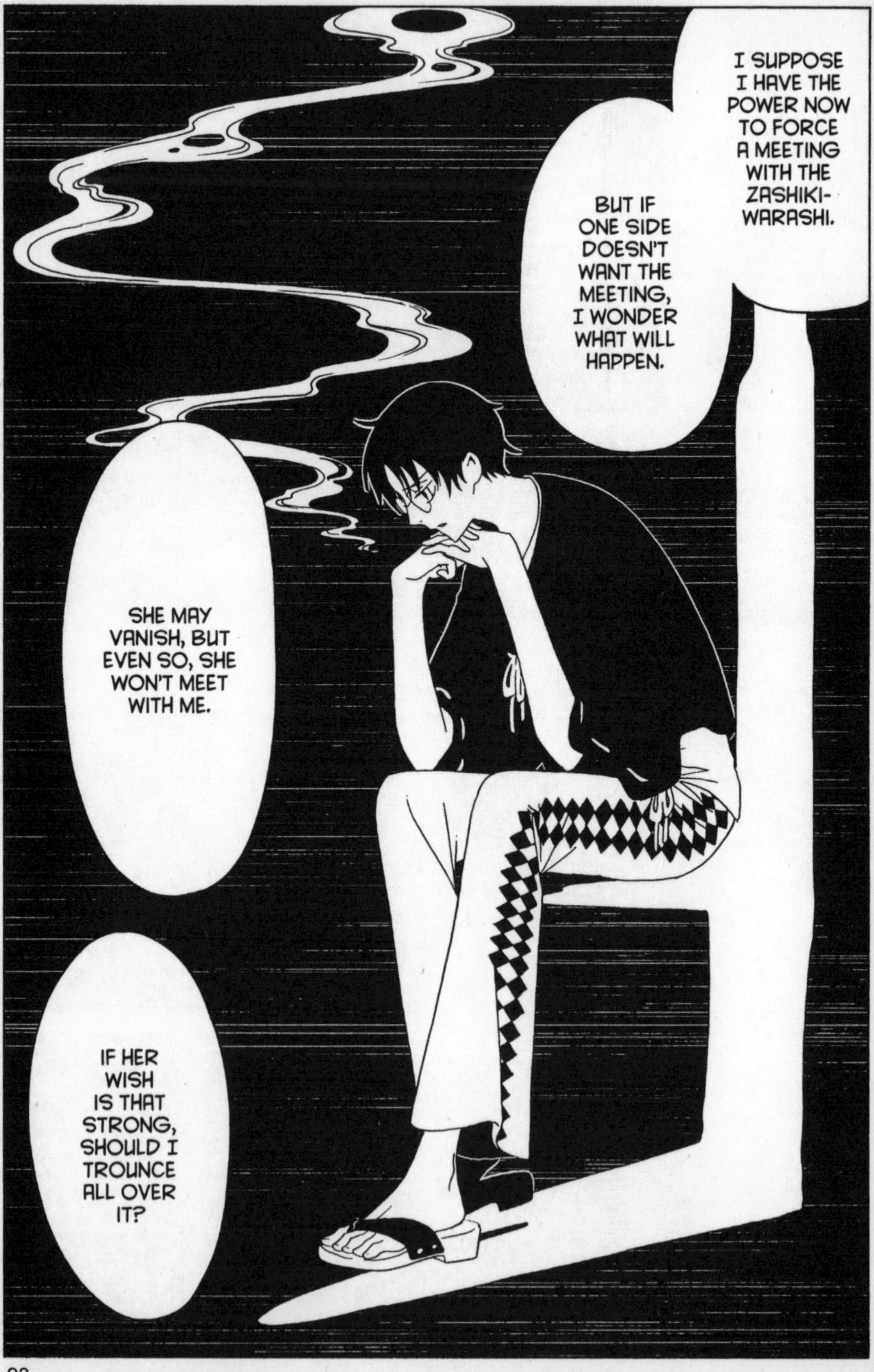
I SUPPOSE I HAVE THE POWER NOW TO FORCE A MEETING WITH THE ZASHIKI-WARASHI.
BUT IF ONE SIDE DOESN'T WANT THE MEETING, I WONDER WHAT WILL HAPPEN.
SHE MAY VANISH, BUT EVEN SO, SHE WON'T MEET WITH ME.
IF HER WISH IS THAT STRONG, SHOULD I TROUNCE ALL OVER IT?

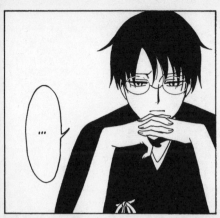

...

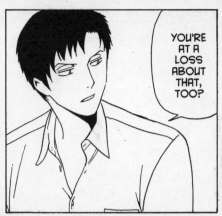

YOU'RE AT A LOSS ABOUT THAT, TOO?

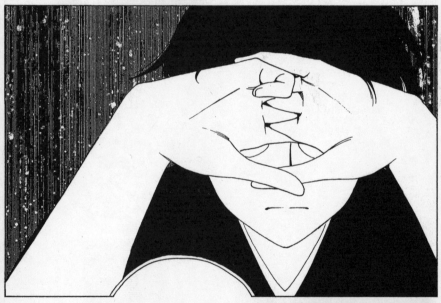

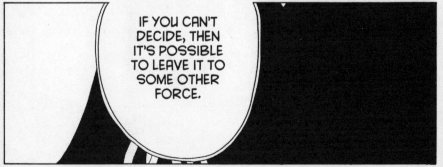

IF YOU CAN'T DECIDE, THEN IT'S POSSIBLE TO LEAVE IT TO SOME OTHER FORCE.

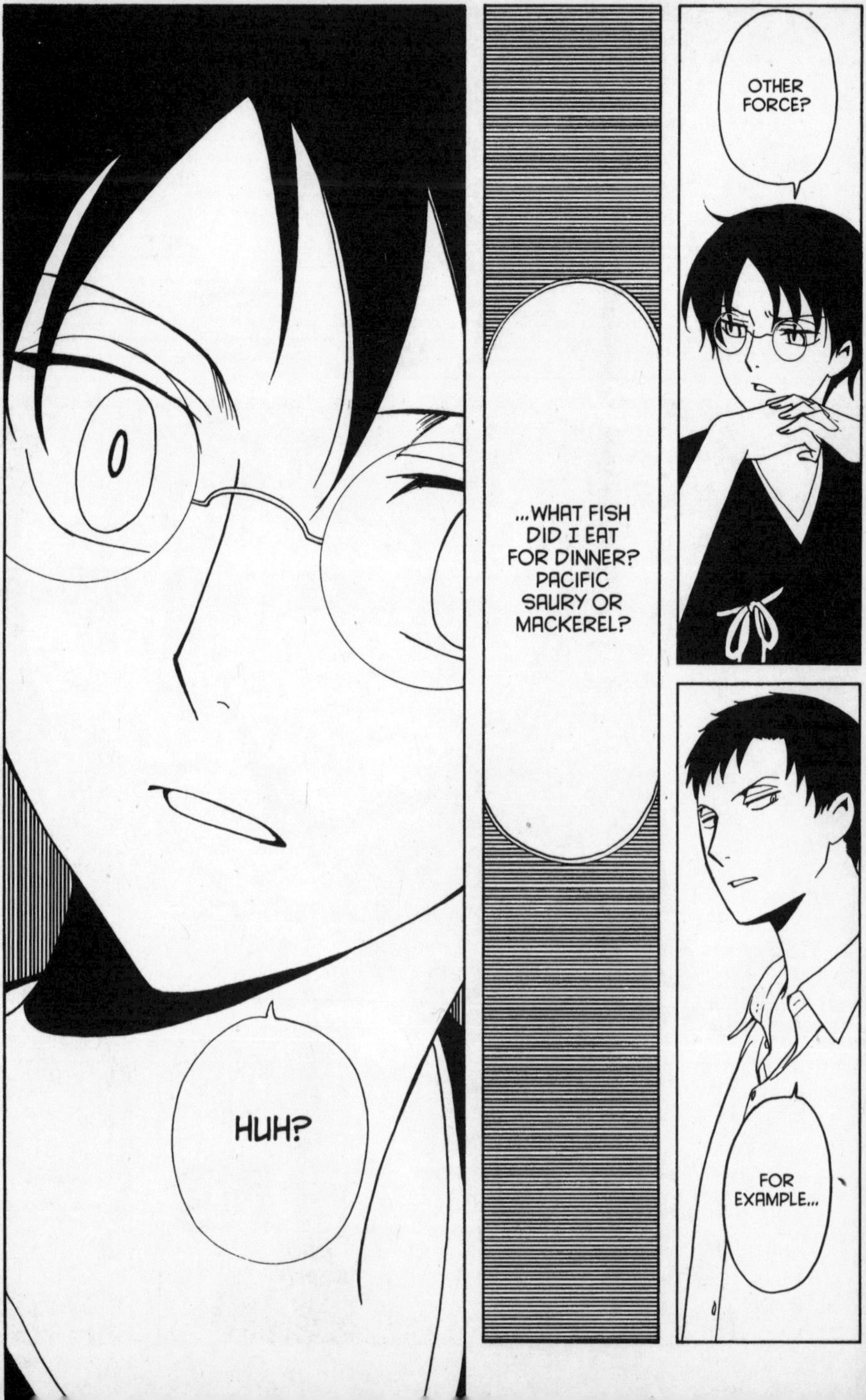
OTHER FORCE?
FOR EXAMPLE...
...WHAT FISH DID I EAT FOR DINNER? PACIFIC SAURY OR MACKEREL?
HUH?

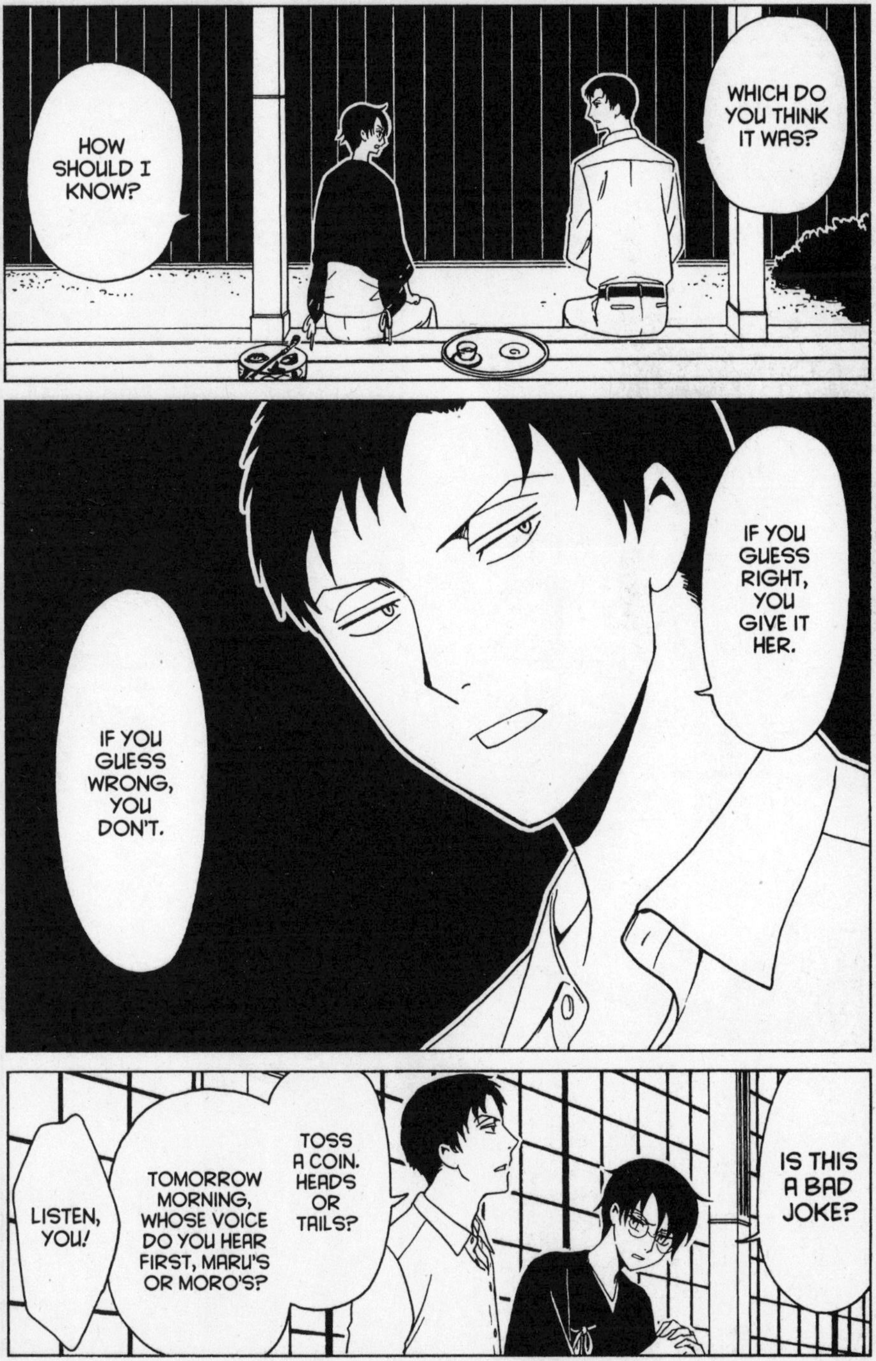
WHICH DO YOU THINK IT WAS?
HOW SHOULD I KNOW?
IF YOU GUESS RIGHT, YOU GIVE IT HER.
IF YOU GUESS WRONG, YOU DON'T.
IS THIS A BAD JOKE?
TOSS A COIN. HEADS OR TAILS?
TOMORROW MORNING, WHOSE VOICE DO YOU HEAR FIRST, MARU'S OR MORO'S?
LISTEN, YOU!

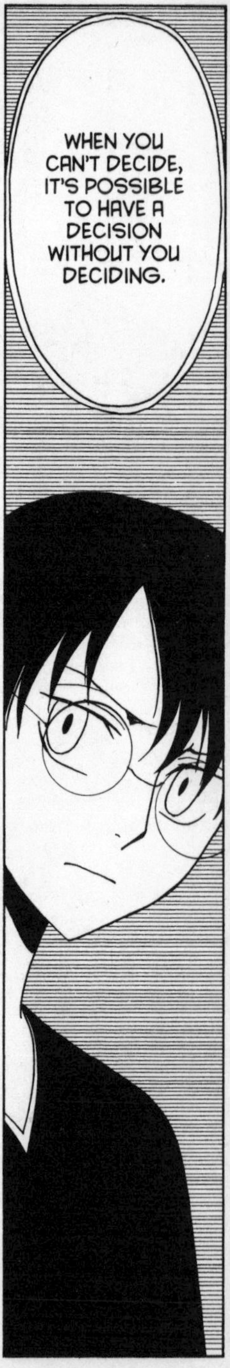
WHEN YOU CAN'T DECIDE, IT'S POSSIBLE TO HAVE A DECISION WITHOUT YOU DECIDING.
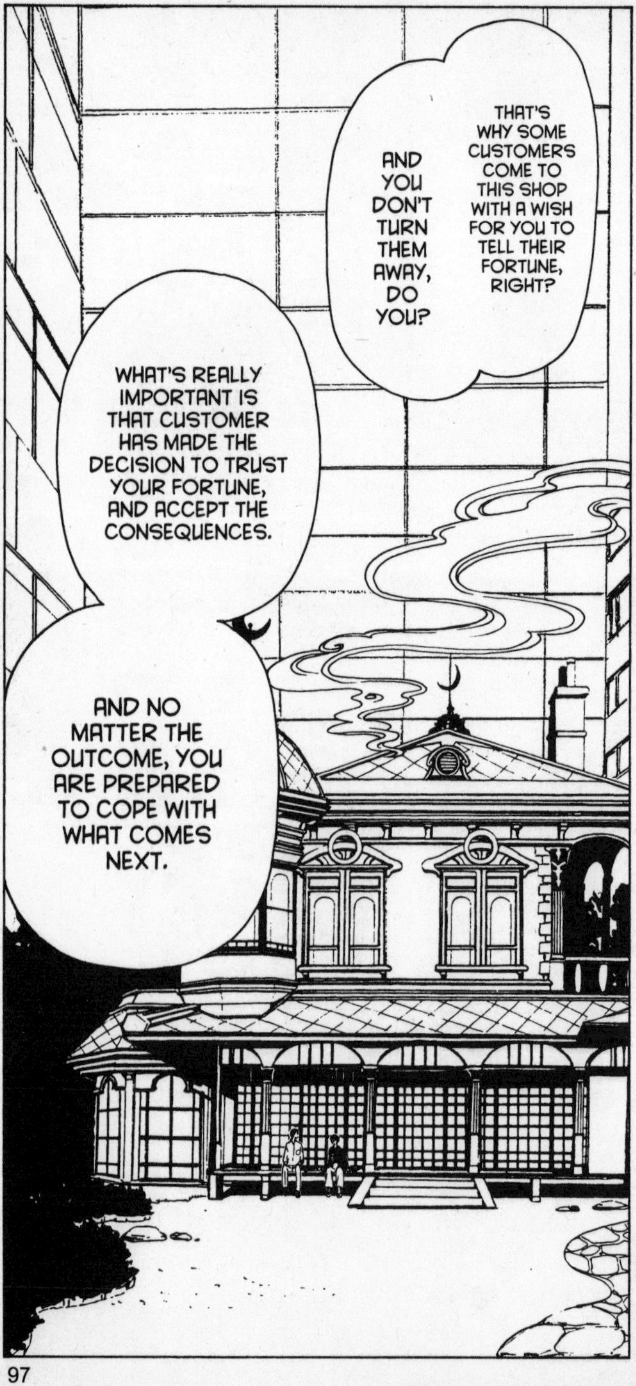
THAT'S WHY SOME CUSTOMERS COME TO THIS SHOP WITH A WISH FOR YOU TO TELL THEIR FORTUNE, RIGHT?
AND YOU DON'T TURN THEM AWAY, DO YOU?
WHAT'S REALLY IMPORTANT IS THAT CUSTOMER HAS MADE THE DECISION TO TRUST YOUR FORTUNE, AND ACCEPT THE CONSEQUENCES.
AND NO MATTER THE OUTCOME, YOU ARE PREPARED TO COPE WITH WHAT COMES NEXT.

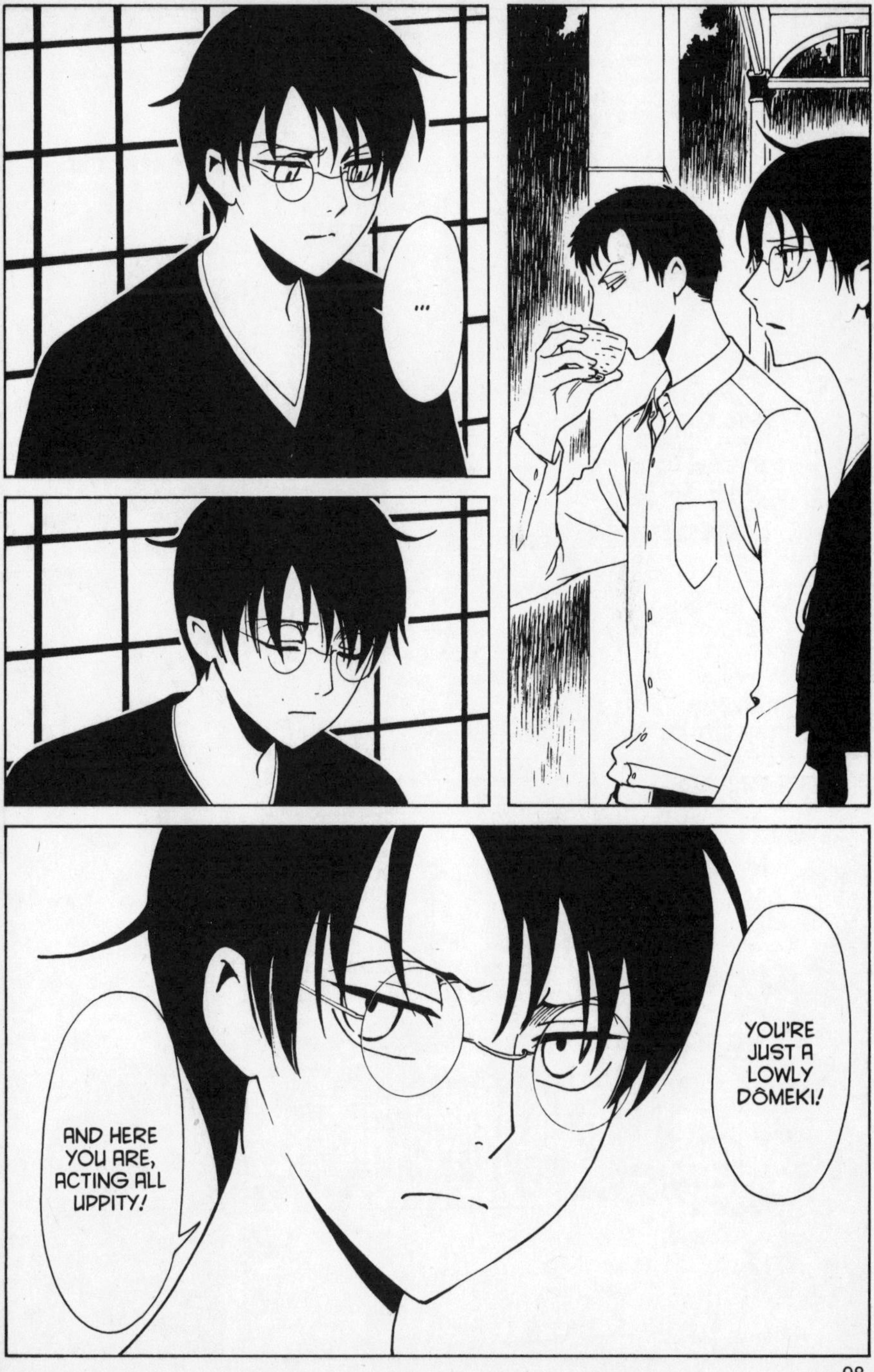
...
YOU'RE JUST A LOWLY DÔMEKI!
AND HERE YOU ARE, ACTING ALL UPPITY!

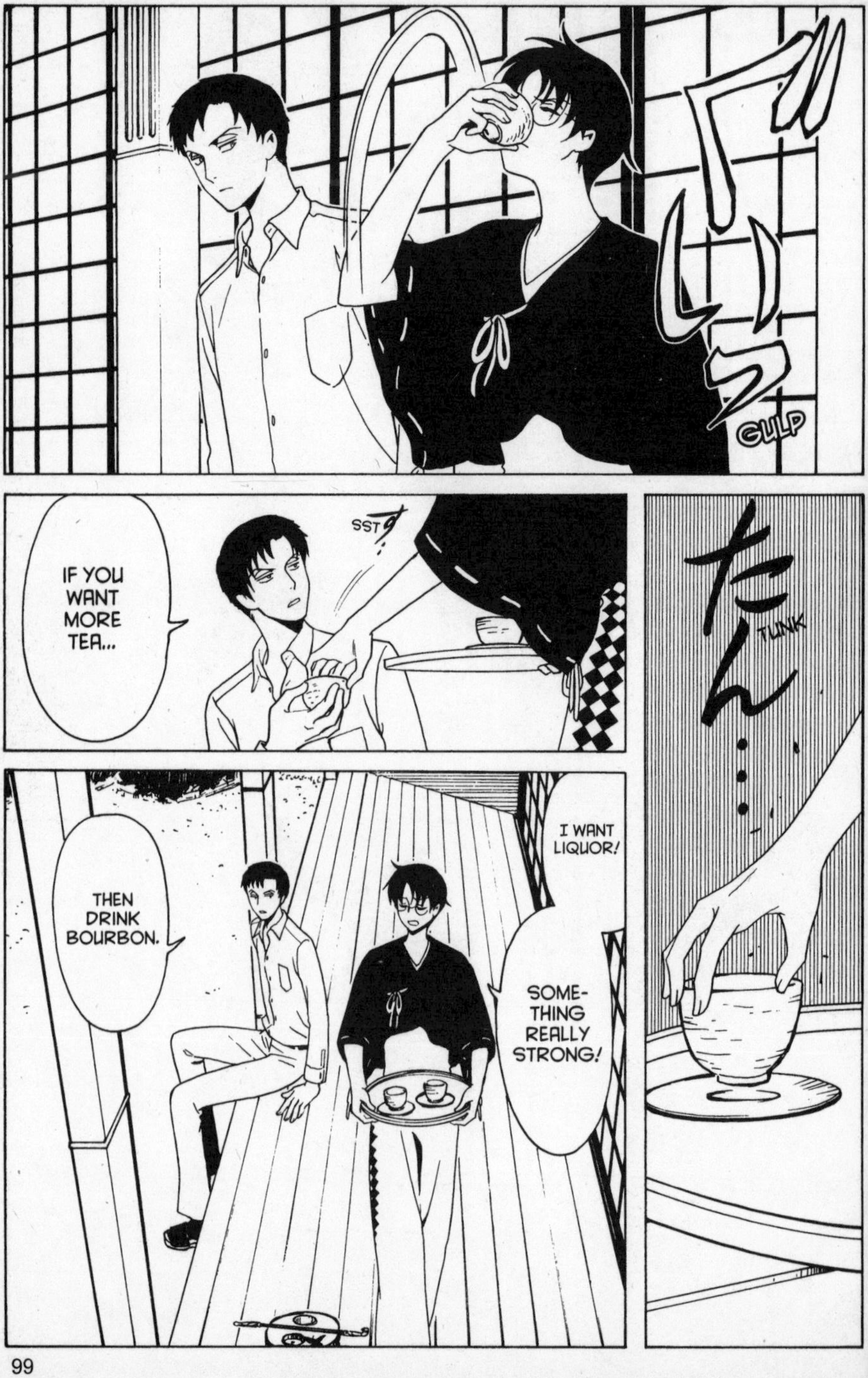
ごくっ
GULP
たん
TUNK
SST
IF YOU WANT MORE TEA...
I WANT LIQUOR!
SOME-THING REALLY STRONG!
THEN DRINK BOURBON.

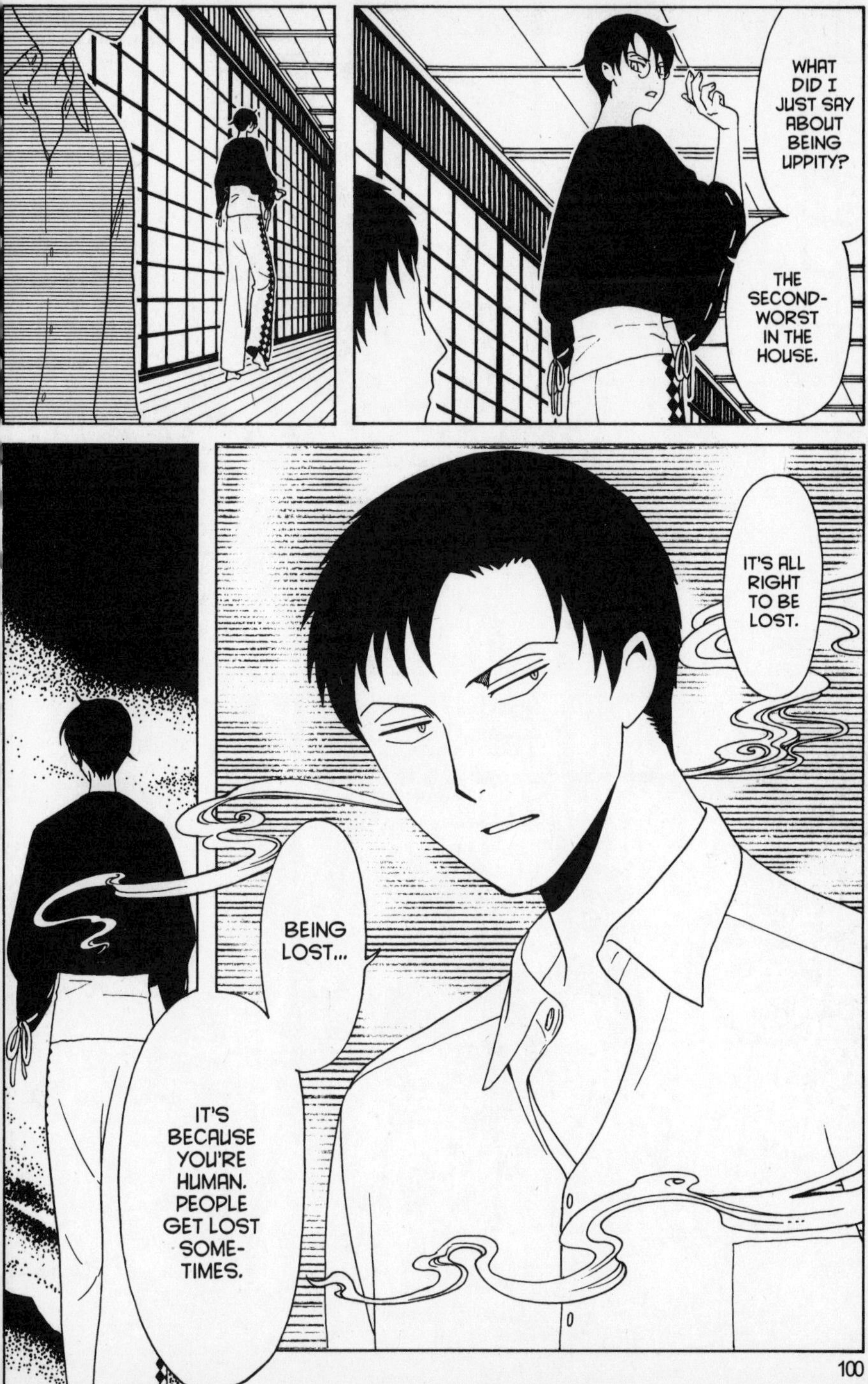
WHAT DID I JUST SAY ABOUT BEING UPPITY?
THE SECOND-WORST IN THE HOUSE.
IT'S ALL RIGHT TO BE LOST.
BEING LOST...
IT'S BECAUSE YOU'RE HUMAN. PEOPLE GET LOST SOME-TIMES.

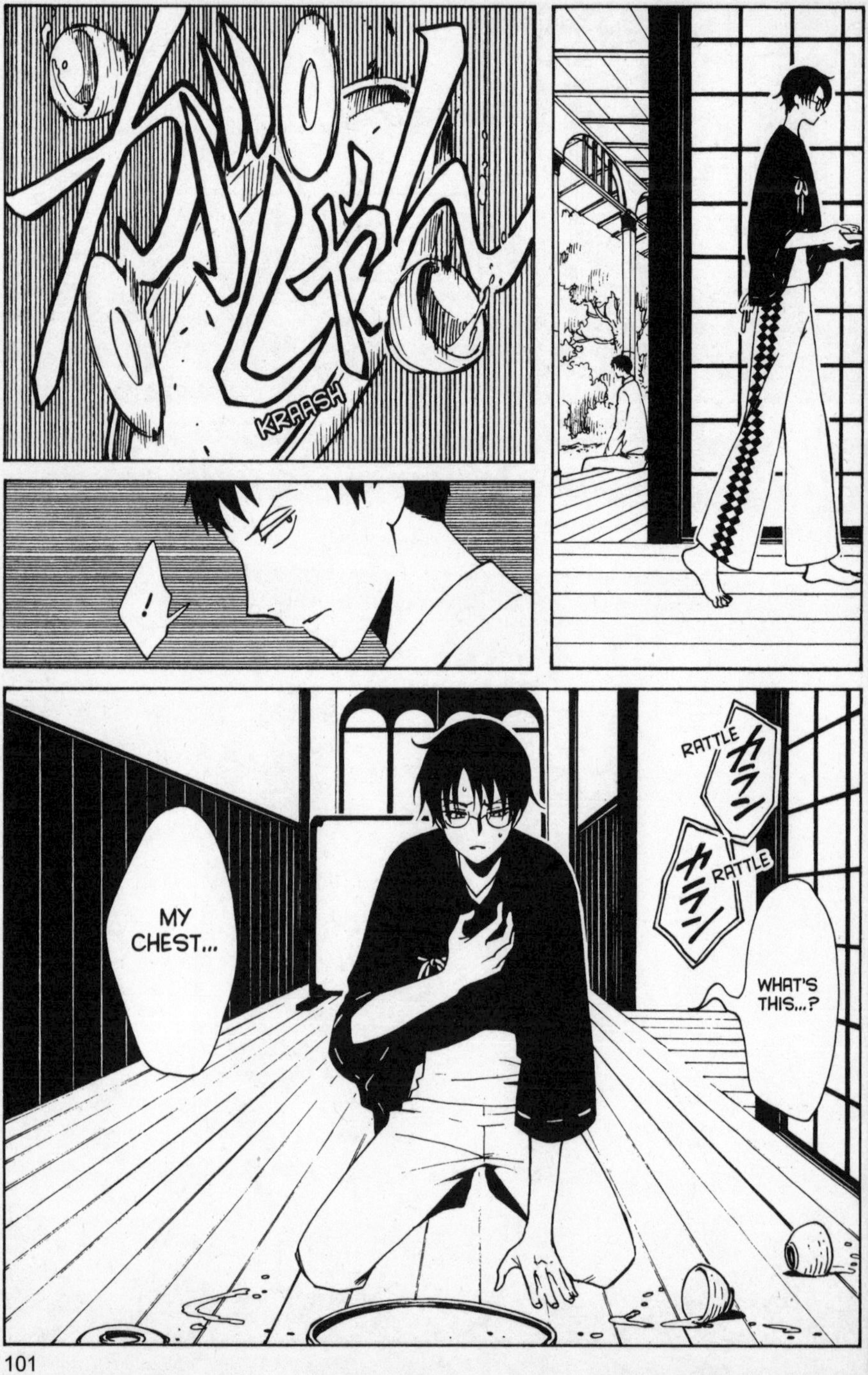
KRAASH
!
RATTLE
カラン
RATTLE
カラン
WHAT'S THIS...?
MY CHEST...

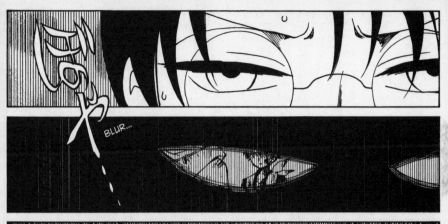

BLUR...

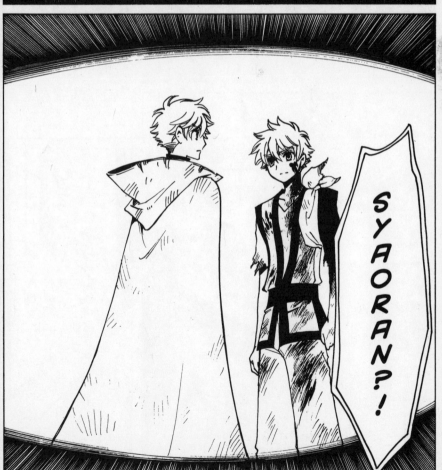

SYAORAN?!

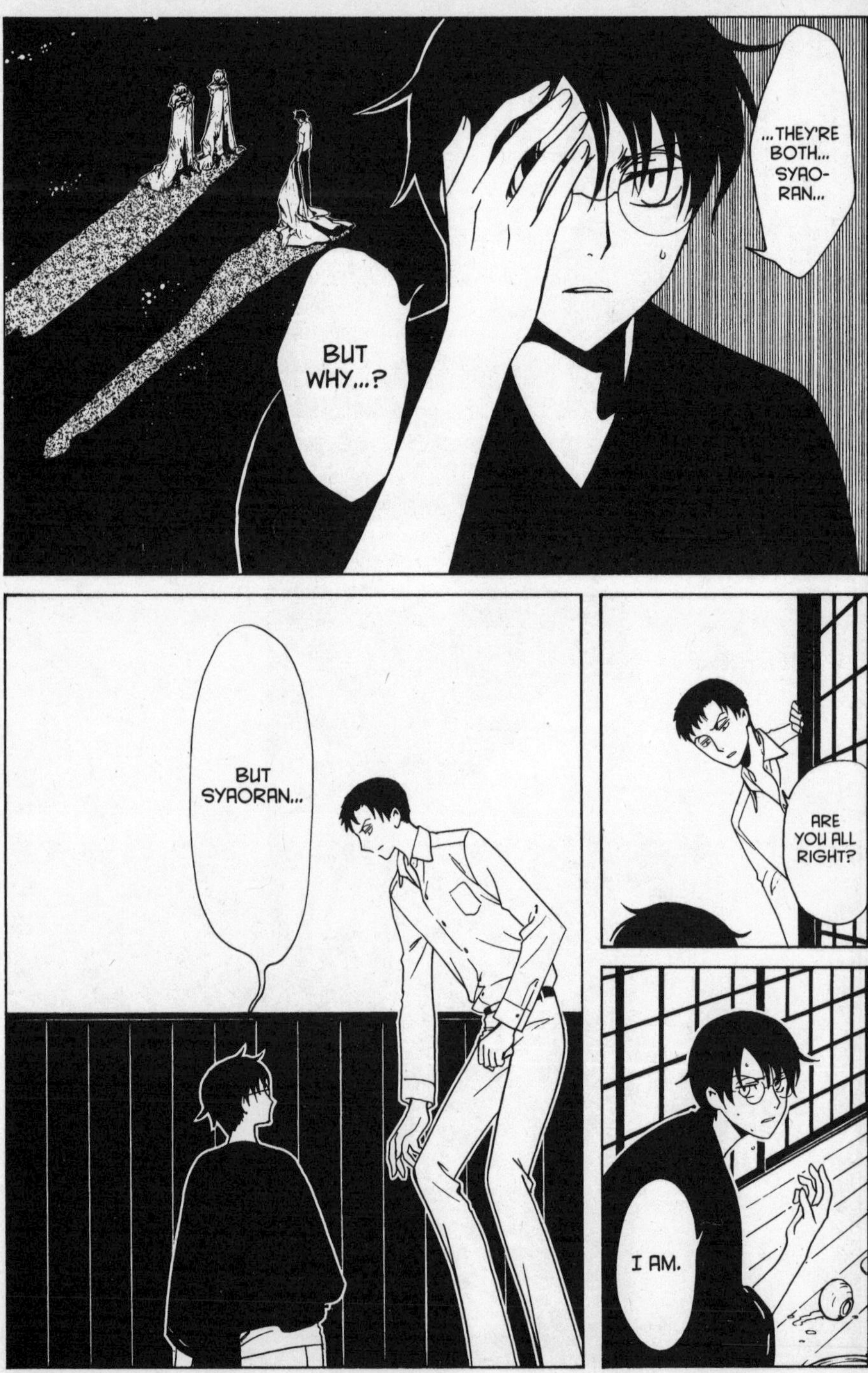
...THEY'RE BOTH... SYAO-RAN...
BUT WHY...?
ARE YOU ALL RIGHT?
BUT SYAORAN...
I AM.

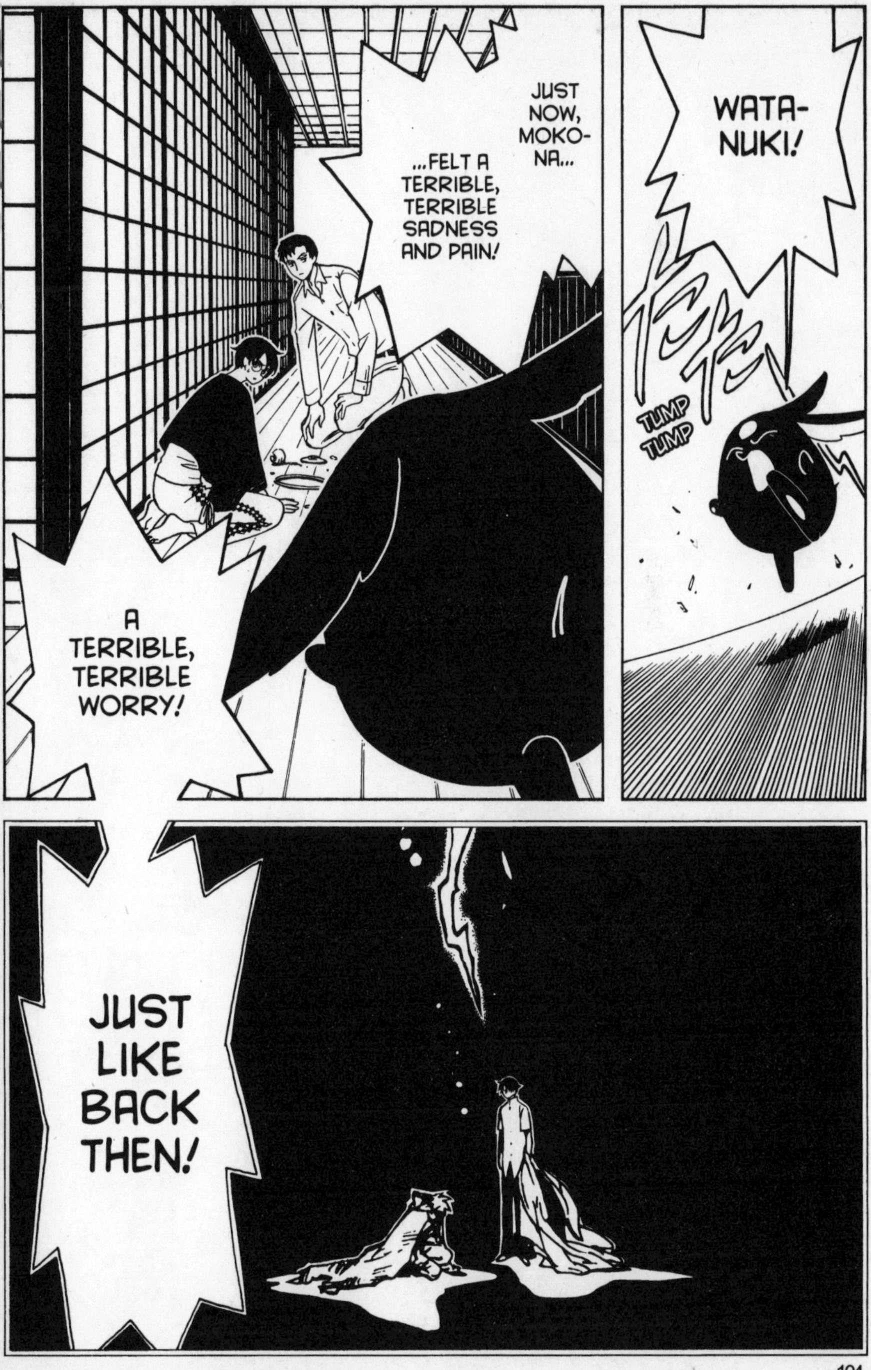
WATA-
NUKI!
TUMP
TUMP
JUST NOW, MOKONA...
...FELT A TERRIBLE, TERRIBLE SADNESS AND PAIN!
A TERRIBLE, TERRIBLE WORRY!
JUST LIKE BACK THEN!

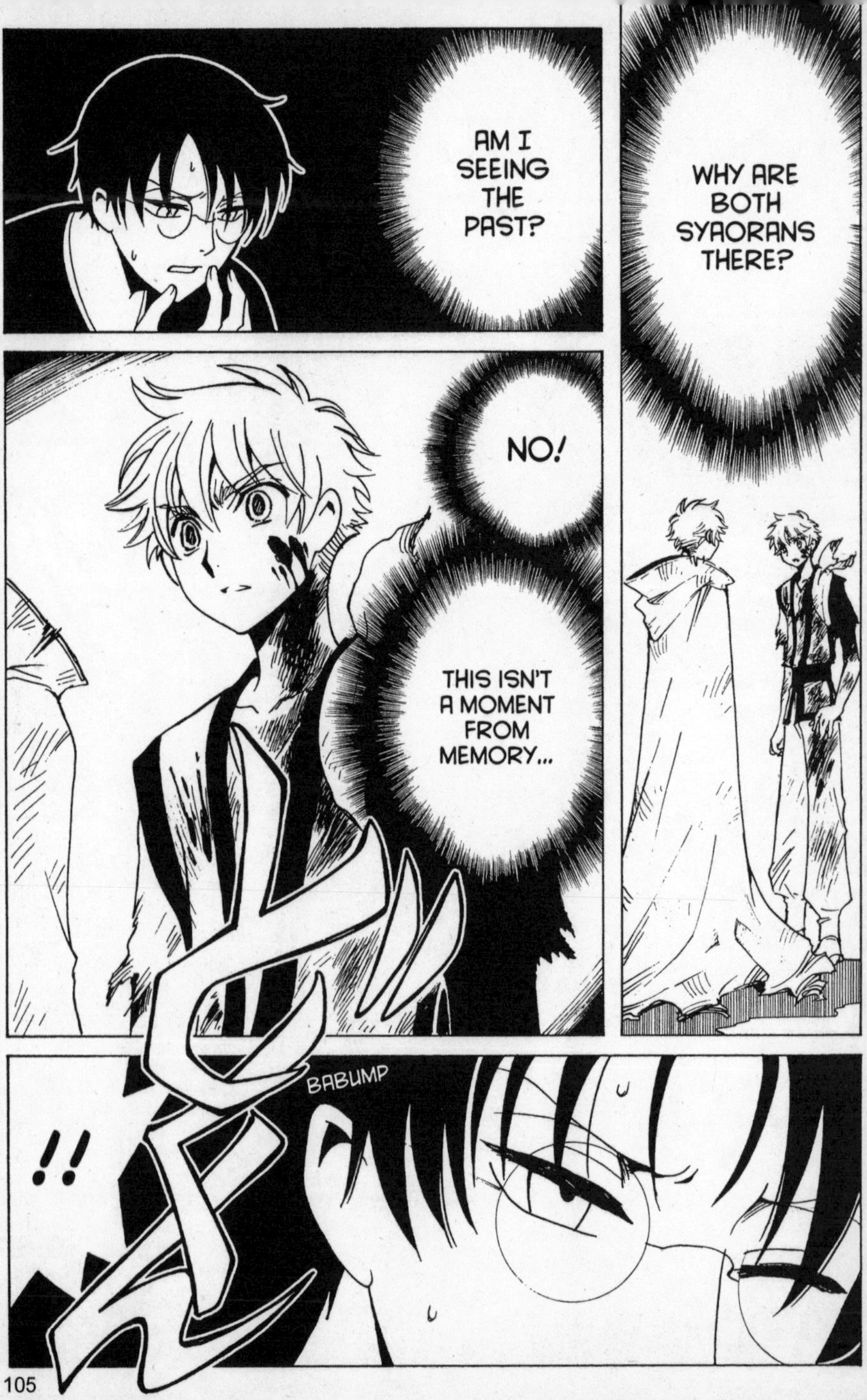
WHY ARE BOTH SYAORANS THERE?
AM I SEEING THE PAST?
NO!
THIS ISN'T A MOMENT FROM MEMORY...
BABUMP
!!

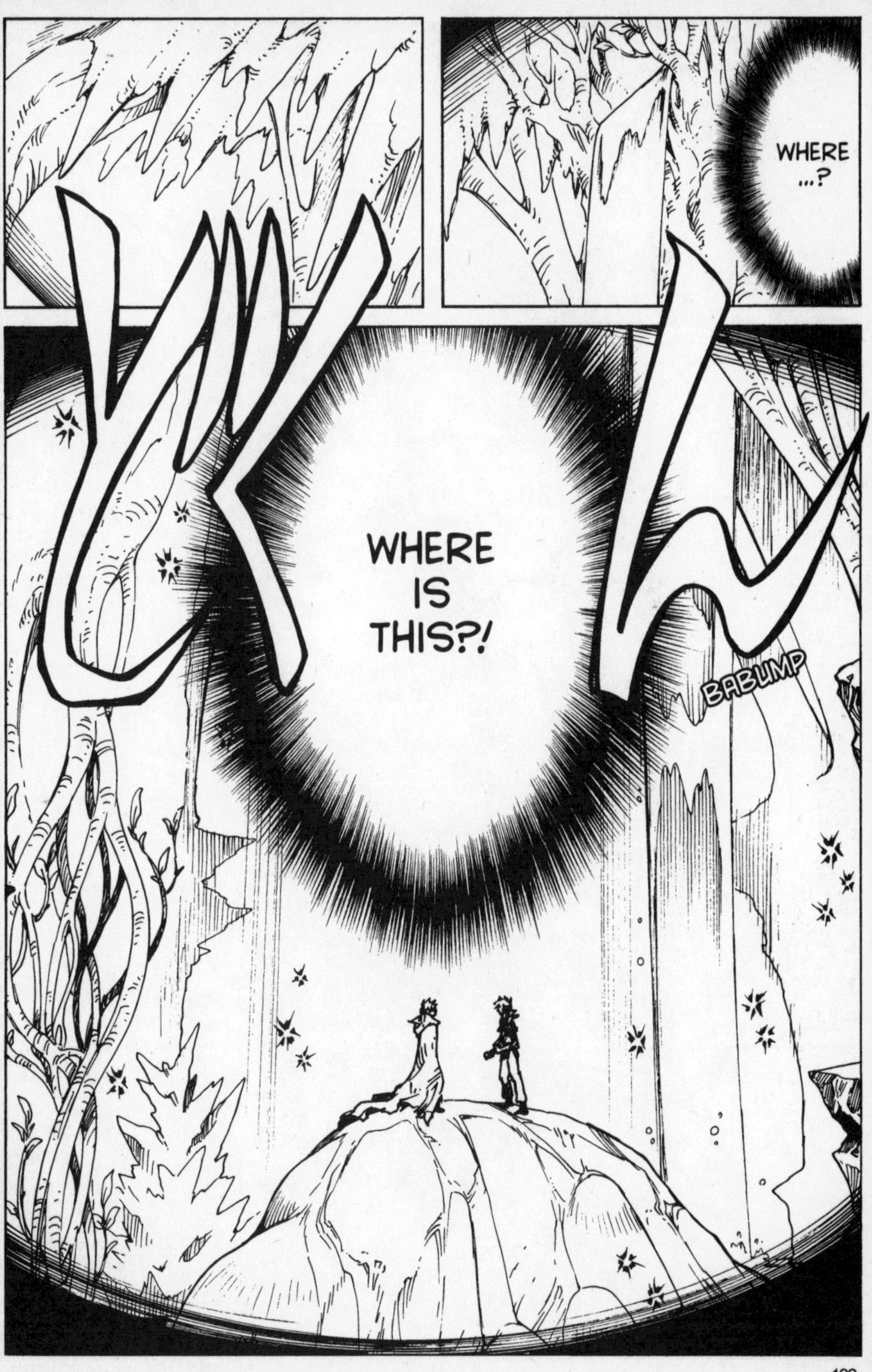
WHERE ...?
WHERE IS THIS?!
BABUMP

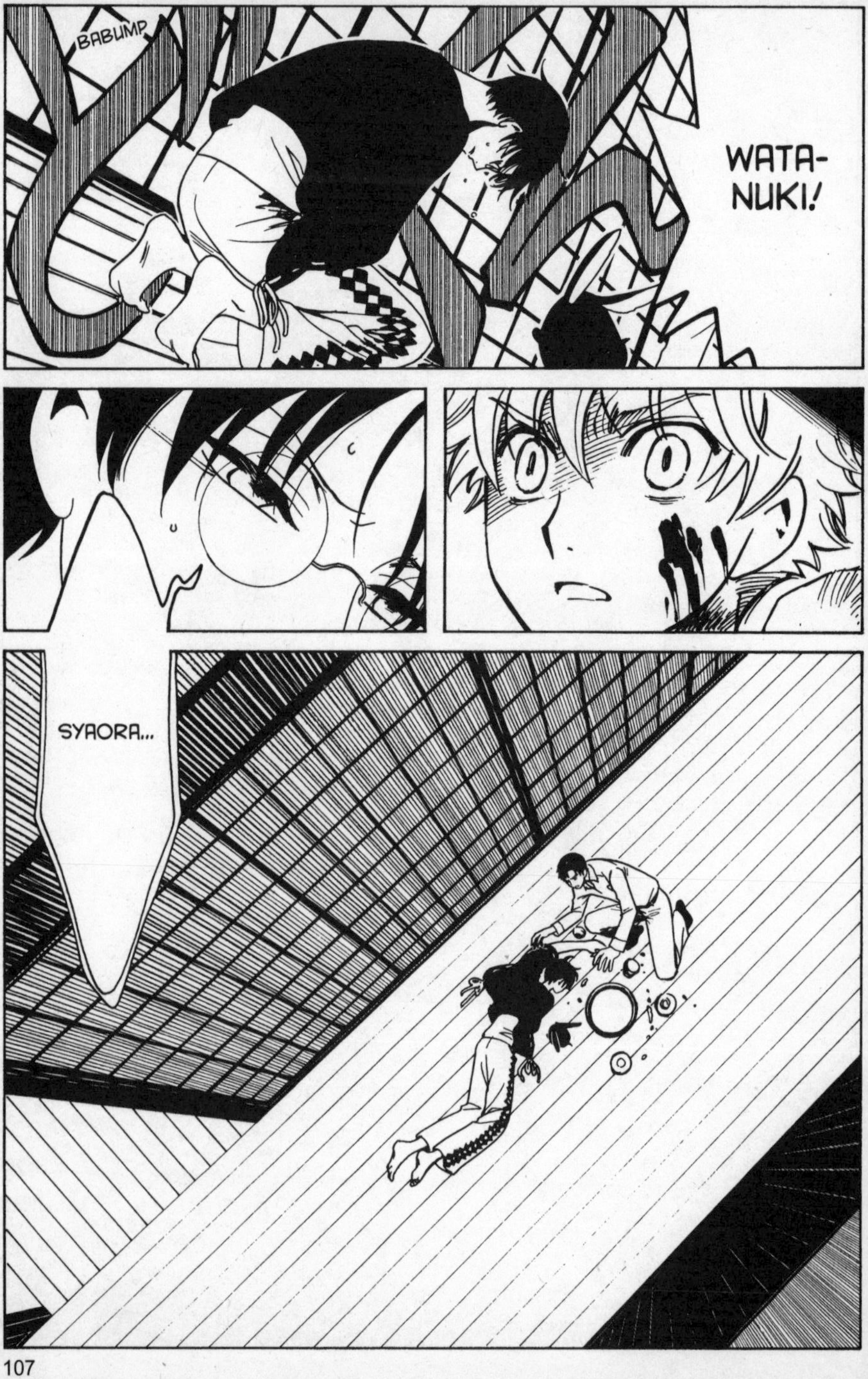
BABUMP
WATA-
NUKI!
SYAORA...

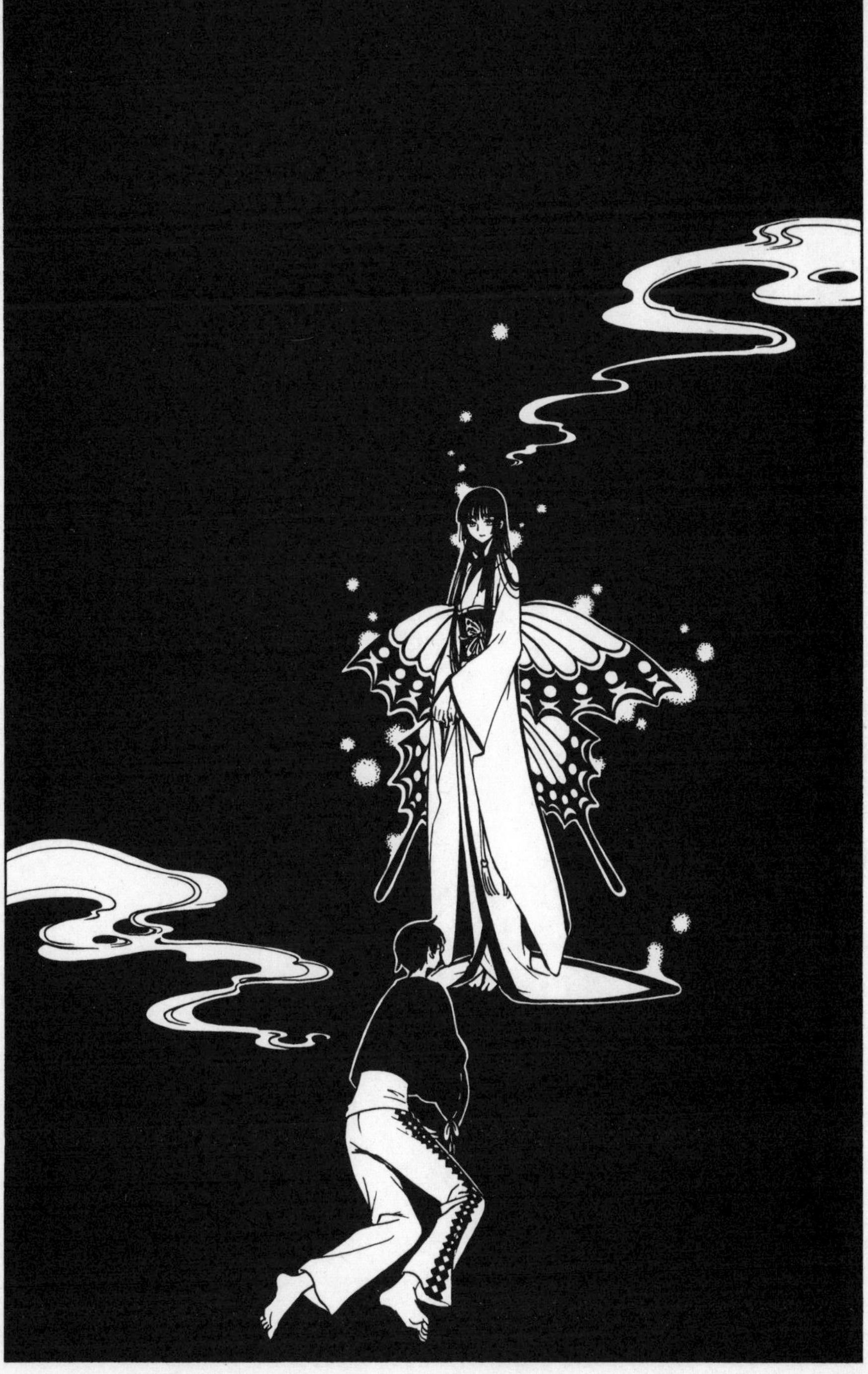

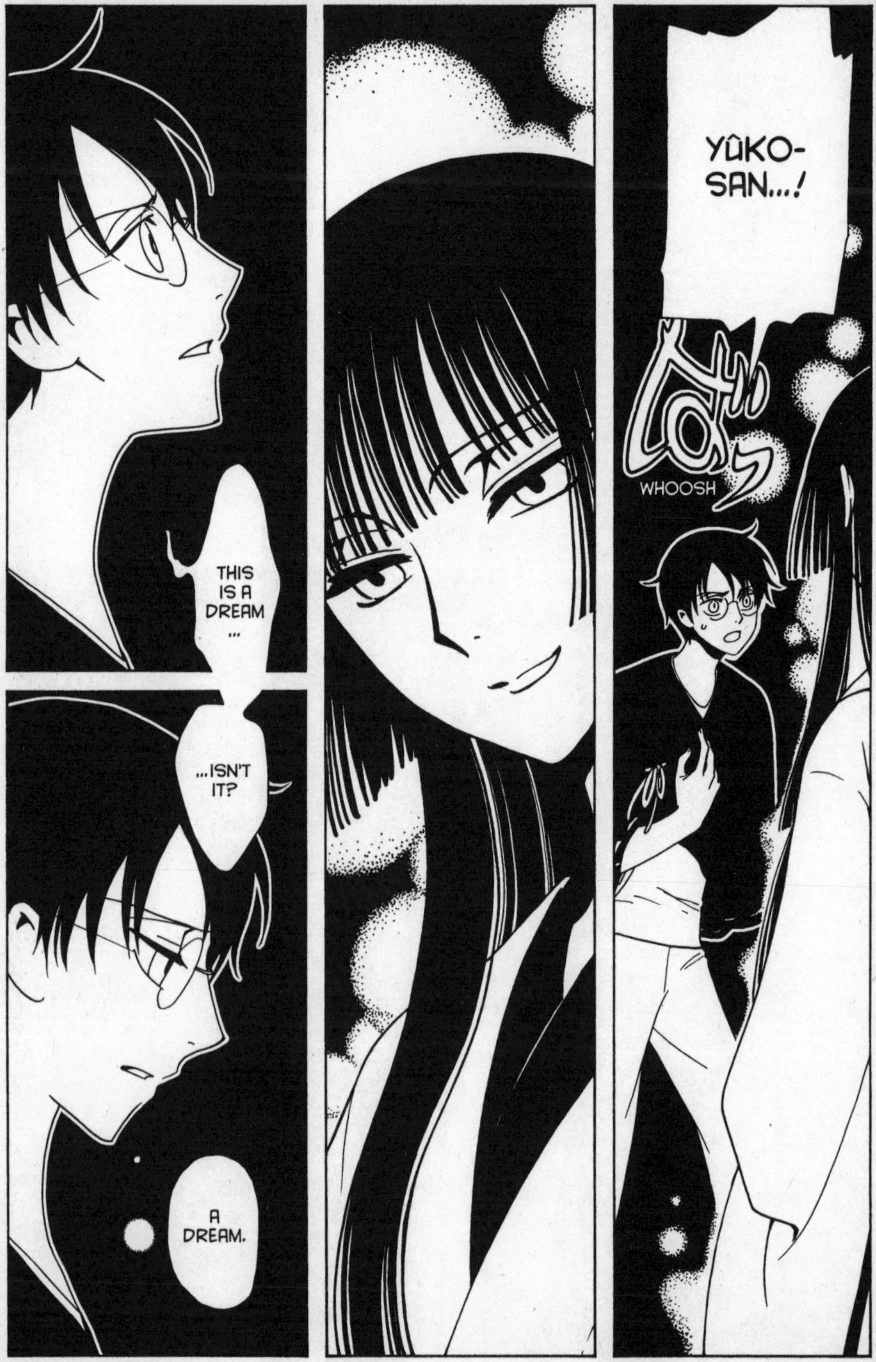
YÛKO-SAN...!
WHOOSH
THIS IS A DREAM ...
...ISN'T IT?
A DREAM.

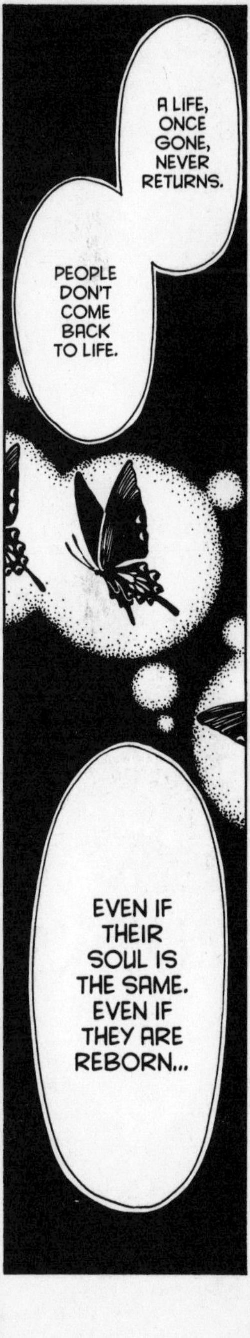
A LIFE, ONCE GONE, NEVER RETURNS.
PEOPLE DON'T COME BACK TO LIFE.
EVEN IF THEIR SOUL IS THE SAME. EVEN IF THEY ARE REBORN...
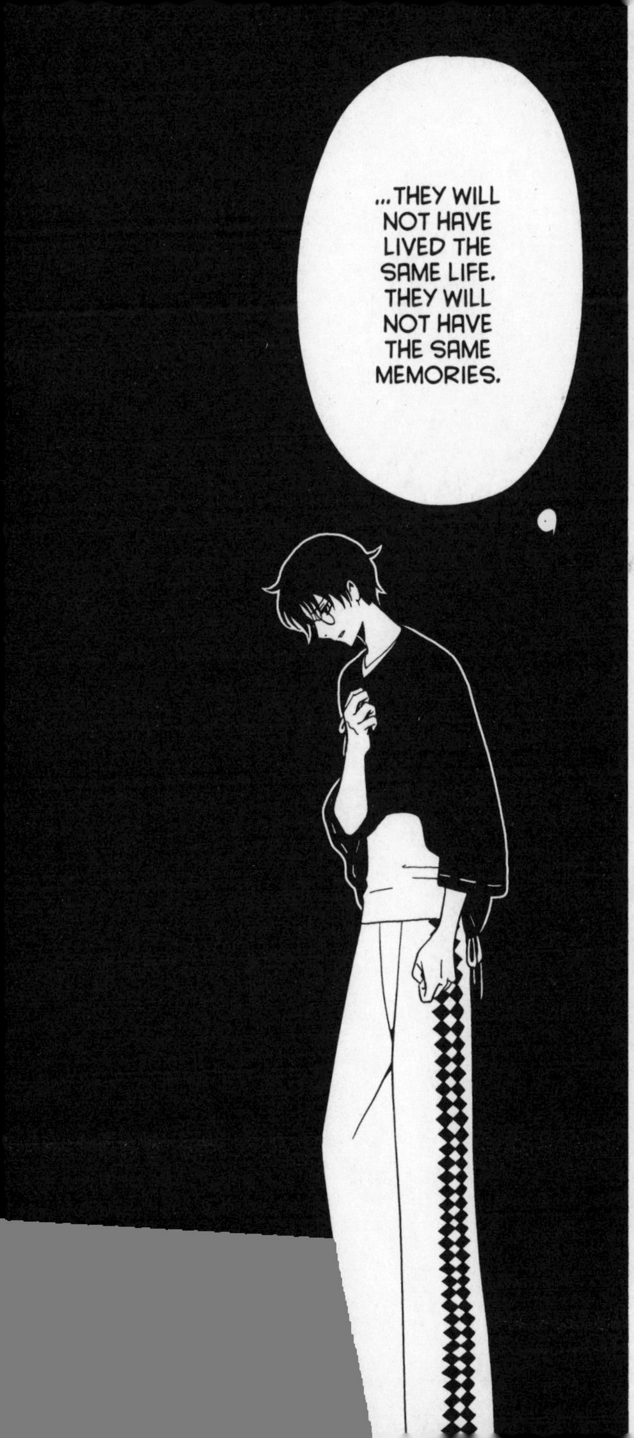
...THEY WILL NOT HAVE LIVED THE SAME LIFE. THEY WILL NOT HAVE THE SAME MEMORIES.

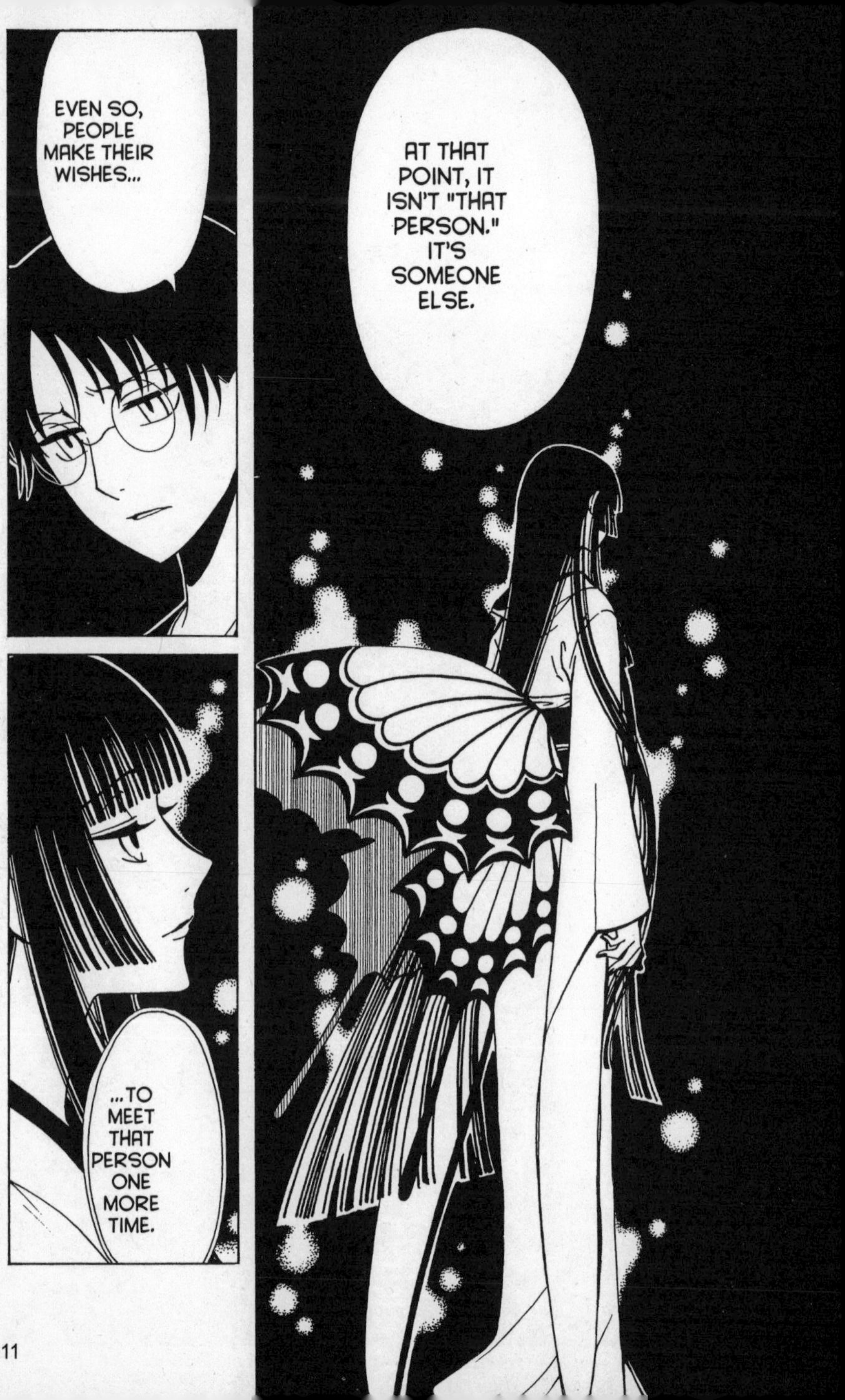

AT THAT POINT, IT ISN'T "THAT PERSON." IT'S SOMEONE ELSE.
EVEN SO, PEOPLE MAKE THEIR WISHES...
...TO MEET THAT PERSON ONE MORE TIME.

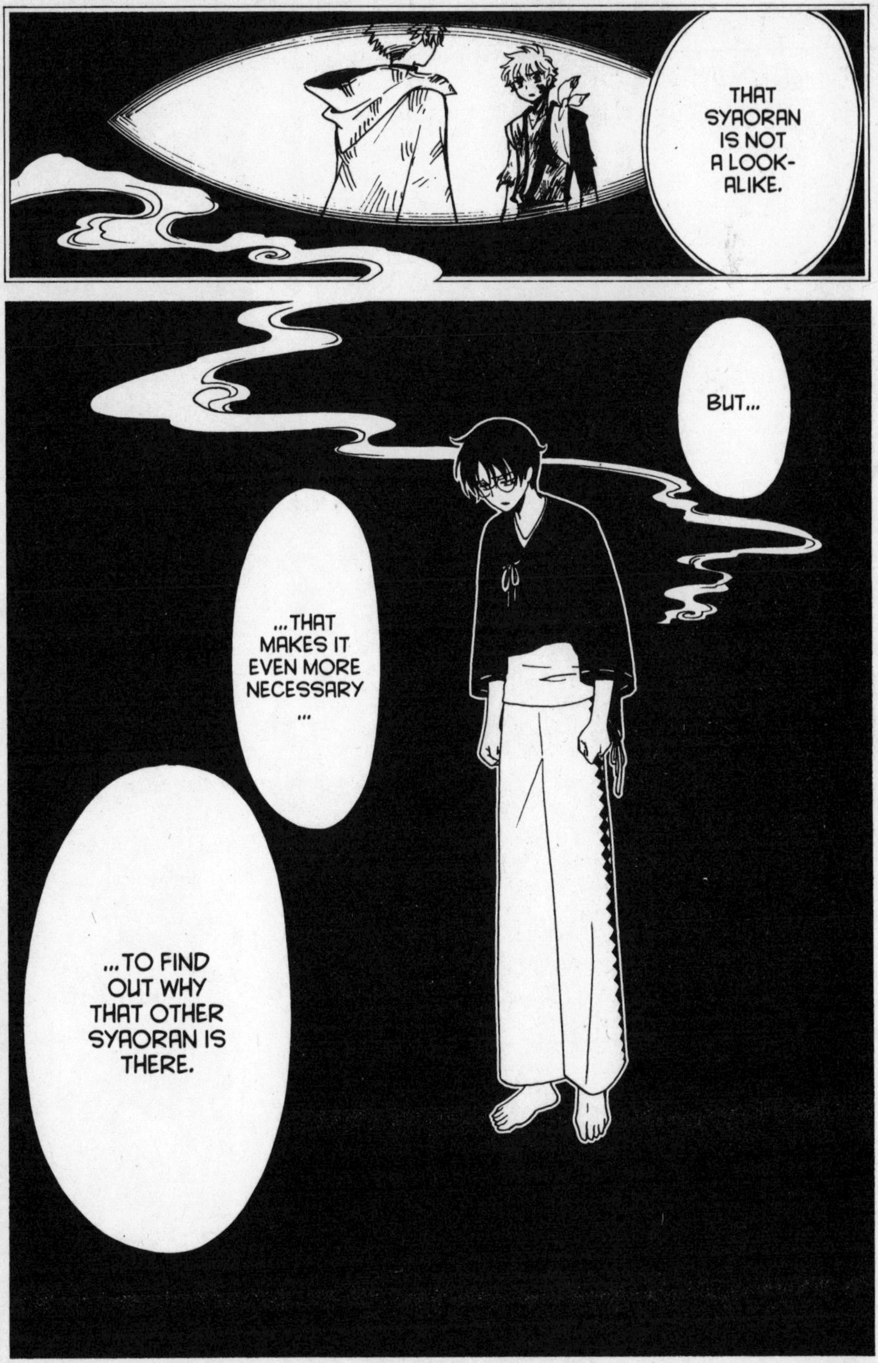
THAT SYAORAN IS NOT A LOOK-ALIKE.
BUT...
...THAT MAKES IT EVEN MORE NECESSARY ...
...TO FIND OUT WHY THAT OTHER SYAORAN IS THERE.

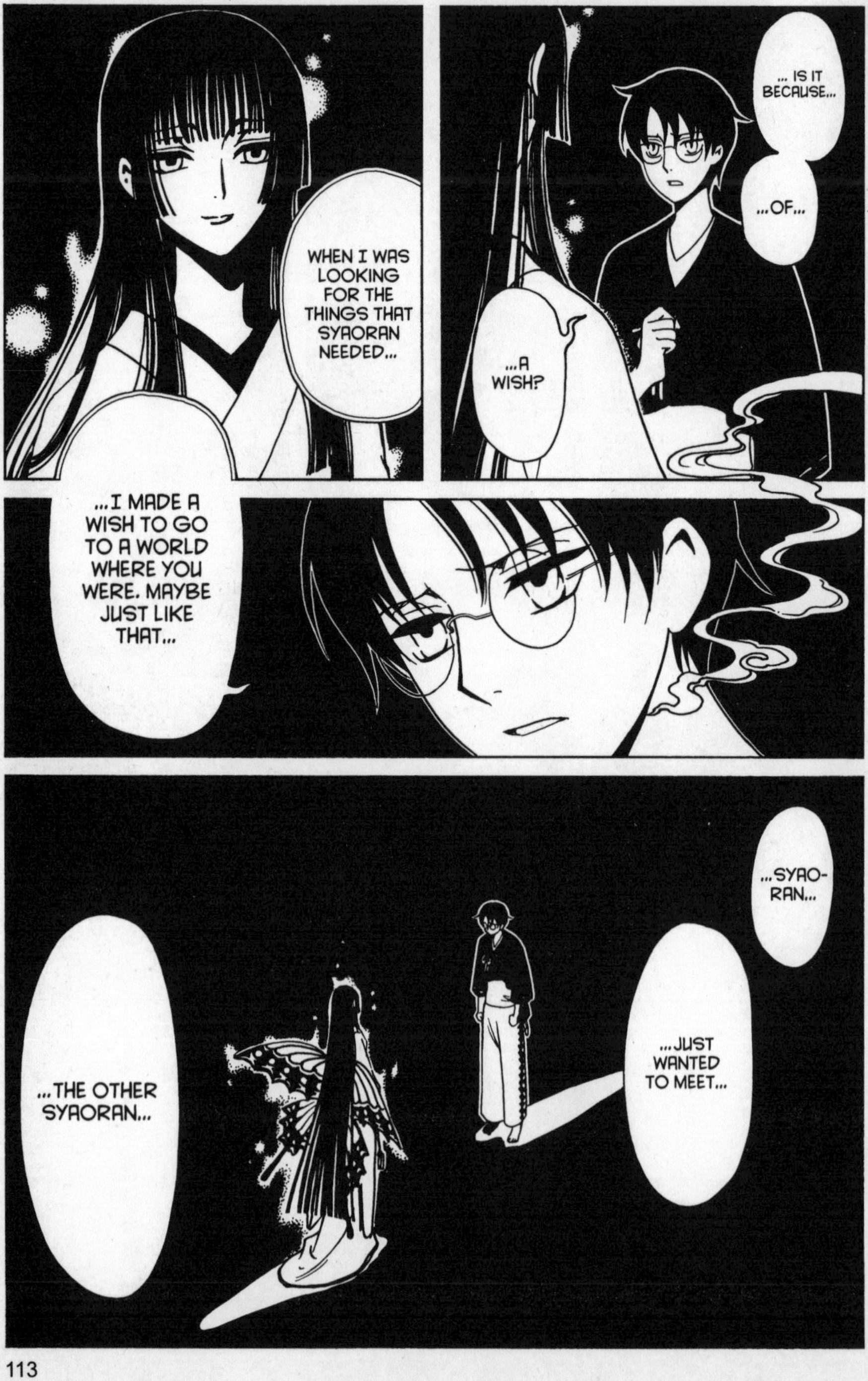
... IS IT BECAUSE...
...OF...
...A WISH?
WHEN I WAS LOOKING FOR THE THINGS THAT SYAORAN NEEDED...
...I MADE A WISH TO GO TO A WORLD WHERE YOU WERE. MAYBE JUST LIKE THAT...
...SYAO-RAN...
...JUST WANTED TO MEET...
...THE OTHER SYAORAN...

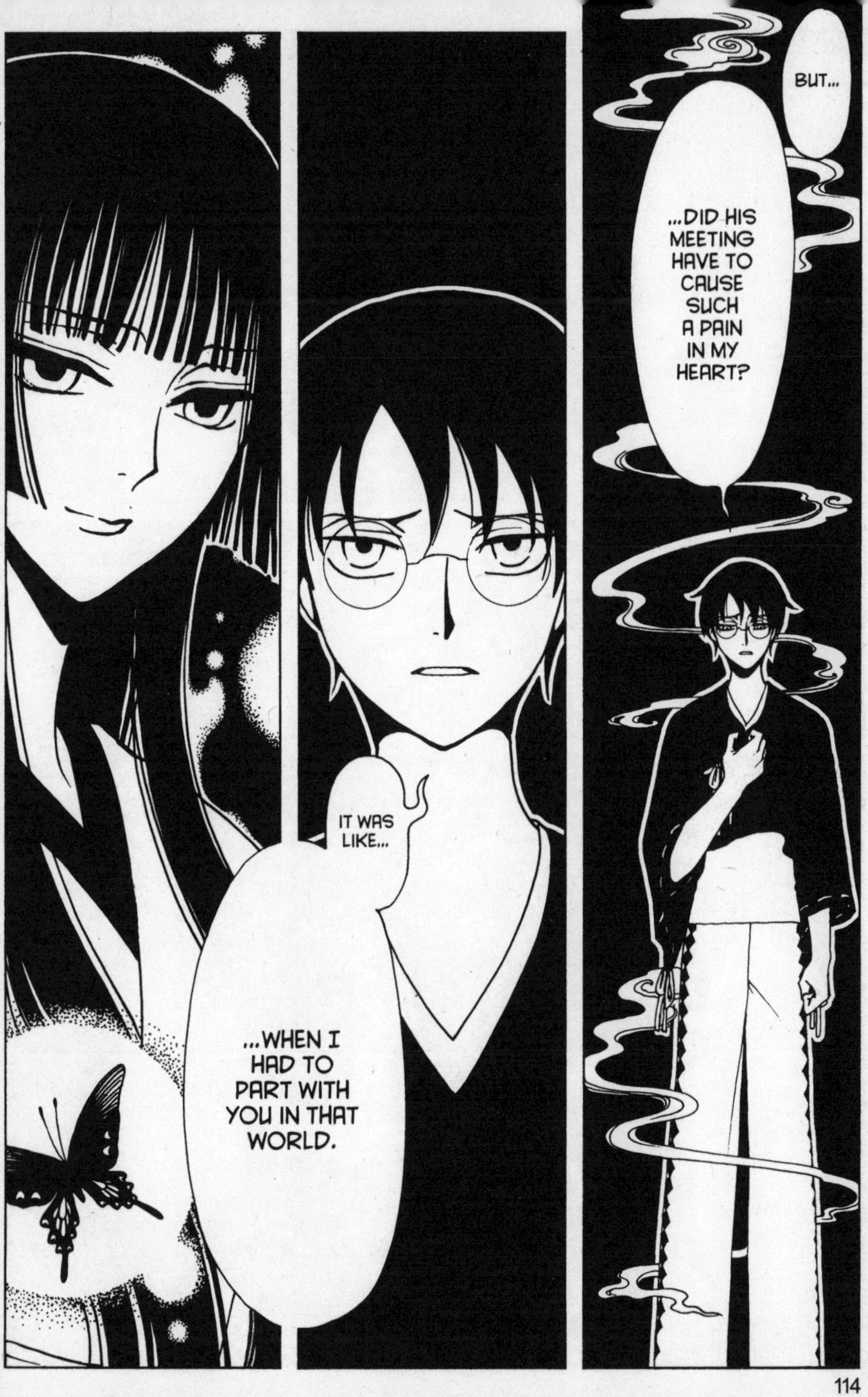
BUT...
...DID HIS MEETING HAVE TO CAUSE SUCH A PAIN IN MY HEART?
IT WAS LIKE...
...WHEN I HAD TO PART WITH YOU IN THAT WORLD.

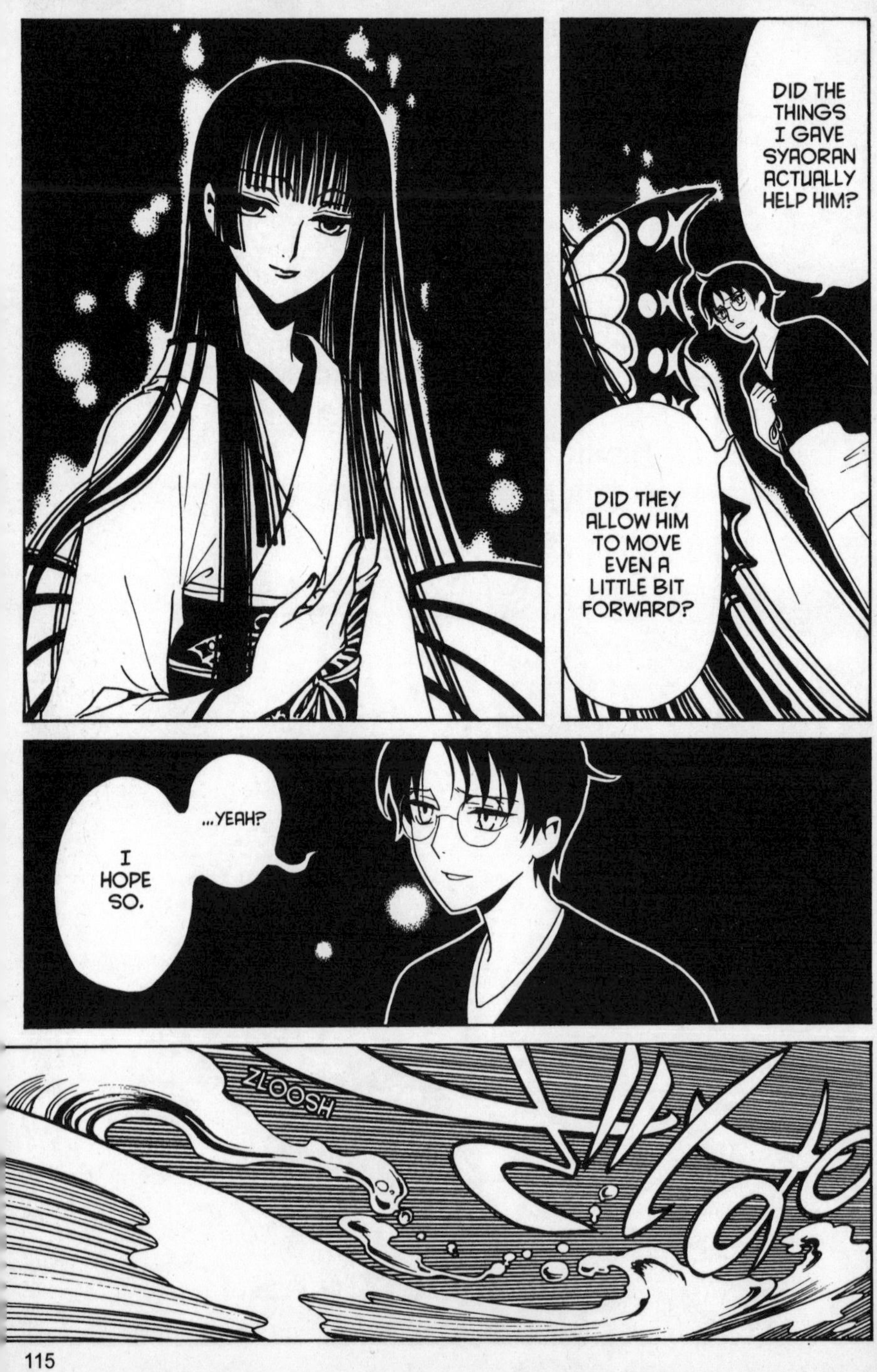

DID THE THINGS I GAVE SYAORAN ACTUALLY HELP HIM?
DID THEY ALLOW HIM TO MOVE EVEN A LITTLE BIT FORWARD?
...YEAH?
I HOPE SO.
ZLOOSH

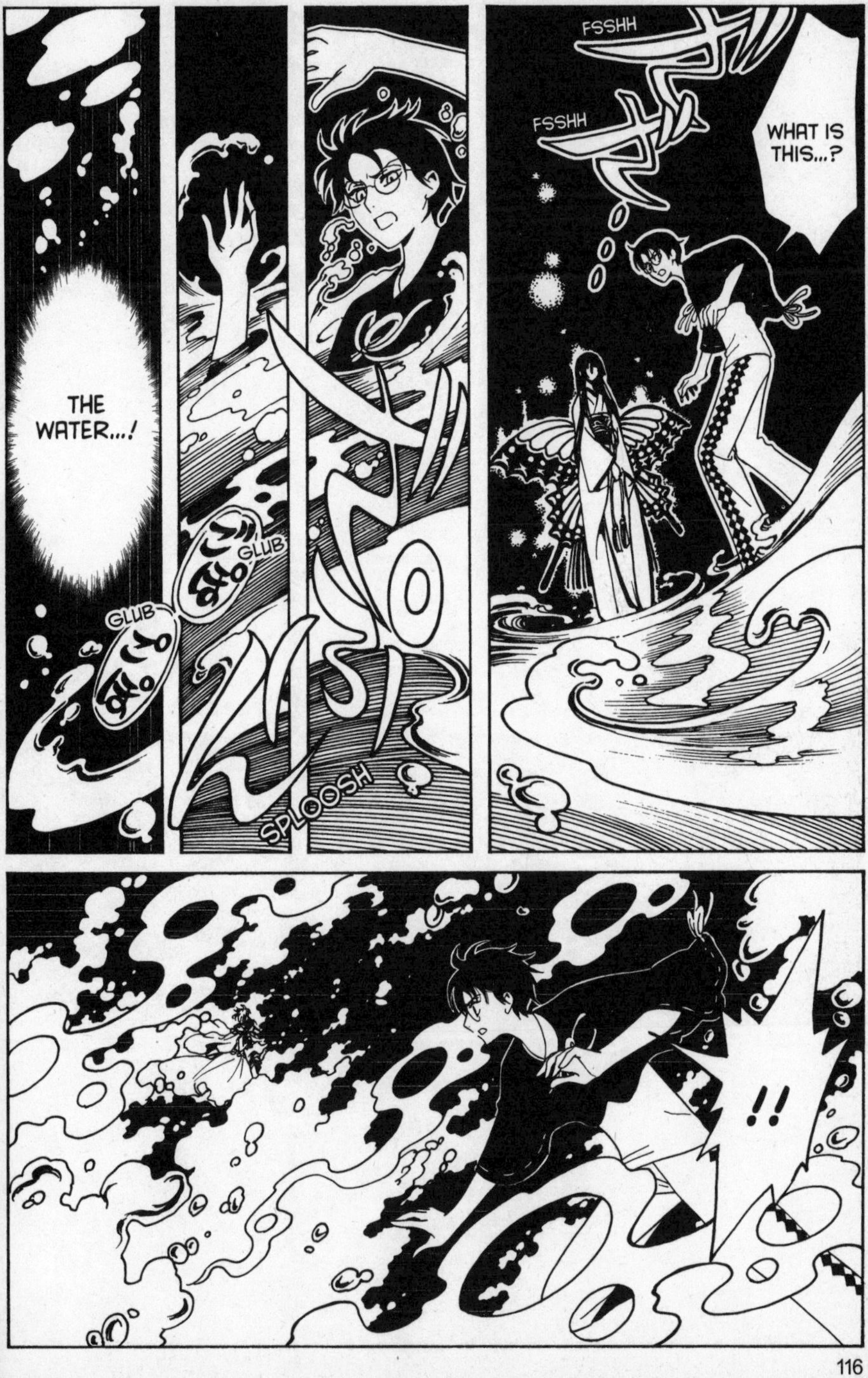
FSSHH
FSSHH
WHAT IS THIS...?
SPLOOSH
GLUB
GLUB
THE WATER...!
!!

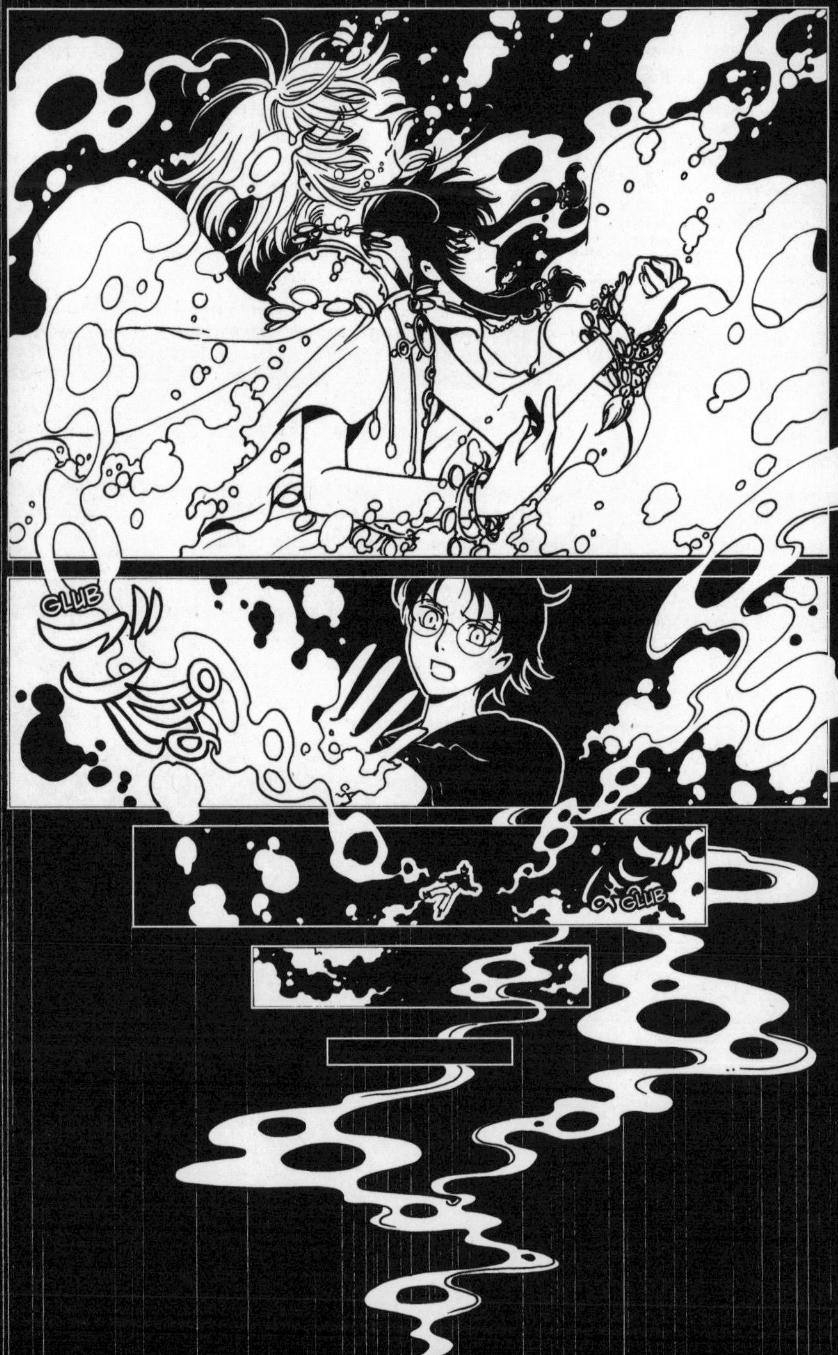
GLUB
GLUB

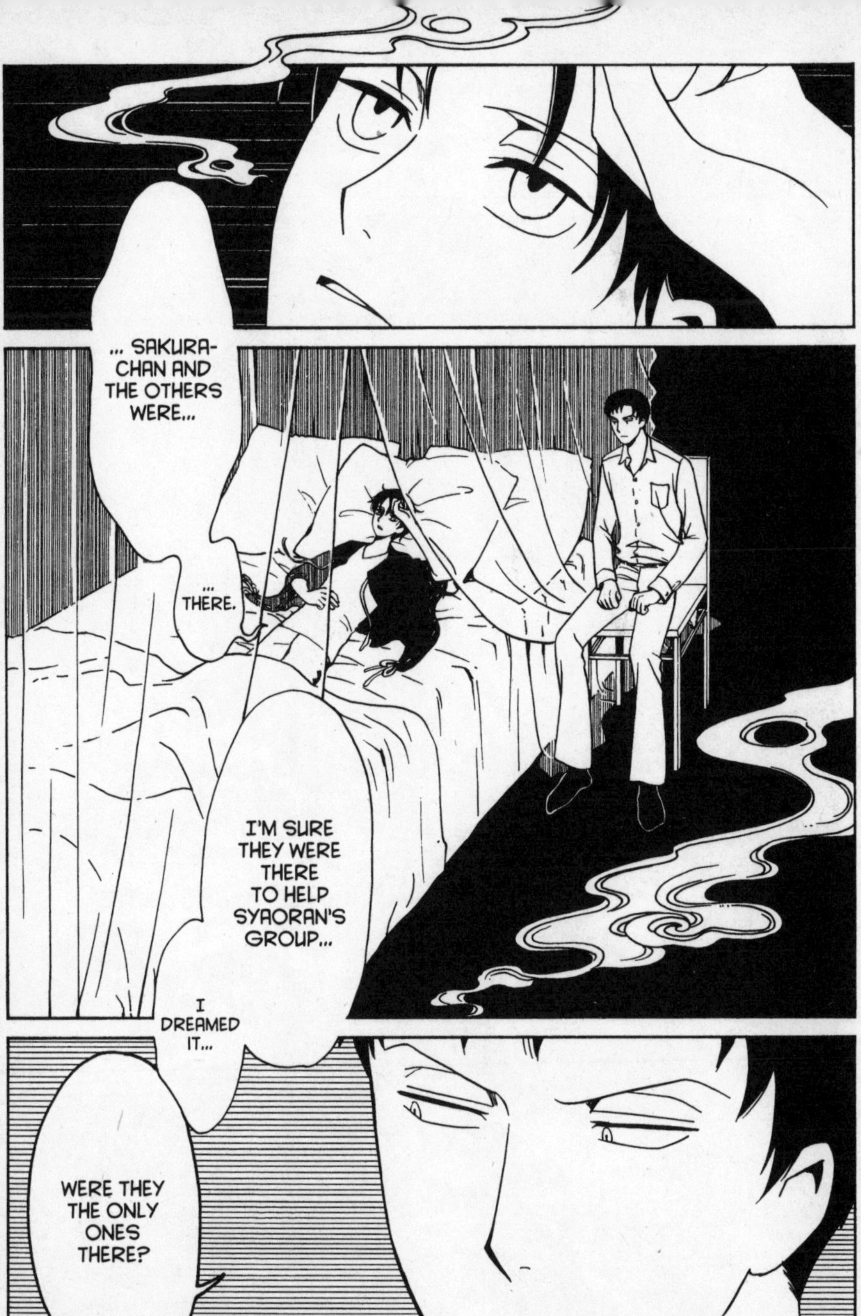
... SAKURA-CHAN AND THE OTHERS WERE...
... THERE.
I'M SURE THEY WERE THERE TO HELP SYAORAN'S GROUP...
I DREAMED IT...
WERE THEY THE ONLY ONES THERE?

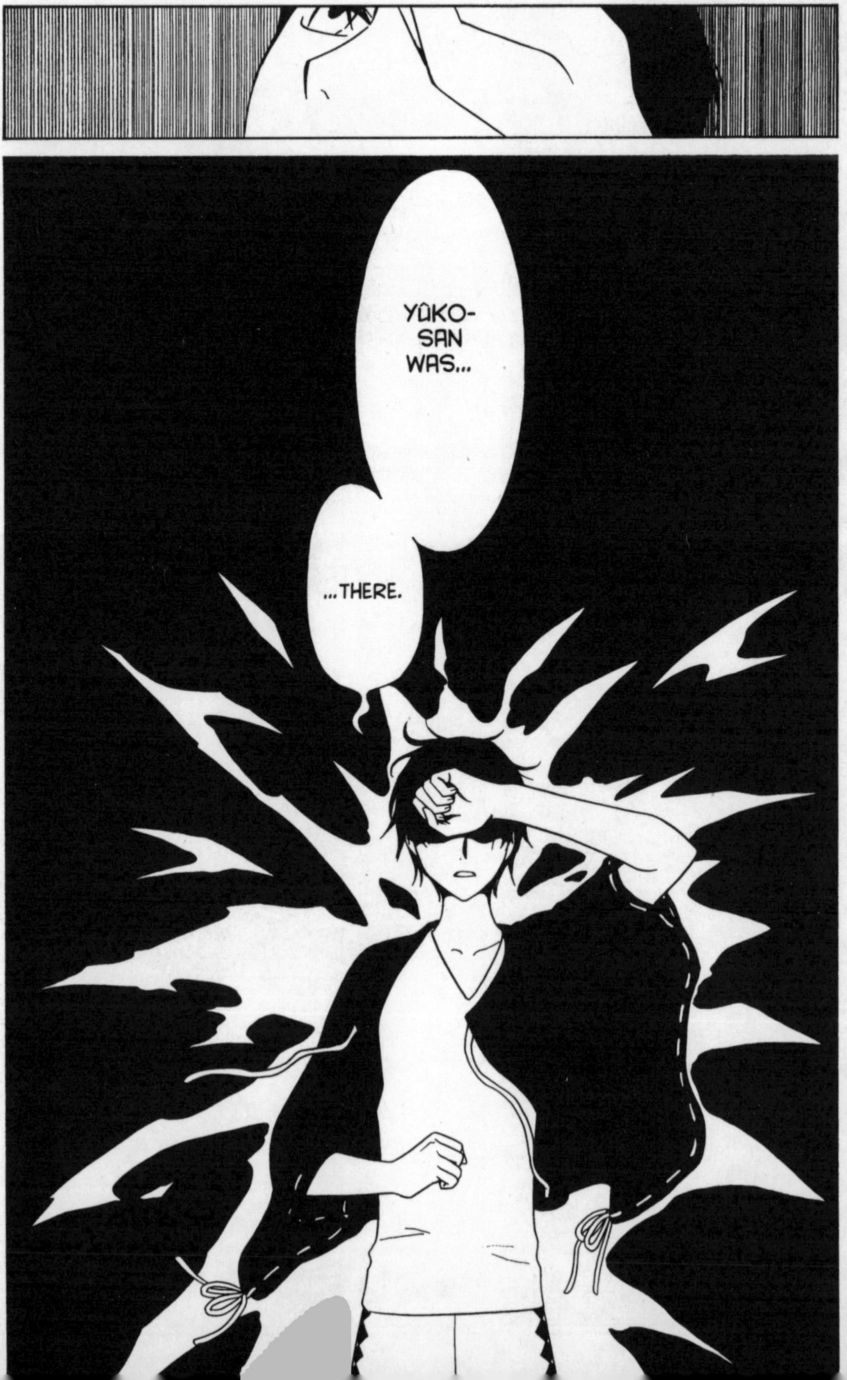
YÛKO-SAN WAS...
...THERE.

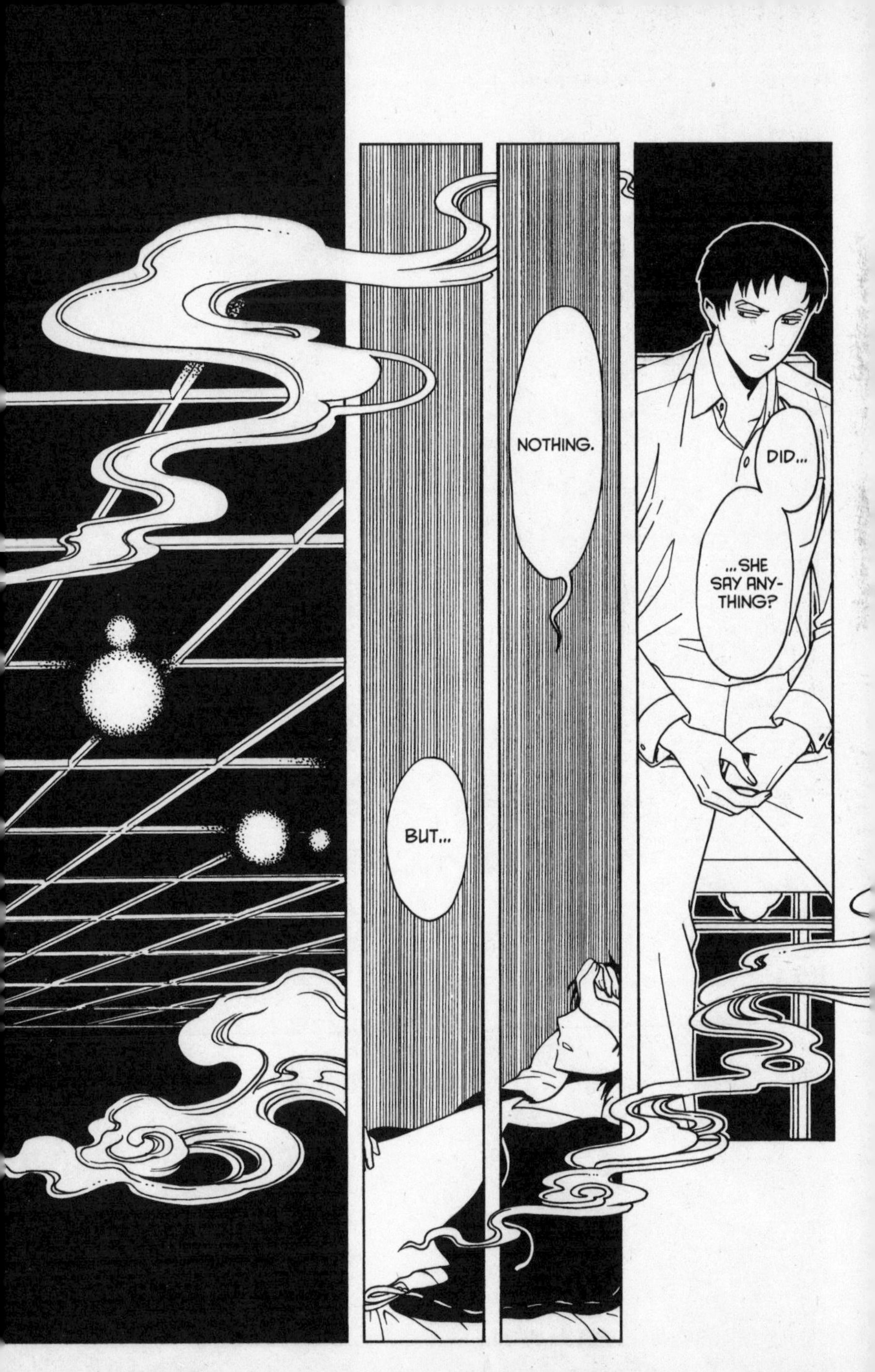
DID...
...SHE SAY ANY-THING?
NOTHING.
BUT...

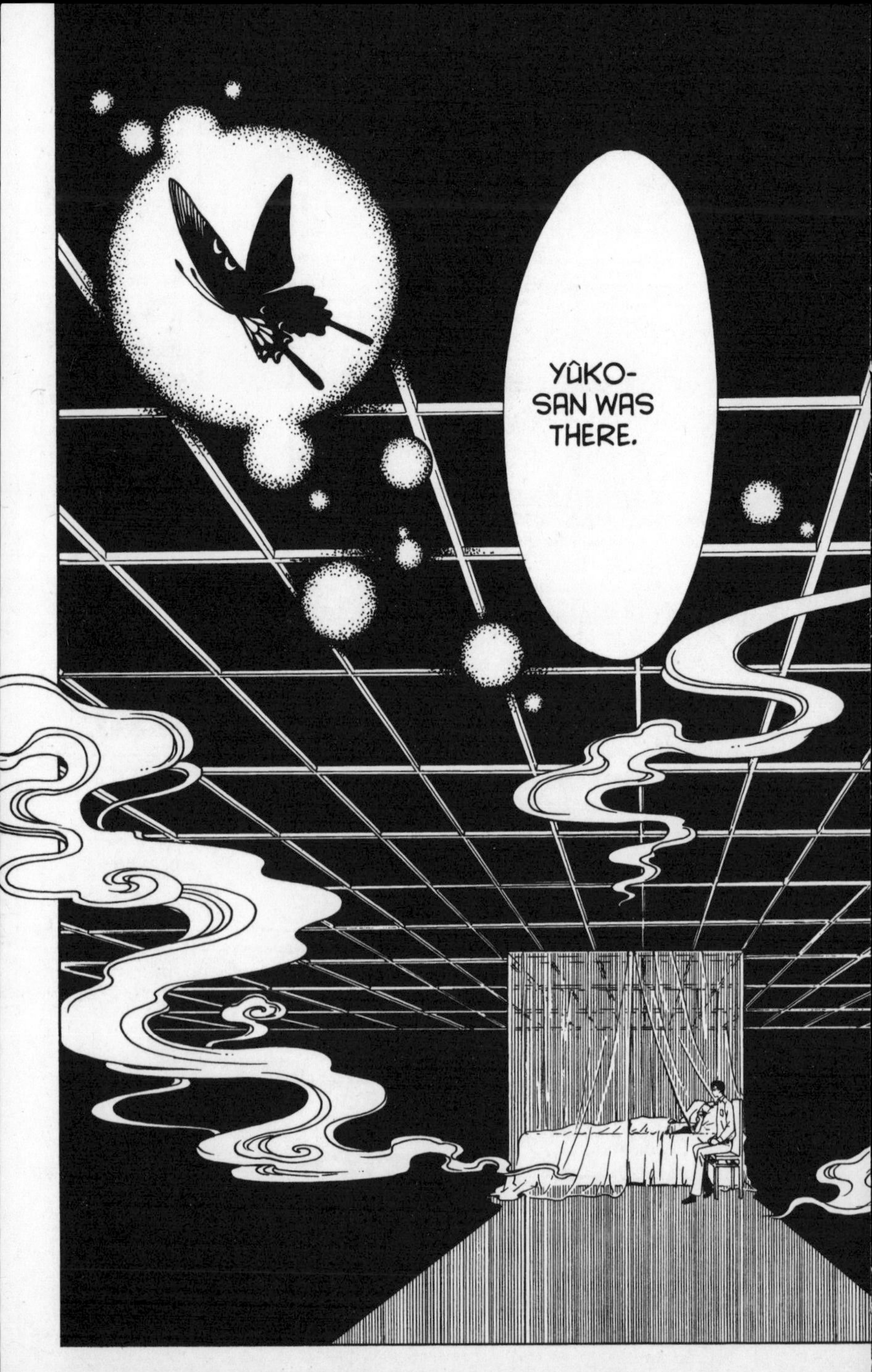
YÛKO-SAN WAS THERE.

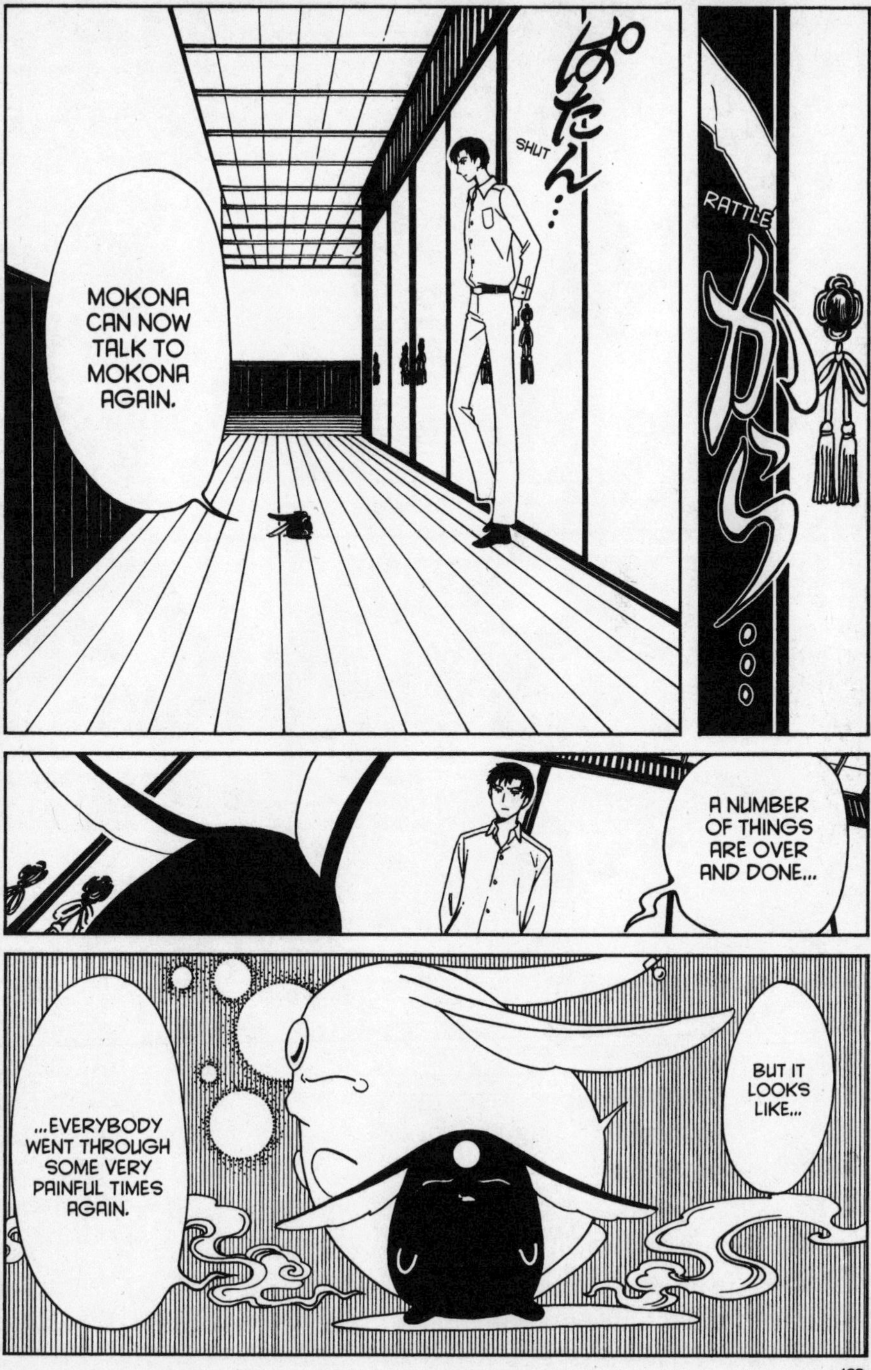
RATTLE
から...
ぱたん...
SHUT
MOKONA CAN NOW TALK TO MOKONA AGAIN.
A NUMBER OF THINGS ARE OVER AND DONE...
BUT IT LOOKS LIKE...
...EVERYBODY WENT THROUGH SOME VERY PAINFUL TIMES AGAIN.

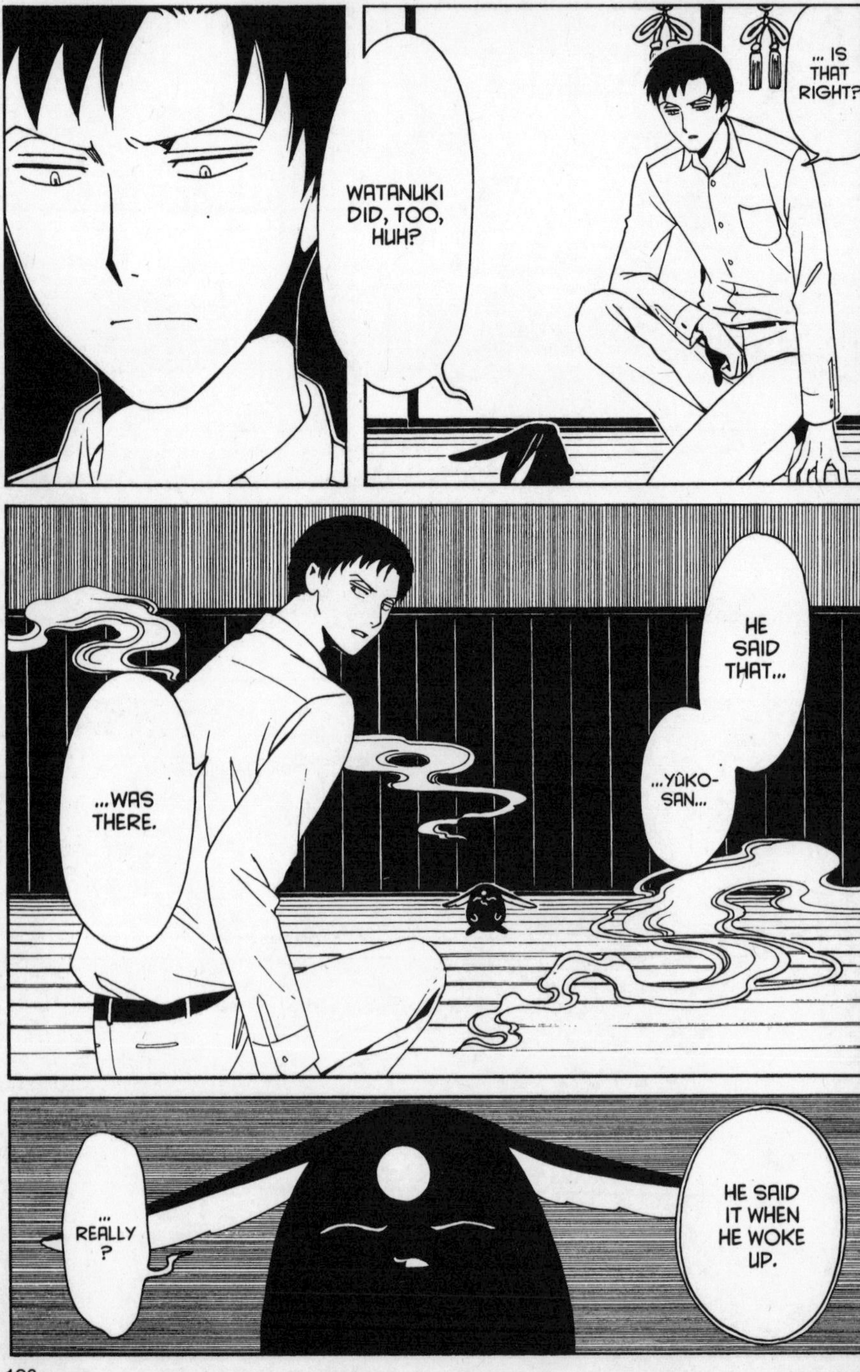
... IS THAT RIGHT?
WATANUKI DID, TOO, HUH?
HE SAID THAT...
...YŪKO-SAN...
...WAS THERE.
HE SAID IT WHEN HE WOKE UP.
... REALLY ?

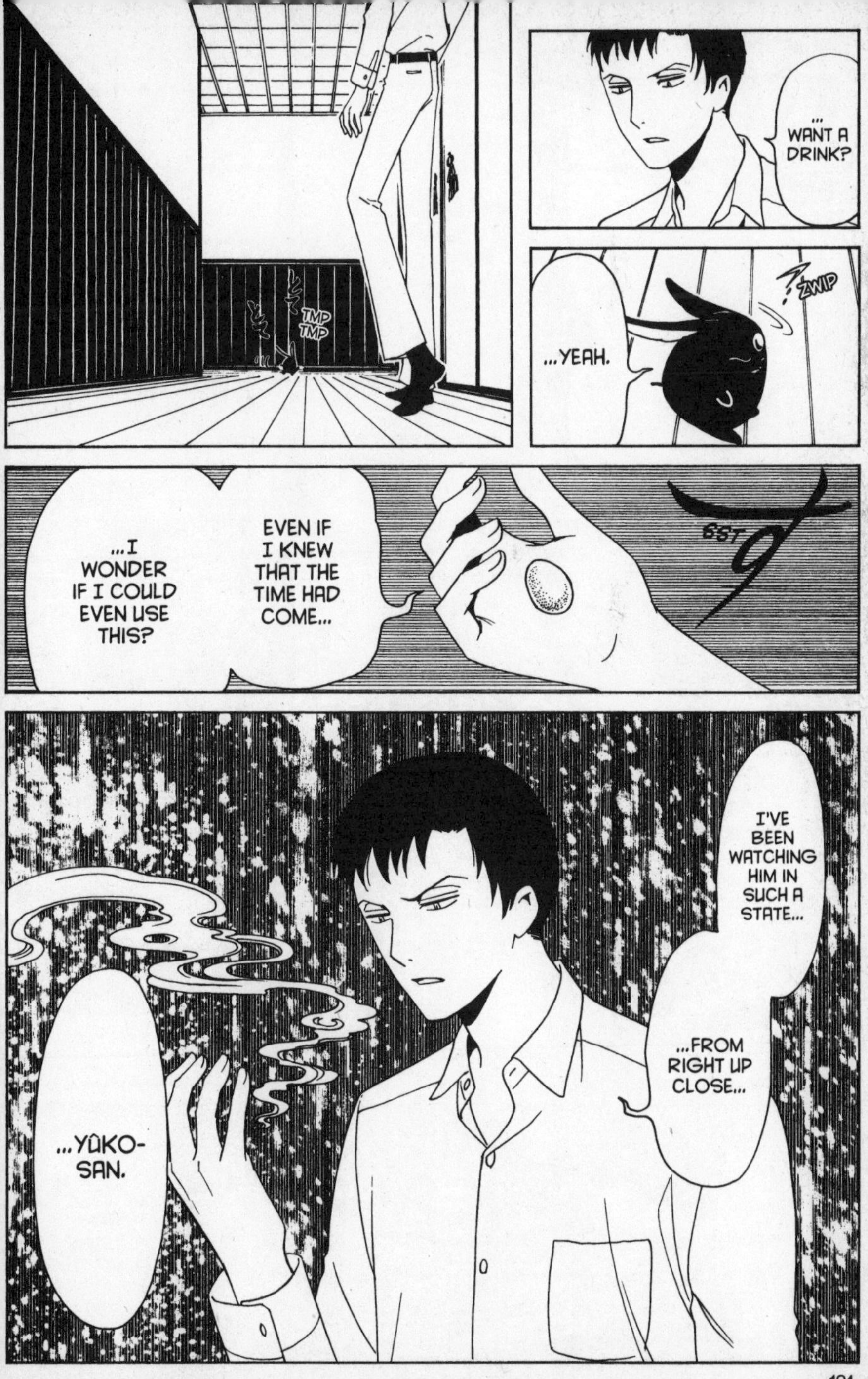
... WANT A DRINK?
ZWIP
...YEAH.
TMP TMP
SST
EVEN IF I KNEW THAT THE TIME HAD COME...
...I WONDER IF I COULD EVEN USE THIS?
I'VE BEEN WATCHING HIM IN SUCH A STATE...
...FROM RIGHT UP CLOSE...
...YÛKO-SAN.

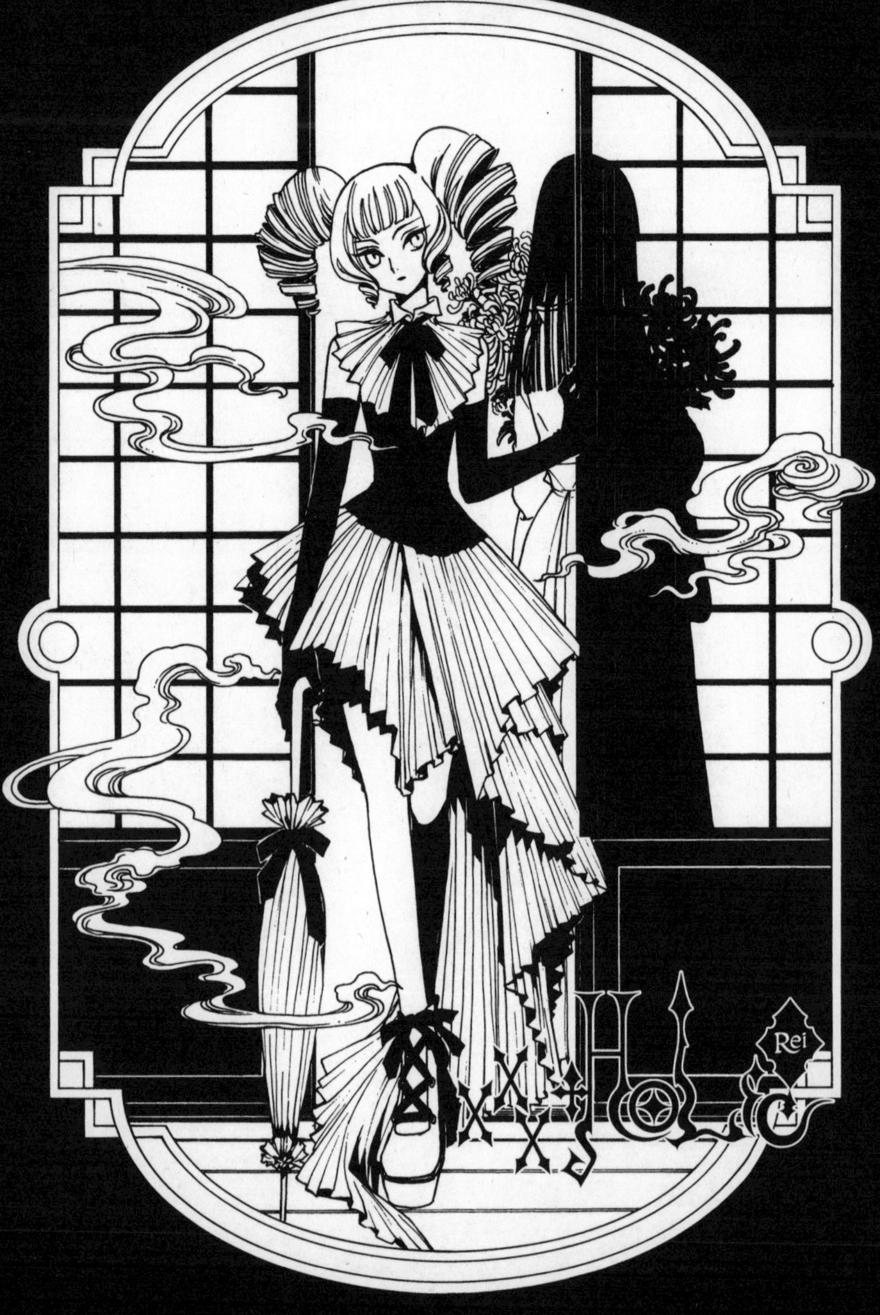
xxxHOLiC
Rei

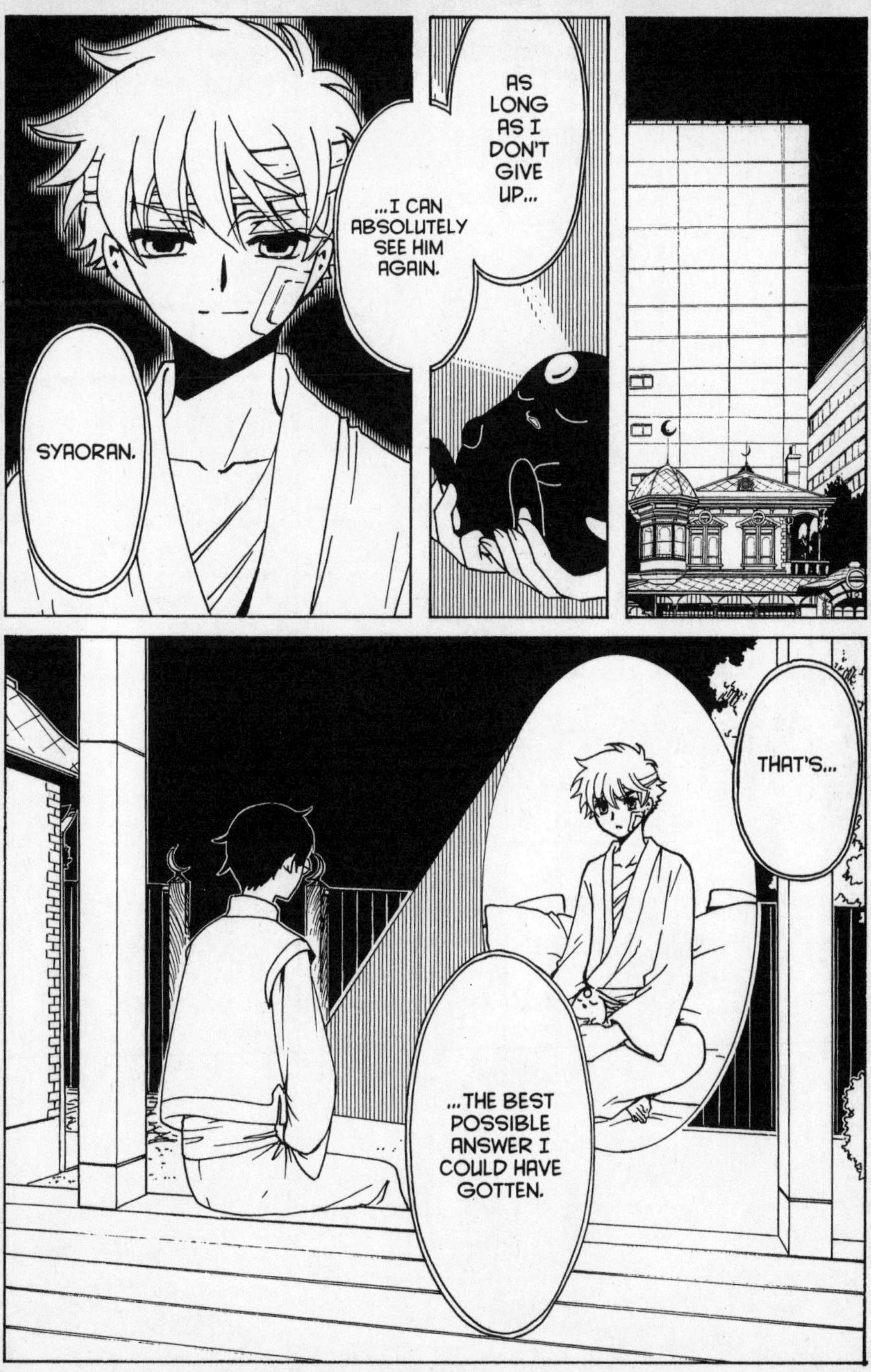
AS LONG AS I DON'T GIVE UP...
...I CAN ABSOLUTELY SEE HIM AGAIN.
SYAORAN.
THAT'S...
...THE BEST POSSIBLE ANSWER I COULD HAVE GOTTEN.

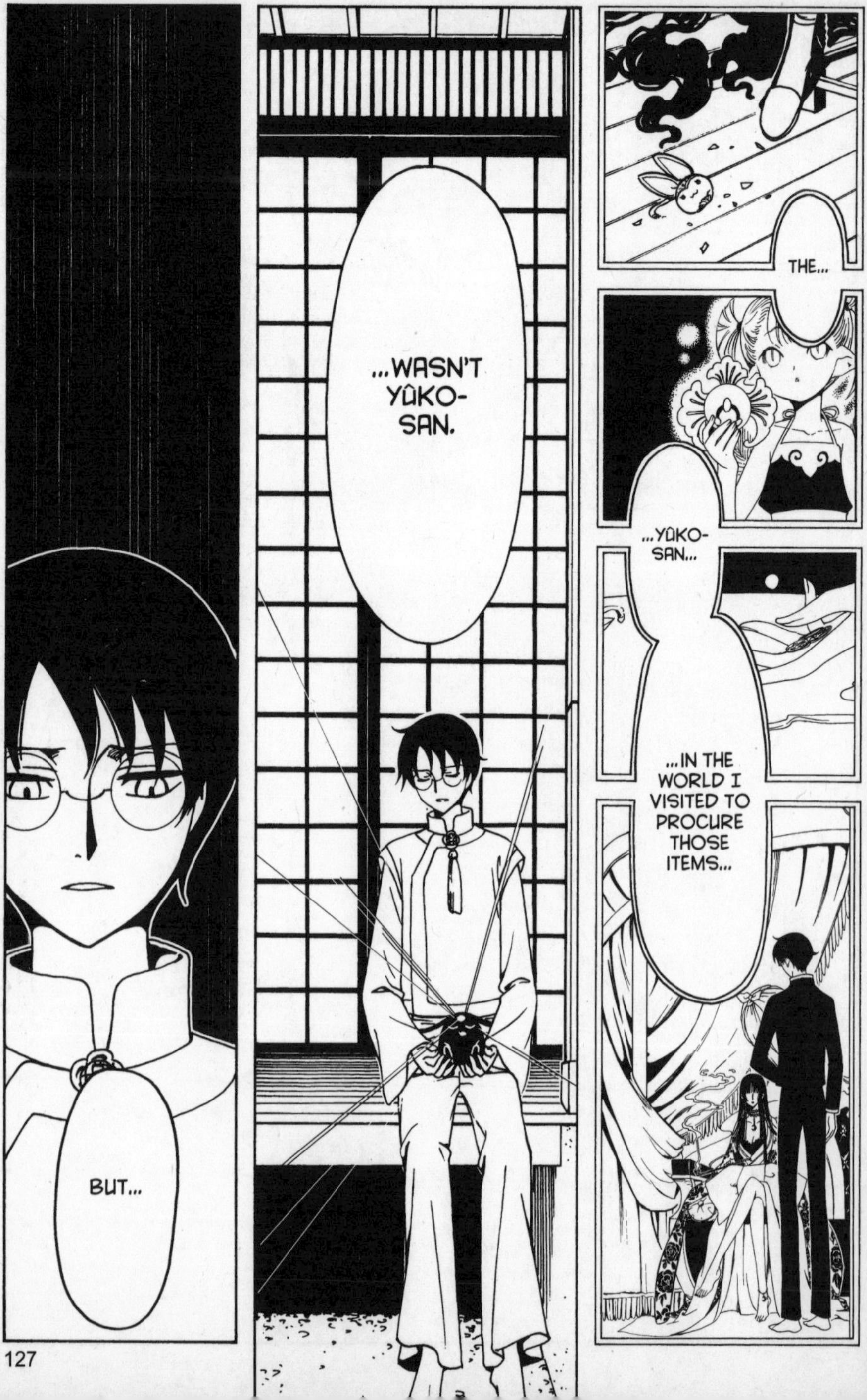
THE...
...YÛKO-SAN...
...IN THE WORLD I VISITED TO PROCURE THOSE ITEMS...
...WASN'T YÛKO-SAN.
BUT...

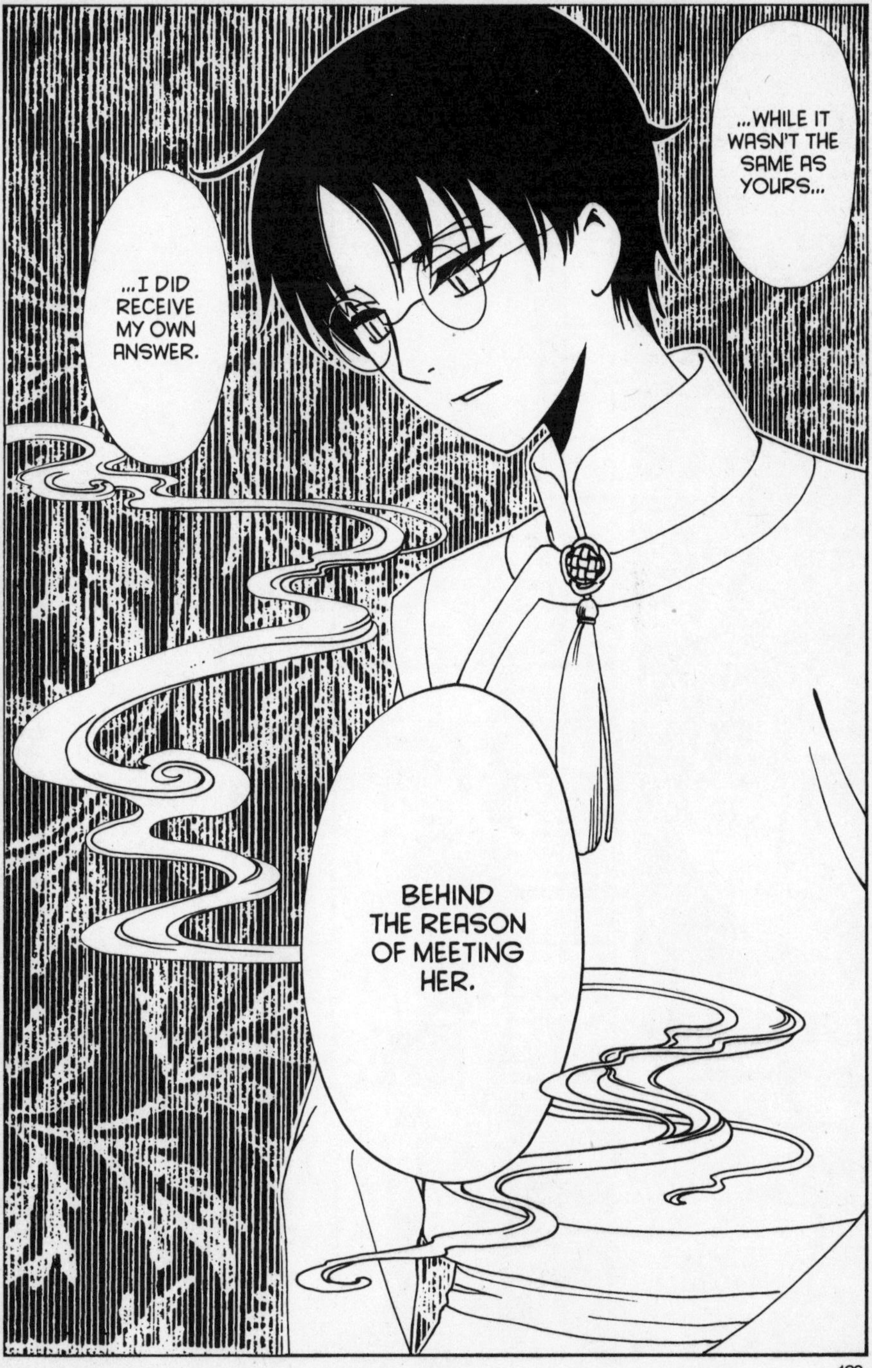
...WHILE IT WASN'T THE SAME AS YOURS...
...I DID RECEIVE MY OWN ANSWER.
BEHIND THE REASON OF MEETING HER.

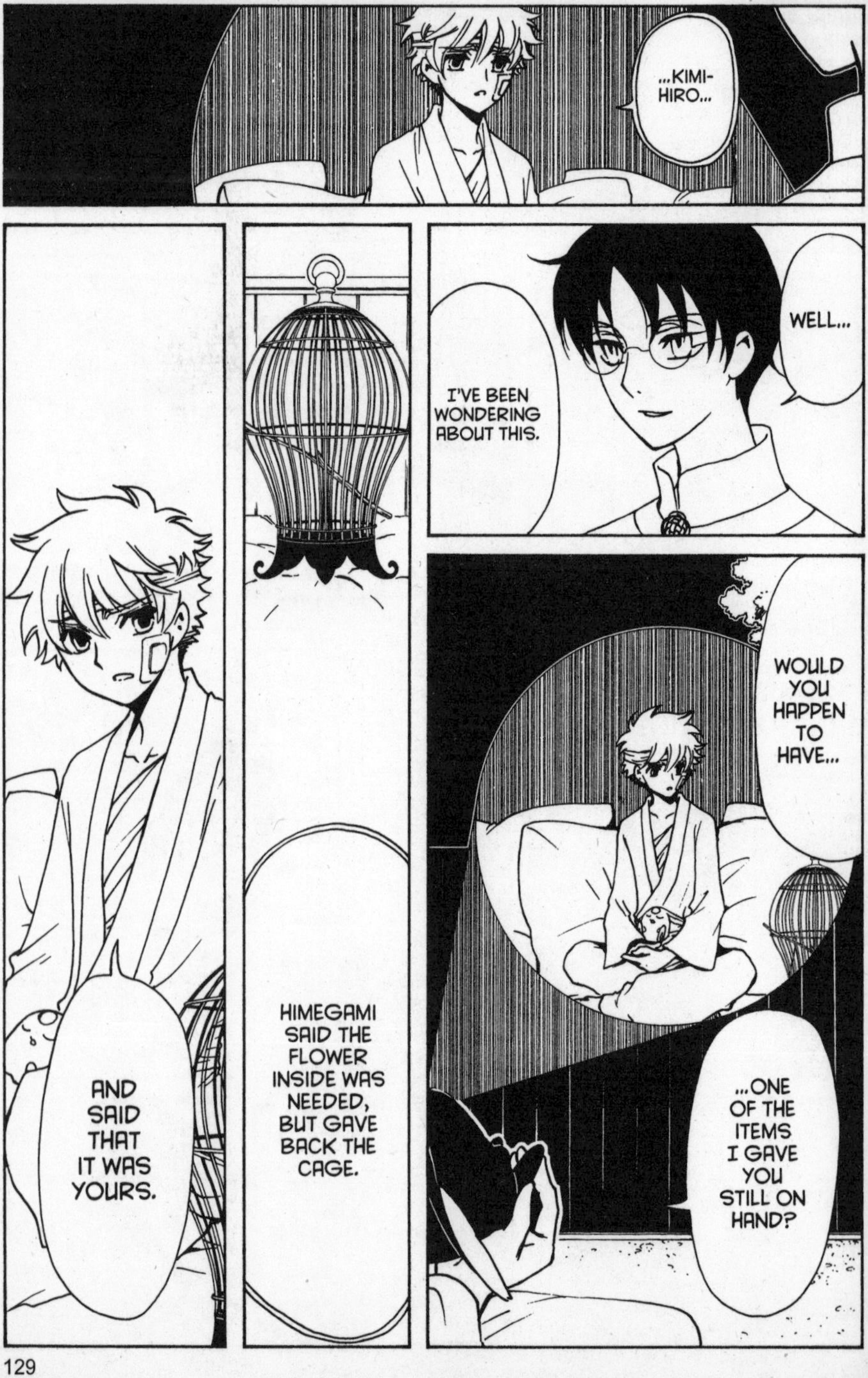
...KIMI-HIRO...
WELL...
I'VE BEEN WONDERING ABOUT THIS.
WOULD YOU HAPPEN TO HAVE...
...ONE OF THE ITEMS I GAVE YOU STILL ON HAND?
HIMEGAMI SAID THE FLOWER INSIDE WAS NEEDED, BUT GAVE BACK THE CAGE.
AND SAID THAT IT WAS YOURS.

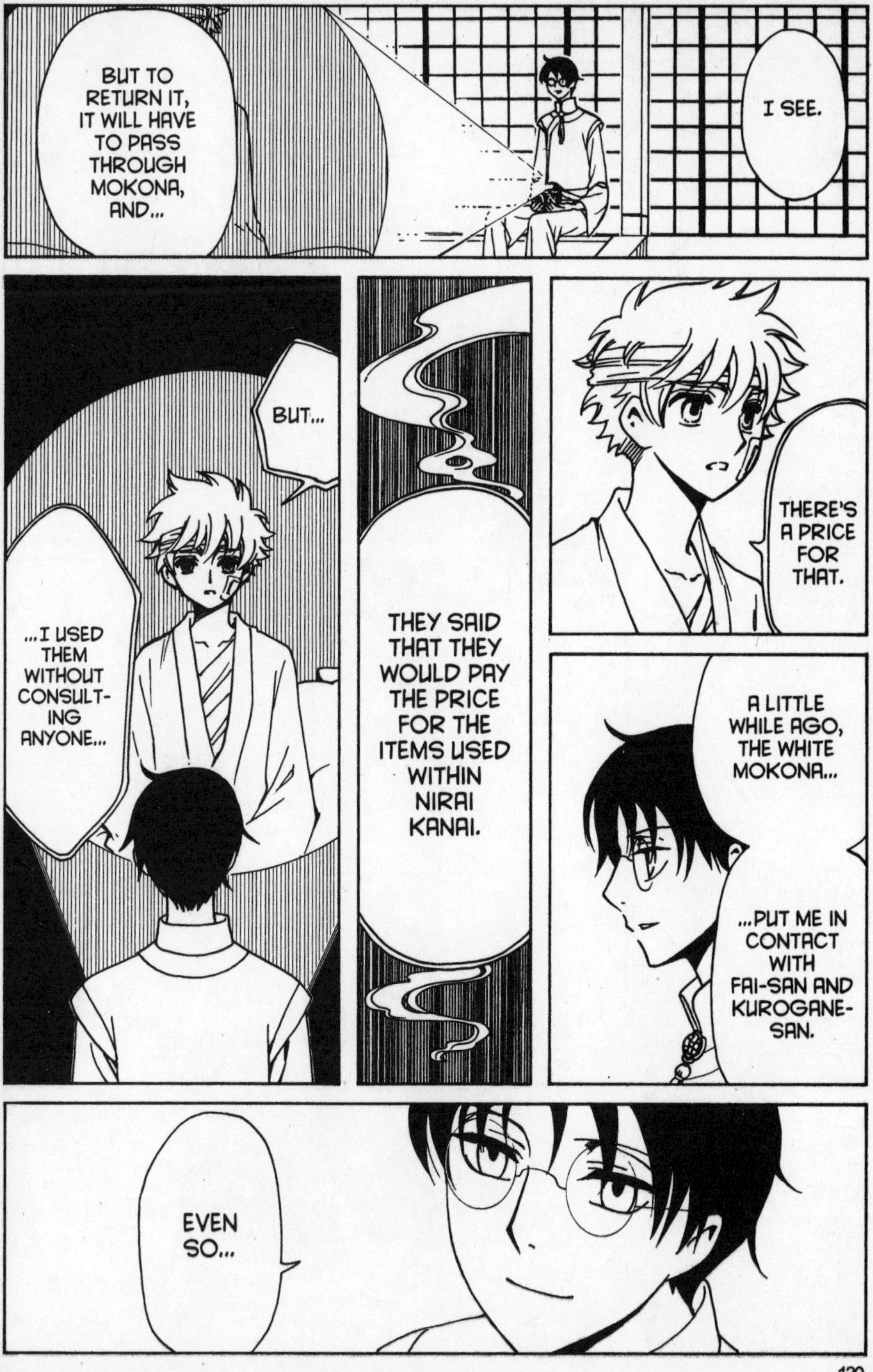
I SEE.
BUT TO RETURN IT, IT WILL HAVE TO PASS THROUGH MOKONA, AND...
THERE'S A PRICE FOR THAT.
A LITTLE WHILE AGO, THE WHITE MOKONA...
...PUT ME IN CONTACT WITH FAI-SAN AND KUROGANE-SAN.
THEY SAID THAT THEY WOULD PAY THE PRICE FOR THE ITEMS USED WITHIN NIRAI KANAI.
BUT...
...I USED THEM WITHOUT CONSULT-ING ANYONE...
EVEN SO...

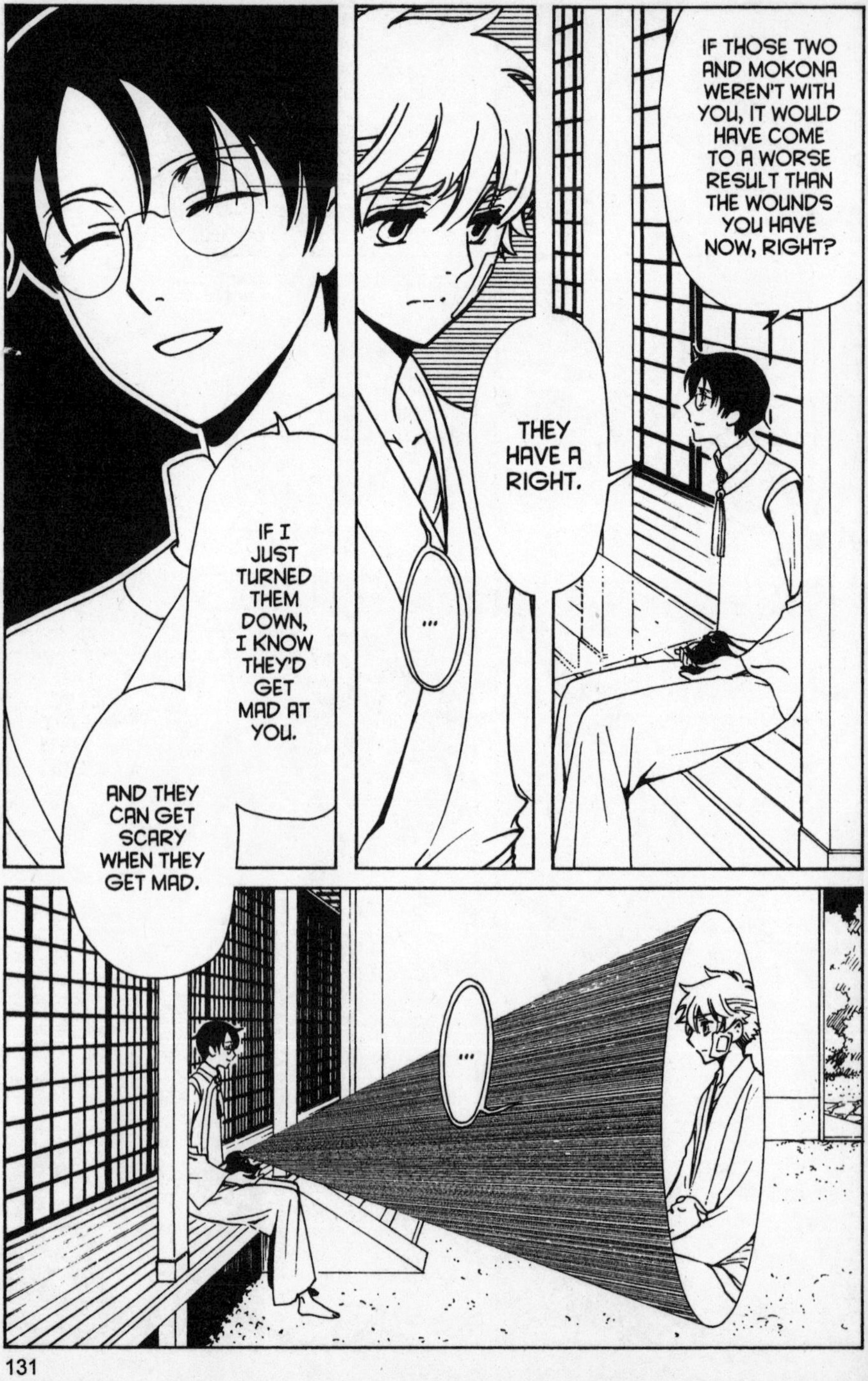
IF THOSE TWO AND MOKONA WEREN'T WITH YOU, IT WOULD HAVE COME TO A WORSE RESULT THAN THE WOUNDS YOU HAVE NOW, RIGHT?
THEY HAVE A RIGHT.
...
IF I JUST TURNED THEM DOWN, I KNOW THEY'D GET MAD AT YOU.
AND THEY CAN GET SCARY WHEN THEY GET MAD.
...

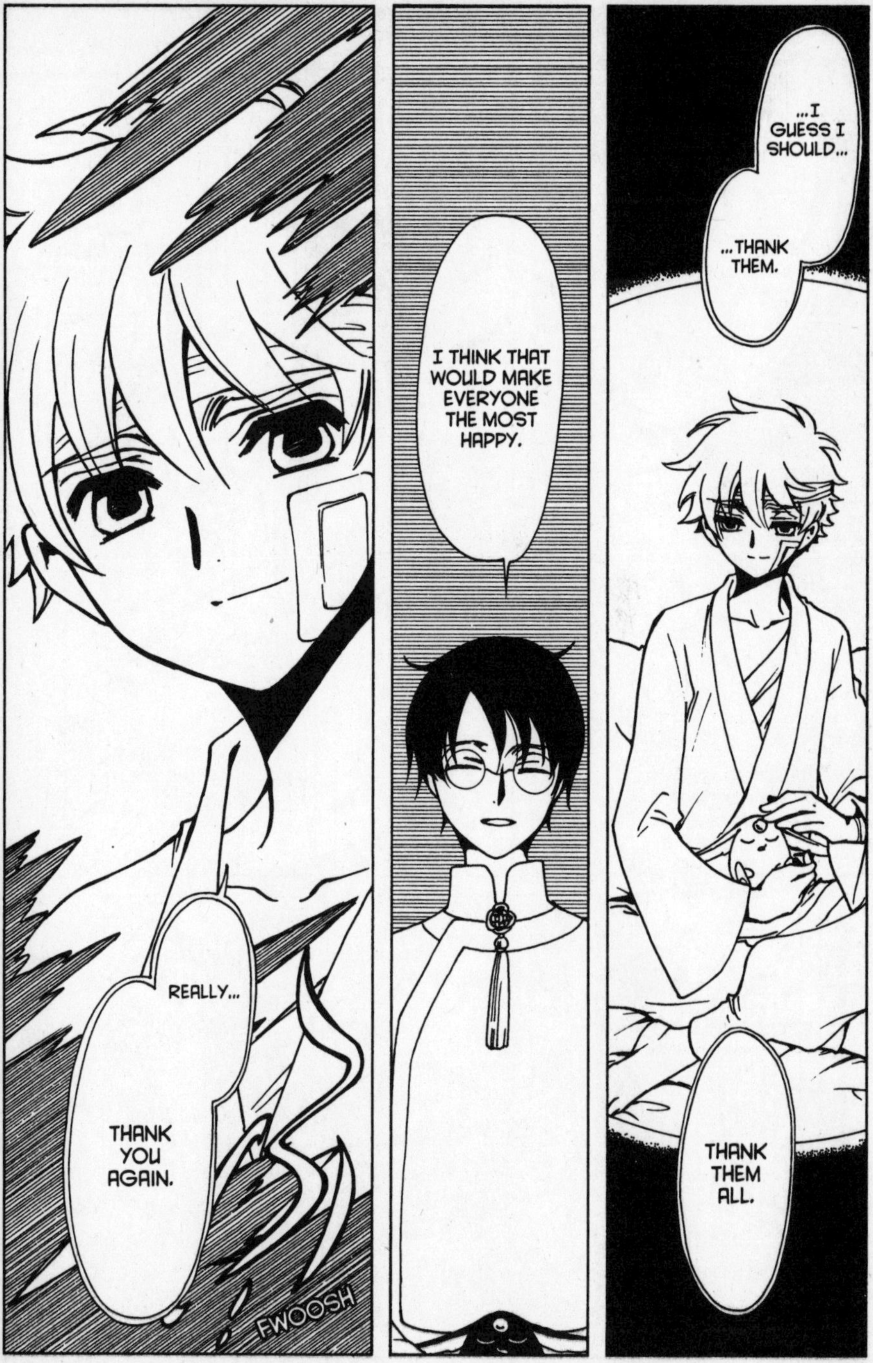
...I GUESS I SHOULD... ...THANK THEM.
THANK THEM ALL.
I THINK THAT WOULD MAKE EVERYONE THE MOST HAPPY.
REALLY... THANK YOU AGAIN.
FWOOSH

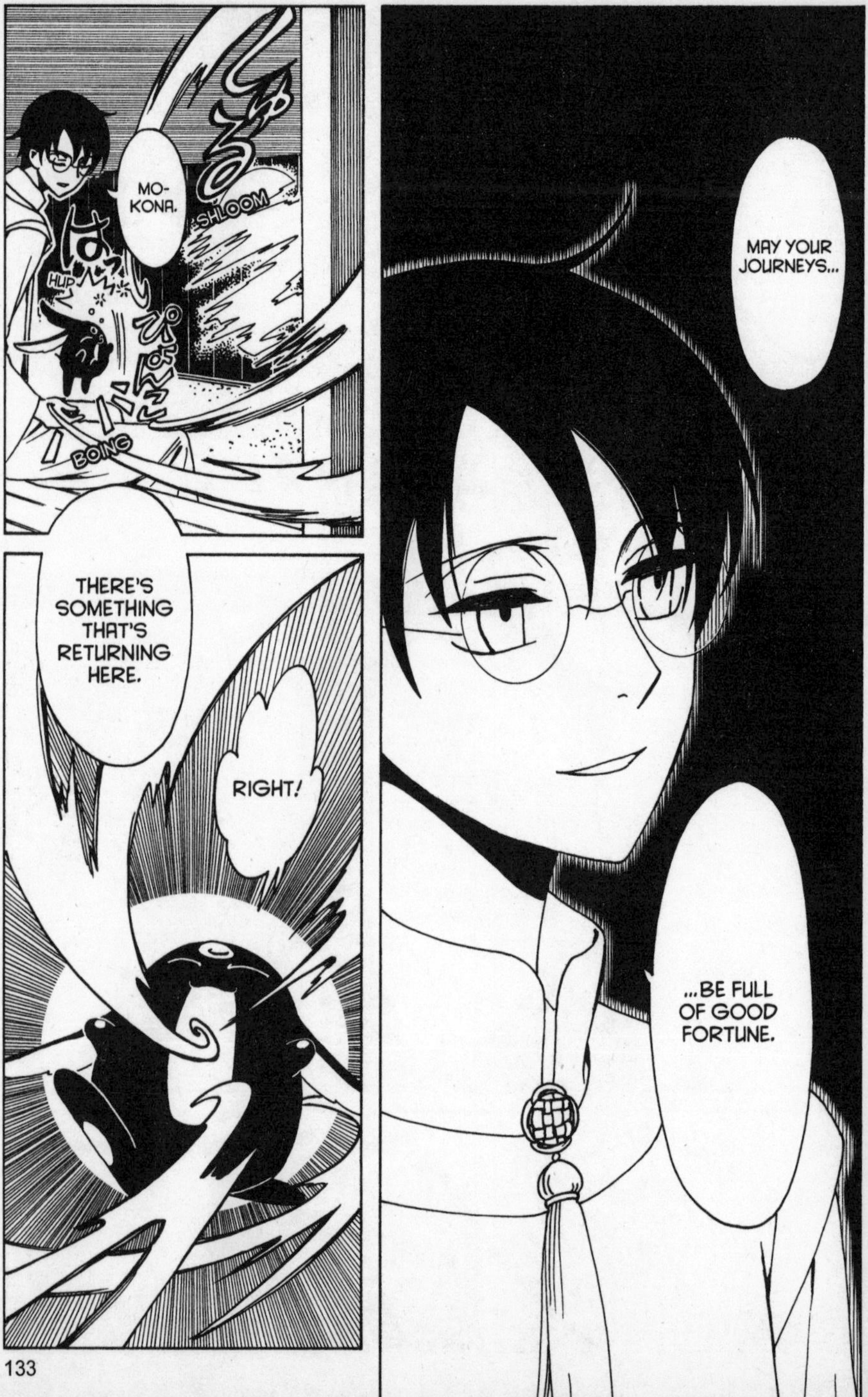
MAY YOUR JOURNEYS...
...BE FULL OF GOOD FORTUNE.
MO-KONA.
SHLOOM
HUP
BOING
THERE'S SOMETHING THAT'S RETURNING HERE.
RIGHT!

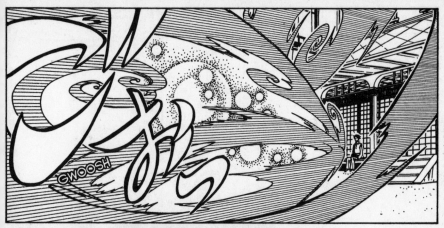

GWOOSH

BUT...

...WHAT THEY RETURNED HAS CHANGED SOMEWHAT FROM WHEN IT WAS GIVEN TO THEM.

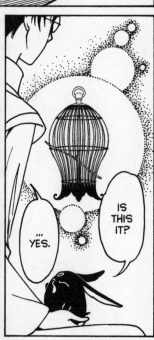

IS THIS IT?

...YES.

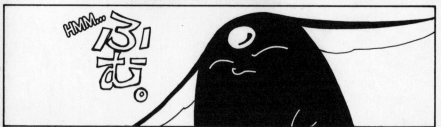

HMM...

134

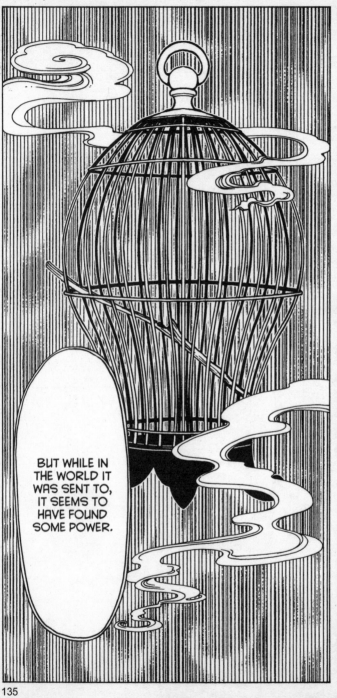

WHEN WE SENT IT, IT WAS JUST A VESSEL CONTAINING FLOWERS.

NOTHING MORE THAN THAT.

BUT WHILE IN THE WORLD IT WAS SENT TO, IT SEEMS TO HAVE FOUND SOME POWER.

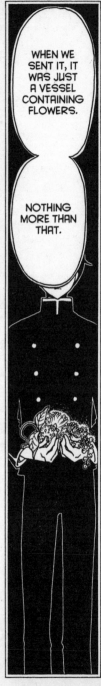

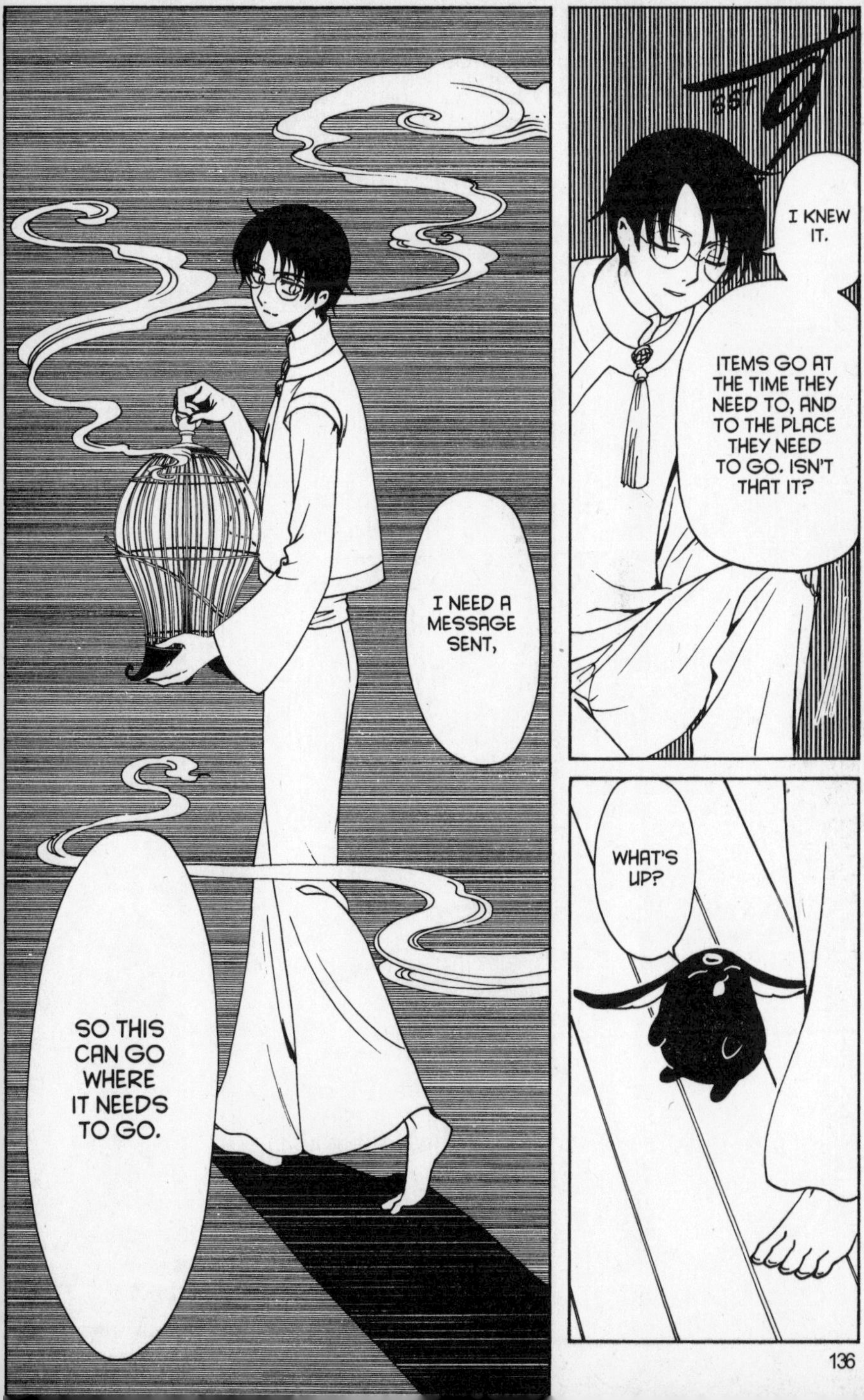
I KNEW IT.
ITEMS GO AT THE TIME THEY NEED TO, AND TO THE PLACE THEY NEED TO GO. ISN'T THAT IT?
WHAT'S UP?
I NEED A MESSAGE SENT,
SO THIS CAN GO WHERE IT NEEDS TO GO.

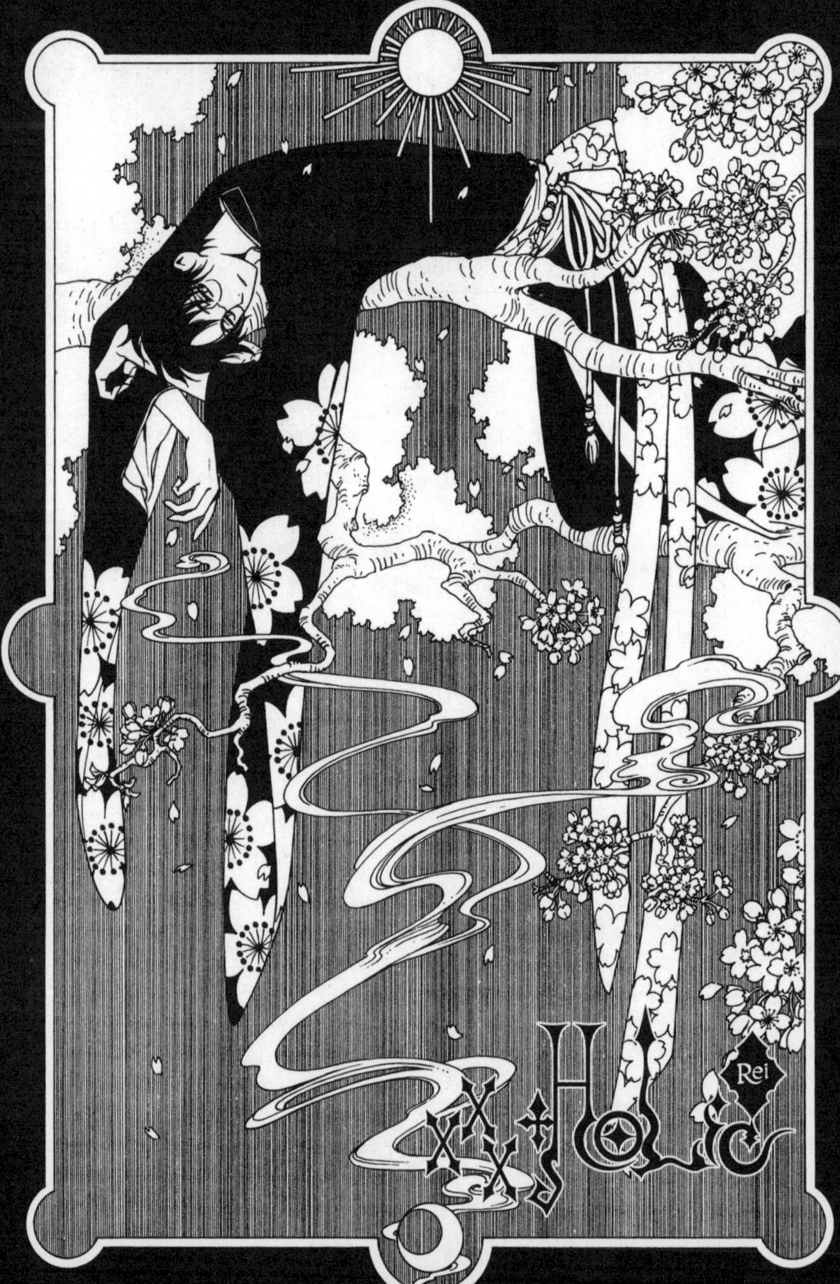
xxxHOLiC
Rei

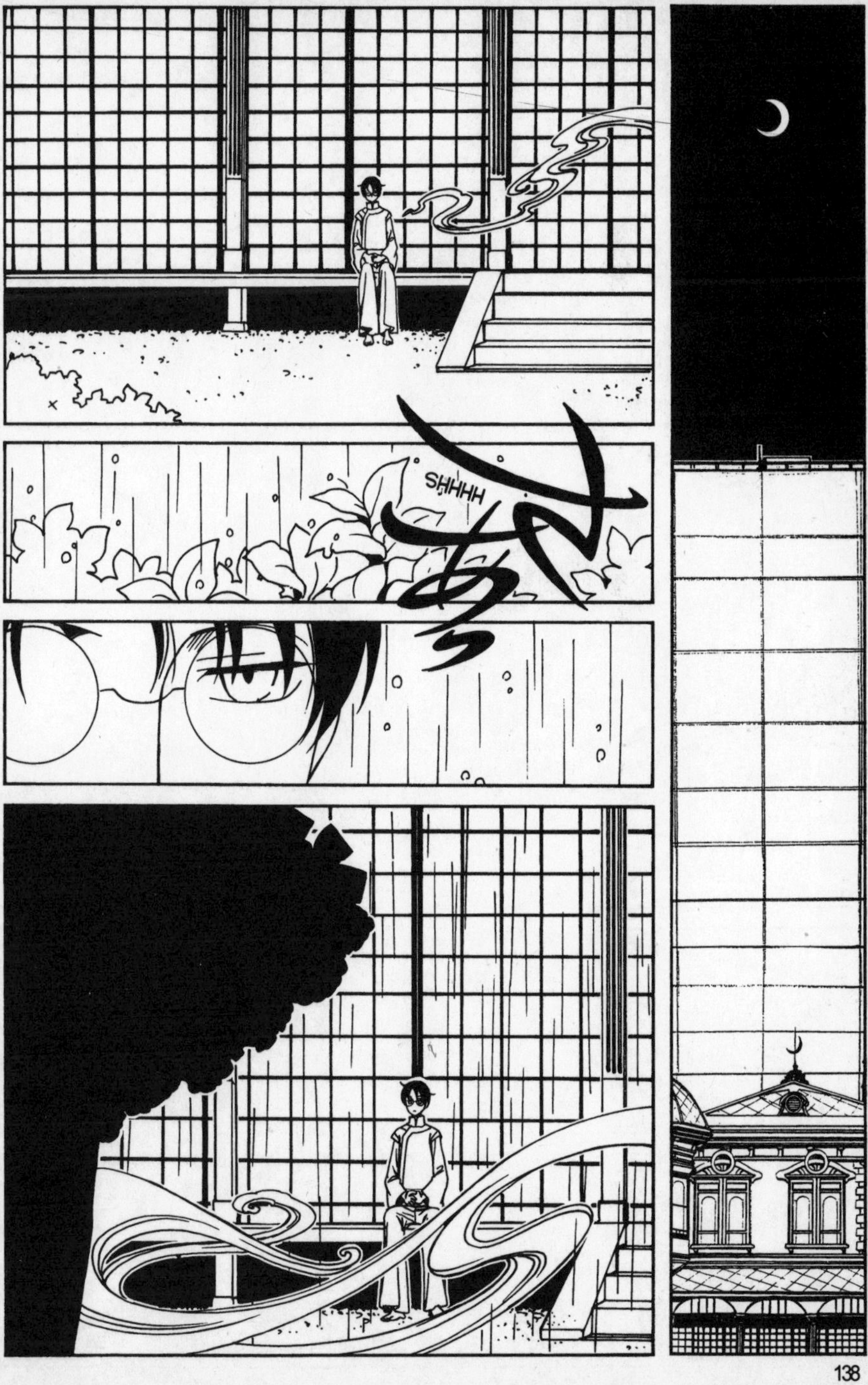
SHHHH

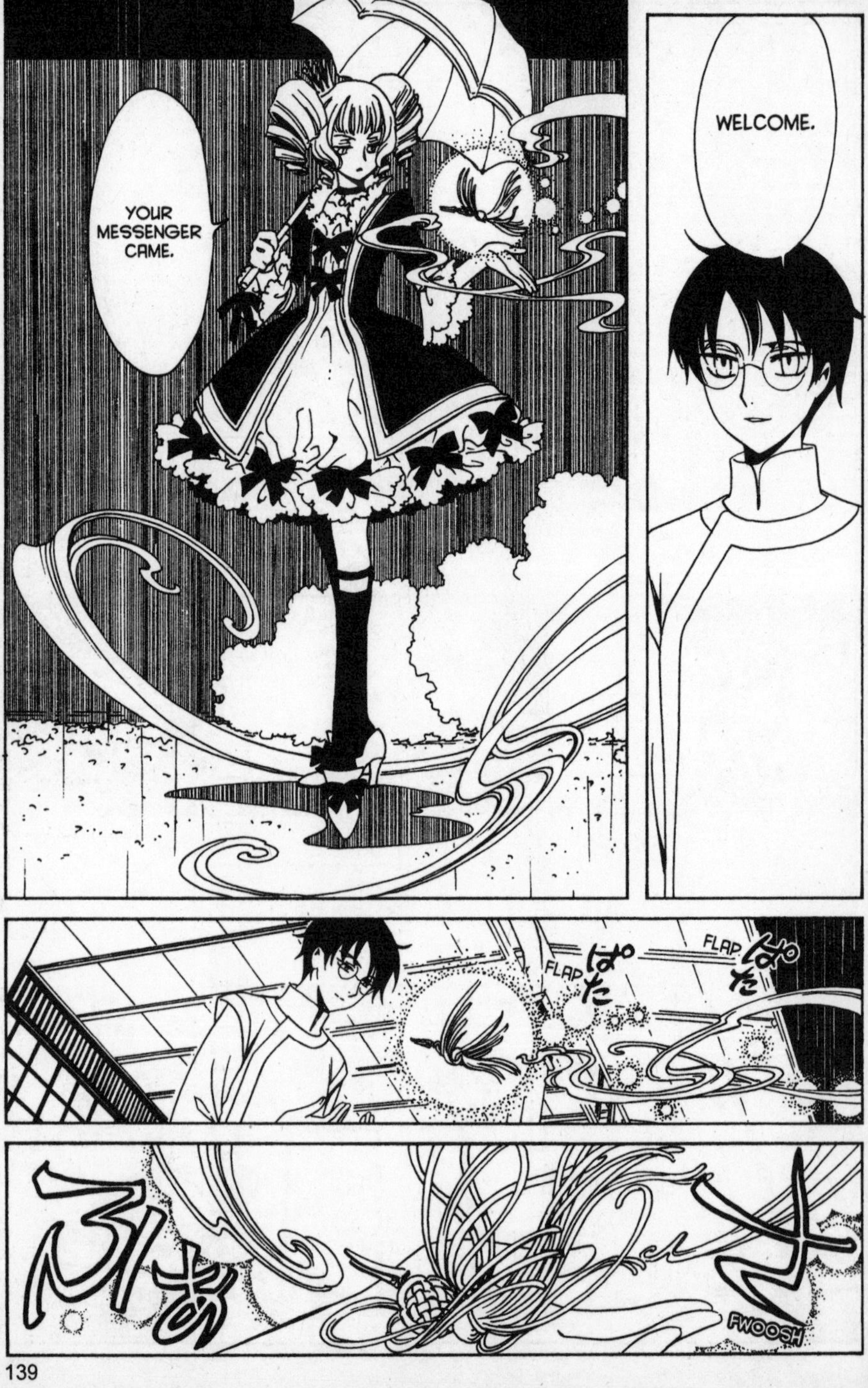
WELCOME.
YOUR MESSENGER CAME.
FLAP
ぱた
FLAP
ぱた
FWOOSH

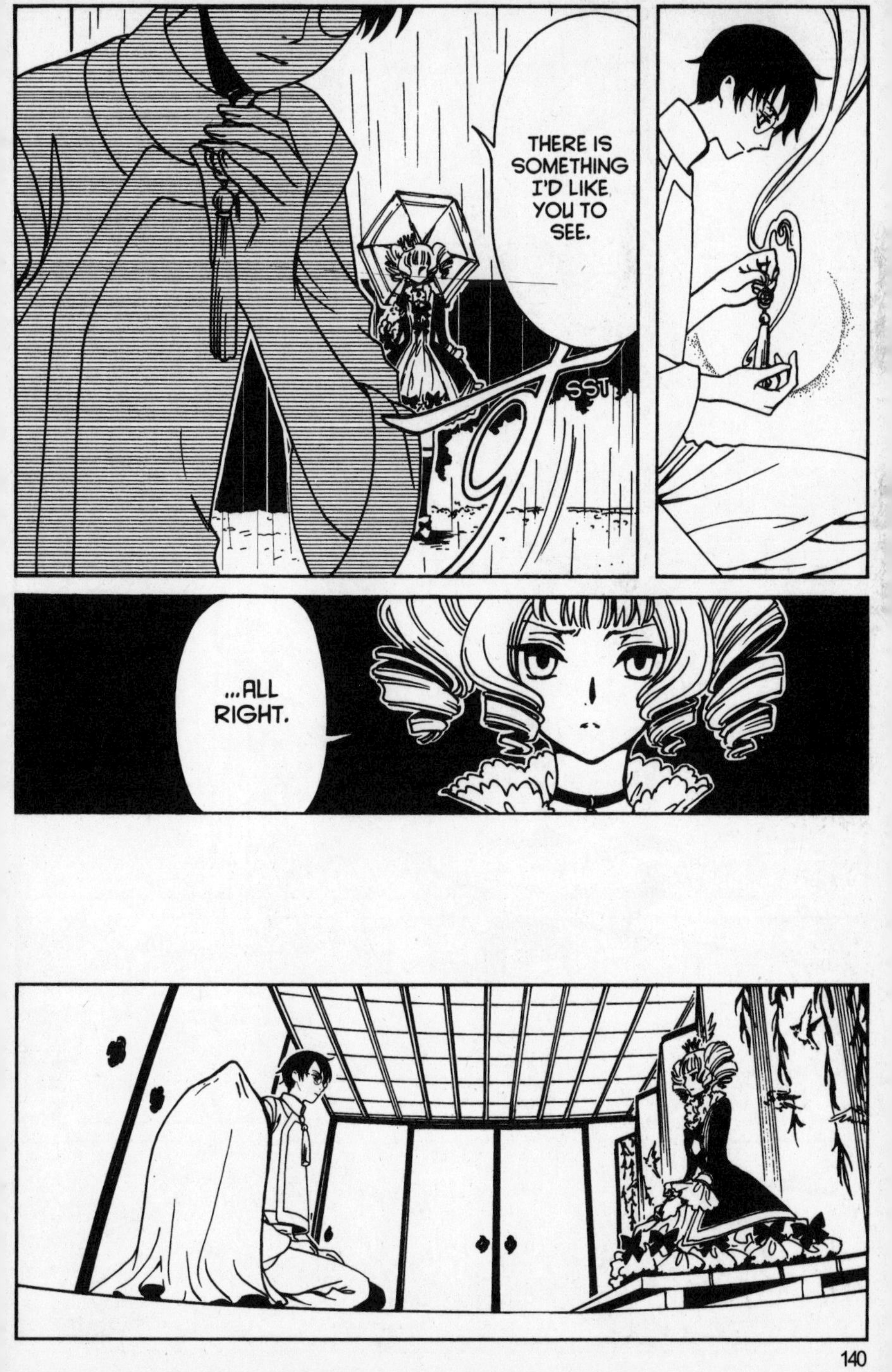
THERE IS SOMETHING I'D LIKE YOU TO SEE.
SST
...ALL RIGHT.

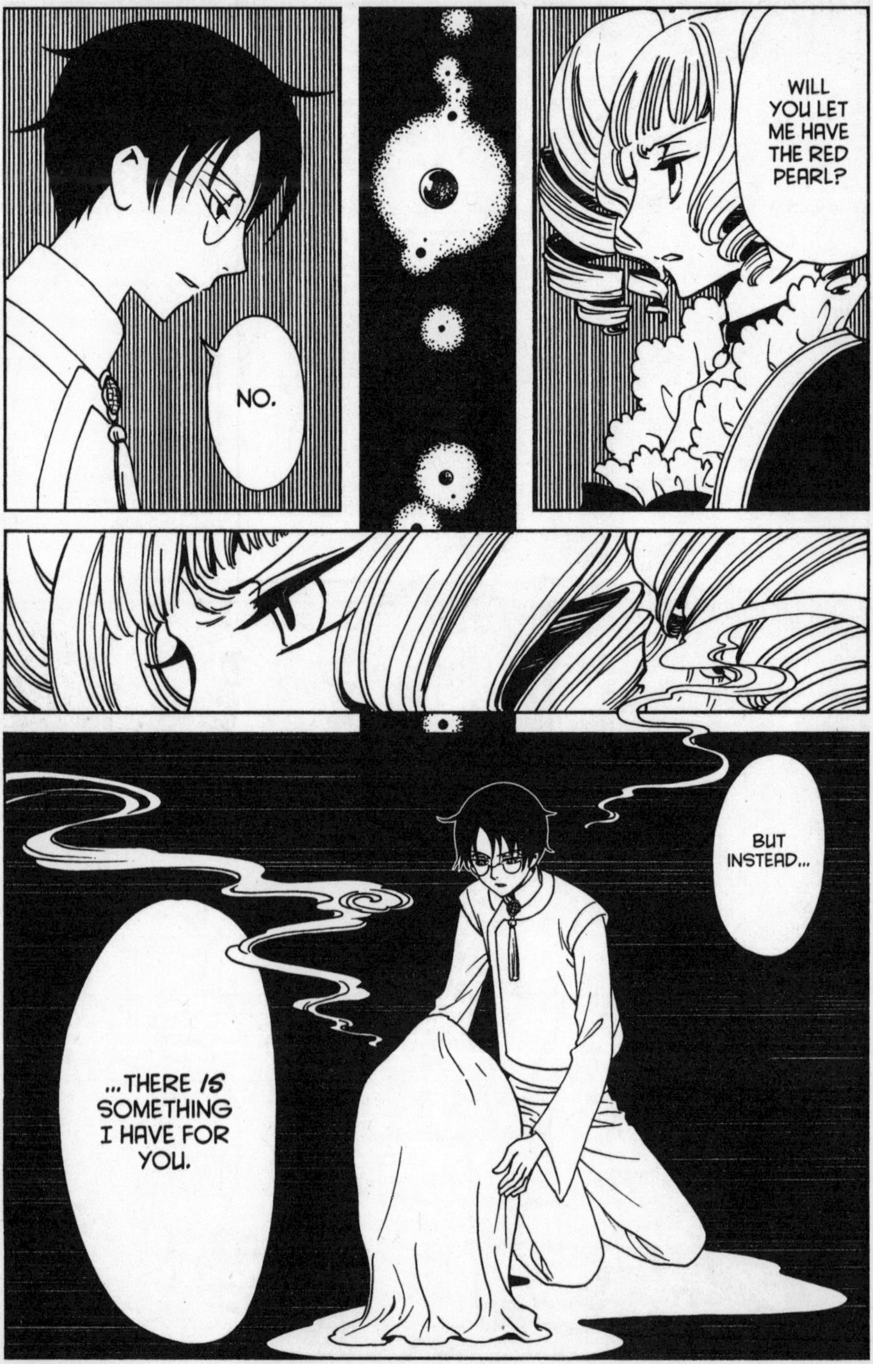
WILL YOU LET ME HAVE THE RED PEARL?
NO.
BUT INSTEAD...
...THERE IS SOMETHING I HAVE FOR YOU.

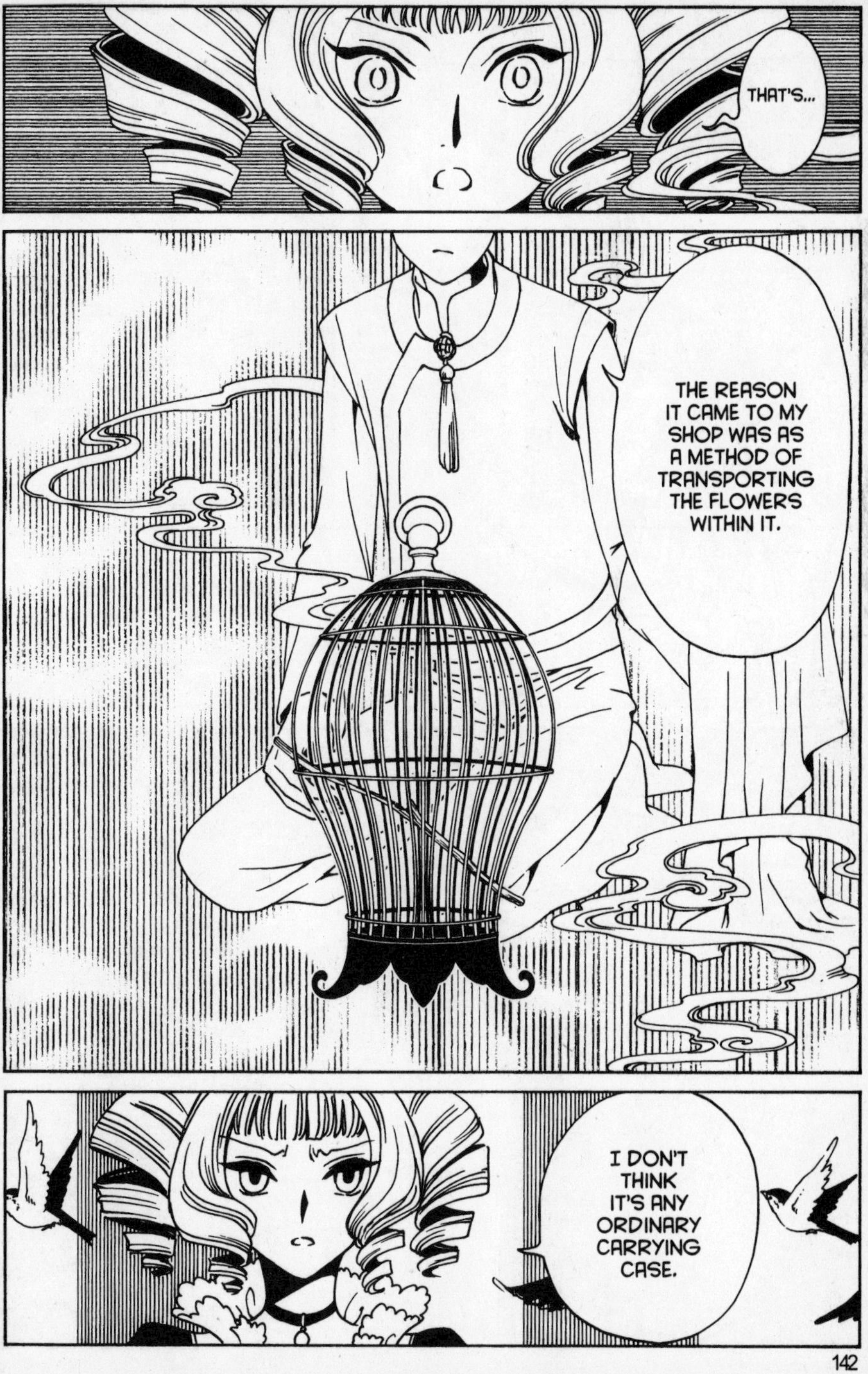
THAT'S...
THE REASON IT CAME TO MY SHOP WAS AS A METHOD OF TRANSPORTING THE FLOWERS WITHIN IT.
I DON'T THINK IT'S ANY ORDINARY CARRYING CASE.

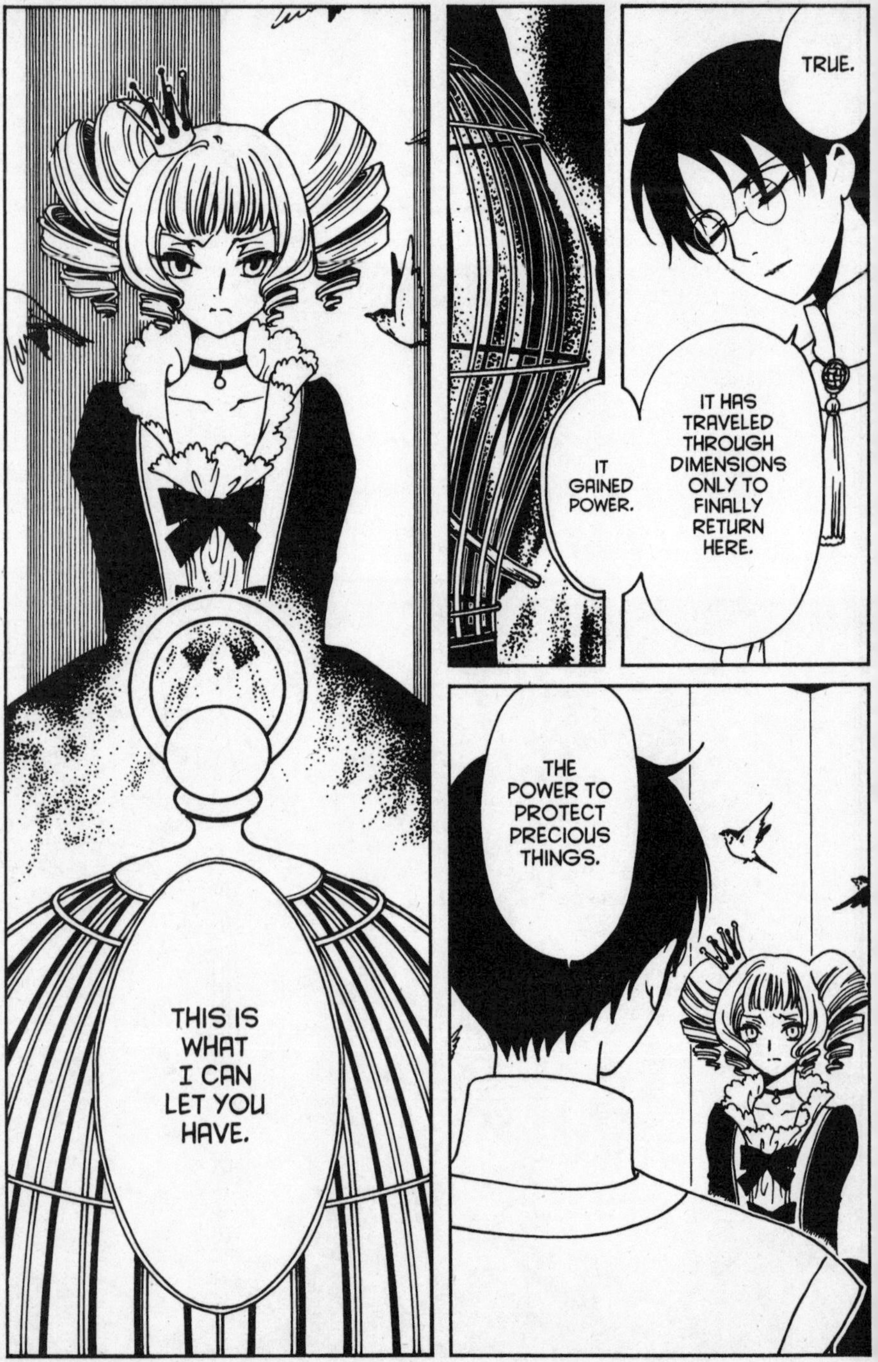
TRUE.
IT HAS TRAVELED THROUGH DIMENSIONS ONLY TO FINALLY RETURN HERE.
IT GAINED POWER.
THE POWER TO PROTECT PRECIOUS THINGS.
THIS IS WHAT I CAN LET YOU HAVE.

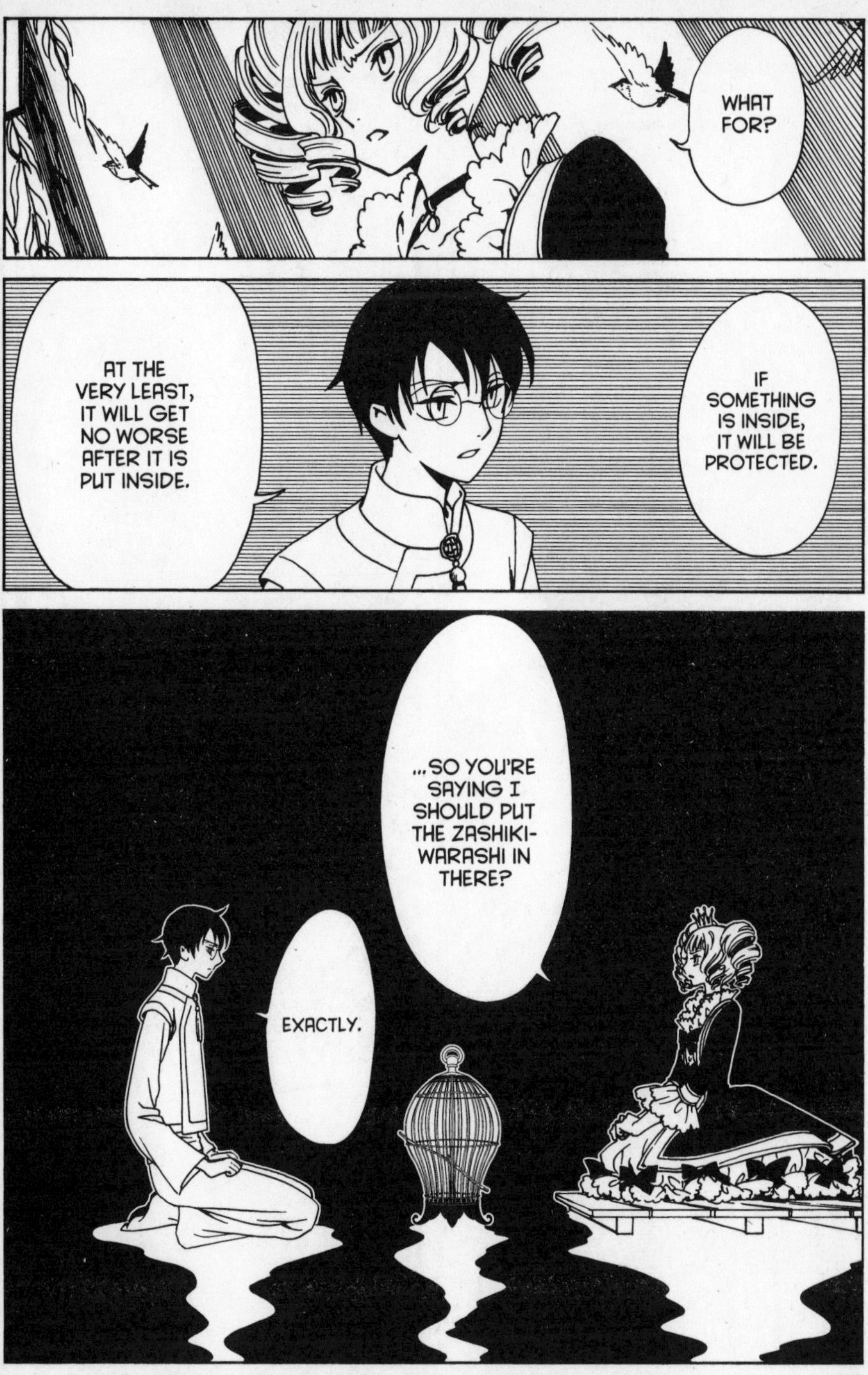
WHAT FOR?
IF SOMETHING IS INSIDE, IT WILL BE PROTECTED.
AT THE VERY LEAST, IT WILL GET NO WORSE AFTER IT IS PUT INSIDE.
...SO YOU'RE SAYING I SHOULD PUT THE ZASHIKI-WARASHI IN THERE?
EXACTLY.

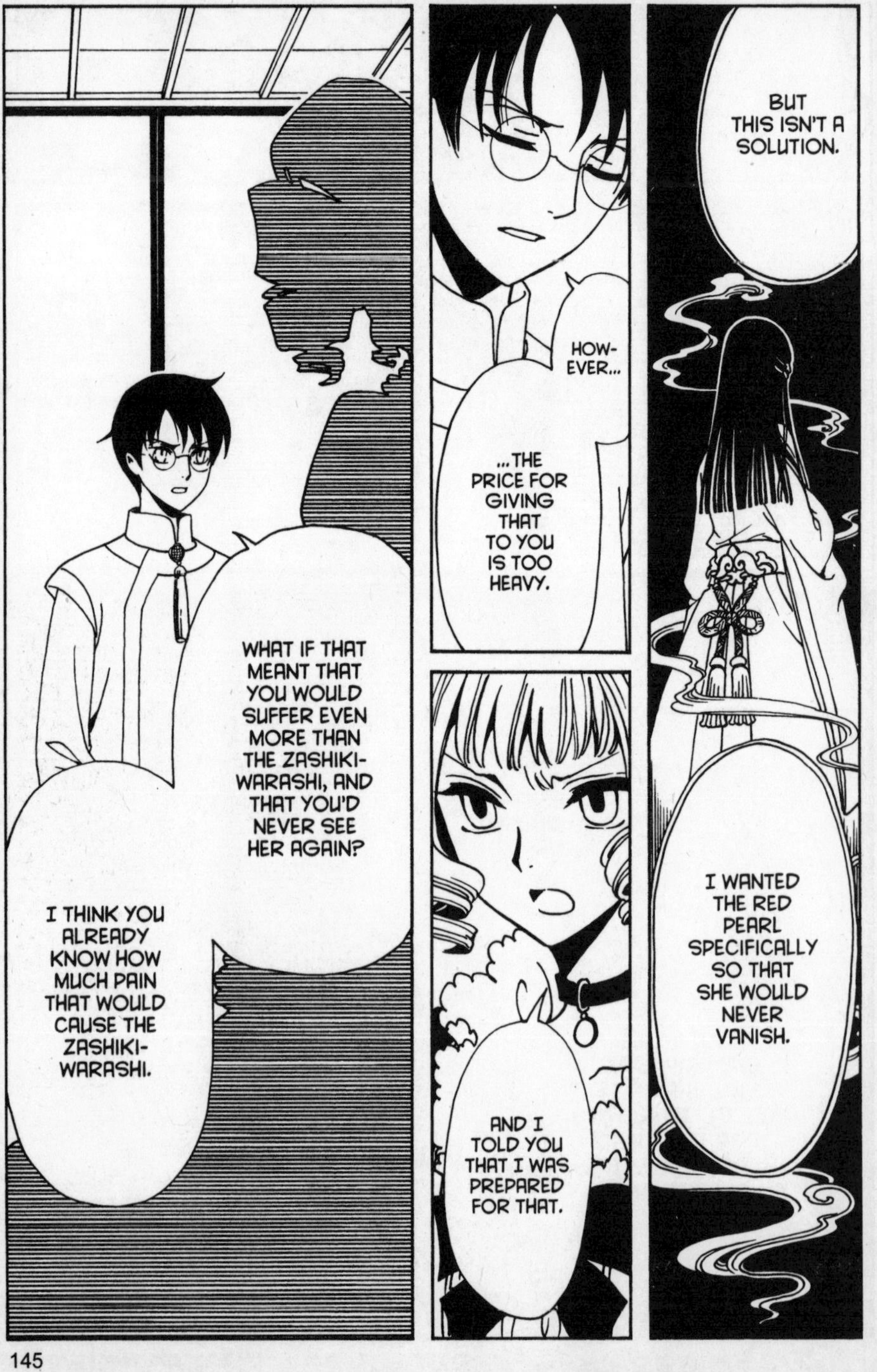
BUT THIS ISN'T A SOLUTION.
I WANTED THE RED PEARL SPECIFICALLY SO THAT SHE WOULD NEVER VANISH.
HOW-EVER...
...THE PRICE FOR GIVING THAT TO YOU IS TOO HEAVY.
AND I TOLD YOU THAT I WAS PREPARED FOR THAT.
WHAT IF THAT MEANT THAT YOU WOULD SUFFER EVEN MORE THAN THE ZASHIKI-WARASHI, AND THAT YOU'D NEVER SEE HER AGAIN?
I THINK YOU ALREADY KNOW HOW MUCH PAIN THAT WOULD CAUSE THE ZASHIKI-WARASHI.

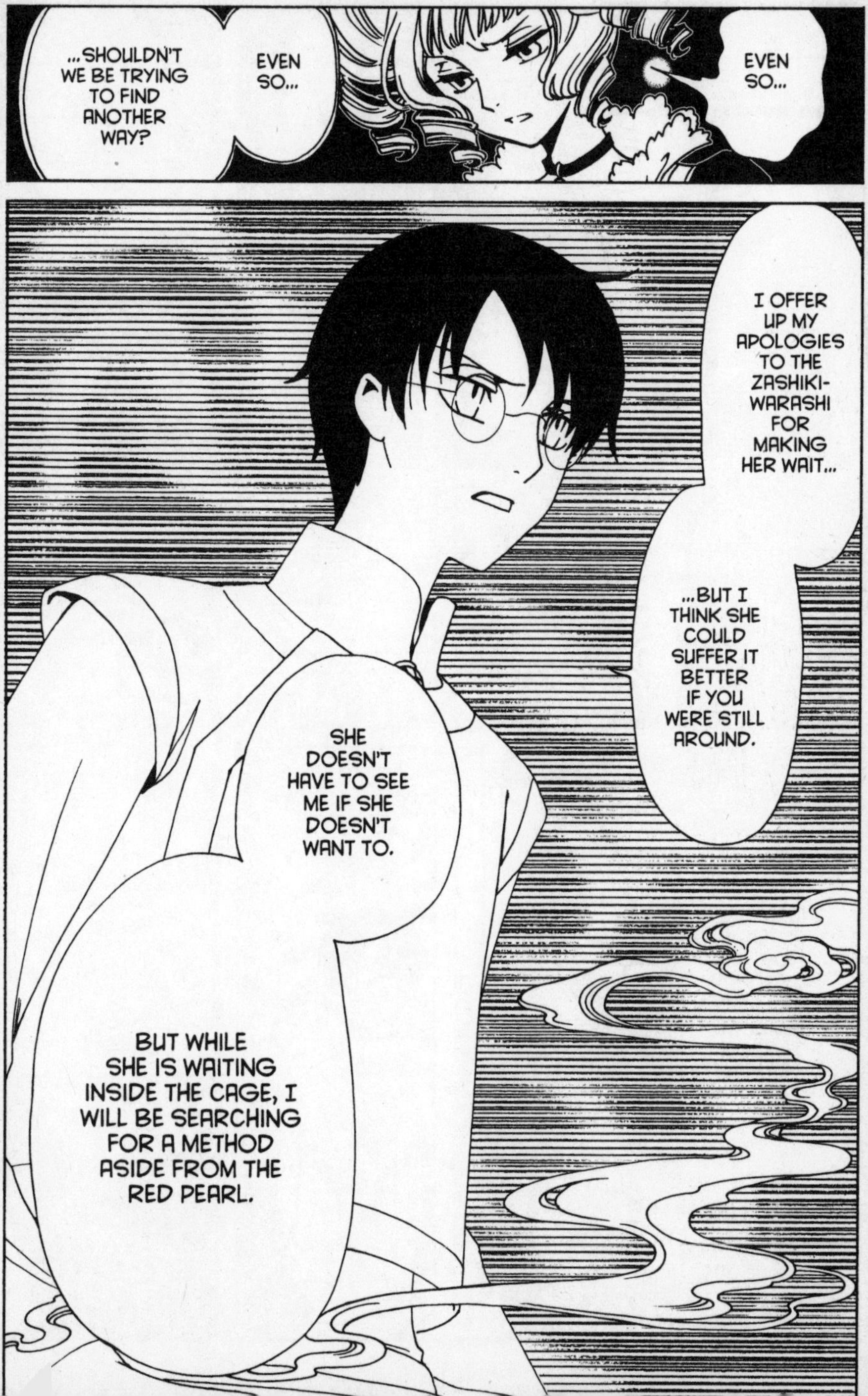
EVEN SO...
EVEN SO...
...SHOULDN'T WE BE TRYING TO FIND ANOTHER WAY?
I OFFER UP MY APOLOGIES TO THE ZASHIKI-WARASHI FOR MAKING HER WAIT...
...BUT I THINK SHE COULD SUFFER IT BETTER IF YOU WERE STILL AROUND.
SHE DOESN'T HAVE TO SEE ME IF SHE DOESN'T WANT TO.
BUT WHILE SHE IS WAITING INSIDE THE CAGE, I WILL BE SEARCHING FOR A METHOD ASIDE FROM THE RED PEARL.

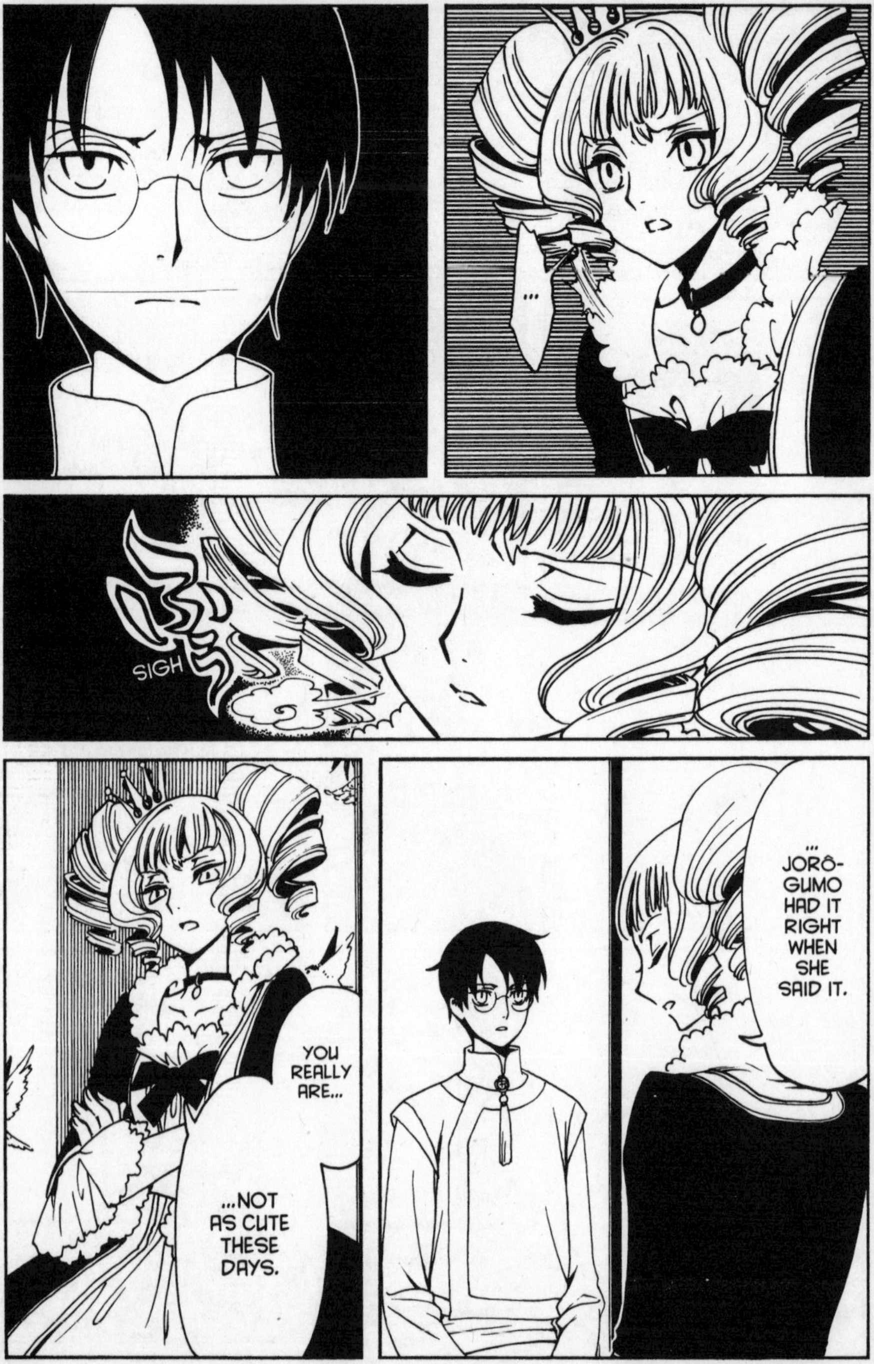
...
SIGH
...JORÔ-GUMO HAD IT RIGHT WHEN SHE SAID IT.
YOU REALLY ARE...
...NOT AS CUTE THESE DAYS.

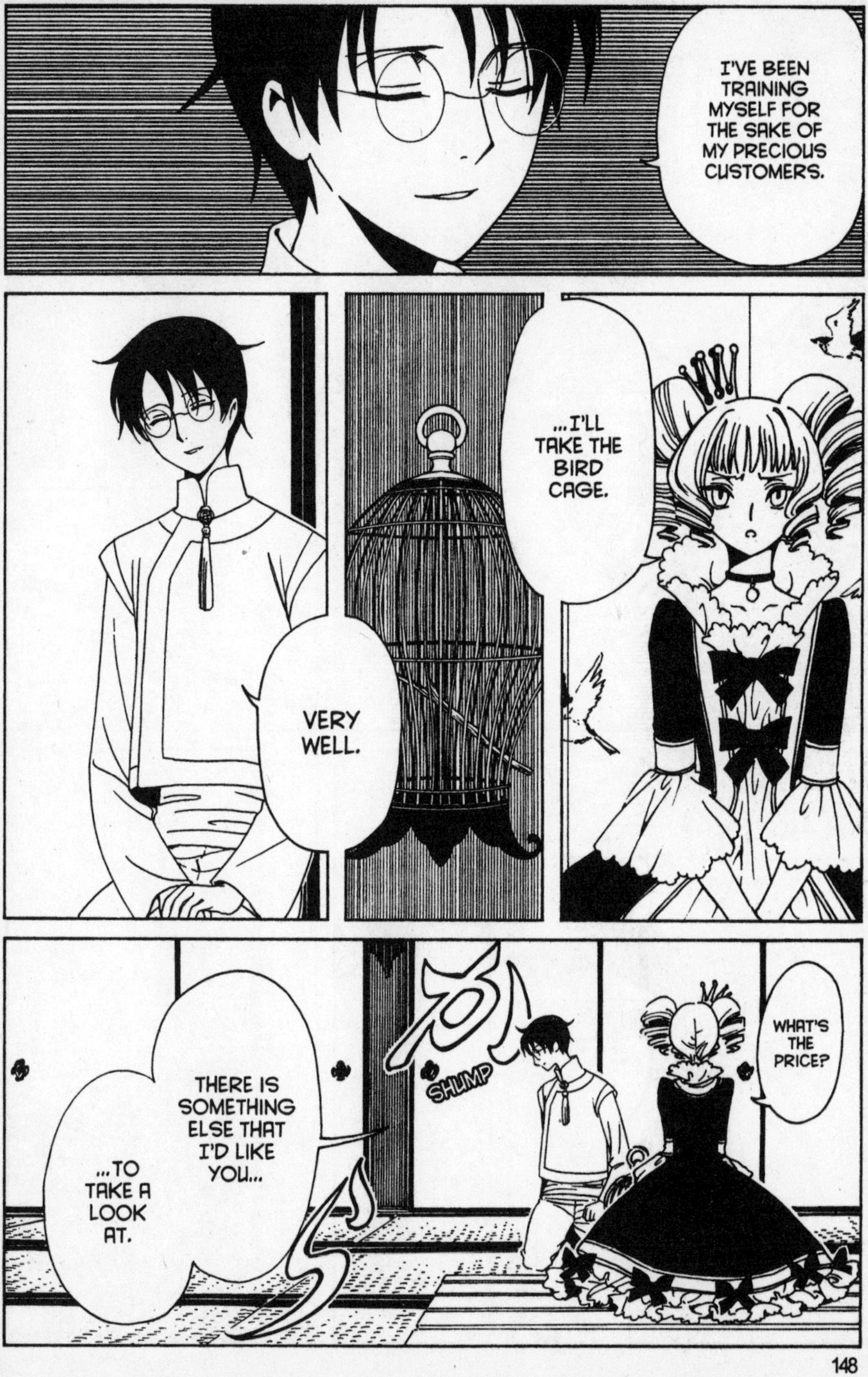
I'VE BEEN TRAINING MYSELF FOR THE SAKE OF MY PRECIOUS CUSTOMERS.
...I'LL TAKE THE BIRD CAGE.
VERY WELL.
WHAT'S THE PRICE?
SHUMP
THERE IS SOMETHING ELSE THAT I'D LIKE YOU...
...TO TAKE A LOOK AT.

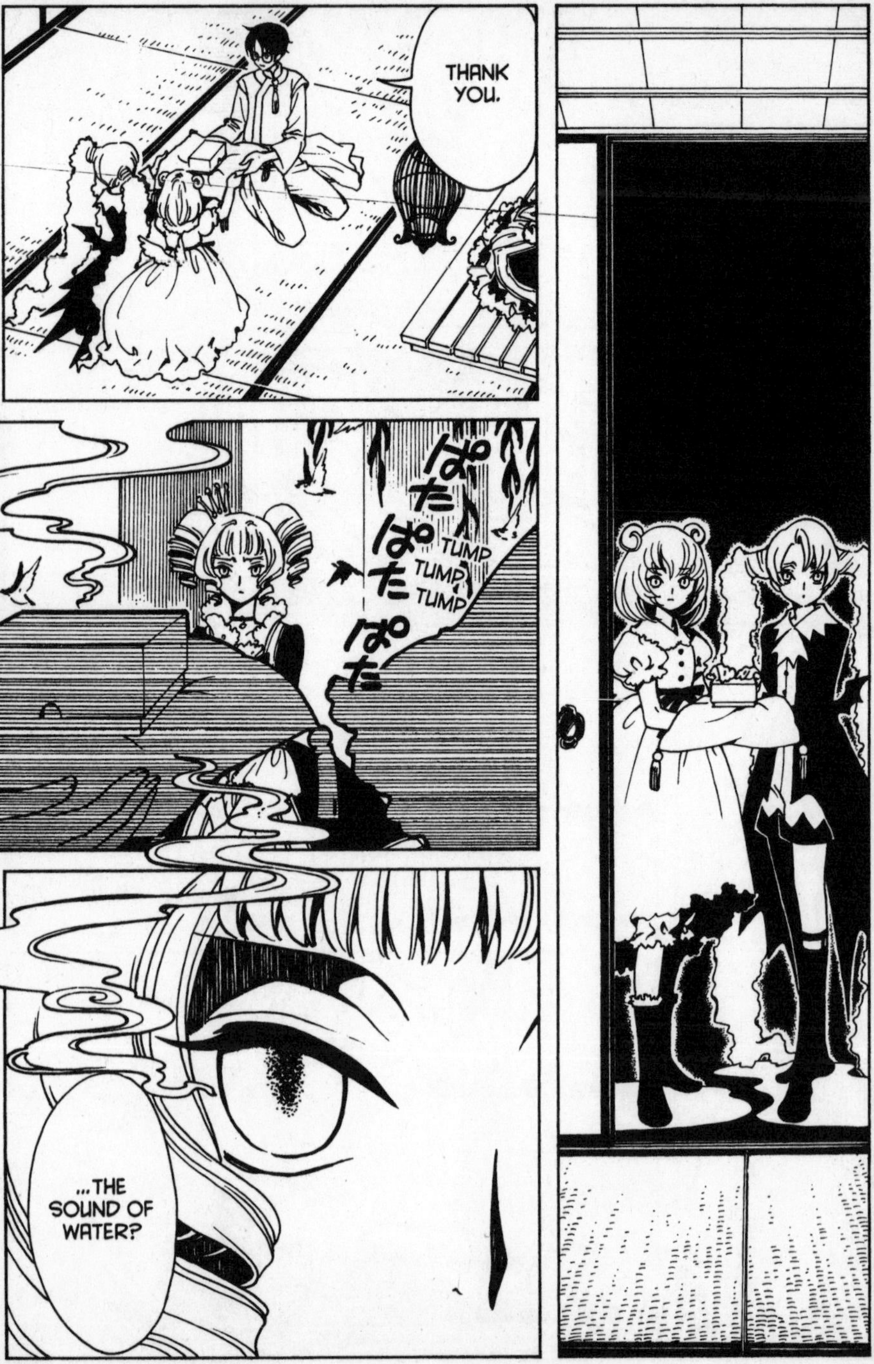
THANK YOU.
ぱたぱたぱた
TUMP TUMP TUMP
...THE SOUND OF WATER?

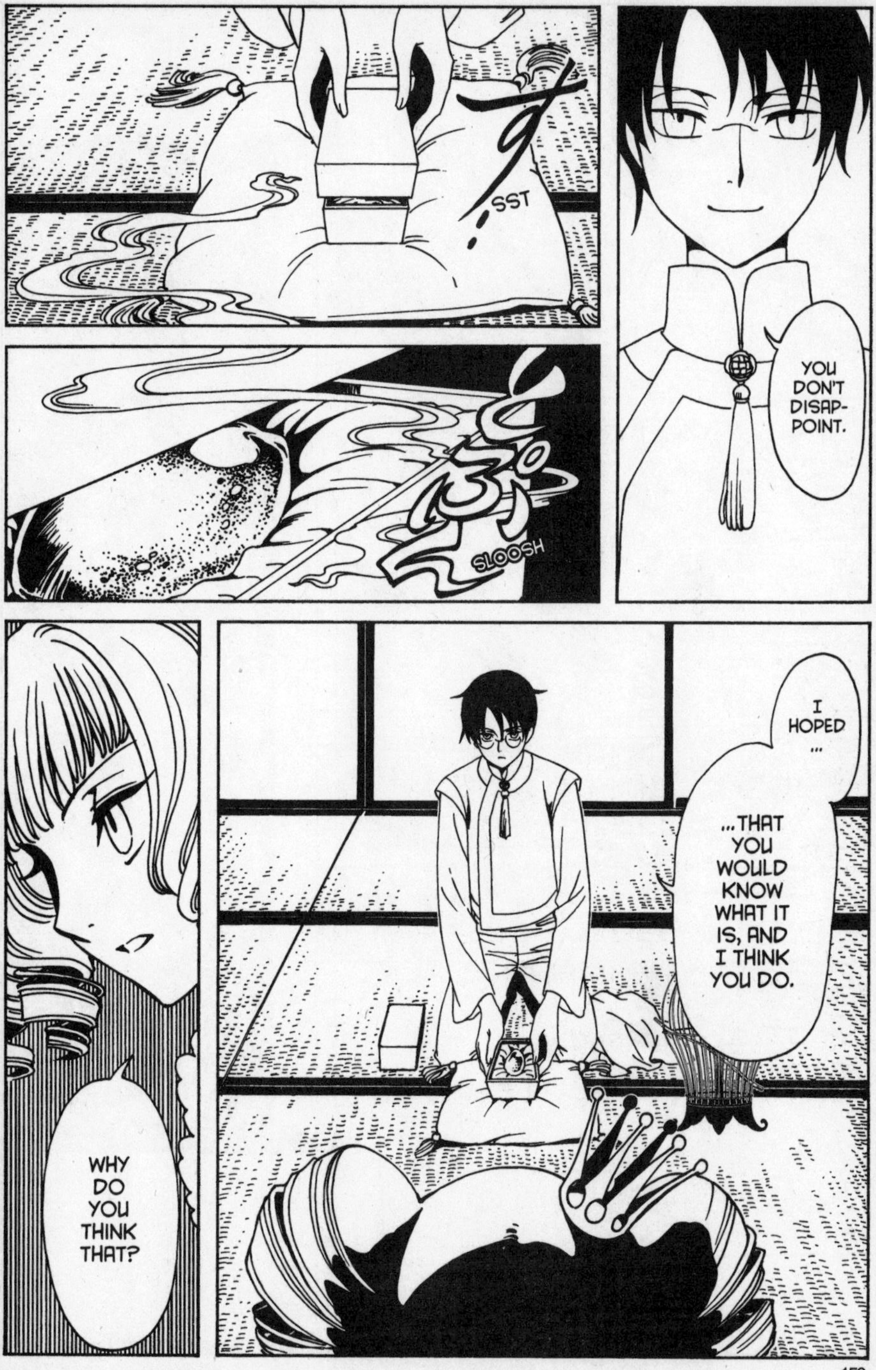
YOU DON'T DISAPPOINT.
SST
SLOOSH
I HOPED ...
...THAT YOU WOULD KNOW WHAT IT IS, AND I THINK YOU DO.
WHY DO YOU THINK THAT?

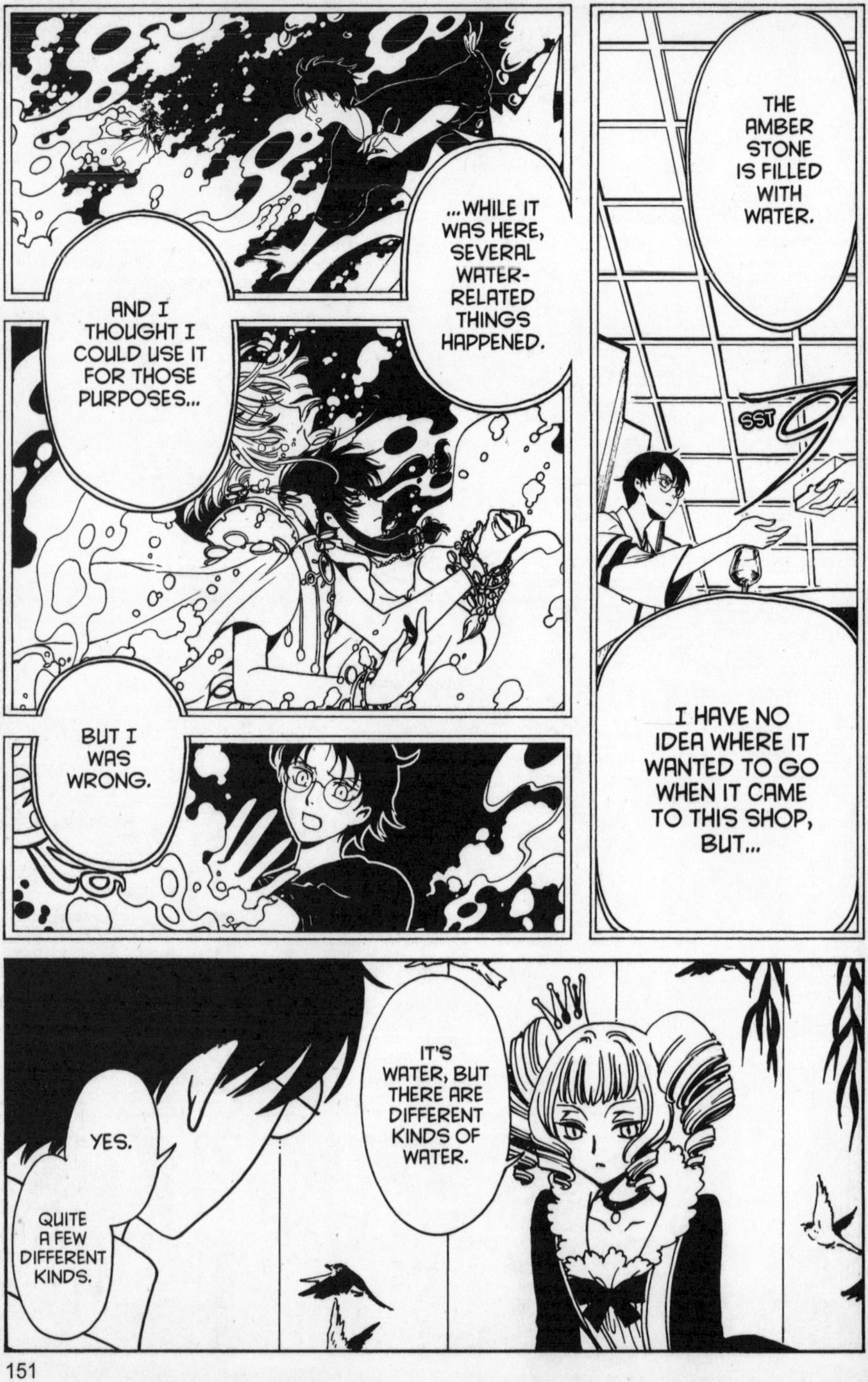
THE AMBER STONE IS FILLED WITH WATER.
SST
I HAVE NO IDEA WHERE IT WANTED TO GO WHEN IT CAME TO THIS SHOP, BUT...
...WHILE IT WAS HERE, SEVERAL WATER-RELATED THINGS HAPPENED.
AND I THOUGHT I COULD USE IT FOR THOSE PURPOSES...
BUT I WAS WRONG.
IT'S WATER, BUT THERE ARE DIFFERENT KINDS OF WATER.
YES.
QUITE A FEW DIFFERENT KINDS.

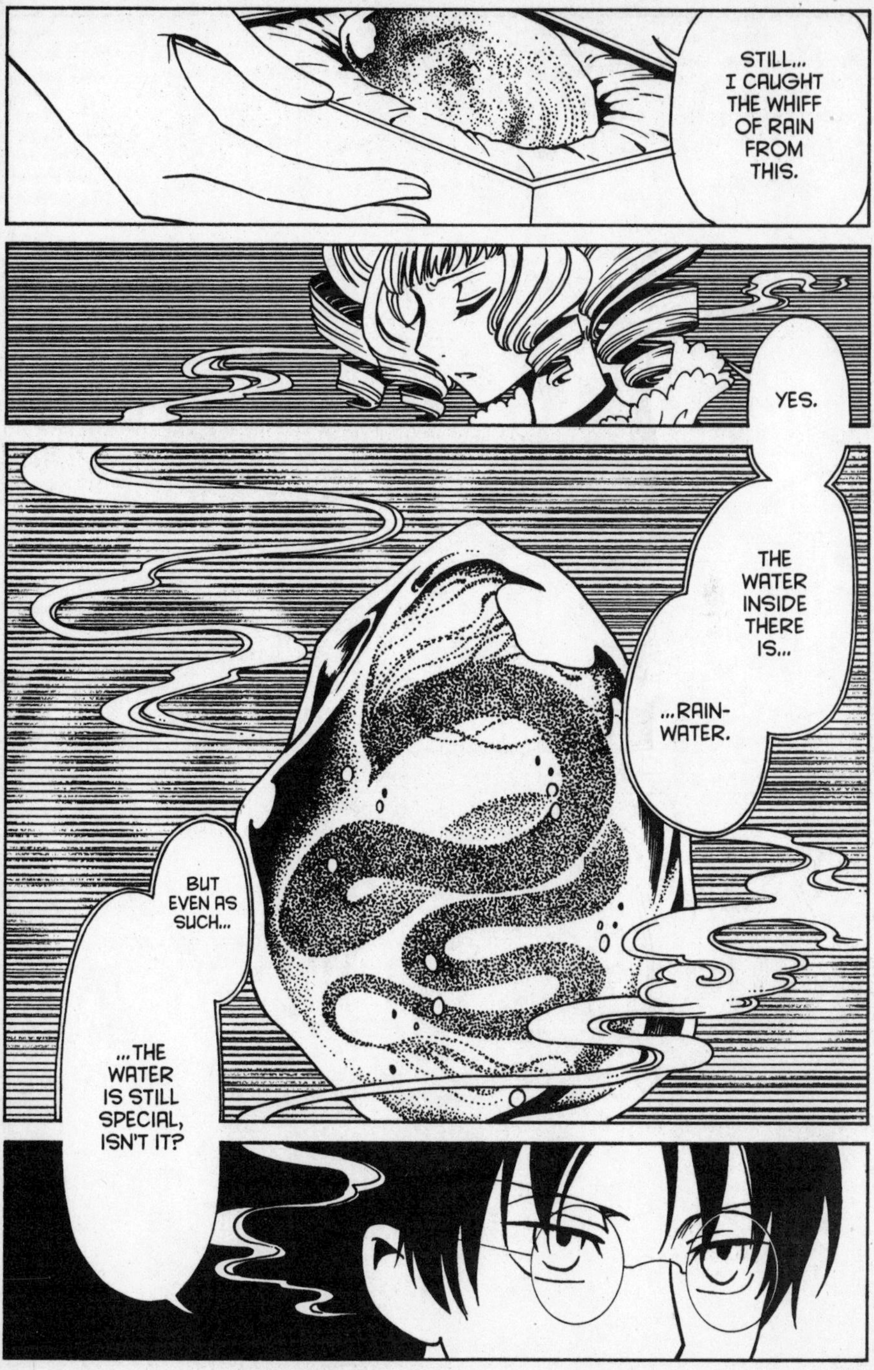
STILL... I CAUGHT THE WHIFF OF RAIN FROM THIS.
YES.
THE WATER INSIDE THERE IS...
...RAIN-WATER.
BUT EVEN AS SUCH...
...THE WATER IS STILL SPECIAL, ISN'T IT?

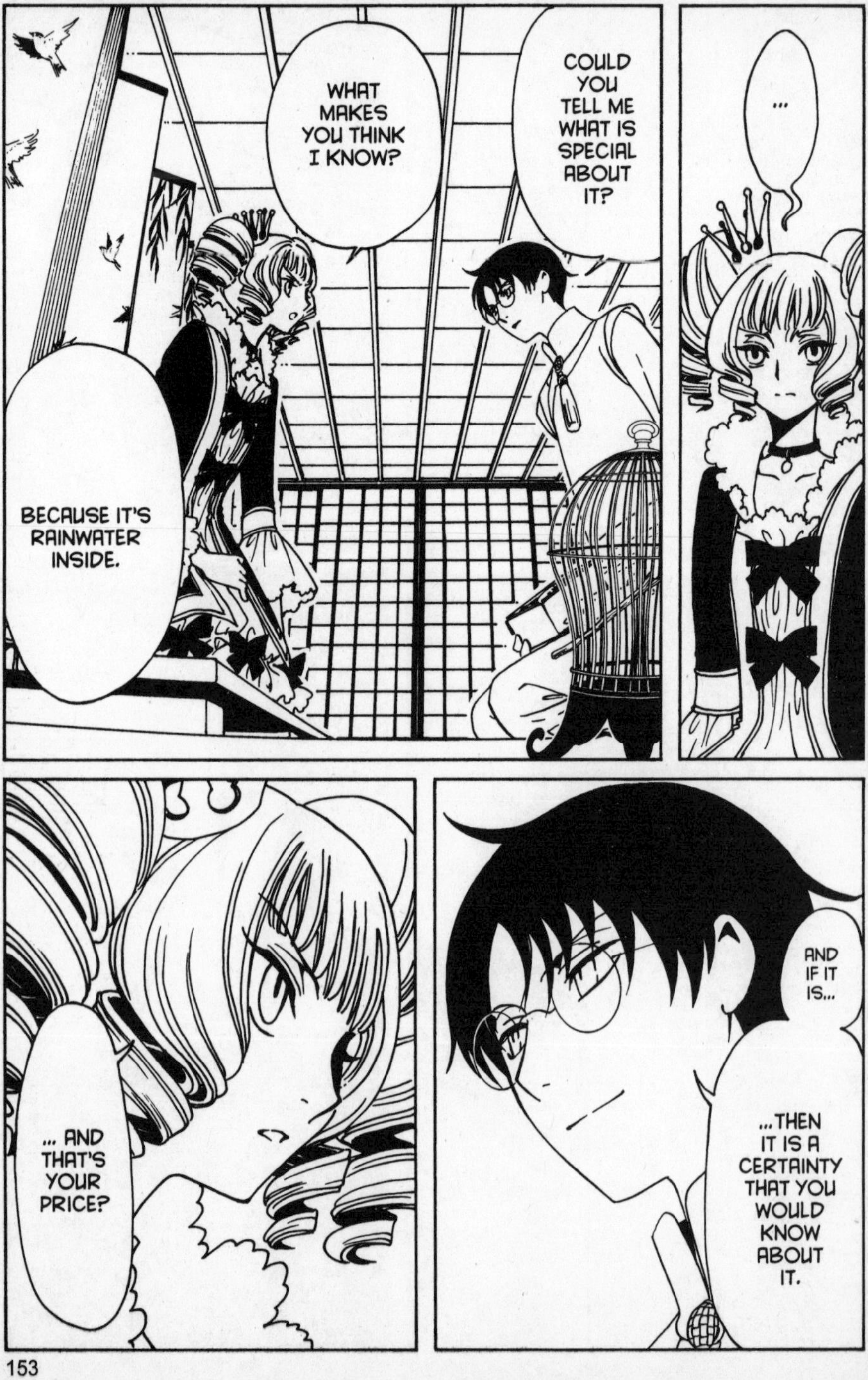
...
COULD YOU TELL ME WHAT IS SPECIAL ABOUT IT?
WHAT MAKES YOU THINK I KNOW?
BECAUSE IT'S RAINWATER INSIDE.
AND IF IT IS...
...THEN IT IS A CERTAINTY THAT YOU WOULD KNOW ABOUT IT.
... AND THAT'S YOUR PRICE?

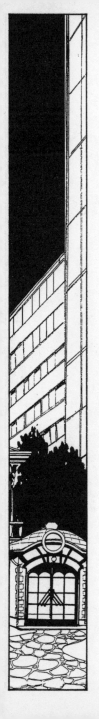

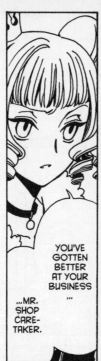

YOU'VE GOTTEN BETTER AT YOUR BUSINESS ...

...MR. SHOP CARE-TAKER.

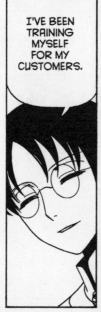

I'VE BEEN TRAINING MYSELF FOR MY CUSTOMERS.

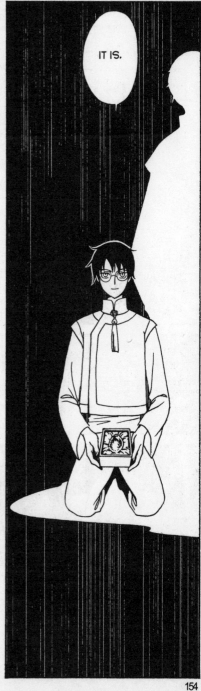

IT IS.

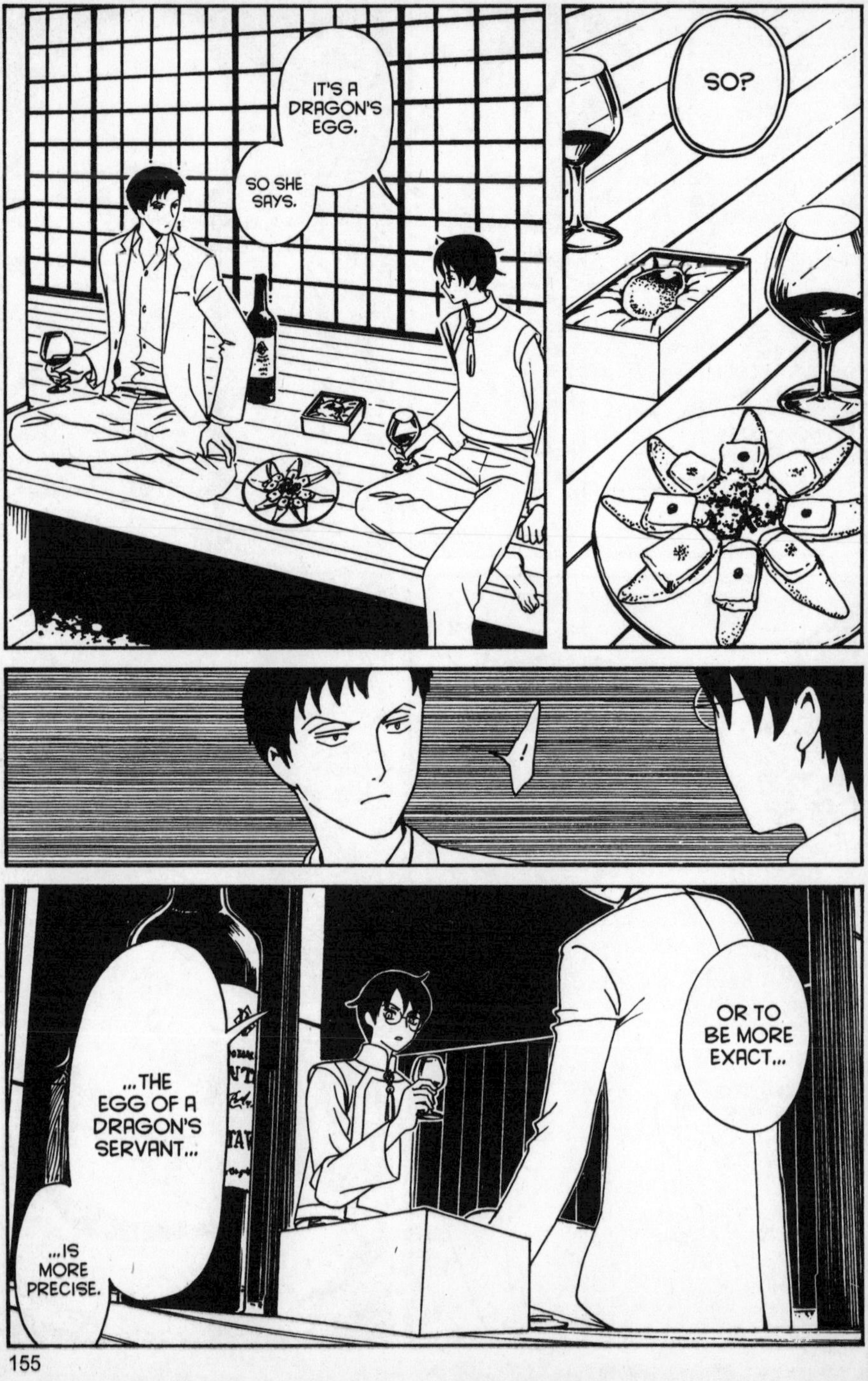
SO?
IT'S A DRAGON'S EGG.
SO SHE SAYS.
OR TO BE MORE EXACT...
...THE EGG OF A DRAGON'S SERVANT...
...IS MORE PRECISE.

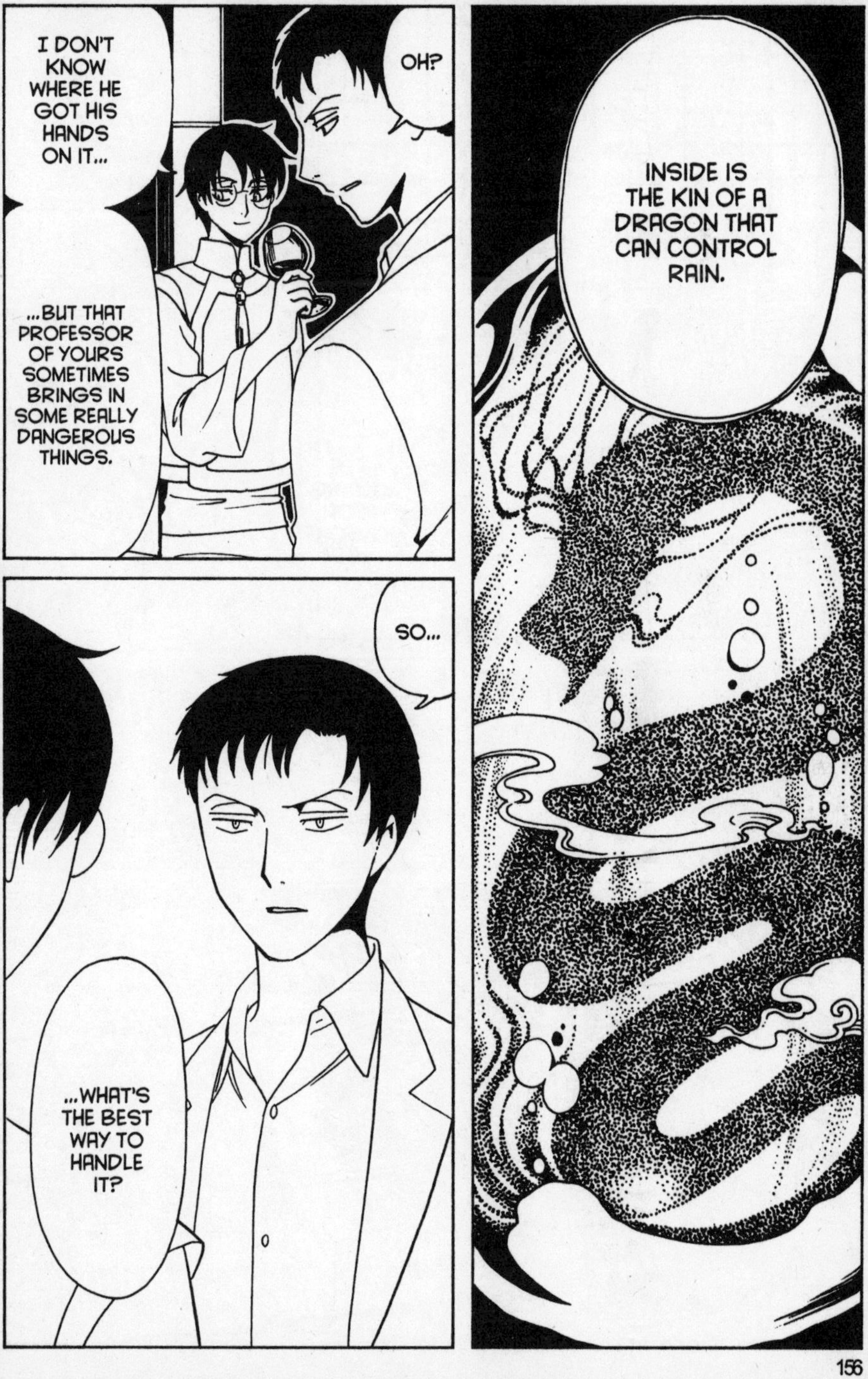
INSIDE IS THE KIN OF A DRAGON THAT CAN CONTROL RAIN.
OH?
I DON'T KNOW WHERE HE GOT HIS HANDS ON IT...
...BUT THAT PROFESSOR OF YOURS SOMETIMES BRINGS IN SOME REALLY DANGEROUS THINGS.
SO...
...WHAT'S THE BEST WAY TO HANDLE IT?

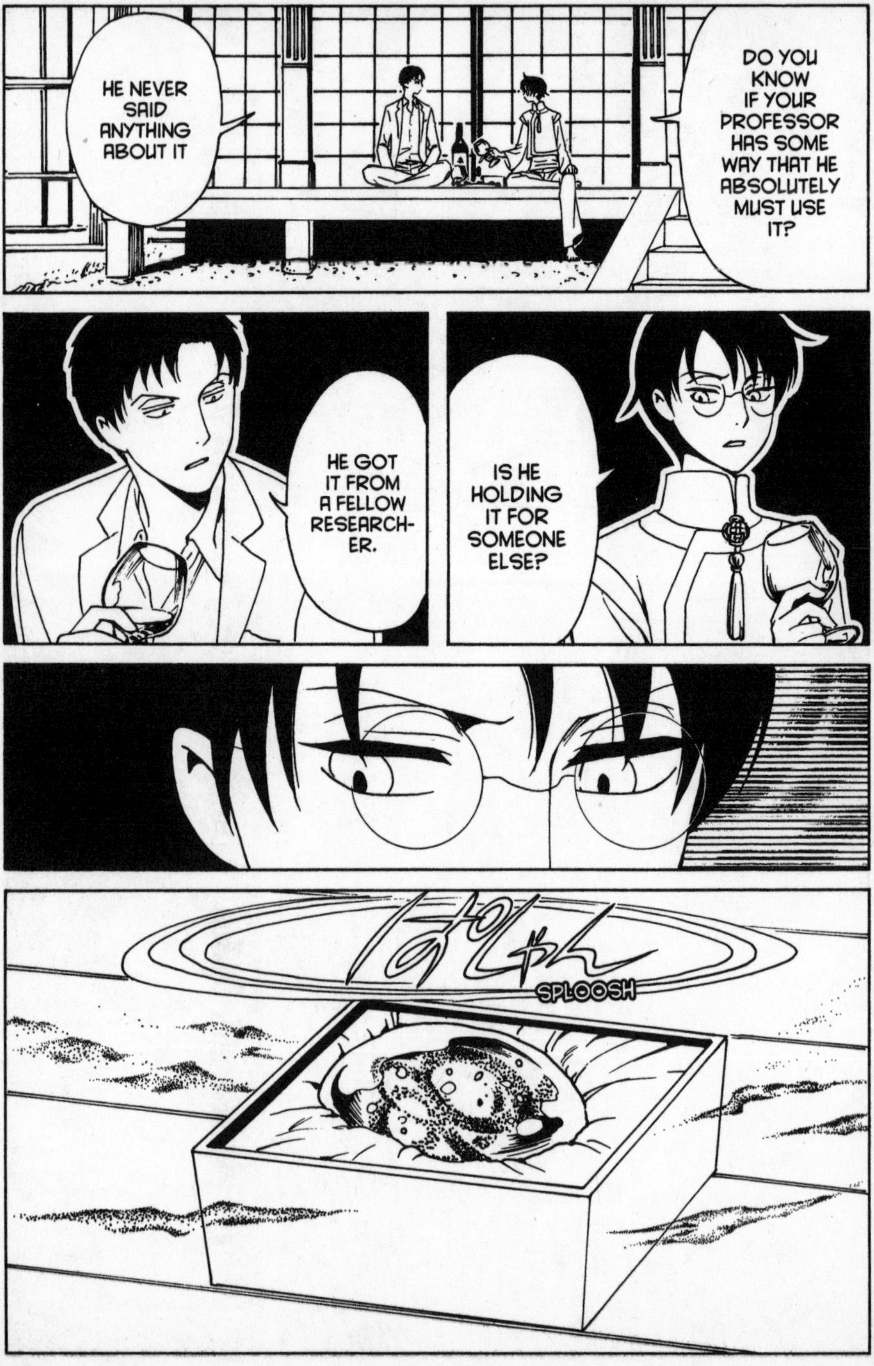
DO YOU KNOW IF YOUR PROFESSOR HAS SOME WAY THAT HE ABSOLUTELY MUST USE IT?
HE NEVER SAID ANYTHING ABOUT IT
IS HE HOLDING IT FOR SOMEONE ELSE?
HE GOT IT FROM A FELLOW RESEARCH-ER.
SPLOOSH

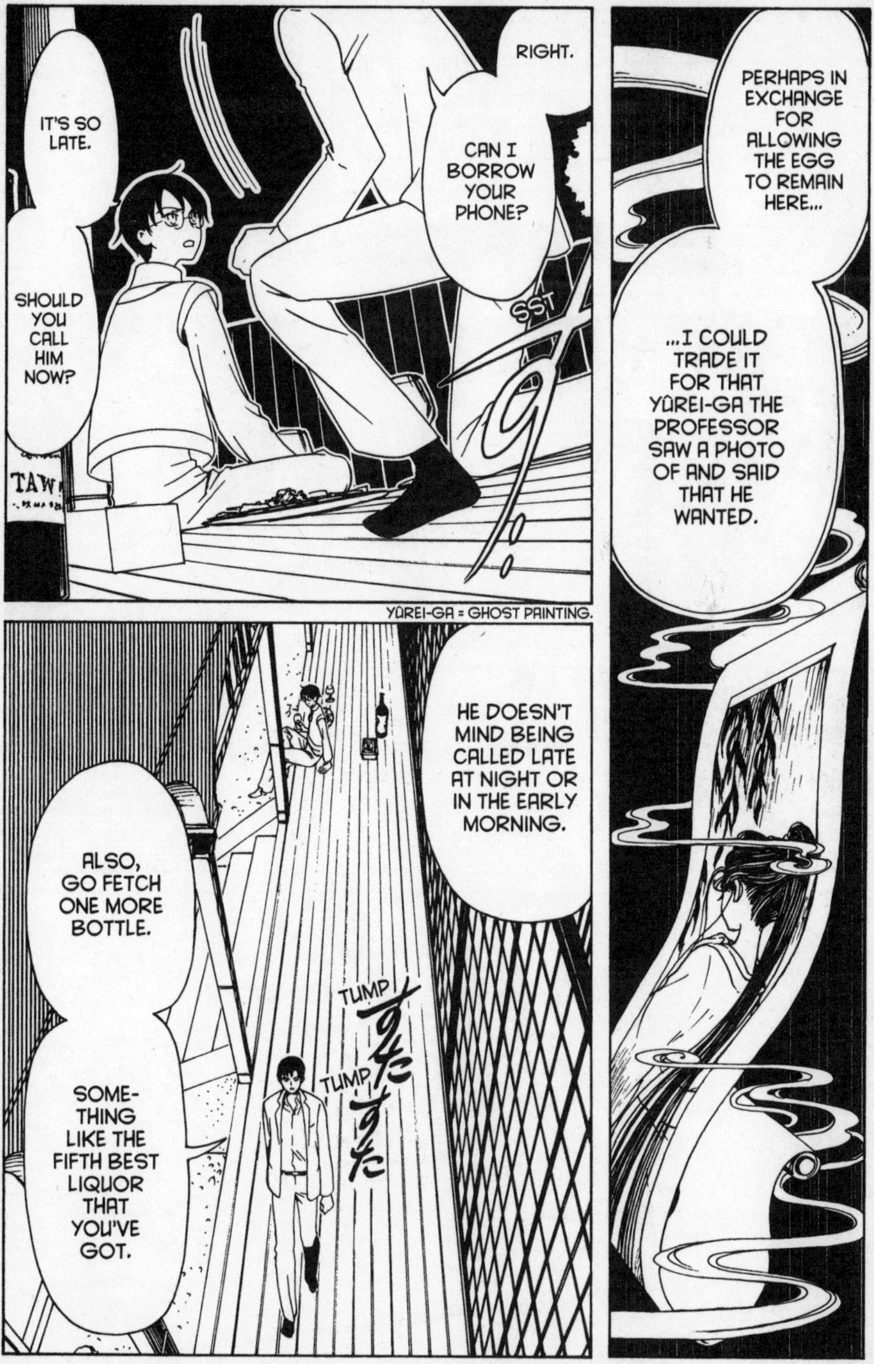
PERHAPS IN EXCHANGE FOR ALLOWING THE EGG TO REMAIN HERE...
...I COULD TRADE IT FOR THAT YÛREI-GA THE PROFESSOR SAW A PHOTO OF AND SAID THAT HE WANTED.
RIGHT.
CAN I BORROW YOUR PHONE?
SST
IT'S SO LATE.
SHOULD YOU CALL HIM NOW?
HE DOESN'T MIND BEING CALLED LATE AT NIGHT OR IN THE EARLY MORNING.
TUMP すた
TUMP すた
ALSO, GO FETCH ONE MORE BOTTLE.
SOME-THING LIKE THE FIFTH BEST LIQUOR THAT YOU'VE GOT.

YÛREI-GA = GHOST PAINTING.

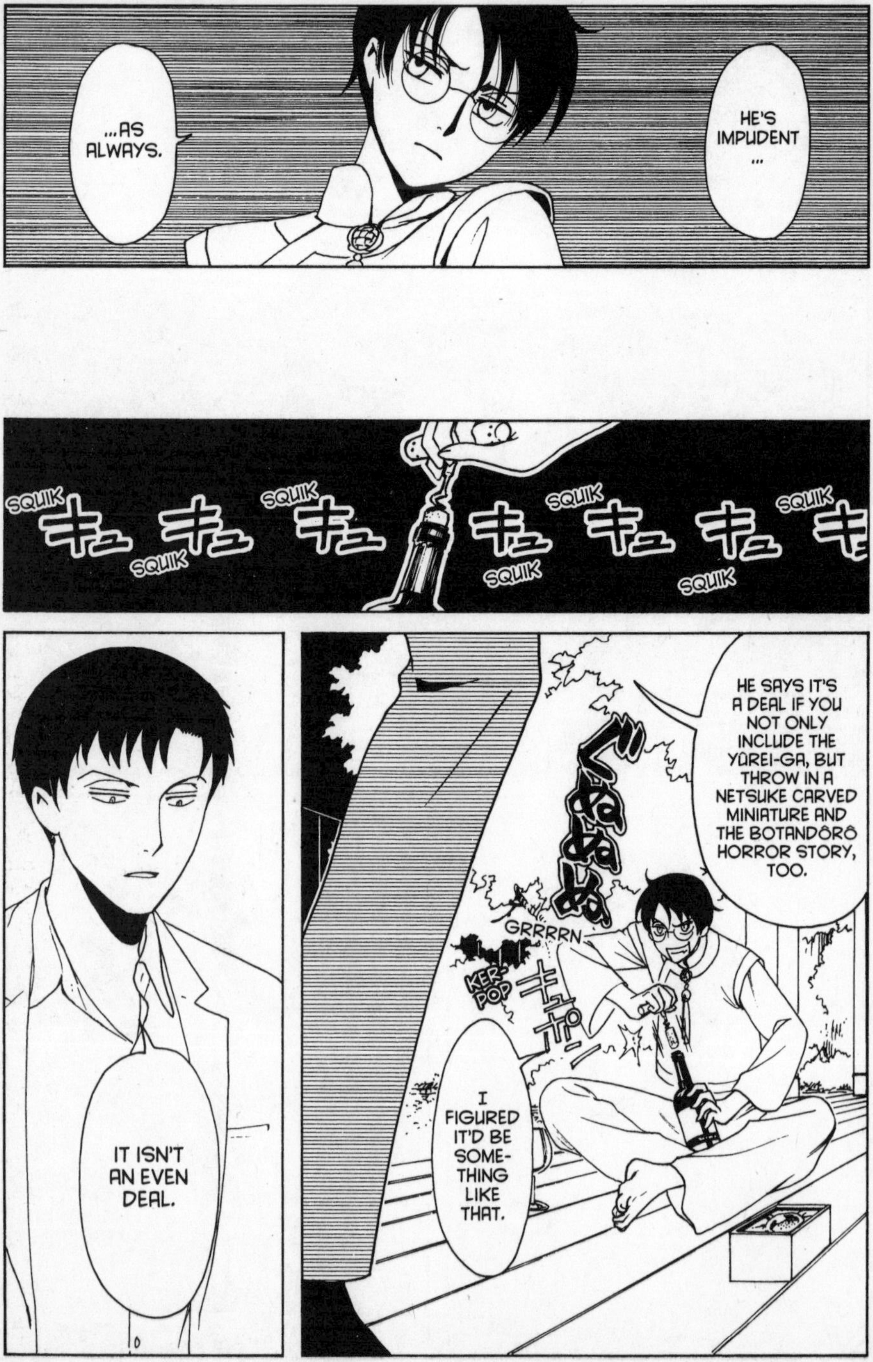
HE'S IMPUDENT ...
...AS ALWAYS.
SQUIK SQUIK SQUIK SQUIK SQUIK SQUIK SQUIK
HE SAYS IT'S A DEAL IF YOU NOT ONLY INCLUDE THE YÛREI-GA, BUT THROW IN A NETSUKE CARVED MINIATURE AND THE BOTANDÔRÔ HORROR STORY, TOO.
GRRRRN
KER-POP
I FIGURED IT'D BE SOME-THING LIKE THAT.
IT ISN'T AN EVEN DEAL.

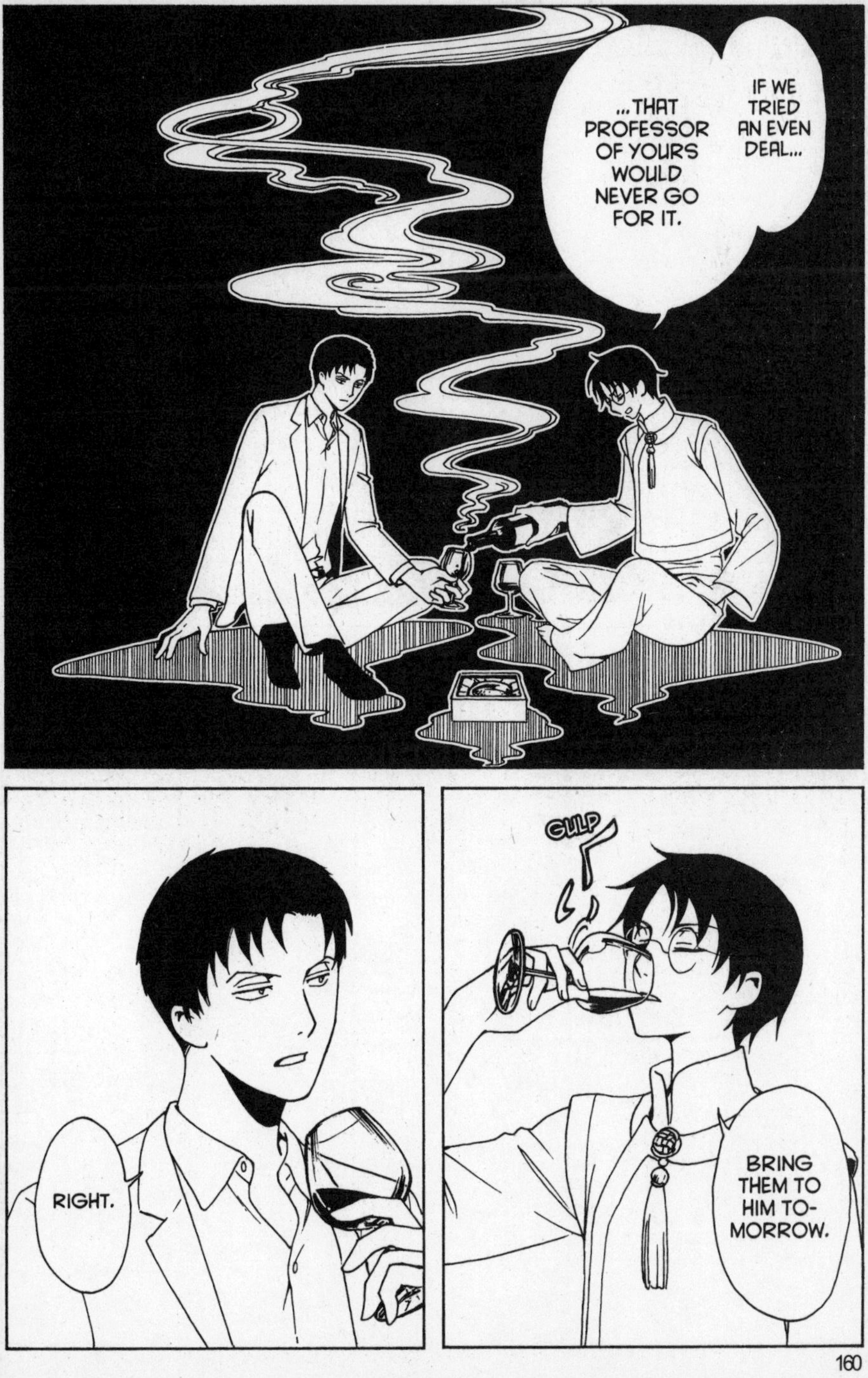
IF WE TRIED AN EVEN DEAL...
...THAT PROFESSOR OF YOURS WOULD NEVER GO FOR IT.
GULP
BRING THEM TO HIM TO-MORROW.
RIGHT.

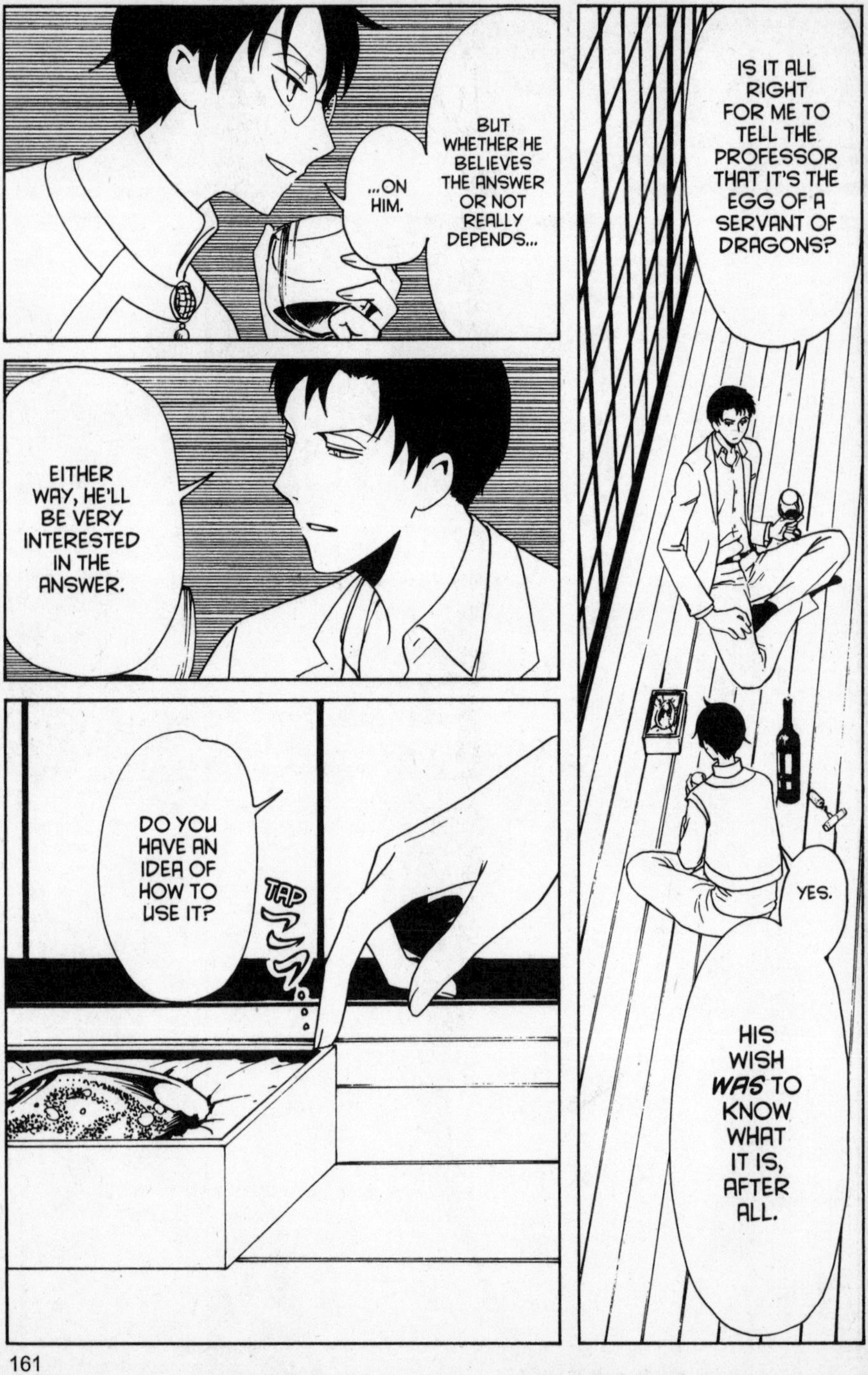
IS IT ALL RIGHT FOR ME TO TELL THE PROFESSOR THAT IT'S THE EGG OF A SERVANT OF DRAGONS?
YES.
HIS WISH *WAS* TO KNOW WHAT IT IS, AFTER ALL.
BUT WHETHER HE BELIEVES THE ANSWER OR NOT REALLY DEPENDS...
...ON HIM.
EITHER WAY, HE'LL BE VERY INTERESTED IN THE ANSWER.
DO YOU HAVE AN IDEA OF HOW TO USE IT?
TAP

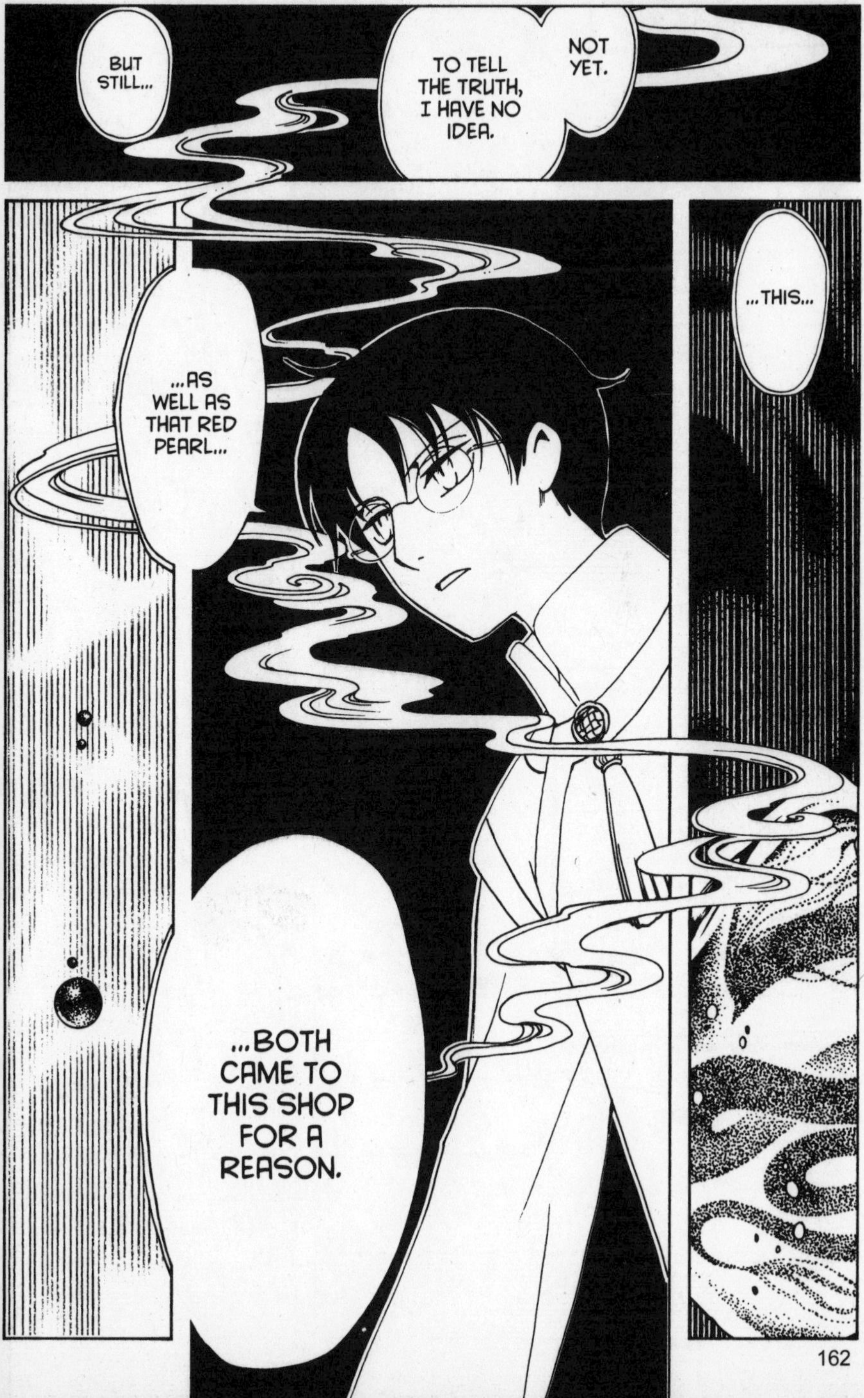
NOT YET.
TO TELL THE TRUTH, I HAVE NO IDEA.
BUT STILL...
...THIS...
...AS WELL AS THAT RED PEARL...
...BOTH CAME TO THIS SHOP FOR A REASON.

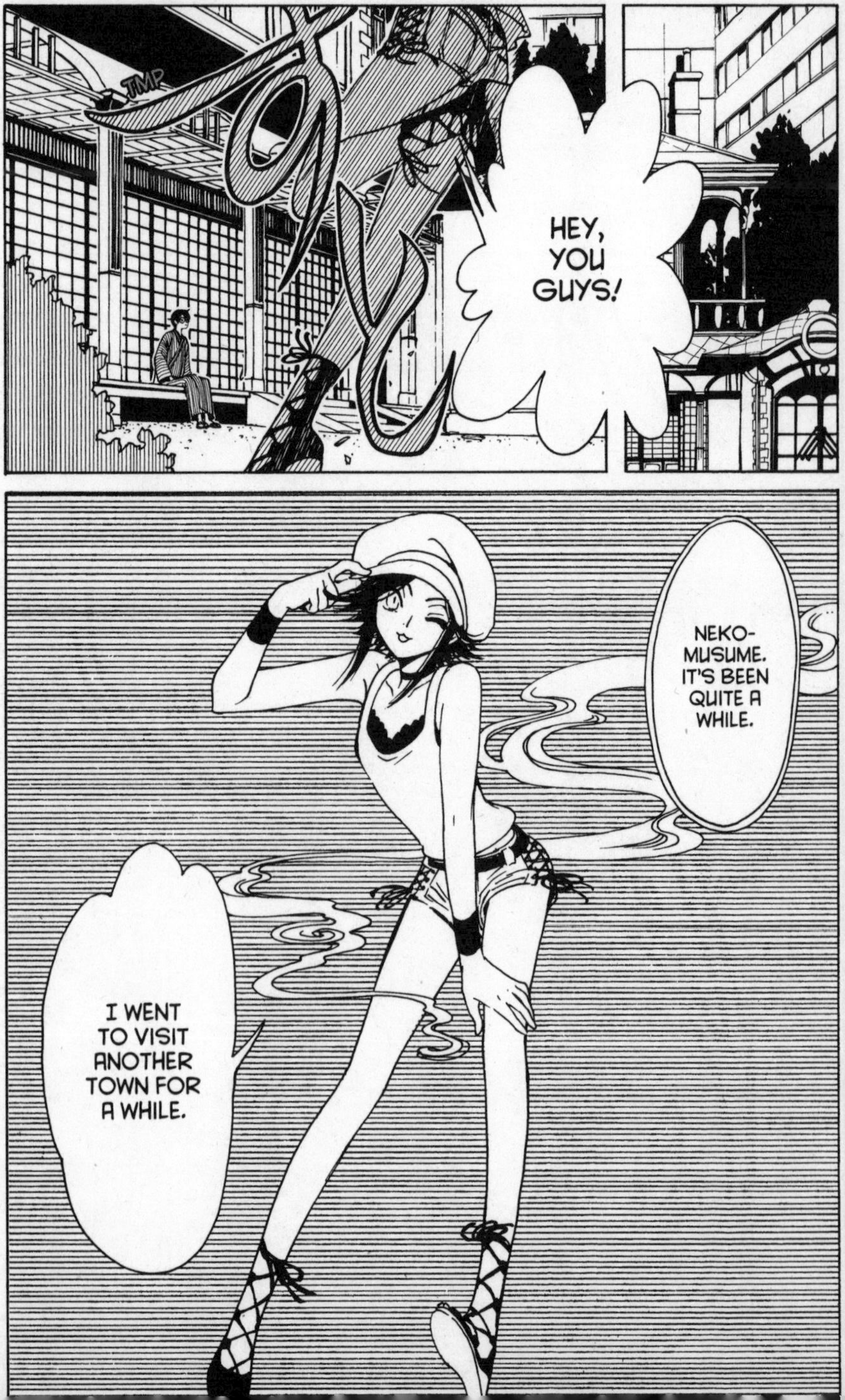
HEY, YOU GUYS!
TMP
NEKO-MUSUME. IT'S BEEN QUITE A WHILE.
I WENT TO VISIT ANOTHER TOWN FOR A WHILE.

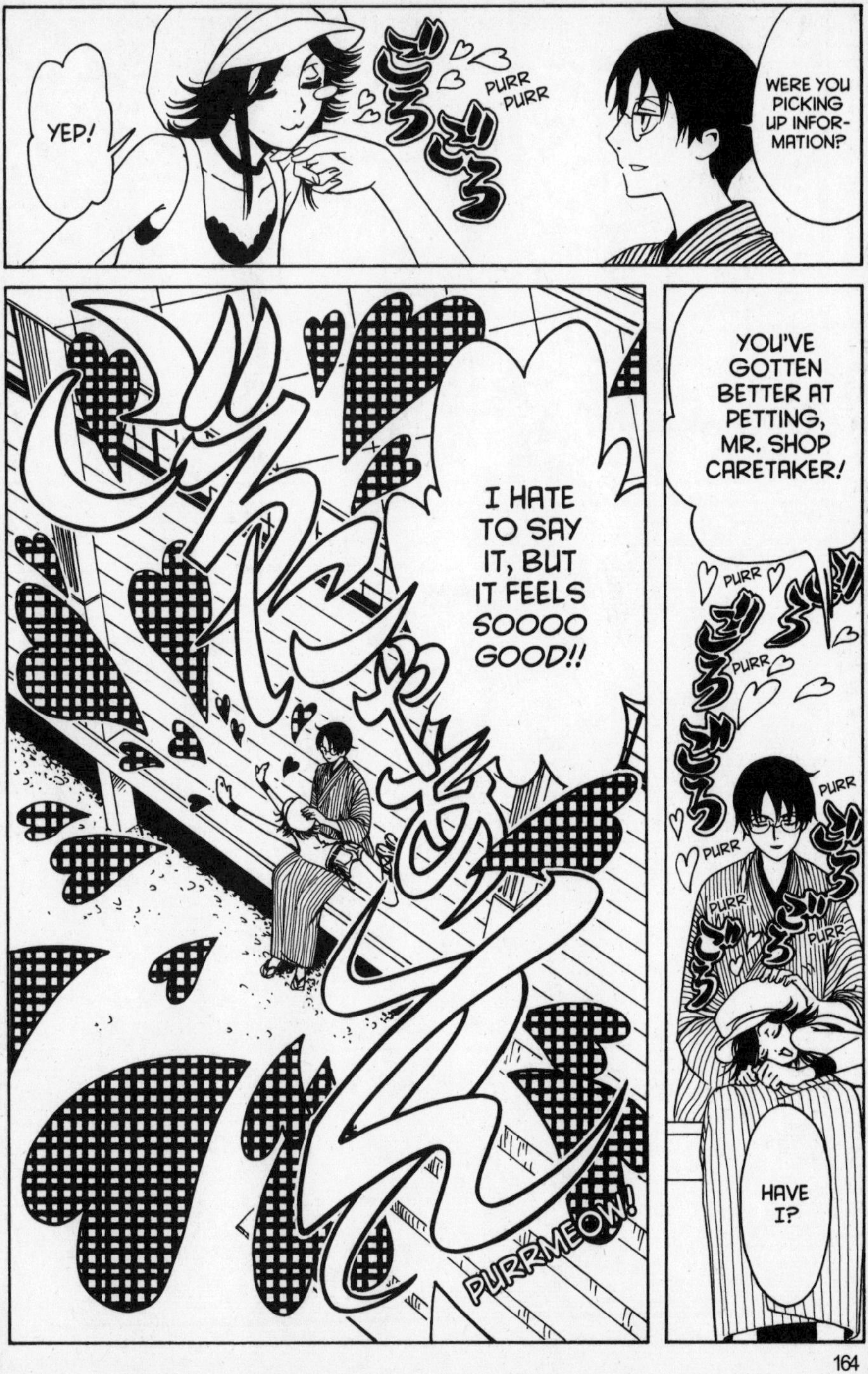
WERE YOU PICKING UP INFORMATION?
ごろごろ
PURR PURR
YEP!
YOU'VE GOTTEN BETTER AT PETTING, MR. SHOP CARETAKER!
PURR
PURR
PURR
PURR
PURR
PURR
HAVE I?
I HATE TO SAY IT, BUT IT FEELS SOOOO GOOD!!
PURRMEOW!

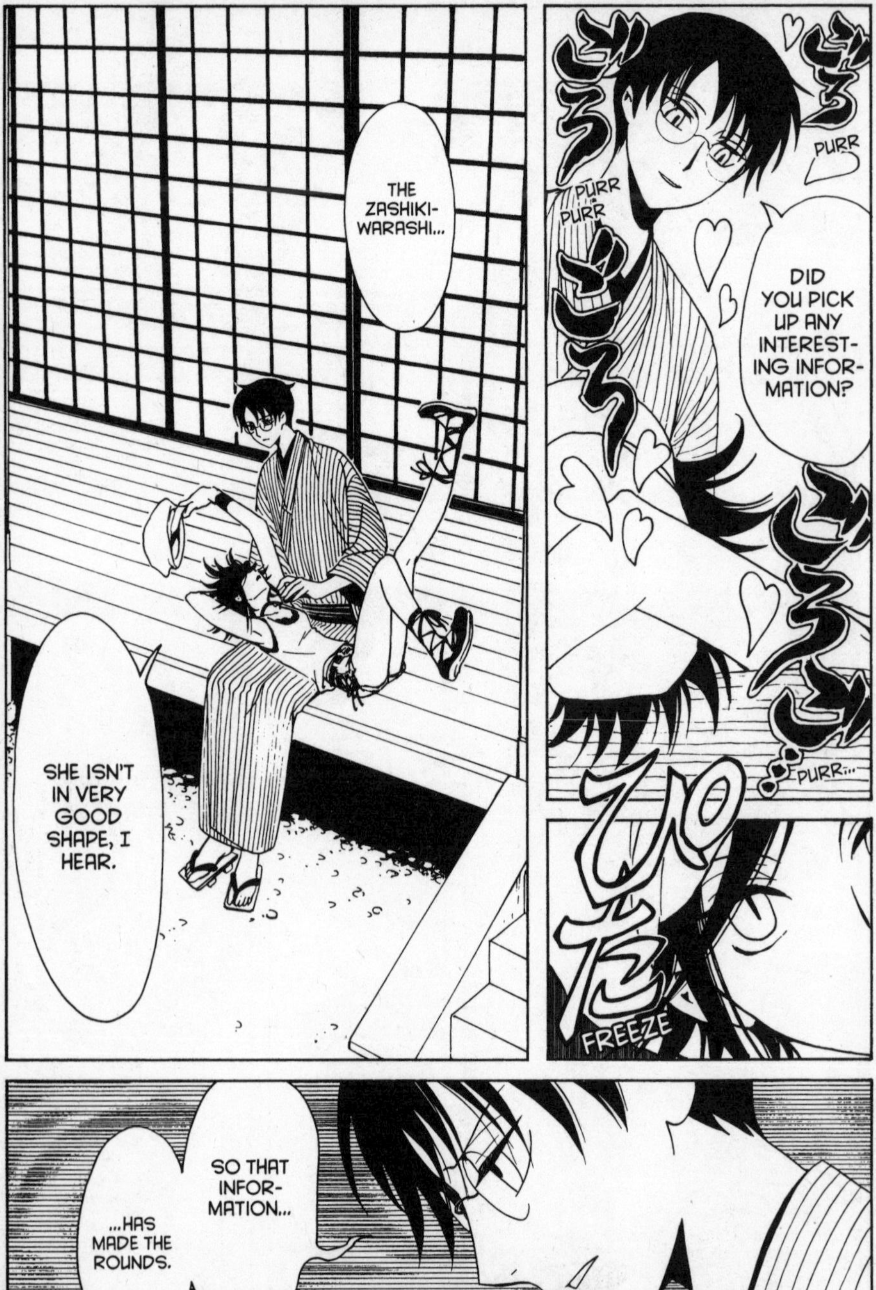
PURR
PURR
PURR
DID YOU PICK UP ANY INTERESTING INFORMATION?
PURR...
FREEZE
THE ZASHIKI-WARASHI...
SHE ISN'T IN VERY GOOD SHAPE, I HEAR.
SO THAT INFORMATION...
...HAS MADE THE ROUNDS.

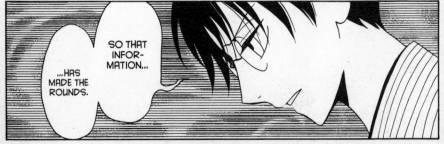

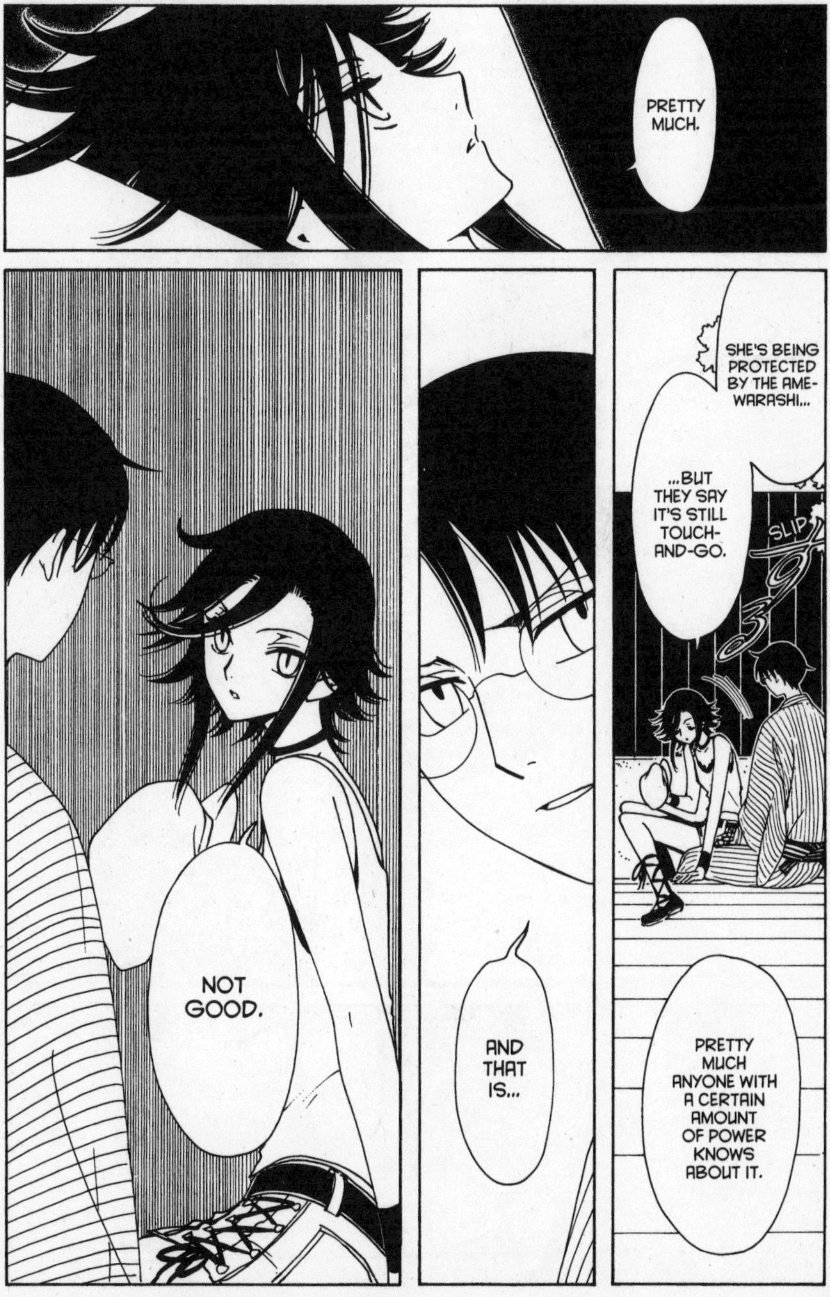
PRETTY MUCH.
SHE'S BEING PROTECTED BY THE AME-WARASHI...
...BUT THEY SAY IT'S STILL TOUCH-AND-GO.
SLIP
PRETTY MUCH ANYONE WITH A CERTAIN AMOUNT OF POWER KNOWS ABOUT IT.
AND THAT IS...
NOT GOOD.

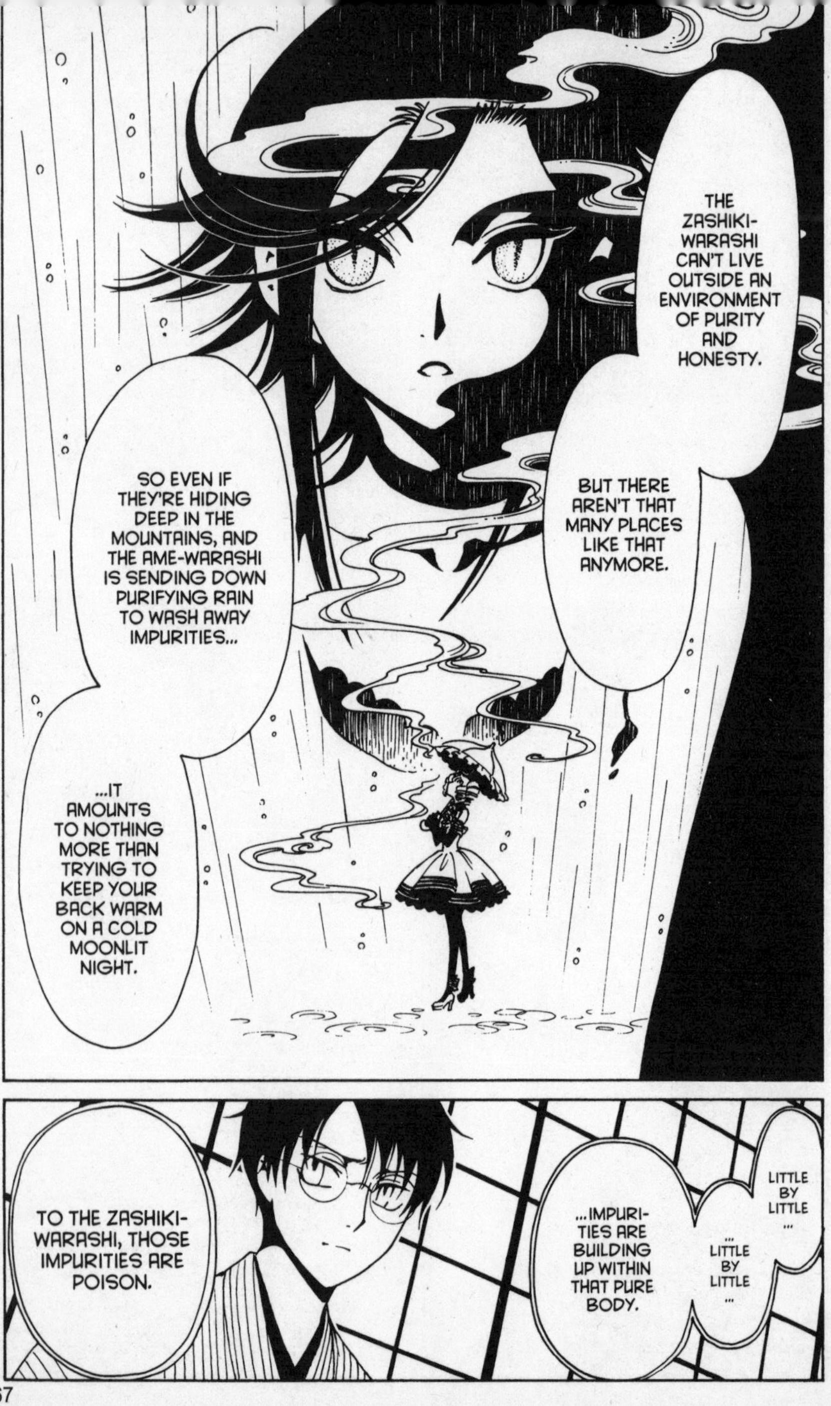
THE ZASHIKI-WARASHI CAN'T LIVE OUTSIDE AN ENVIRONMENT OF PURITY AND HONESTY.
BUT THERE AREN'T THAT MANY PLACES LIKE THAT ANYMORE.
SO EVEN IF THEY'RE HIDING DEEP IN THE MOUNTAINS, AND THE AME-WARASHI IS SENDING DOWN PURIFYING RAIN TO WASH AWAY IMPURITIES...
...IT AMOUNTS TO NOTHING MORE THAN TRYING TO KEEP YOUR BACK WARM ON A COLD MOONLIT NIGHT.
LITTLE BY LITTLE ...
... LITTLE BY LITTLE ...
...IMPURI-TIES ARE BUILDING UP WITHIN THAT PURE BODY.
TO THE ZASHIKI-WARASHI, THOSE IMPURITIES ARE POISON.

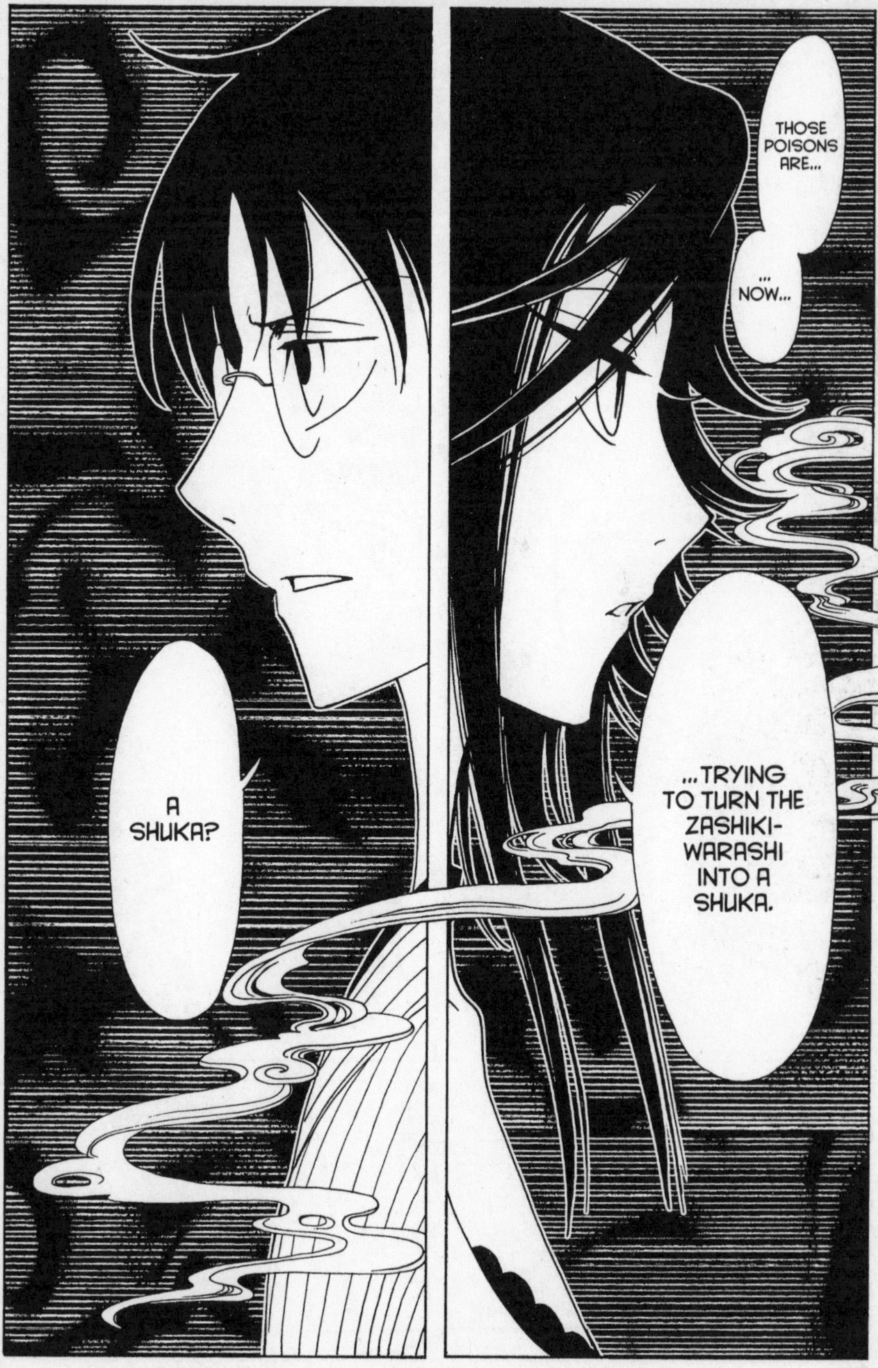
THOSE POISONS ARE...
... NOW...
...TRYING TO TURN THE ZASHIKI-WARASHI INTO A SHUKA.
A SHUKA?

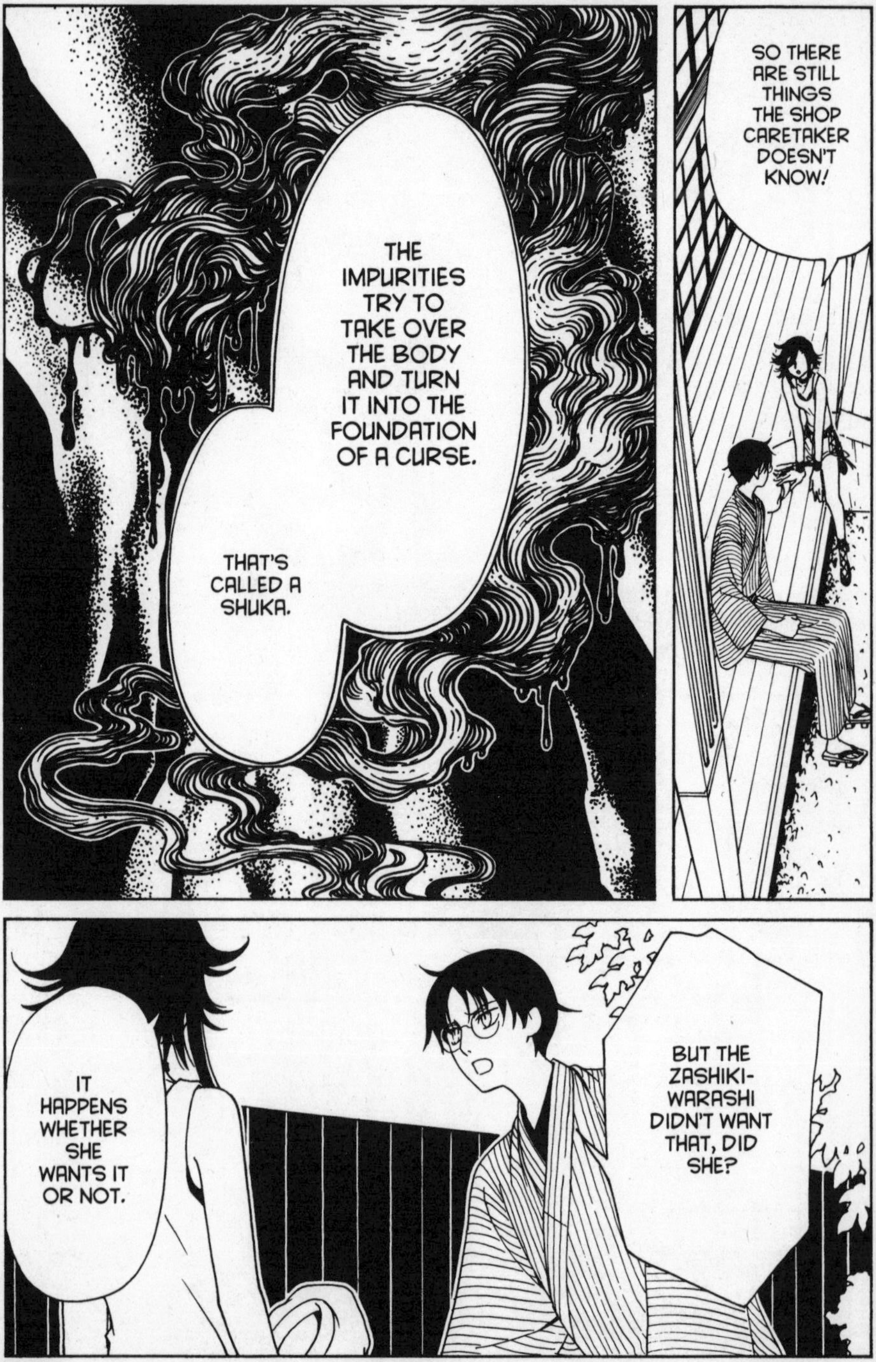
SO THERE ARE STILL THINGS THE SHOP CARETAKER DOESN'T KNOW!
THE IMPURITIES TRY TO TAKE OVER THE BODY AND TURN IT INTO THE FOUNDATION OF A CURSE.
THAT'S CALLED A SHUKA.
BUT THE ZASHIKI-WARASHI DIDN'T WANT THAT, DID SHE?
IT HAPPENS WHETHER SHE WANTS IT OR NOT.

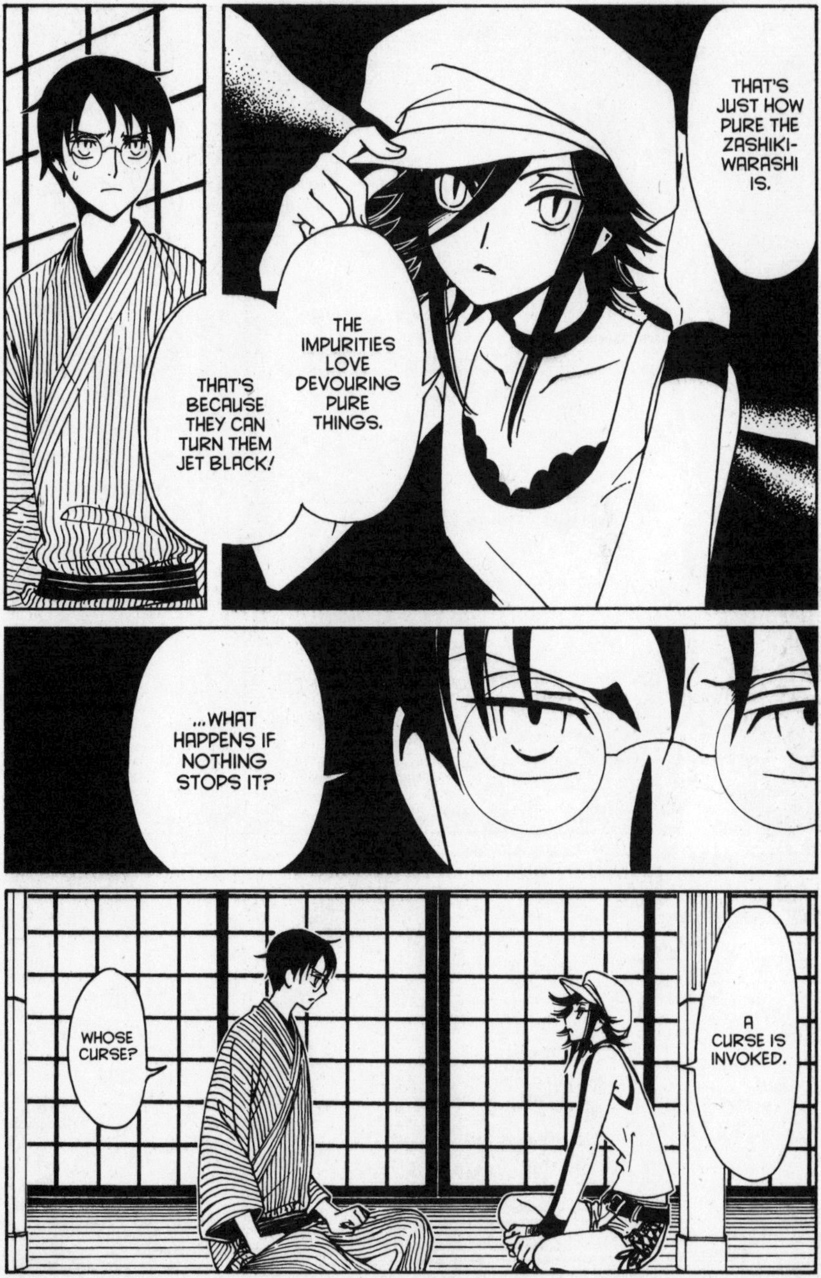
THAT'S JUST HOW PURE THE ZASHIKI-WARASHI IS.
THE IMPURITIES LOVE DEVOURING PURE THINGS.
THAT'S BECAUSE THEY CAN TURN THEM JET BLACK!
...WHAT HAPPENS IF NOTHING STOPS IT?
A CURSE IS INVOKED.
WHOSE CURSE?

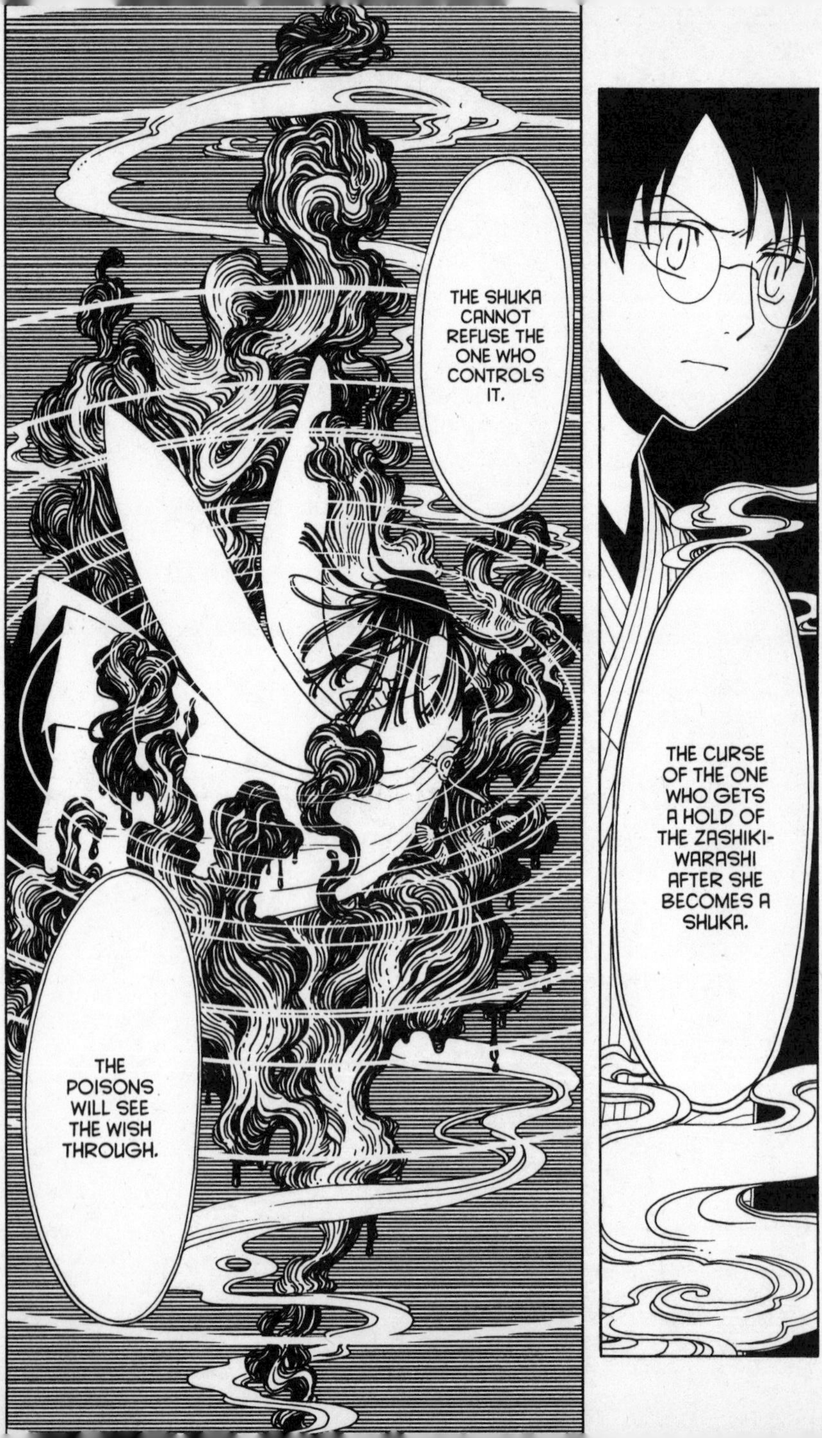
THE CURSE OF THE ONE WHO GETS A HOLD OF THE ZASHIKI-WARASHI AFTER SHE BECOMES A SHUKA.
THE SHUKA CANNOT REFUSE THE ONE WHO CONTROLS IT.
THE POISONS WILL SEE THE WISH THROUGH.

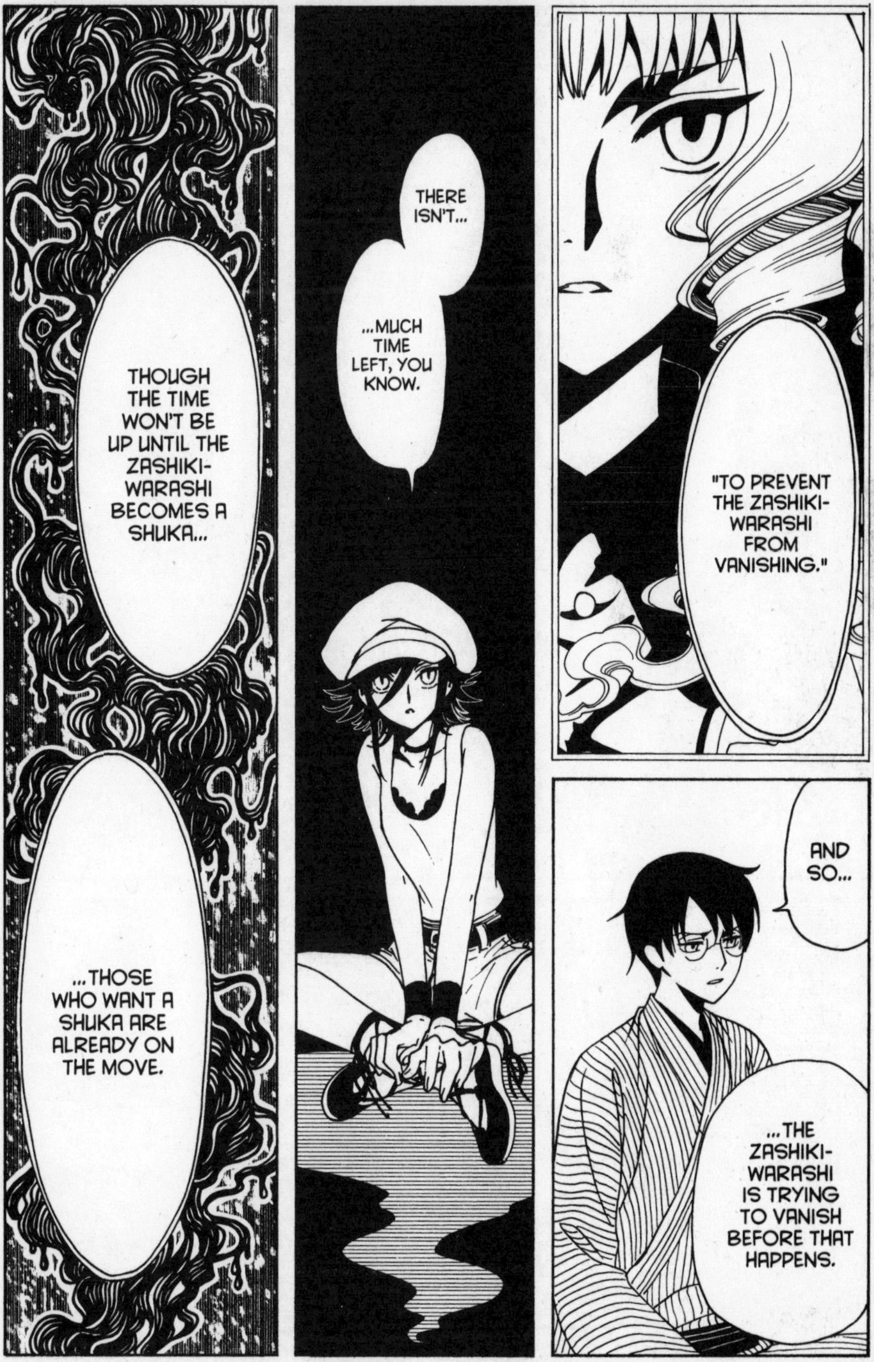
"TO PREVENT THE ZASHIKI-WARASHI FROM VANISHING."
AND SO...
...THE ZASHIKI-WARASHI IS TRYING TO VANISH BEFORE THAT HAPPENS.
THERE ISN'T...
...MUCH TIME LEFT, YOU KNOW.
THOUGH THE TIME WON'T BE UP UNTIL THE ZASHIKI-WARASHI BECOMES A SHUKA...
...THOSE WHO WANT A SHUKA ARE ALREADY ON THE MOVE.

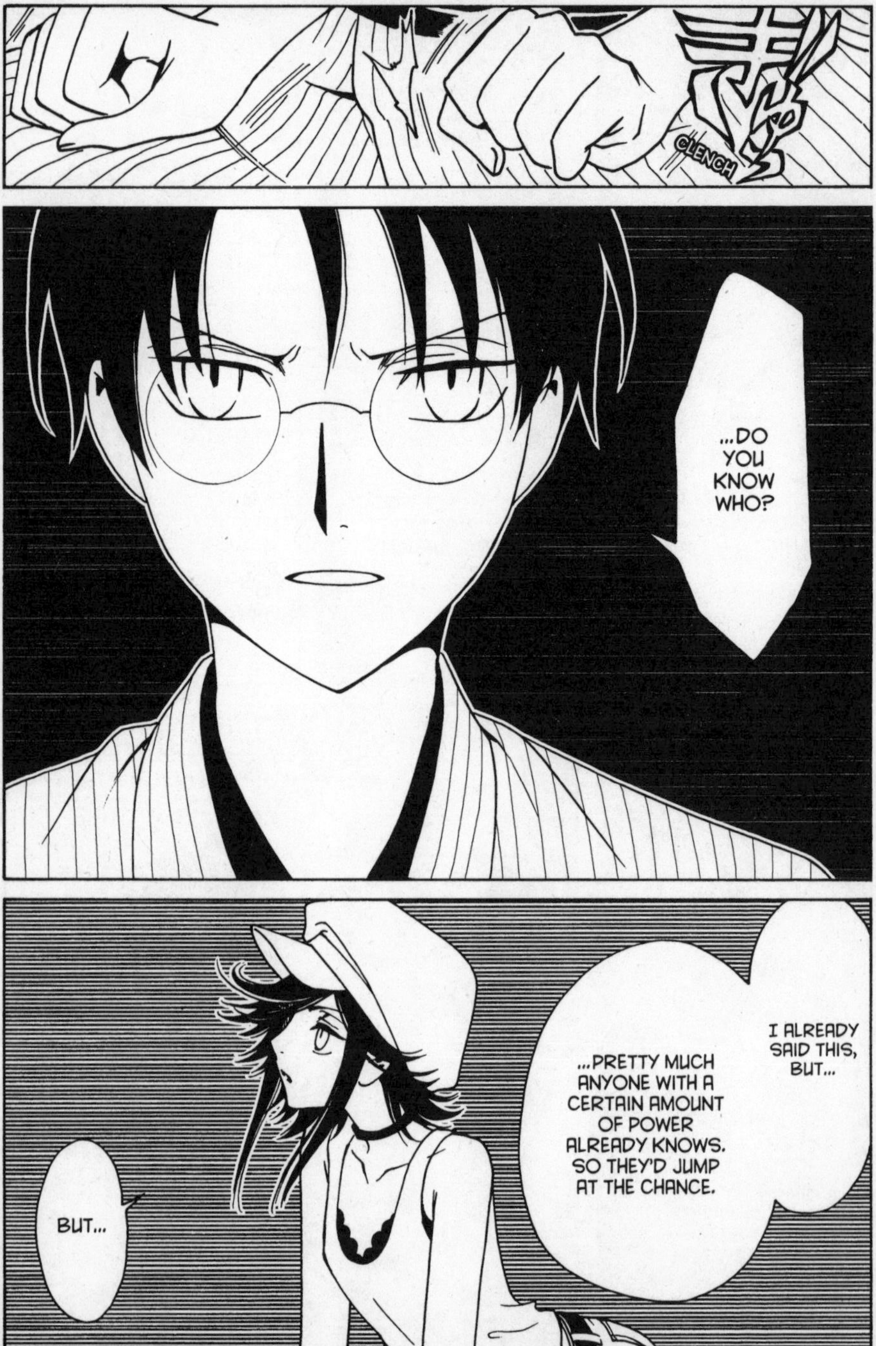
CLENCH
...DO YOU KNOW WHO?
I ALREADY SAID THIS, BUT...
...PRETTY MUCH ANYONE WITH A CERTAIN AMOUNT OF POWER ALREADY KNOWS. SO THEY'D JUMP AT THE CHANCE.
BUT...

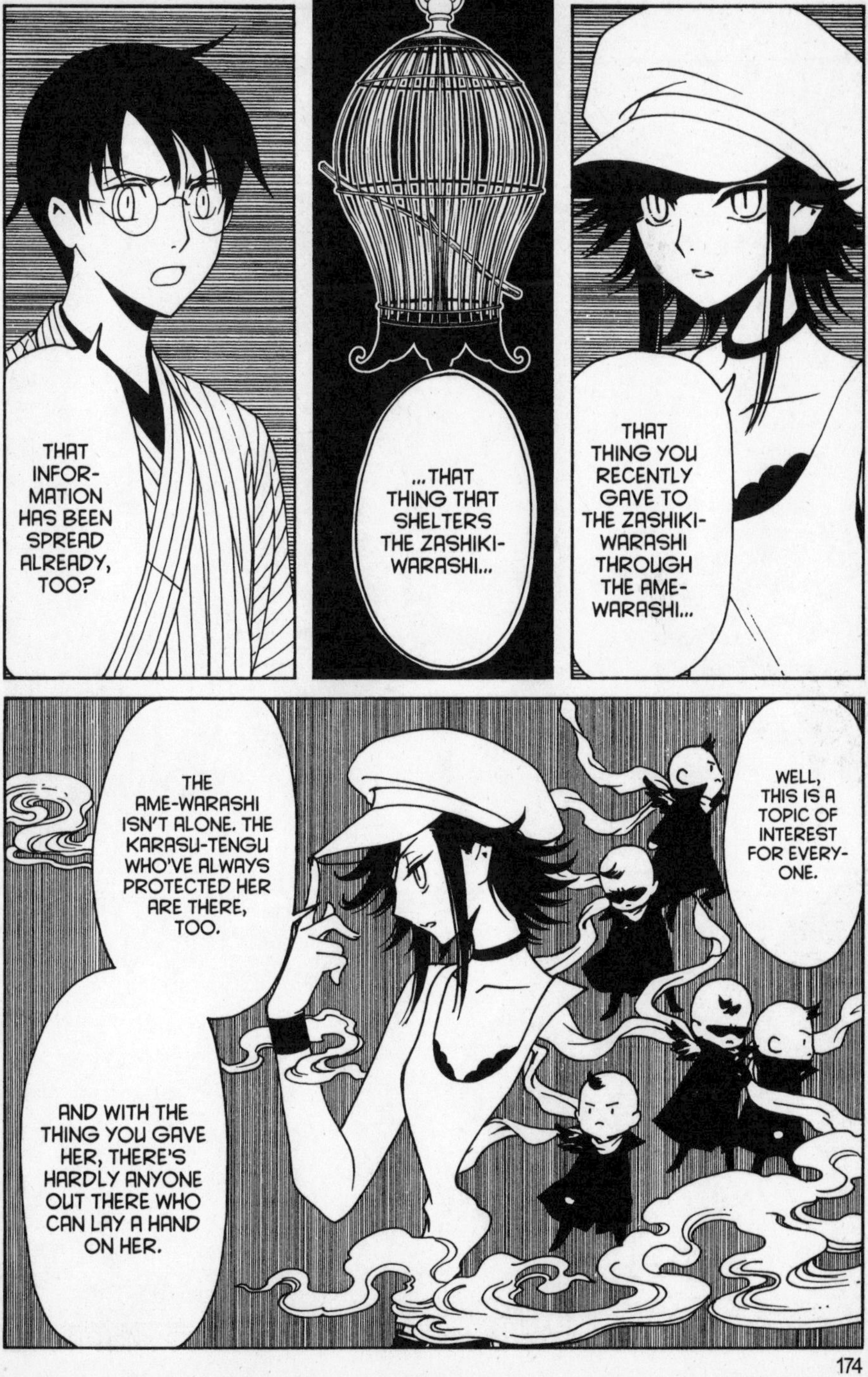
THAT THING YOU RECENTLY GAVE TO THE ZASHIKI-WARASHI THROUGH THE AME-WARASHI...
...THAT THING THAT SHELTERS THE ZASHIKI-WARASHI...
THAT INFOR-MATION HAS BEEN SPREAD ALREADY, TOO?
WELL, THIS IS A TOPIC OF INTEREST FOR EVERY-ONE.
THE AME-WARASHI ISN'T ALONE. THE KARASU-TENGU WHO'VE ALWAYS PROTECTED HER ARE THERE, TOO.
AND WITH THE THING YOU GAVE HER, THERE'S HARDLY ANYONE OUT THERE WHO CAN LAY A HAND ON HER.

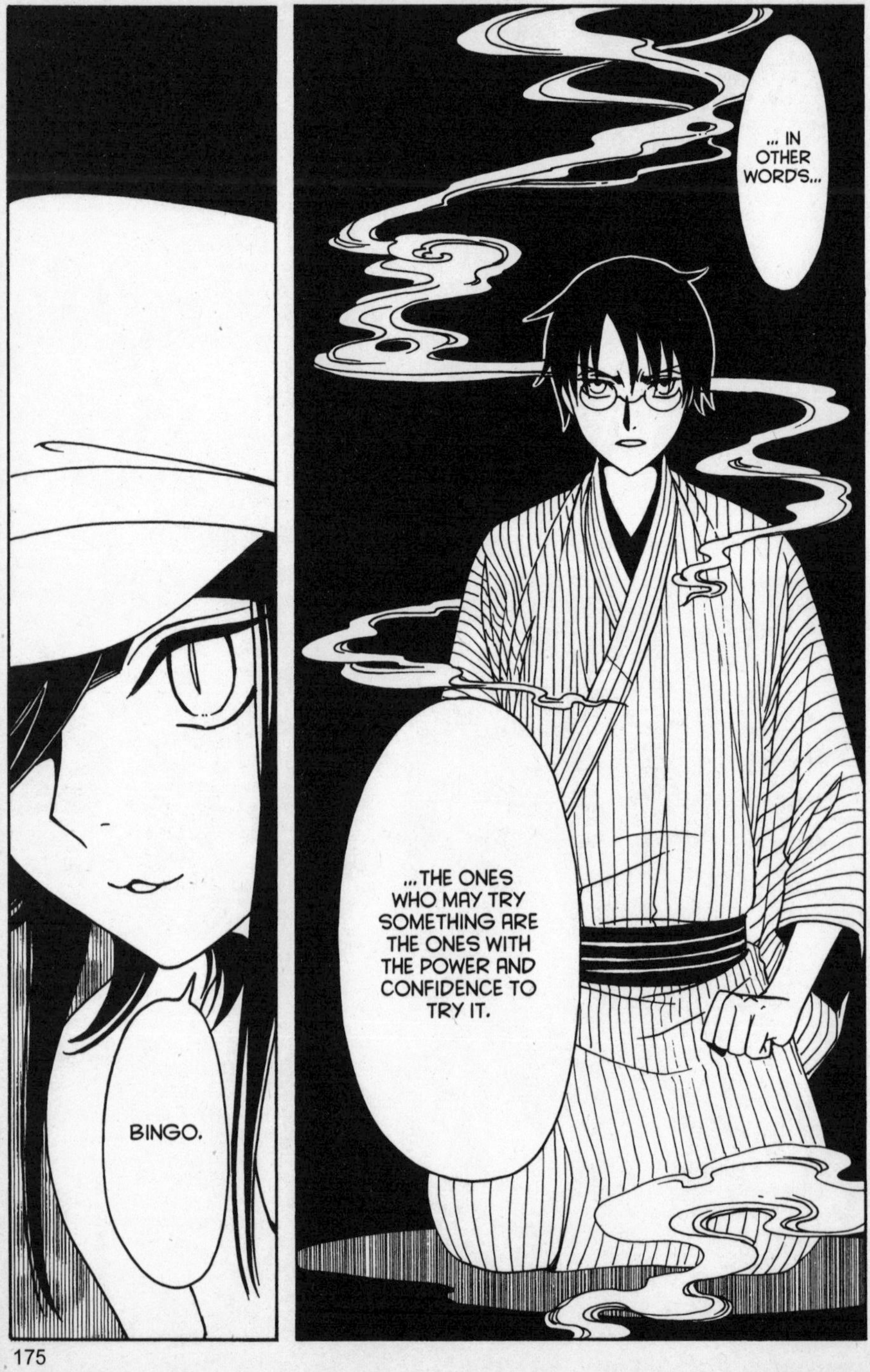
... IN OTHER WORDS...
...THE ONES WHO MAY TRY SOMETHING ARE THE ONES WITH THE POWER AND CONFIDENCE TO TRY IT.
BINGO.

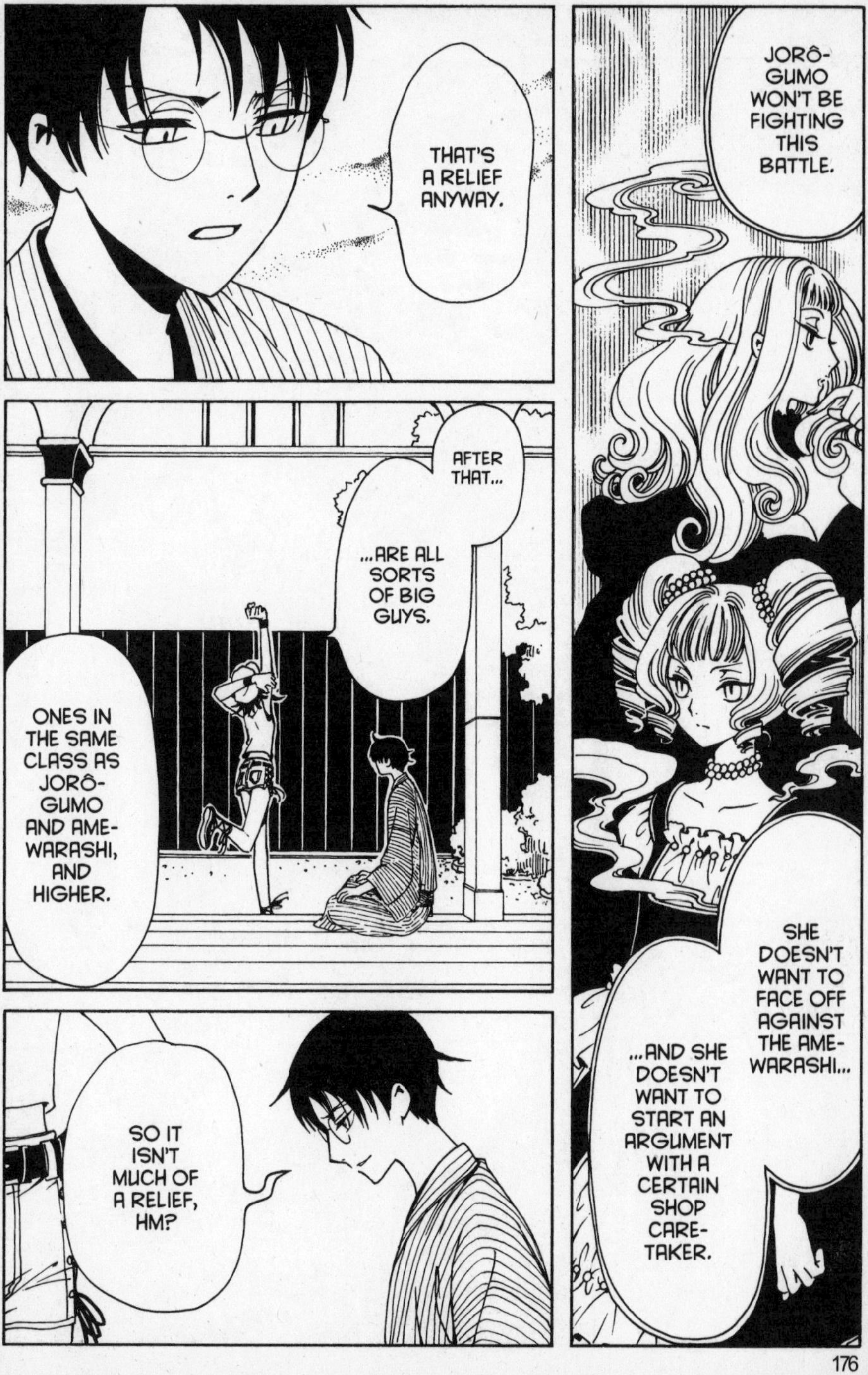
JORÔ-GUMO WON'T BE FIGHTING THIS BATTLE.
SHE DOESN'T WANT TO FACE OFF AGAINST THE AME-WARASHI...
...AND SHE DOESN'T WANT TO START AN ARGUMENT WITH A CERTAIN SHOP CARE-TAKER.
THAT'S A RELIEF ANYWAY.
AFTER THAT...
...ARE ALL SORTS OF BIG GUYS.
ONES IN THE SAME CLASS AS JORÔ-GUMO AND AME-WARASHI, AND HIGHER.
SO IT ISN'T MUCH OF A RELIEF, HM?

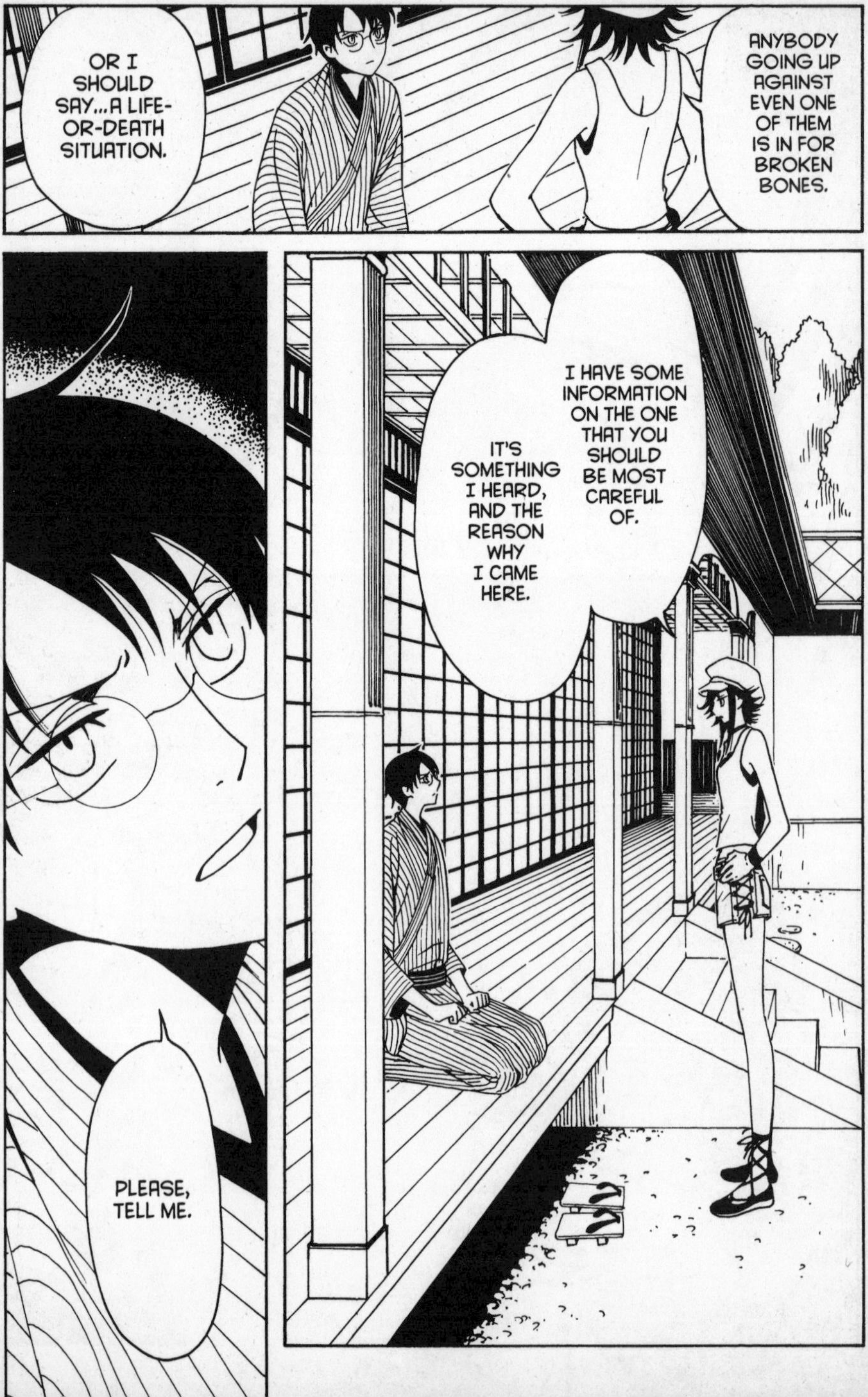
ANYBODY GOING UP AGAINST EVEN ONE OF THEM IS IN FOR BROKEN BONES.
OR I SHOULD SAY...A LIFE-OR-DEATH SITUATION.
I HAVE SOME INFORMATION ON THE ONE THAT YOU SHOULD BE MOST CAREFUL OF.
IT'S SOMETHING I HEARD, AND THE REASON WHY I CAME HERE.
PLEASE, TELL ME.

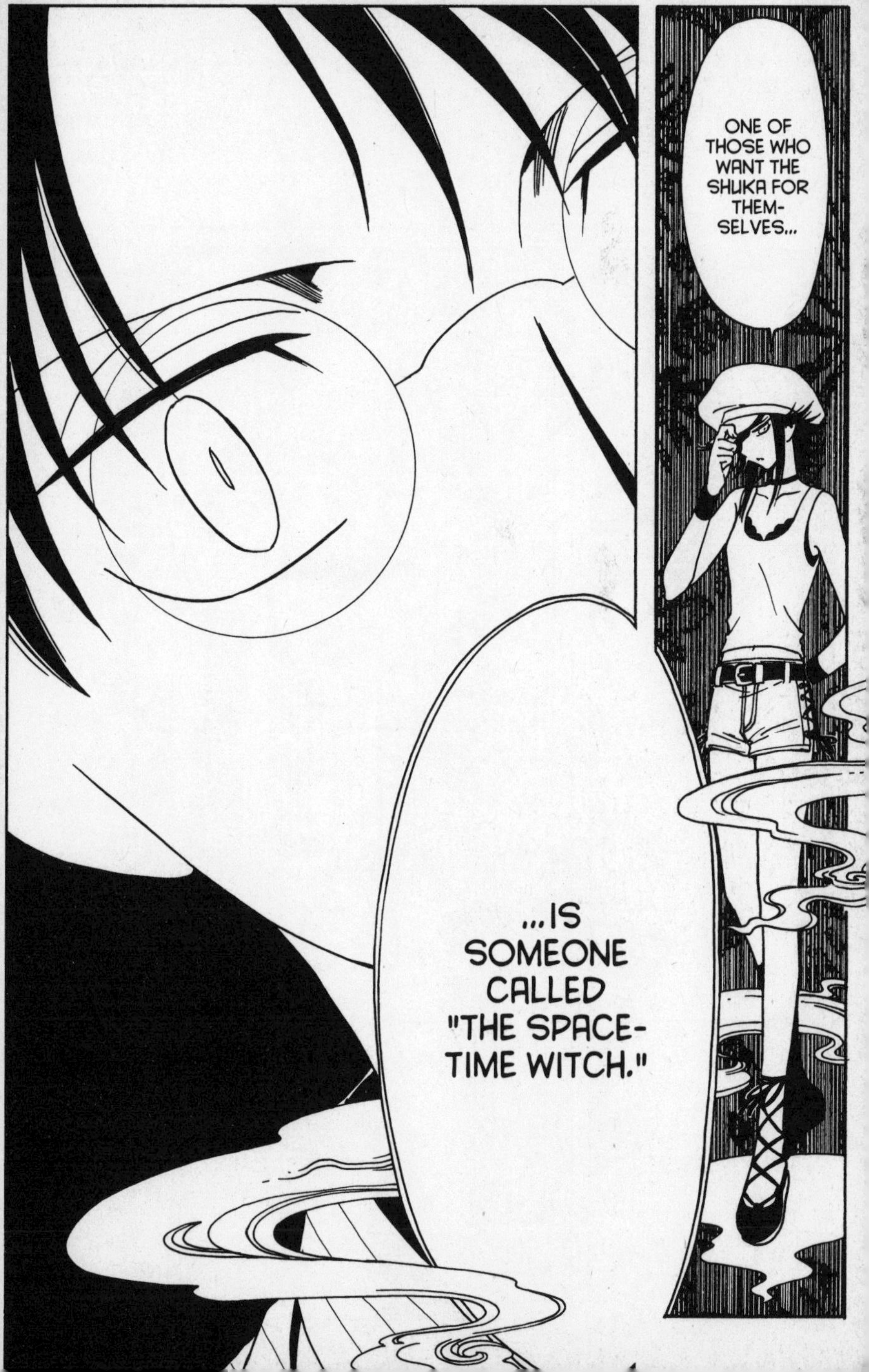
ONE OF THOSE WHO WANT THE SHUKA FOR THEM-SELVES...
...IS SOMEONE CALLED "THE SPACE-TIME WITCH."

~ TO BE CONTINUED ~

Translation Notes

Japanese is a difficult language and translation is often more art than science. For your edification and reading pleasure, here are notes on some of the places where we could have gone in a different direction in our translation of the work, or where a Japanese cultural reference is used.

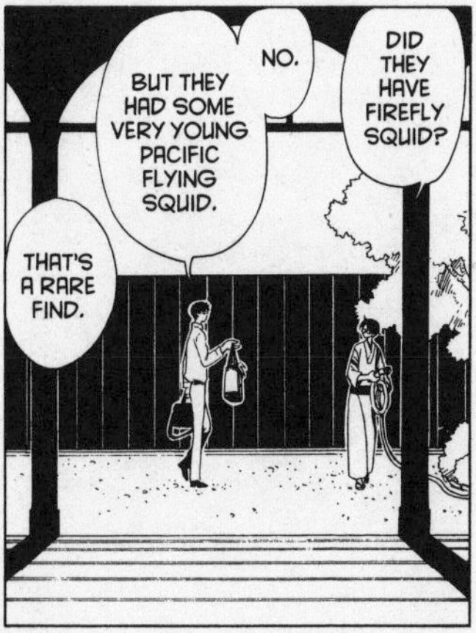
DID THEY HAVE FIREFLY SQUID?
NO.
BUT THEY HAD SOME VERY YOUNG PACIFIC FLYING SQUID.
THAT'S A RARE FIND.

Firefly squid, page 13

Firefly squid are a type of squid found in fairly deep waters (about 1,000 feet) and are bioluminescent. They have photophores on their bodies and arms that produce light. They are considered a delicacy in upper-echelon sushi bars and other Japanese seafood establishments.

Pacific Flying Squid, page 13

These squid are found in the waters around Japan (and in other places in the Pacific), and are known for their ability to launch themselves into the air and "fly" up to about 30 feet through the use of a biological high-pressure water jet.

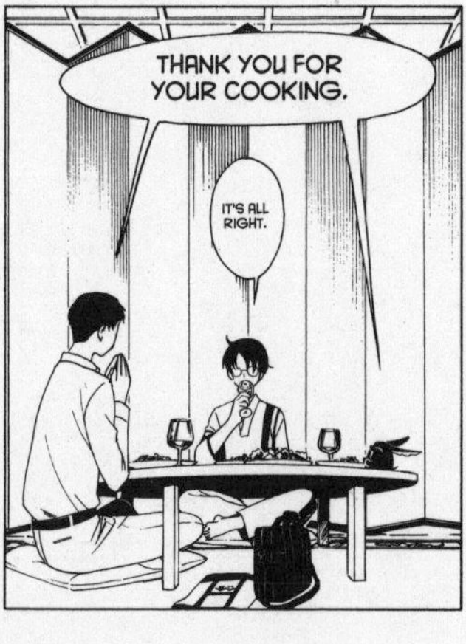
THANK YOU FOR YOUR COOKING.
IT'S ALL RIGHT.

Thank you for your cooking!, page 18

As noted in the notes for the original *xxxHolic* series in Volume 7, there is a tradition that mirrors "saying grace" in Christian tradition. Nearly all Japanese people say the word *itadakimasu* before eating. *Itadaku* is the formal verb meaning "receive," combined with the formal verb ending *-masu*. The literal meaning would be, "I shall receive," but now it is something said by custom before eating. It's translated as "thank you for your cooking," because it would only be polite for Mokona and Dômeki to thank the cook.

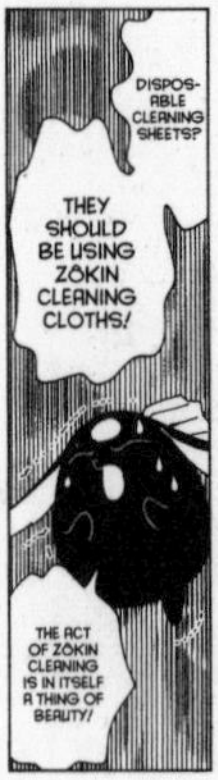
DISPOS-ABLE CLEANING SHEETS?
THEY SHOULD BE USING ZÔKIN CLEANING CLOTHS!
THE ACT OF ZÔKIN CLEANING IS IN ITSELF A THING OF BEAUTY!

Disposable cleaning sheets and Zôkin, page 37

The traditional way of "mopping" Japanese floors was with a folded and quilted towel called a zôkin, dipped in cleaning water and pushed along the floor by hand in a bent-over run. But since this is pretty hard on the cleaner, more modern manufacturers have created disposable cleaning cloths that can be attached to a specially made pole with a base to do the same job without the need for bending over. Of course traditionalists hate it, but it's hard to argue that it's any less effective than cleaning with a zôkin.

Yaobikuni, page 44

The kanji that make up the word "Yaobikuni" mean "800 years," but like some other uses of the term "yao," it carries the nuance of "uncountable." Or in this case, extremely long-lived.

Manga fans may have come across the "mermaid meat" legend before, where the consumption of mermaid meat can either make one immortal, or turn one into a hideous monster. This Yaobikuni became a central figure in the original *xxxHolic* series, volume 17.

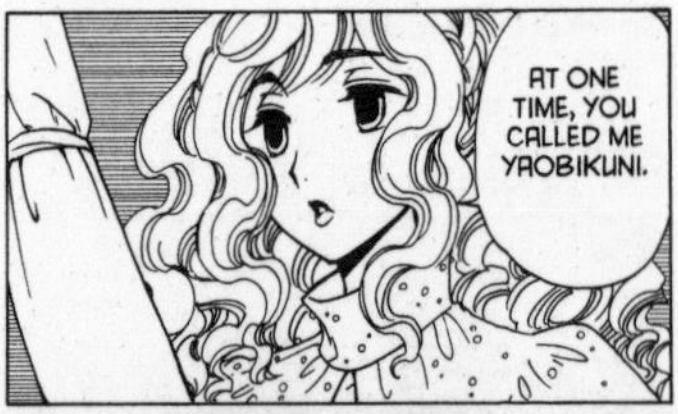
AT ONE TIME, YOU CALLED ME YAOBIKUNI.

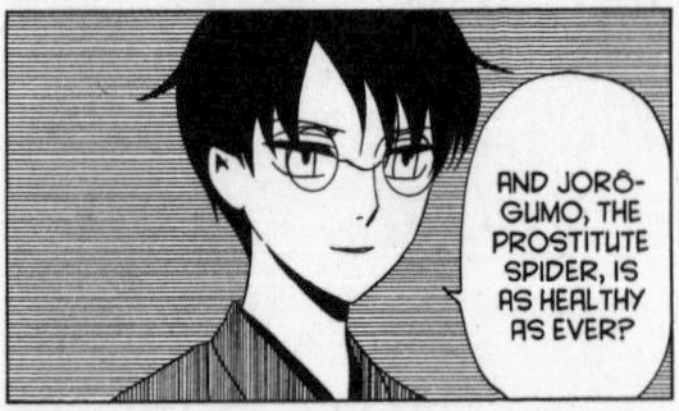
AND JORÔ-GUMO, THE PROSTITUTE SPIDER, IS AS HEALTHY AS EVER?

Jorô-Gumo, page 44

The English name for the jorô-gumo spider is the prostitute spider, and that's what this character is called as well. There are tales from the Izu peninsula of a spirit prostitute spider that sends a man to his death or gets revenge for broken promises. She first appeared in the original *xxxHolic* series in Volume 8, where she obtains Kimihiro's eye, eventually eating it (he gets a replacement), and later in Volume 17, where she becomes a customer of Kimihiro's and through him, becomes the partner of the Yaobikuni.

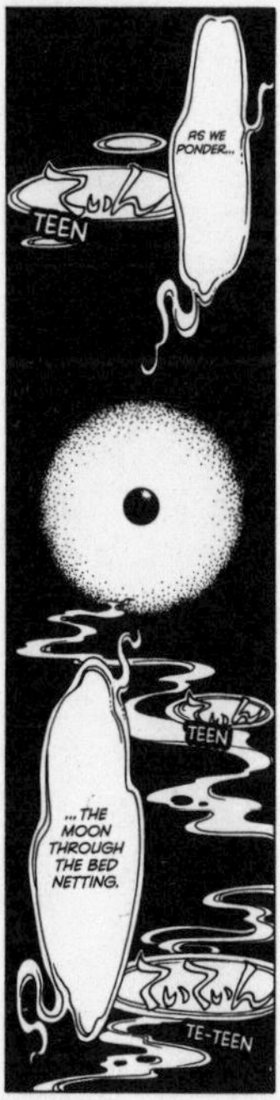
AS WE PONDER...
TEEN
TEEN
...THE MOON THROUGH THE BED NETTING.
TE-TEEN

Bed netting, page 63

The Japanese song was a bit more subtle. It spoke of two people pondering the moon through "kaya," the netting that keeps out mosquitoes at night. However if two people are pondering the moon through the same netting, it would imply that they're sleeping together on the same futon. Although the word "bed" was used in the translation, the Japanese version only implied it in a round-about way.

Yûrei-ga, page 158

These are 19th and early 20th-century paintings of ghosts (yûrei is Japanese for "ghosts"), but also demons and otherworldly creatures. These paintings usually are painted on cloth and hung as wall scrolls in people's houses.

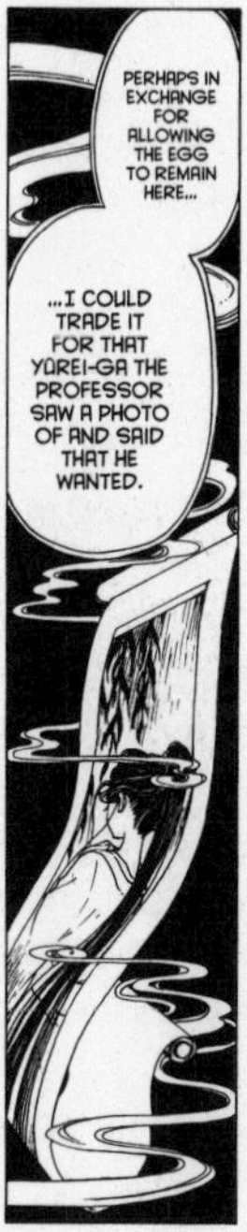
PERHAPS IN EXCHANGE FOR ALLOWING THE EGG TO REMAIN HERE...
...I COULD TRADE IT FOR THAT YŪREI-GA THE PROFESSOR SAW A PHOTO OF AND SAID THAT HE WANTED.

Botandôrô, page 159

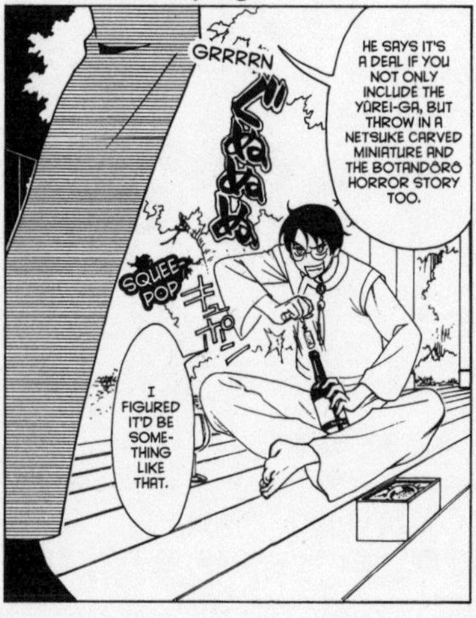
GRRRRN
HE SAYS IT'S A DEAL IF YOU NOT ONLY INCLUDE THE YŪREI-GA, BUT THROW IN A NETSUKE CARVED MINIATURE AND THE BOTANDŌRŌ HORROR STORY TOO.
SQUEE-POP
I FIGURED IT'D BE SOME-THING LIKE THAT.

This is a story of a widowed samurai for whom life holds no meaning until he meets a beautiful woman one night whose servant holds a peony lantern. It's only after falling in love and having an affair with the woman that he learns that to anyone's eye but his, she is a rotting corpse, and she will soon take him to the world of the dead. This story started as a Chinese ghost story, then became a kabuki theater play, novels, movies, and other entertainment. Botandôrô means "peony lantern."

Neko Musume, page 163

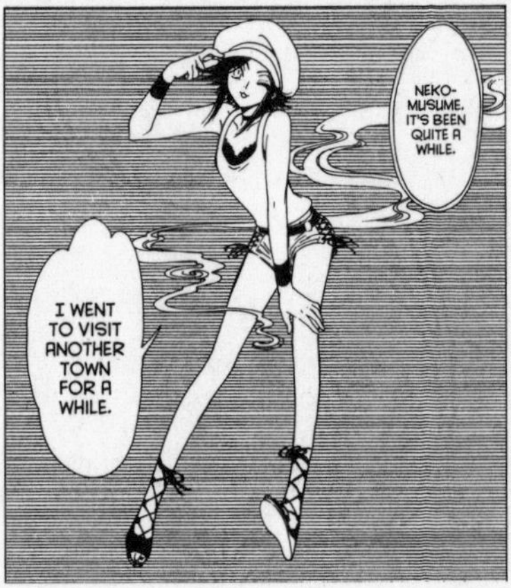
NEKO-MUSUME. IT'S BEEN QUITE A WHILE.
I WENT TO VISIT ANOTHER TOWN FOR A WHILE.

As included in the notes for Volume 8 of the original *xxxHolic* series, Neko-Musume is a cat that can transform into the shape of a young girl. Sometimes her cat-like attributes stay in place (ears, eyes, tail, etc.) and sometimes they don't. As a Neko-Musume gets older, it can become a Nekomata and can gain additional odd powers. This Neko Musume appears to let Watanuki know that many in the spirit world were out to get his right eye (which Jorô-Gumo eventually ate, see previous note), and later told Yûko of a source for special water she needed in exchange for a hat that cools in the summer. This Neko Musume has access to a lot of information.

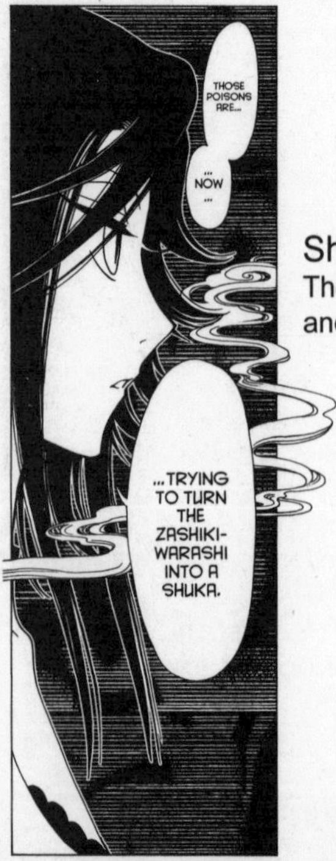
THOSE POISONS ARE...
...NOW...
...TRYING TO TURN THE ZASHIKI-WARASHI INTO A SHUKA.

Shuka, page 168

The word Shuka is made up of kanji for "curse," and a lesser-known kanji for "song" or "poem."

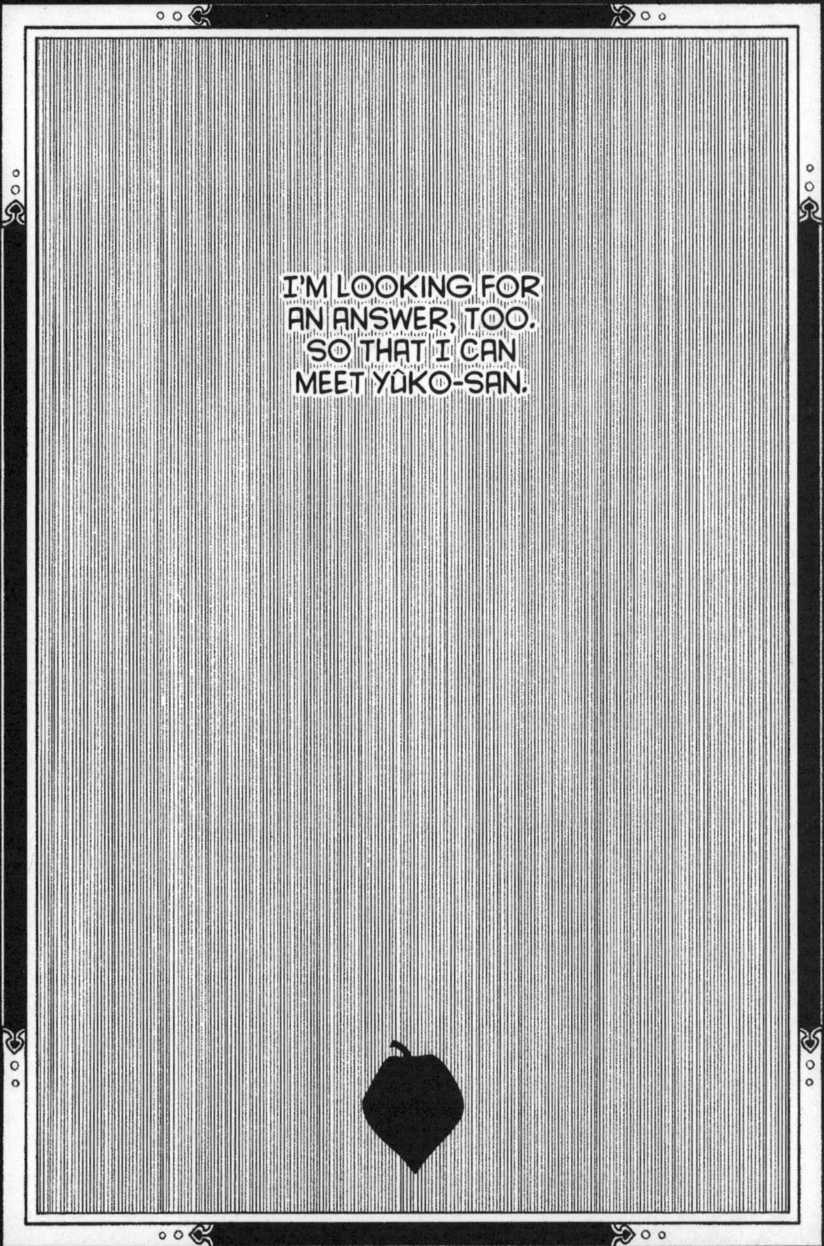
I'M LOOKING FOR AN ANSWER, TOO. SO THAT I CAN MEET YÛKO-SAN.

A Kodansha Comics Trade Paperback Original.

xxxHOLiC Rei volume 4 copyright © 2016 CLAMP • ShigatsuTsuitachi CO., LTD./Kodansha English translation copyright © 2017 CLAMP • ShigatsuTsuitachi CO., LTD./Kodansha

Published in the United States by Kodansha Comics, an imprint of Kodansha USA Publishing, LLC, New York.

Publication rights for this English edition arranged through Kodansha Ltd., Tokyo.

First published in Japan in 2016 by Kodansha Ltd., Tokyo.

ISBN 978-1-61262-586-7

Printed in the United States of America.

www.kodanshacomics.com

9 8 7 6 5 4 3 2 1

Translation: Bill Flanagan
Lettering: Paige Pumphrey
Editing: David Yoo, Haruko Hashimoto

Japan's most powerful spirit medium delves into the ghost world's greatest mysteries!

Story by Kyo Shirodaira, famed author of mystery fiction and creator of *Spiral*, *Blast of Tempest*, and *The Record of a Fallen Vampire*.

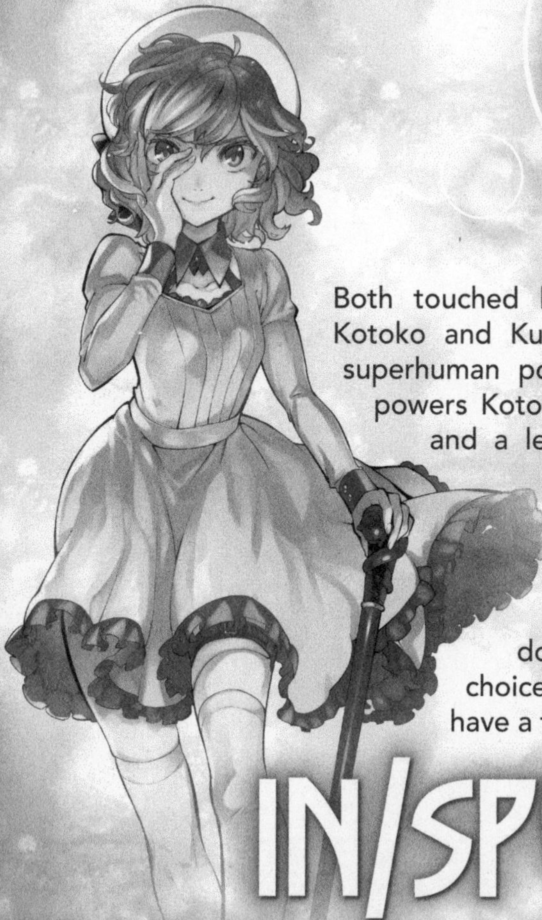

Both touched by spirits called yôkai, Kotoko and Kurô have gained unique superhuman powers. But to gain her powers Kotoko has given up an eye and a leg, and Kurô's personal life is in shambles. So when Kotoko suggests they team up to deal with renegades from the spirit world, Kurô doesn't have many other choices, but Kotoko might just have a few ulterior motives...

IN/SPECTRE

STORY BY **KYO SHIRODAIRA**
ART BY **CHASHIBA KATASE**

"I'm pleasantly surprised to find modern shojo using cross-dressing as a dramatic device to deliver social commentary... Recommended."

-Otaku USA Magazine

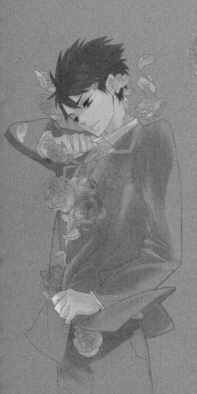

The prince in his dark days

By Hico Yamanaka

A drunkard for a father, a household of poverty... For 17-year-old Atsuko, misfortune is all she knows and believes in. Until one day, a chance encounter with Itaru–the wealthy heir of a huge corporation–changes everything. The two look identical, uncannily so. When Itaru curiously goes missing, Atsuko is roped into being his stand-in. There, in his shoes, Atsuko must parade like a prince in a palace. She encounters many new experiences, but at what cost...?

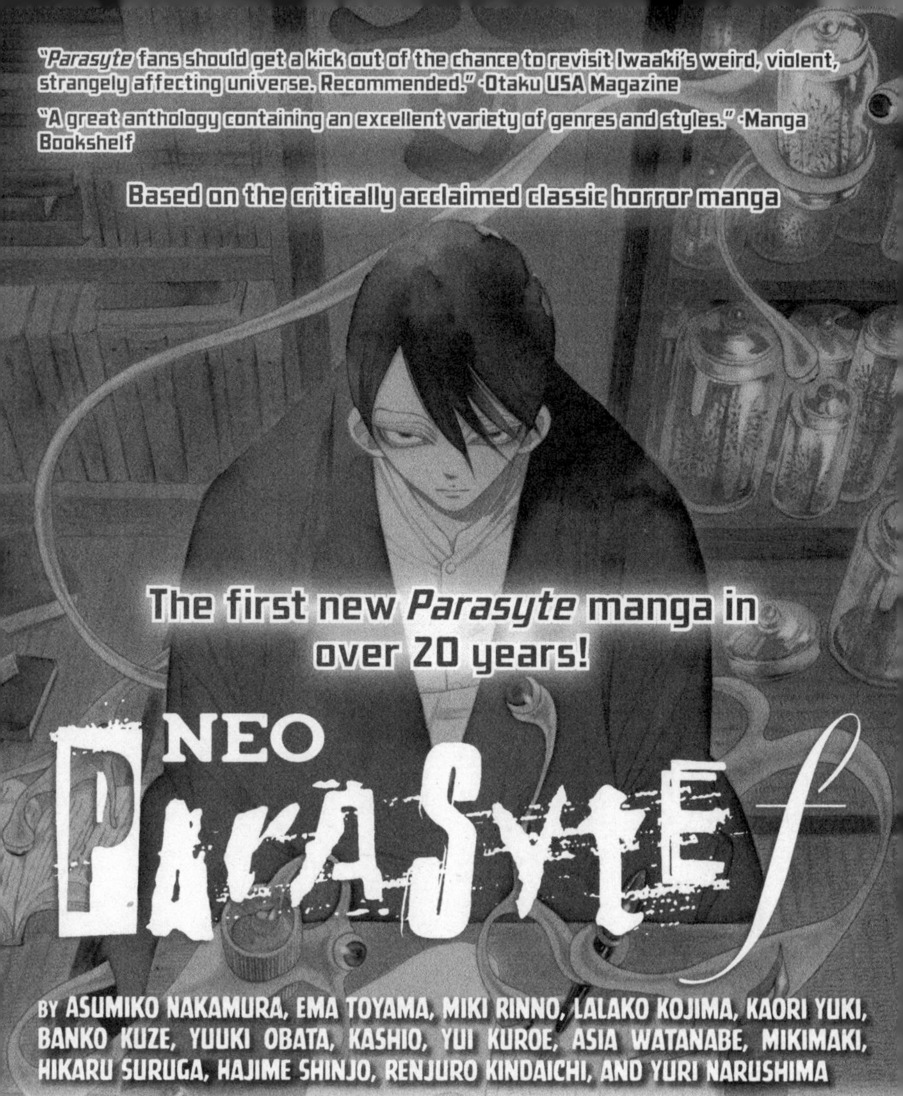

Based on the critically acclaimed classic horror manga

The first new *Parasyte* manga in over 20 years!

NEO PARASYTE f

BY ASUMIKO NAKAMURA, EMA TOYAMA, MIKI RINNO, LALAKO KOJIMA, KAORI YUKI, BANKO KUZE, YUUKI OBATA, KASHIO, YUI KUROE, ASIA WATANABE, MIKIMAKI, HIKARU SURUGA, HAJIME SHINJO, RENJURO KINDAICHI, AND YURI NARUSHIMA

A collection of chilling new *Parasyte* stories from Japan's top shojo artists!

Parasites: shape-shifting aliens whose only purpose is to assimilate with and consume the human race... but do these monsters have a different side? A parasite becomes a prince to save his romance-obsessed female host from a dangerous stalker. Another hosts a cooking show, in which the real monsters are revealed. These and 13 more stories, from some of the greatest shojo manga artists alive today, together make up a chilling, funny, and entertaining tribute to one of manga's horror classics!

KC KODANSHA COMICS

HAPPINESS

——ハピネス——

By Shuzo Oshimi

From the creator of *The Flowers of Evil*

Nothing interesting is happening in Makoto Ozaki's first year of high school. HIs life is a series of quiet humiliations: low-grade bullies, unreliable friends, and the constant frustration of his adolescent lust. But one night, a pale, thin girl knocks him to the ground in an alley and offers him a choice.

Now everything is different. Daylight is searingly bright. Food tastes awful. And worse than anything is the terrible, consuming thirst...

Praise for Shuzo Oshimi's *The Flowers of Evil*

"A shockingly readable story that vividly—one might even say queasily—evokes the fear and confusion of discovering one's own sexuality. Recommended." —The Manga Critic

"A page-turning tale of sordid middle school blackmail." —Otaku USA Magazine

"A stunning new horror manga." —Third Eye Comics

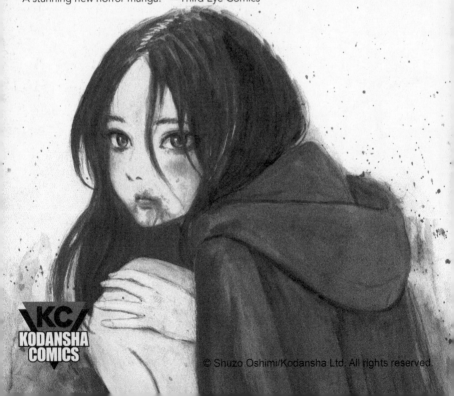

KC KODANSHA COMICS

New action series from Hiroyuki Takei, creator of the classic shonen franchise Shaman King!

In medieval Japan, a bell hanging on the collar is a sign that a cat has a master. Norachiyo's bell hangs from his katana sheath, but he is nonetheless a stray — a ronin. This one-eyed cat samurai travels across a dishonest world, cutting through pretense and deception with his blade.

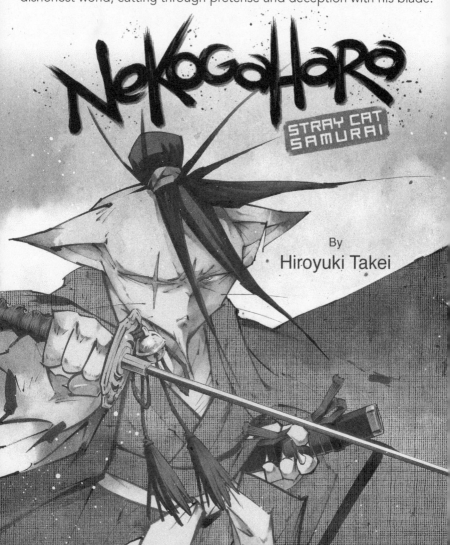

NEKOGAHARA

STRAY CAT SAMURAI

By
Hiroyuki Takei

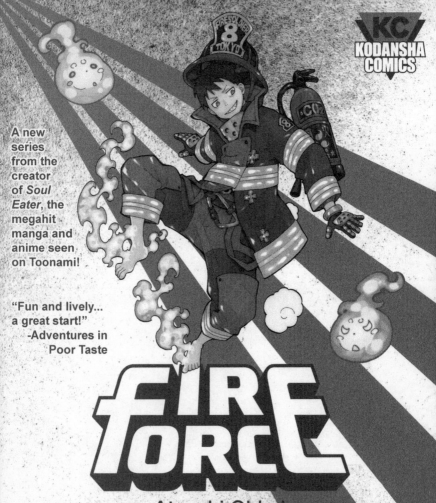

A new series from the creator of *Soul Eater*, the megahit manga and anime seen on Toonami!

"Fun and lively... a great start!"
-Adventures in Poor Taste

FIRE FORCE

By Atsushi Ohkubo

The city of Tokyo is plagued by a deadly phenomenon: spontaneous human combustion! Luckily, a special team is there to quench the inferno: The Fire Force! The fire soldiers at Special Fire Cathedral 8 are about to get a unique addition. Enter Shinra, a boy who possesses the power to run at the speed of a rocket, leaving behind the famous "devil's footprints" (and destroying his shoes in the process). Can Shinra and his colleagues discover the source of this strange epidemic before the city burns to ashes?

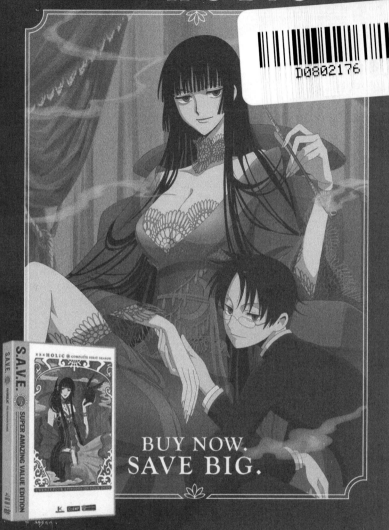